ABRAHAM
KUYPER

Collected Works in Public Theology

GENERAL EDITORS
JORDAN J. BALLOR
MELVIN FLIKKEMA

AbrahamKuyper.com

ON CHARITY
& JUSTICE

ABRAHAM
KUYPER

Edited by Matthew J. Tuininga

Introduction by John Witte Jr.

LEXHAM PRESS

ACTON INSTITUTE
FOR THE STUDY OF RELIGION AND LIBERTY

On Charity & Justice

Abraham Kuyper Collected Works in Public Theology

Lexham Press, 1313 Commercial St., Bellingham, WA 98225
LexhamPress.com

Print ISBN 9781577996736
Digital ISBN 9781683595960
Library of Congress Control Number 2021942207

Lexham Editorial: David Bomar, Claire Brubaker, Justin Marr, Abigail Stocker
    Mandi Newell
Cover Design: Christine Christophersen
Typesetting: ProjectLuz.com

CONTENTS

ABRAHAM KUYPER AND THE SOCIAL ORDER: PRINCIPLES FOR CHRISTIAN LIBERALISM

MATTHEW J. TUININGA

Abraham Kuyper believed that the salvation proclaimed in the gospel of Jesus Christ extends to every part of creation. The good news is not simply that the souls of individual Christians will be saved for an eternity in heaven. Nor is it merely that the church will be ransomed out of the world for a fresh start in the future kingdom of God. Rather, Jesus came to bring salvation to the material creation, including the social life of embodied human beings. And while that salvation will not be complete until the age to come, it nevertheless begins during the present age. As a result, a programmatic dimension of faithful Christian witness is the collective Christian commitment to promoting love and justice in every sphere of human life—from economics to politics, from journalism to the household, from the most turbulent of social questions to the basic motivations of human life. Kuyper believed Christians were dangerously neglecting this witness in his day, even as the secularism, materialism, and individualism of the French Revolution were tearing modern society apart. The gospel demanded a vigorous, socially aware, gospel-centered Christian response.

Though he clearly did not get everything right, the prescience of Kuyper's analysis of the crisis of modernity at the dawn of the twentieth century is impressive. Even his practical proposals, logically designed for his late-nineteenth-century Dutch context, remain surprisingly relevant to the contexts of twenty-first-century Christians across the globe. Kuyper's evaluation of liberalism and conservatism, democracy and socialism, materialism and individualism, capitalism and secularism, pluralism and consumerism remains so apt for our times that it is sometimes easy to forget that Kuyper wrote these words more than a hundred years ago.

For all the differences between our time and Kuyper's, Christians today face largely the same daunting task as did Kuyper: to articulate a vigorous, socially aware, gospel-centered Christian vision for a world that is in danger of fracturing under the diffusive and secularizing pressures of modernity. Here I offer my assessment of how Kuyper's writings on charity and justice might help us do this.

THE GOSPEL POLITICS OF CHARITY AND JUSTICE

Abraham Kuyper was not impressed with the Dutch Reformed church's social teaching. In a series of articles eventually published as *Christ and the Needy* in 1895, he complains that "for so many years the preaching in our churches has neglected to proclaim Jesus' direct teaching about social relationships." Kuyper notes the irony that while Christians found all kinds of reasons to assume that Jesus' social teaching had no contemporary relevance, it was often nonbelieving socialists who took Jesus' teaching most seriously. The chief problem was that too many pastors and teachers spiritualized Scripture. Where the Gospels speak of Jesus' poverty and humble identification with the poor, these leaders "used it to exhort to heavenly mindedness." Jesus proclaimed blessings on the poor and woes on the rich, but

> one can hardly approve of the constant *spiritualization* of all these statements in today's preaching such that every connection with life is eliminated from them by ignoring the social meaning implicit in them. ... Once one imagines that all such statements by Jesus apply only to the condition of the soul, one

breaks the connection between *soul* and *body*, between our
inner and outer life situation—a connection to which both
Scripture and Jesus hold fast.[1]

Such spiritualizing tendencies reflected the "spiritual poverty" of a church
that failed to grasp the depth of sin and evil and therefore failed to preach
the "full Christ" and the *whole* gospel.[2] The result was a Christian society
in which few Christians could be said to be followers of Christ "in *social
respects*," and in which "prevailing conditions and personal relationships ...
blaspheme the person and word of our blessed Savior." Kuyper has harsh
words for pastors guilty of such spiritualization: "Woe unto you if you
take just half the gospel of our Savior and admonish submission, while
concealing the divine mercy of the Christ of God for the socially oppressed
and for those who must bear a cross."[3]

Kuyper's antidote is to remind his readers of the comprehensive nature
of the gospel. Jesus brought "deliverance from the social needs of his time,"
first and foremost by breaking the power of the sin that lay at the root of
so much poverty. He not only secured justification through the forgiveness
of sins; he called his followers to conform to the justice of God, from which
such justification could not be separated. He therefore condemned the
"service of mammon" and the idolatry of capital. He consistently chose the
side of the poor, the "have-nots," wherever "poor and rich were at odds."[4]
Understanding this, the Protestant Reformers, "precisely by emphasizing
justification, reinforced justice among the people, deepened their sense of
justice, and promoted justice throughout the land."[5]

But—and this point was crucial for Kuyper—Jesus did not stop with
such spiritual deliverance, moral exhortation, and personal example. "He
also *organized*."[6] He established the church as a social body centered on the
ministry of the word, a ministry that encompassed his social teaching. Even
more poignantly, he established "an organized *ministry of benevolence* which
in the name of the Lord, who is the single owner of all goods, demands the

---

1. Abraham Kuyper, "Christ and the Needy," in this volume, p. 23.
2. Abraham Kuyper, "The Workers' Issue and the Church," in *OBE*, 1; Kuyper, "Christ
   and the Needy," 42.
3. Kuyper, "Christ and the Needy," 43.
4. Abraham Kuyper, "The Social Question and the Christian Religion," in *OBE*, 17.
5. Abraham Kuyper, "Income and Expenditure," in *OBE*, 4.
6. Kuyper, "Social Question and the Christian Religion," 19.

community of goods in the sense that it will not be tolerated in the circle of believers that a man or a woman should go hungry or lack clothing." Finally, he established the church on the principle of *"equality."* "He abolished all artificial divisions between men by joining rich and poor in one holy food at the Lord's Supper."[7]

The social principles of the gospel were taught by Jesus and embedded in the institutional structure of the church in order that they might gradually infuse the broader social order. And over time the gospel did indeed have a real, if imperfect, impact. Slavery was ended, the poor were cared for, and the moral principle of fundamental human equality was established. Indeed, "if the church had not strayed from her simplicity and heavenly ideal, the influence of the Christian religion on political institutions and societal relationships would eventually have become dominant."[8]

The diaconate was a particularly important expression of the church's social identity in Christ. Kuyper observed that Calvinism was unique among the major branches of Protestantism in its reinstating of the ecclesiastical office of poor relief.[9] He claimed that the original diaconate operated according to two important principles. First, it served the nonbelieving and believing poor alike, just as God shows mercy to both the just and the unjust. Second, it was intended "exclusively for the needy," not for "the aged, the widows and orphans among our working classes." In other words, it was not intended to replace ordinary means of care and support. Rather, it was designed for emergencies, for those poor and destitute who slipped through the ordinary network of care. Kuyper believed the social crisis of his own day had overwhelmed the resources of the diaconate and of families. Because the system had broken down, it was necessary for the state to intervene. But the eclipse of the diaconate could not be tolerated, because it was an expression of a fundamental Christian principle: the "diaconate is the expression of the morally elevating thought that help and care for the

---

7. Kuyper, "Social Question and the Christian Religion," 20.

8. Kuyper, "Social Question and the Christian Religion," 21. Kuyper maintained that "Christianity is preeminently social," and, "rightly viewed, the original organism of humanity, now purified, has been resurrected in the church of Christ" ("Social Question and the Christian Religion," 30n73).

9. See Matthew J. Tuininga, "Good News for the Poor: An Analysis of Calvin's Concept of Poor Relief and the Diaconate in Light of His Two Kingdoms Paradigm," *Calvin Theological Journal* 49, no. 2 (November 2014): 221–47.

needy do not come from man but from God. ... He receives his alms from the same God from whom the rich man receives his wealth."[10]

Kuyper argues that because care for the poor is rooted in the gospel, it must be conducted according to the gospel principles of love and justice. The poor do not merely have civil or political rights to relief, he maintained, nor should their needs be relieved merely to satisfy the economic purposes of the state. Rather, the poor are brothers and sisters made in the image of God, members of the social body whose well-being is an essential requirement of the health of that body. The people of any given country make up "a *community* willed by God, a living human *organism* ... standing under the law of life that we are all members of one another, so that the eye cannot do without the foot or the foot without the eye." As he puts it in *The Social Question and the Christian Religion*, "The really decisive question in all this is simply whether you recognize in the less fortunate, indeed in the poorest of the poor, not just a *persona miserabilis*, a wretched creature, but someone of your own flesh and blood and, for Christ's sake, your *brother*."[11]

The sort of love Kuyper had in mind therefore implied social solidarity as an expression of basic Christian equality. Following leading theologians of the Christian tradition such as Ambrose, Aquinas, and Calvin, Kuyper emphasizes that a certain "para-equality" with respect to the "ordinary requirements of life," matters such as shelter, bed, food, and clothing, is a demand of justice and right. "This is the right that the poor have, for Christ's sake, with respect to those possessing more. Those who possess more but fall short in this matter are not only unmerciful but commit an injustice, and for that injustice they will suffer the punishment of eternal judgment in eternal pain." Lest his readers imagine that he is exaggerating, Kuyper is ready with a stern appeal to Matthew 25, where Jesus declares that in the final judgment he will separate the sheep from the goats on precisely this basis. The lesson to Kuyper was as clear as it was sobering: "These *basic* ideas of Jesus about social relationships are at the same time the *main* ideas in his teaching about the kingdom." No one could read the Bible seriously and claim that "social relationships were a side issue for Jesus. In the Gospels the issue comes up again and again. It is explained both theoretically and practically in every possible manner. It forms one

---

10. Abraham Kuyper, "Draft Pension Scheme for Wage Earners," in *OBE*, 9–10. In this way Kuyper contrasted the diaconate with private charity and state provision.
11. Kuyper, "Social Question and the Christian Religion," 30, 54.

of the *salient* points in the whole of Jesus' preaching. Anyone who denies or disputes this is lacking in respect for the Word of the Lord. Anyone who bows before this Word must stand on our side in this matter."[12]

THE GODLESS POLITICS OF REVOLUTION AND MATERIALISM

While the gospel calls for a politics of charity and justice, Kuyper believed that the forces of the revolution were driving modern society toward secularism, materialism, and individualism. The crises of labor, poverty, democracy, journalism, education, and the family were all products of its godless and anti-social emphasis on human autonomy. At the same time, Kuyper found the conservative reaction to the forces of modernity to be just as troubling. Because the revolution's ideology ultimately consisted of rebellion against God, the solution was not conservatism but what Kuyper called social Christianity.

Kuyper's critique of revolutionary ideology often focuses on its radical individualism, which he places in sharp antithesis to the inherently social nature of Christianity. The French Revolution's rejection of the oppressive tyranny of the *ancien régime* was in many ways justified and even "horribly necessary," but its effect was the "demolition of all social organization" in a misguided attempt to return to "undeveloped nature." In the name of nature, the Revolution ripped apart the organic social ties that bind human beings to one another. It "separated, contrary to God's ordinances, nature from history and replaced the will of the *Creator of nations* with the will of the *individual*." Its ultimate effect was to run roughshod over nature itself, casting each individual onto a sea of ruthless competition. Thus "while the Christian religion seeks the dignity of the human person in the relationships of an organically integrated society, the French Revolution disrupted that organic tissue, severed those social bonds, and finally, with its atomistic tinkering, left us with nothing but the solitary, self-seeking individual that asserts its independence." Whereas the Christian religion, "as the fruit of divine compassion, introduced the world to a love that wells up from God, the French Revolution opposed this with the egoism of a passionate struggle for possessions." The Revolution "made the possession of money the highest good; and then it set every man against his fellow-man in the pursuit of money." This, Kuyper stresses, was the "pivot on which the whole social

---

12. Kuyper, "Christ and the Needy," 38.

question turns. The French Revolution, and so too present-day liberalism, is anti-social; and the social distress which today disturbs Europe is the evil fruit of the individualism that was enthroned with the French Revolution."[13]

The competition provoked by the Revolution's individualism was made all the worse by the "mercantile gospel" of "*laissez faire, laissez passer*," according to which economic competition among individuals was to be unrestrained by government. The constant need for efficiency and a competitive edge exacerbated the ever-increasing division of labor and drastically lowered the conditions of labor. The old organic ties of lord and servant gave way to the brittle ties of contracts easily severed. Labor was just another commodity managed according to the principles of supply and demand without regard for the well-being of workers or their families as human beings. The need for surplus capital encouraged the exploitation of labor, leaving "the broad lower strata of society with only so much as appeared strictly necessary for keeping them alive as instruments for feeding capital (for in this system labor counted for nothing more)."[14] Capitalism thus gave rise to unprecedented class warfare. Covetousness was unleashed and unrestrained.[15] The new capitalist "*aristocracy of money*" was more powerful than that of the *ancien régime*, and it had lost any sense of social obligation to the lower classes.

The Revolution could not offer individuals any god other than mammon "because it cut off the prospect of eternal life and directed men to seek happiness on earth, hence in earthly things. This created a base atmosphere in which everything was valued in terms of money and anything was sacrificed for money." The glitz and glitter of the rich was only the tip of the iceberg of materialism, advertising, and consumerism that trickled down to all classes. Kuyper indicts even the "bourgeois practice of instilling false needs in the poor by making a display of its wealth, and of undermining the contentment that can leave men happy with little by igniting in them ... a feverish passion for pleasure." Money—or mammon—was the god of capitalism, and it fixed the minds of the have-nots on their lack even as inequality between rich and poor rose to unprecedented heights. The Revolution preached liberty, equality, and fraternity. "But alas, the equality

---

13. Kuyper, "Social Question and the Christian Religion," 10n20, 12n22, 23-24.
14. Kuyper, "Social Question and the Christian Religion," 24-25. See Abraham Kuyper, "The Family, Society, and the State," in this volume.
15. See Abraham Kuyper, "You Shall Not Covet," in this volume.

they dreamed of turned out to be an increasingly offensive inequality, and for the promised fraternity they got a replay of the fable of the wolf and the lamb."[16]

The result was a social crisis in which the eventual demand of the lower classes for social democracy was inevitable. The protests of the free-market liberal elites notwithstanding, there was no rational reason why the lower classes should not push the logic of revolution to the point where they too might benefit from liberty, equality, and fraternity. "It must be stressed," Kuyper writes, "that the liberal calls a totally arbitrary halt on a trajectory which according to his theory has to be followed. Thus the liberal not only has spiritual kinship with the social democrat, but unlike him he is in the wrong, because he is arbitrary, self-serving, and inconsistent."[17]

Socialism emphasized "a rising sense of community, of the rights of community and the organic nature of society, in opposition to the one-dimensional individualism with which the French Revolution has impregnated our society, along with its corresponding economic school of *laissez faire, laissez passer*." But this "zeal for the *social* principle" led to "a battle over property rights and a war on capitalism, given that the individual finds his strongest bulwark precisely in his property." Absolute property rights were now viewed as the "insurmountable obstacle preventing society from doing justice to its sociological nature."[18] In fact, the social crisis spawned by the Revolution was giving way to all manner of reactions ranging from nihilism and anarchy to state socialism and social democracy. Those liberals who refused to embrace social democracy were the new conservatives. But they all shared a common foundation: commitment to the basic principle of the French Revolution.

Kuyper recognized the seeming contradiction in his claim that socialism was the logical and necessary outworking of the French Revolution even though it opposed the Revolution's liberal individualism. "This apparent contradiction stems from the fact that the individualistic character of the French Revolution is only a derived principle. It is not its root principle from which it drew its dynamic. That root principle is its defiant cry *Ni Dieu, ni maître!* Or, if you will: man's emancipation from God and from

---

16. Kuyper, "Social Question and the Christian Religion," 24, 26. See also Kuyper, "You Shall Not Covet."
17. Kuyper, "Social Question and the Christian Religion," 27n61.
18. Kuyper, "Social Question and the Christian Religion," 33–34.

the order instituted by him."[19] For all of his rhetoric about the antithesis between liberal individualism and social Christianity, Kuyper believed that the true conflict of the future was between secularist materialism and social Christianity, or, as he saw it, between godless revolution and fidelity to the creation ordinances of God. The heirs of the Revolution, whether from the left or the right, inevitably elevated the god of mammon in the place of the Creator. Class warfare continued to intensify because the rich and the poor and all those in between subjected their lives to the overriding purpose of material prosperity, each seeking control of the state in order to advance their own interests. "Thus, however idealistic social democracy may present itself, its striving remains focused, at bottom, on nothing other than acquiring more *financial* power. It calls for more material well-being but to the neglect of every other element."[20]

Much of Kuyper's critique of democracy as a political philosophy rests on this point. Five of the six chief dangers facing democracy that he identifies in "The Reefs of Democracy" (1895) revolve around materialism in one way or another. One of those reefs is the "materialization" of political life. Kuyper praised the social democrats for denouncing the inequality in society but charged that they sought to replace that inequality with a thoroughly materialistic understanding of human well-being that left no place for the spiritual. Yet humans consist of both body and soul. "If you invert the order of things, in defiance of our nature, of Christ's command, and of the moral character of politics, and push *material* interests so emphatically to the foreground that the spiritual aspect becomes a *side issue*, then you debase our life as human beings. ... You materialize law and justice." Thus while Christ called people to "Seek ye first the kingdom of God, and his righteousness; and all these things shall be added unto you," the social democrats effectively called people to "Seek ye first the improvement of your material needs, and the spiritual goods will follow."[21]

A further reef facing democracy was its tendency to exacerbate class warfare. To be sure, some measure of class conflict was the inevitable result of necessary inequality in a sinful world, but democracy "tempts one class in society to avail itself of the state machine as a tool to break the neck of the other class." No longer did the classes regard the state as an expression of

---

19. Kuyper, "Social Question and the Christian Religion," 38.
20. Kuyper, "Christ and the Needy," 69. See also Kuyper, "You Shall Not Covet."
21. Abraham Kuyper, "The Reefs of Democracy," in this volume, p. 67.

the sovereignty of God designed to transcend partisan interests by serving the common good of the organic community. Locked in conflict with one another, they threatened to "destroy all social harmony," debasing government into "an instrument for promoting economic interests."[22]

Along with materialism and class conflict, Kuyper identified the further danger of "rudeness and vulgarity" that would follow from the efforts of parties and demagogues to pander to crass popular interests. Political life would decline as uneducated people spurned the "finer nuances" of careful political reasoning in favor of "toxic slogans and glittering generalities," and the press would no doubt pander to such delusion. In the end all public solidarity would give way to the egoism of class interest. With its power increasingly reaching into the affairs of banks and corporations, government would fall prey to corruption. Respect for government and law would fall in proportion to the extent to which they came to serve the interests of money.[23]

The dangers Kuyper associated with materialism and class conflict ultimately pointed to the deeper problem with the Revolution's commitment to human autonomy. Its heirs increasingly proclaimed a role for the state that ran roughshod over nature. The first phase led it to "dismantle the existing order and leave nothing standing except the individual with his own free will and his supposed supremacy." In the second phase its adherents sought to "push God and his order aside ... and, deifying yourself, sit in the seat of God, ... and from your own brain create a new order of things." The socialists "look upon the entire structure of contemporary society as nothing but a product of human convention." The social democrats allowed the state to be absorbed into society, while the state socialists allowed society to be absorbed by the state, but both were totalizing in their efforts to make humanity "the maker of society in the strictest sense of the word," even where that required "violat[ing] natural laws wherever they stand in the way or push[ing] aside the moral law whenever it forms an obstacle." No sphere of life was left to develop organically according to the creation ordinances of God. "The social edifice has to be erected according to man's whim and caprice. That is why God has to go, so that men, no longer restrained by

---

22. Kuyper, "Reefs of Democracy," 69.
23. Kuyper, "Reefs of Democracy," 74.

natural bonds, can invert every moral precept into its opposite and subvert every pillar of human society."[24]

In "The Reefs of Democracy" Kuyper identifies this as the "pernicious idea" of "popular sovereignty" or "universal suffrage," the most dangerous reef threatening democracy. Kuyper opposed giving the ballot to all adult individuals, preferring a household-based society, but it was not the expansion of the right to vote about which he was concerned. Rather, by the terms "popular sovereignty" and "universal suffrage" he referred to "a system that opposes God's sovereignty with the proposition that governing authority resides in the latent will of the state, and that every inhabitant as a member of the body politic contributes toward expressing the will of the state. Then the state no longer depends on God but is self-sufficient, and the people acts politically on a foundation of atheism." In short, by popular sovereignty Kuyper denoted an inherently atheistic system in which government was seen to rest on human beings' "arbitrary will" rather than on the "ordinances of God."[25] It was a system in which majority rule was deemed a sufficient basis for any given policy, regardless of the rights of individuals or the integrity of various spheres of life. Such a theory of authority would inevitably grow more and more radical as it sought to remake society according to human desires, even tearing down such traditional bulwarks of the social order as the Christian household.

CHRISTIAN DEMOCRACY: KUYPER'S SOCIAL POLICY

It is against this revolutionary backdrop that Kuyper's ideas of sphere sovereignty and the rule of divine law are best understood. For Kuyper the central conflict of human history was the conflict between human sovereignty and divine sovereignty. The Revolution was merely the latest and most profound expression of human rebellion against the Creator. Yet in the gospel of Christ God had already asserted his own decisive claim: "There is not a square inch in the whole domain of our human existence over which Christ, who is sovereign over all, does not call out: 'Mine!'" This was not, for Kuyper, mere rhetoric. Nor was the appeal to Christ's lordship designed to justify the claims of a particular political party or agenda. Rather, by consigning all of God's authority to Christ, Kuyper sought to uncover all *other* human pretensions to illegitimate sovereignty. To be sure, God regularly

---

24. Kuyper, "Social Question and the Christian Religion," 34, 38, 43.
25. Kuyper, "Reefs of Democracy," 63.

delegates his authority to human beings, his image-bearers. But he does not delegate his "all-encompassing sovereignty" to any one human authority or institution. On the contrary, rooted in the creation itself are a myriad of creation ordinances, each governing its own sphere. As Kuyper puts it, "There are in life all kinds of spheres as numerous as constellations in the sky," each with "a unique principle as its center or focal point. ... Just as we speak of a moral world, a world of science, a world of business, an art world, so we speak still more properly of a sphere of morality, a family sphere, a sphere of socioeconomic life, each having its own *domain*."[26]

Kuyper made no attempt to articulate an authoritative list of the spheres. To do so would miss the point. What Kuyper did point out is that because the spheres are mutually interdependent—"all these spheres interlock like cogwheels"—they constantly threaten to disrupt or suppress one another. The task of the state is "to enable the various spheres, insofar as they manifest themselves visibly, to interact in a healthy way and to keep each of them within proper bounds."[27] Government exists to administer and uphold justice, but

> its duty is not to take over the tasks of family and society; the state should withdraw its hands from them. But as soon as collisions arise from contacts between the different spheres of life, so that one sphere encroaches upon or violates the divinely ordained domain of another, then a government has the God-given duty to uphold rights against arbitrary acts and to push back the stronger party in the name of God's rights to both spheres.[28]

A Christian political vision will therefore call the state to fulfill its proper responsibility with respect to each social sphere, including that of education, which was Kuyper's particular concern in the address "Sphere Sovereignty" that he delivered at the founding of the Free University.[29] The

---

26. Abraham Kuyper, "Sphere Sovereignty," in this volume, p. 120.
27. Kuyper, "Sphere Sovereignty," 121.
28. Kuyper, "Social Question and the Christian Religion," 51.
29. Kuyper believed that education had long been dominated by an "authoritarian" state whose policy of secularization served to "weaken private initiative and dampen personal energy" with severe religious, economic, and political consequences. Securing equal support for religious schools therefore became one of Kuyper's most dynamic policy initiatives. See Kuyper, "Reefs of Democracy."

state is to do this without usurping the sovereignty of God delegated to each sphere. In this sense liberty is a fundamental commitment of Christian political theology. Christians must always be at the forefront of attempts to defend the liberty of organic human life from the invasive tendencies of the revolutionary state.

At its heart Kuyper's public theology was fundamentally deontological. Underlying all human flourishing was the sovereignty of God as communicated through his law. In its purest form, Kuyper believed, this law was expressed in the Ten Commandments. Properly understood and fulfilled, the law "coincides ... with the image of the Son of God. ... In its ultimate completion the law and the Christ are one. Thus the law explicates the Christ to you, and Christ shows you the unity of the law in its completion." This was a radical claim, designed to encourage pastors "finely and strictly and sternly" to preach the law, and Kuyper went to great lengths to dispel concerns that his emphasis on the law was contrary to the teaching of the apostle Paul. Yet at the heart of Kuyper's defense of the law in his commentary on Lord's Day 44b is not a nuanced biblical theology of law but a practical reflection on what the Christian tradition has called God's moral law. For Kuyper, that moral law was best communicated in the Ten Commandments, but it was also "woven into our creaturely existence through creation." While sin has undermined humans' "awareness and knowledge of the law," through common grace God has restrained the power of sin such that "also in the unregenerated and unconverted there is still always a remnant of knowledge of the law." This law, which the Christian tradition historically called natural law, but which Kuyper preferred to describe as God's creation ordinances, helps to preserve "a certain civil justice which does not accomplish anything for salvation but makes a humane life in human society possible and thus provides a place for the church to find a foothold."[30] Both the state and the church have the responsibility to maintain it.

But law itself could not save a sinful society. Only the gospel offered a sufficient response to the Revolution and its god of mammon: "Legislation by itself will not cure our sick society unless at the same time drops of the medicine enter the hearts of rich and poor." The poor required much more than outward possessions and sensual pleasures. They needed "spiritual well-being" and the "peace of God."[31] For this reason, material effi-

---

30. Abraham Kuyper, "Our Relationship to the Law," in this volume, p. 376.
31. Kuyper, "Social Question and the Christian Religion," 52–53.

ciency could not be the sole criteria by which to evaluate a social system. Christianity highlighted "deeper-lying principles" that had to be taken into account. As far as Kuyper was concerned, "either coercion will make way again for love, for God's sake and to the church's credit; or else coercion will gain the upper hand, but only to have the state absorbed into society and at last to see society and government sink away into communism."[32]

Kuyper understood the argument of the social democrats that material improvement would elevate the lives of oppressed people "*morally* and *intellectually*." But, he charged, "For the time being these are just so many words, and meanwhile they restrict people's horizon to existence in this life." Moral and intellectual well-being would not simply emerge by themselves in a context of plenty. They had to be actively promoted. Just as Jesus' social teaching was part of his announcement of the kingdom of heaven, so the problem of poverty required that Christians, like Jesus, "do not for a moment wage even the struggle against social injustice otherwise than in connection with the kingdom of heaven."[33] It was this that distinguished Christians from socialists.

On the other hand, it was only a complete Christianity, a *social* Christianity, that would be of any use. "If you fail to realize this and think the evil can be exorcized by fostering greater piety, kindlier treatment and ampler charity, you may think that we face a religious question, or a philanthropic question, but not a *social* question. The social question is not a reality for you until you level an *architectonic critique* at human society as such and accordingly deem a different arrangement of the social order desirable, and also possible." Christians had to reject the anti-social individualism of laissez-faire liberalism. "If ... the question is raised whether our human society is an *aggregate of individuals* or an *organic body*, then all those who are Christians must place themselves on the side of the social movement and against liberalism."[34] Nor could Christians approve of a state that remained passive in the face of grinding poverty, for the sake of free-market principles.

Kuyper's insistence on a social Christian approach to politics led him to articulate distinct Christian perspectives on classic liberal themes of property, human dignity, rights, and democracy. Invoking the Christian

---

32. Kuyper, "Draft Pension Scheme," 11.
33. Kuyper, "Christ and the Needy," 35.
34. Kuyper, "Social Question and the Christian Religion," 29, 44. See also n112.

moral tradition, he utterly rejected the liberal notion of absolute property rights that some conservative Christians were defending. It was legitimate to appeal to the eighth commandment, "You shall not steal," as warrant for the ownership of resources necessary for one's life. This was a basic principle of natural law. But "it is most incorrect the way many people have appealed to the eighth commandment in order to defend *today's* distribution of wealth as well as the notion of ownership rights as they are *currently* exercised." If property owners "try to deduce from the eighth commandment that all they have is their lawful property and that God has given them the freedom to do with it as they please, Christian ethics has the duty and call to break down all such false notions." One only has the right to dispose of one's belongings "*in order to do good.*" The church is called to preach "constantly and unceasingly" that God alone possesses full ownership of goods; human beings are merely stewards.[35]

A corollary of this principle, for Kuyper, again following the Christian tradition, is that "we can never have any other property right than in association with the organic coherence of mankind, hence also with the organic coherence of mankind's goods."[36] Thus while communism is inherently wrong, a social system in which, say, land is held in common might not be. The eighth commandment could *not*, therefore, be used as a weapon against the social democrats. Its prohibition of theft "does not as such have anything to say about the nature of the distribution of earthly goods and makes room for different forms of the distribution of wealth." Indeed, Kuyper invokes the Heidelberg Catechism's broad definition of theft as justification for the claim that "*a very large part* of the belongings in this world are stolen property."[37] He condemns excessive land ownership, insisting that the rights of the poor were violated if they were left in poverty while others amassed wealth.[38]

Kuyper also argues that the eighth commandment requires government to regulate property in accord with principles of justice. "The supposition that the right of ownership is regulated on its own by social relationships is as a whole false, and to the degree that it does contain some truth, it does

---

35. Abraham Kuyper, "You Shall Not Steal," in *OBE*, 716–17, 720, emphasis added.
36. Kuyper, "Social Question and the Christian Religion," 45.
37. Kuyper, "You Shall Not Steal," 717–18. See also Kuyper, "Social Question and the Christian Religion,"46–47.
38. Kuyper asserted in a meditation on Isaiah 5:8, "Large landholding is rooted in sin. It militates against the ordinances of God." See Abraham Kuyper, "Woe unto Them That Join House to House," in *OBE*, 1.

not exonerate the government that as God's handmaid has indeed been charged with the responsibility to ensure that the regulation of the right of ownership does not lead to the ruin of society." Thus, Kuyper insists, "the government is to direct the distribution of wealth" in accord with biblical principles. Such regulation must extend to "land ownership, interest rates, firstborn rights, and rights of inheritance," and it must ensure "that the repulsive inequality between powerful capitalists and defenseless citizens remains within certain limits."[39] Scripture does not provide particular details here, but it does provide general principles from which Christians could discern that the theory of absolute property rights and the laissez-faire economic theory that went with it were unjust.[40] The social situation of Kuyper's day "aroused situations that cry out loudly for God's justice," and all conscientious Christians were obligated to work to improve the laws in accord with that justice.[41]

Kuyper also articulates a Christian conception of fundamental human dignity in contrast to the sort of human dignity envisioned by the Revolution. The Revolution imagined human beings to be autonomous individuals, each seeking their own self-fulfillment. In contrast, Christianity characterizes human beings as subjects of God created for loving service within "the relationships of an organically integrated society." The Revolution embraced human pride, launching a program of social deconstruction that wrenched apart "everything that gives human life its dignified coherence." Christianity recognizes all persons to be sinful and needful of grace and repentance. Whereas the Revolution robbed the poor of their dignity by suggesting that they lacked the chief things worth living for—"outward possessions, material goods and sensual pleasures"—Christianity offers the poor the hope and happiness that comes from the fear of God.[42] Christ himself had identified with the poor and the oppressed, not the rich and the powerful. It angered Kuyper that many of the poor were tempted to follow social democracy because Christians had failed to proclaim the full social implications of the gospel.[43] "When from the side of democratic socialism

---

39. Kuyper, "You Shall Not Steal," 736–37, 739.
40. Kuyper, "Social Question and the Christian Religion," 46n115.
41. Kuyper, "You Shall Not Steal," 743.
42. Kuyper, "Social Question and the Christian Religion," 22–23, 53.
43. Kuyper recognized that the *demoralization* that follows on the heels of material need" led many to abandon Christianity. "Were not almost all those who now rage once baptized? And following their baptism, what has been spent on those thousands to

and anarchism an enticing, defiant call is targeted also at *our* working people and little folk [*kleine luyden*], with the aim of making them forsake their God, stimulate their greed, and inflame their passions, is it then not our calling, our bounden duty, to make the voice of our Savior heard in reply to those cries out of the depths?"[44]

For Kuyper equality in human dignity called for at least a "para-equality" of possessions. Absolute equality was out of the question, but it was unjust that some could not meet their most basic needs while others lived in luxury. "The worker, too, must be able to live as a person created in the image of God. He must be able to fulfill his calling as husband and father. He too has a soul to lose, and therefore he must be able to serve his God just as well as you. ... To treat the workingman simply as a 'factor of production' is to violate his human dignity."[45] This concept of human dignity led Kuyper to use the language of rights to describe the claims persons might take to government. For instance, people who have spent their lives working responsibly "have a moral right to a pension when their strength begins to fail." This right does not come from government or from human beings but is "grounded in ordinances imposed by God on mankind."[46] He likewise argued that the people collectively "has a right to defend, *before* the government and if need be *against* the government, those God-given liberties which it has received in its organic components." Such a right came from God, not from government. "This is not a legal but a moral right, and on that ground alone it never stops in its quest for a political voice."[47]

It was this right that grounded Kuyper's conviction that while government receives its authority from the sovereign God (hence nullifying the principle of popular sovereignty), the people maintain the right to voice their concerns and defend their liberties. This is a right properly exercised through broad popular suffrage and through a democratic parliament that possesses the power of the purse. In fact, Kuyper argued that according to

---

make them understand, instead of the caricature of the Christian religion against which they now utter their curses, something—at least something—of the true love of God that there is in Christ Jesus?" Christian theologians and intellectuals had utterly failed the working class. See Kuyper, "Social Question and the Christian Religion," 41–42. See also Kuyper, "Reefs of Democracy."

44. Kuyper, "Christ and the Needy," 44.
45. Kuyper, "Social Question and the Christian Religion," 50.
46. Kuyper, "Draft Pension Scheme," 1.
47. Kuyper, "Reefs of Democracy," 49.

God's ordinances, as a people matures its political forms should become more democratic. "As a tree trunk during its growth expands and splits every bond and obstacle, so the natural growth of a people bursts every shackle with which its development is being held back." To oppose democracy was to oppose a "developmental law of national life." Kuyper declared that "the task of each of us as Christians is to foster that development and at the same time to guide it into proper channels." He defended expanding the franchise to the lower class not as a natural (that is, human-derived) or civil right but as a *"moral* right." Where that right was not honored, "injustice is done to one segment of the nation because the other segment arrogates to itself the right to reserve all representative power for itself."[48]

But the modern tendency was to collapse everything into the all-powerful social state. While Kuyper advocated a stronger role for government in protecting the rights of the poor, he insisted that government do so in a way that preserved the integrity of the other spheres. One of those spheres was that of private enterprise. Laissez-faire economics represented the autonomy of the market taken to an extreme, to the point of trampling over the other spheres, and should therefore be rejected. But the market should nevertheless be free to develop according to its own principles in accord with the proper development of the other spheres. Capital and business had their rights, even though these could not be permitted to run roughshod over the rights of laborers to good working conditions, to a living wage, and to the organization of unions.[49]

Kuyper was especially concerned about the family. In opposition to the anti-social atomism of the Revolution, Kuyper argued that the family, not the individual, was the true basis for the social order. It was in the family, more than any other social institution, that individuals learned the meaning of justice and the virtues of citizenship. Indeed, Kuyper argued, "The basic premise of our antirevolutionary politics is rooted in the family." The family "is the first to give shape to all the veins of the network along which the state sends out its life-blood to its widest circumference and back again to its center." The relationship of parents and children communicated the organic nature of human society, putting the lie to myths of individualism and the social contract. Fathers and mothers taught their children practices of justice, fairness, reconciliation, and arbitration, providing a foundation

---

48. Kuyper, "Reefs of Democracy," 80.
49. Kuyper, "Reefs of Democracy."

for peaceful judicial systems and constitutional arrangements of power. In fact, the true meaning of the revolutionary slogan of "liberty, equality, and fraternity" was revealed in the relationships of brothers and sisters in the Christian household rather than among individuals in the secular state.[50] The relationships of husbands and wives embodied the fundamental social virtues of trust, accommodation, and honor, all in a context of faithfulness. Even the relationships of masters and servants fostered virtues of service and care that organically knit the different classes of society together as one body.

Kuyper was unabashedly patriarchal in his vision of the family. As he saw it, the Christian household revealed the proper balance between principles of equality and inequality. On the one hand, the members of a family are fundamentally equal to one another before God.[51] On the other hand, in numerous respects, including authority, they are profoundly unequal. God has ordained certain expressions of authority that are inviolable, including that of husbands over wives, parents over children, and masters over servants. "Households where the woman is number one and the man plays a subordinate role have become all too common. Such arrangements are sinful. Households like that have been turned inside out by the Revolution and are in conflict with God's ordinance." For Christians to be antirevolutionary was to be committed to maintaining these relationships in accord with "the solid ground of the Word of God."[52]

In accord with his theory of sphere sovereignty, Kuyper argued that the family needed to be promoted and protected so that it could develop freely in accord with God's will, and so remain "that wondrous creation from which the rich fabric of man's organic life is to evolve. ... We do not have to organize society; we have only to develop the germ of organization which God himself implanted in our human nature." The various movements spawned by the Revolution, however, trampled over the family in the name of individualism and social reconstruction. "Away, therefore, with false individualism, and anathema on every effort to break up the family!"[53] Because sexual immorality was a threat to the family it was also a matter

---

50. Kuyper, "The Family, Society, and the State."
51. Interestingly, here Kuyper rejected "natural" superiority as a basis for household hierarchy, preferring to rest his case for household authority on Scripture alone ("The Family, Society, and the State").
52. Kuyper, "The Family, Society, and the State," 320
53. Kuyper, "Social Question and the Christian Religion," 49.

of proper political concern. "It is especially for this reason that adultery, prostitution, and all unchastity constitute a direct threat to the welfare of the state. These sins will gradually produce a generation without any faithfulness or trust, without any sense of mutual accommodation, and without any sense of honor for the nation."[54]

Taken together, all of these principles made Kuyper's social policy balanced and nuanced. His workers' pension plan, which he proposed in the Dutch Parliament in 1895, serves as a helpful illustration. Kuyper saw his pension plan—which would guarantee workers the continuation of a living wage in their declining years—as a partial solution to the disintegration of the organic social relationships that had once provided such support. He argued that while the abolition of traditional social bonds such as serfdom and guilds had increased individual liberty, it had reduced economic solidarity and security. Due to ruthless competition workers could no longer negotiate living wages with their employers in order to provide for their families, nor could they band together in unions to limit competition in the labor market. Kuyper's conclusion was simple. "Clearly, only the government can help."[55]

But, Kuyper insisted, government should not ordinarily take up the permanent responsibility of caring for workers. Such a permanent role on the part of government would usurp the role of various other spheres, so hindering the organic development of society. It would take away from the dignity of workers by eliminating room for private initiative. And it would greatly constrict the possibilities for private charity and bonds of care that aimed to serve the whole person. The work of charity for the poor was a task for individuals, churches, and other social organizations, not the task of government.[56] Nevertheless, "when pauperism spreads and philanthropy falls short and starvation is imminent, government *inaction* would

---

54. Kuyper, "The Family, Society, and the State," 282.
55. Kuyper, "Draft Pension Scheme," 3.
56. Kuyper defined charity as material assistance to those who are poor and unable or unwilling to work, whether "through their own fault or through no fault of their own." Such persons are rightly left to the care of the church and to private generosity. The draft pension plan, on the other hand, was concerned with those individuals who had worked hard their entire life yet had insufficient resources to care for themselves, those who had been disabled by sickness or accident, those who were unemployed despite a desire to work, or family members whose working caregivers had died. See Kuyper, "Draft Pension Scheme," 6, 13.

be criminal." When the social crisis is so desperate that "private initiative cannot hope to rectify" it, government must step in. As Kuyper defined the principle, "government is duty-bound to protect rights if injustice results when they are left in the care of the private sector." "Such intervention should not permanently displace private initiative, but instead should assist private initiative, strengthen it, and so conduct affairs that before long government can withdraw again."[57]

On the other hand, sometimes a state of affairs required permanent legislation backed by coercive force. Kuyper believed that just as the government regulated trade and commerce, so "wage labor has come to need enduring legislation to guide and protect it. And this level of involvement by government will not be temporary but permanent." Just as there was a commercial code, so there needed to be a labor code. It was not sufficient simply to establish a voluntary insurance plan. For while many workers could be expected to save voluntarily, "sloth and sin" would prevent others from doing so.[58] On the other hand, the government could not be expected to finance such a plan. A government-funded program that amounted to a system of handouts would paralyze private initiative rather than strengthen it. It would amount to "distributing money, not justice." Material assistance on the part of the state had to be limited to the "smallest dimensions" if it was not to "weaken the working classes and break their natural resilience."[59]

Kuyper's solution was "mandatory participation." Workers would be required on a weekly basis to contribute to a retirement fund that was payable to themselves and their families. Employers would be required to provide funds for sickness and disability insurance. Workers would collectively contribute to a fund providing unemployment insurance. Initially government would supplement these programs, but its role would gradually diminish to that of oversight. The goal was to secure the just rights of workers and their families without making government relief permanent, as well as to reduce the number of people requiring charity, to the point that the resources of churches and private initiative would again be sufficient to serve their needs. Those who had earned care as a matter of justice and right could do so through the pension plan, while those who were "destitute"

---

57. Kuyper, "Draft Pension Scheme," 3–4, 6.
58. Kuyper, "Draft Pension Scheme," 4.
59. Kuyper, "Social Question and the Christian Religion," 51–52.

or who "hit bottom through their own fault" could experience the care of God through the diaconate of the church.[60]

In this way the dignity of those who sought to earn a living wage and provide for their families would be preserved through the combined contributions of capital and labor, without swallowing any of these spheres into the all-powerful grasp of the state. For their part, the destitute and otherwise poor could be served in a way that served their spiritual needs as well as their material needs. It was a plan of government intervention that respected the social and private purposes of property, preserved the integrity of organic society and private initiative, secured the rights of workers and their families in accord with their equal dignity, and promoted loving care for the spiritual and material needs of the poor by granting due place to the social ministry of the church.

CONCLUSION: KUYPER'S SOCIAL THOUGHT FOR TODAY

Abraham Kuyper was deeply conscious of the eclipse of orthodox Christianity in modern Europe. He accepted pluralism as a defining feature of his world, and he thought long and hard about how Christians might participate politically in a pluralistic society from a principled theological standpoint. For all of his skepticism about the future of a world increasingly distancing itself from Christianity, Kuyper could be breathtakingly optimistic about progress and modernity. His writings reflect the hubris of his day with respect to matters of race, nationality, and colonialism, and Kuyper maintained thoroughly conservative patriarchal views with respect to gender and the household. Yet in the areas of poor relief, labor, health care, and education he was a committed progressive. In short, Kuyper's social thought exhibited all the paradoxes one might expect from a late-nineteenth-century European Christian democrat. His intellectual brilliance and proclivity toward dialectical thought enabled him to offer a social and political perspective that defied the reactionary categories of the right or the left. He embraced key ideas from the conservatives, liberals,

---

60. Kuyper, "Draft Pension Scheme," 4, 6–8, 12; see also 8–13; Kuyper, "Social Question and the Christian Religion," 41.

and socialists alike, while showing how a Christian perspective must ultimately differ from all three.[61]

A striking feature of Kuyper's thought is his ruthless criticism of the liberal tradition and laissez-faire capitalism, both of which he associated with the French Revolution. And yet, in the irony of all ironies, Kuyper waxed eloquently about the virtues of the United States and its glorious future, despite the fact that in some respects the United States displayed its liberal and capitalist commitments with even greater vigor than did nineteenth-century France. Kuyper quickly forgot his penetrating criticism of the liberal tradition when he took the United States into his sights, viewing America through rose-colored glasses. In part he was able to do this because of his selective historiography. Kuyper argued that, like the Netherlands and Britain, the United States owed its commitment to liberty to its Calvinist inheritance, an inheritance transmitted to America by the Puritans, secured through an essentially conservative revolution, and carefully institutionalized by pious founding fathers. True, he acknowledged, America was a republic that vested sovereignty in its people. But Americans were a deeply religious people who acknowledged the sovereignty of God. This was in stark contrast to the form of liberalism that had emerged in France with its godless revolution.

Kuyper's optimism about America stemmed from his belief in the possibility of a sort of Christian democracy (or what we might call Christian liberalism). It was not democracy *itself* to which he was opposed. On the contrary, he viewed it as the moral right of a mature people. Nor was Kuyper opposed to regulated free-market capitalism. On the contrary, he advocated policies that would secure social justice with minimal government interference in other spheres. Kuyper's disciplined Christian reflection on politics enabled him to transcend the categories of left and right. He discerned that liberalism and conservatism, capitalism and socialism alike

---

61. Kuyper's proposals also reflected the political context that he inhabited: the parliamentary constitutional monarchy of the modern Netherlands. The version of democracy he defended, with its rejection of popular sovereignty and its distinction between the parliament and the government, made little sense in republican contexts that differed from constitutional monarchies such as the Netherlands or Britain. Likewise, his insistence that Reformed Christians should maintain their own minority political party, constructing alliances with other parties on specific issues while avoiding anything like a permanent alliance, presupposed the existence of a multiparty parliamentary system quite different from that of the United States.

rested on the atheistic, individualistic, and materialistic assumptions of modernity, and he grasped how crucial it was for Christians to refuse to allow such modern assumptions to dictate the shape of Christian political thought. Christians needed to articulate an alternative political theology rooted in the creation ordinances through which God has enabled human society to flourish in all of its diversity. What is more, it was insufficient for Christians to seek a social order that merely conformed to God's law outwardly. Christians needed to seek the welfare and salvation of the whole person—body and soul—and the whole society—material and spiritual. In short, Kuyper offered a vision of charity and justice that was ultimately rooted in the Christian gospel.

How might we apply Kuyper's ideas in our own pluralistic and often deeply polarized contexts? Certainly not by pandering to the politics of the right or the left (although no doubt Kuyper would have incorporated key insights of both the right and the left). Nor can it be by offering simplistic appeals to the lordship of Christ as crass justification for imposing our political predilections on others. Like Christ, Christians are called to witness to the lordship of Christ through sacrificial service, not domination (see Phil 2:5-11). As Kuyper grasped, such service calls us to seek charity and justice for all people.

Two core commitments must define any Kuyperian political or social vision. First, Christian public engagement must be grounded in a core commitment to divine sovereignty as the fundamental principle of creation. Kuyper shared the classic Christian conviction that God does not rule creation simply through his word, from the outside, so to speak. Rather, his moral law—what Christians have classically called natural law and what Kuyper called creation ordinances—is written into creation itself. Thus for any human society to flourish, its practices, customs, and laws must arise from creation itself. This is true for every sphere, from economics and journalism, to sexuality and marriage. Government's task is not to usurp the work of these spheres, even when we want it to. Rather, its task is to secure order, stability, and justice, in order that humans might freely serve God in every area of organic society.

Second, Christian public engagement must be social in orientation. We cannot flourish as isolated individuals, each pursuing our own happiness according to our own lights, just so long as we do no harm to another. Rather, we are called to stand in solidarity with one another as brothers and sisters called to be united in Christ. The tendency of modernity has been to reduce all social ties to the level of the easily broken contract. Kuyper grasped the classic Christian insistence that we are one another's keepers. Whether in our stewardship of resources, our faithfulness to the bonds of embodied life, or our struggles against injustice, we are called to bear one another's burdens. This solidarity should characterize our churches and our communities, but it must also characterize our politics.

ABRAHAM KUYPER: ALWAYS REFORMING

JOHN WITTE JR.

English historian Herbert Butterfield once wrote of the habit of his fellow English Protestants "to hold some German up their sleeves ... and at appropriate moments to strike the unwary Philistine on the head with this secret weapon, the German scholar having decided in a final manner whatever point may have been at issue."[1] Many American Protestants have had a similar habit of holding a secret Dutchman up their sleeves with which to strike unwary Philistines on the head—whether in the classroom, courtroom, or conference hall.

The "secret Dutchman" is the author of the work you are holding, Abraham Kuyper (1837-1920), one of the great polymaths in the history of the Netherlands. Kuyper was a formidable theologian and philosopher, journalist and educator, churchman and statesman of extraordinary accomplishment. He was the author of some 223 scholarly works, and thousands of devotionals, sermons, speeches, lectures, letters, op-eds, briefing papers,

---

1. Herbert Butterfield, *Christianity and History* (New York: Charles Scribner's Sons, 1949), 1.

and media quotes.[2] He served for nearly half a century as editor-in-chief of both the Dutch daily *Standaard* and the weekly *Heraut*. He founded the Free University of Amsterdam in 1880 and taught there intermittently for two decades. Throughout much of his career, Kuyper was a leader of the Protestant Antirevolutionary Party in the Netherlands, and served as member of Parliament, minister of justice, and then prime minister from 1901 to 1905. On the national celebration of his seventieth birthday in 1907, his toastmaster declared: "The history of the Netherlands, in Church, in State, in Society, in Press, in School, and in the Sciences of the last forty years, cannot be written without the mention of his name on almost every page, for during this period the biography of Dr. Kuyper is to a considerable extent the history of the Netherlands."[3]

Happily, Kuyper's life and work are no longer so secret in the English-speaking world, or indeed well beyond now too in the Global South and on the Pacific Rim. Over the past generation, several of Kuyper's writings have been (re)published in English, along with a score of major new academic studies, and hundreds of articles and dissertations.[4] These earlier

---

2. See *AKCR*, xi. See also the invaluable 756-page guide, *AKB*; George Harinck, "Foreword," in *AKB*, xiii (referencing roughly 2,200 devotionals).

3. Quoted by John Hendrik de Vries, "Biographical Note," in Abraham Kuyper, *Lectures on Calvinism*, repr. ed. (Grand Rapids: Eerdmans, 1981), ii.

4. Kuyper's writings: see *AKB*, 660–711. Major new academic studies: see, among others, Brant M. Himes, *For a Better Worldliness: Abraham Kuyper, Dieterich Bonhoeffer, and Discipleship for the Common Good* (Eugene, OR: Wipf & Stock, 2018); Craig G. Bartholomew, *Contours of the Kuyperian Tradition* (Downers Grove, IL: IVP Academic, 2017); James D. Bratt, *Abraham Kuyper: Modern Calvinist, Christian Democrat* (Grand Rapids: Eerdmans, 2013); John Halsey Wood, *Going Dutch in the Modern Age: Abraham Kuyper's Struggle for a Free Church in the Nineteenth-Century Netherlands* (Oxford: Oxford University Press, 2013); Ernst N. Conradie, ed., *Creation and Salvation: Dialogue on Abraham Kuyper's Legacy for Contemporary Ecotheology* (Leiden: Brill, 2011); Richard J. Mouw, *Abraham Kuyper: A Short and Personal Introduction* (Grand Rapids: Eerdmans, 2011); Steve Bishop and John H. Kok, *Abraham Kuyper: A Collection of Readings on the Life, Work, and Legacy of Abraham Kuyper* (Sioux Center, IA: Dordt College Press, 2013); Richard J. Mouw, *The Challenges of Cultural Discipleship: Essays in the Line of Abraham Kuyper* (Grand Rapids: Eerdmans, 2011); Vincent E. Bacote, *The Spirit in Public Theology: Appropriating the Legacy of Abraham Kuyper* (Grand Rapids: Baker Academic, 2005); Jasper Vree and Johan Zwaan, *Abraham Kuyper's Commentatio (1860): The Young Kuyper about Calvin, a Lasco, and the Church*, 2 vols. (Leiden: Brill, 2005); John Bolt, *A Free Church, A Holy Nation: Abraham Kuyper's American Public Theology* (Grand Rapids: Eerdmans, 2001); Luis E. Lugo, ed., *Religion, Pluralism, and Public Life: Abraham Kuyper's Legacy for the Twenty-First Century*

efforts have been greatly enhanced by the production of Kuyper's twelve volumes of Abraham Kuyper Collected Works of Public Theology, all published in crisp English edition, expertly translated, judiciously edited, and handsomely produced. Here readers can find an excellent cross-section of his work over a long career—multivolume theological tomes, expansive political platforms and policy statements, learned sermons and speeches, pithy op-eds and popular articles.

All these new publications have not only solidified Kuyper's place high on the honor roll of great Dutch Calvinists. They have also helped secure his standing as a towering Christian public intellectual of the later nineteenth century, whose teachings offer an enduring and edifying witness to modern churches, states, and societies alike. Much as his contemporary Pope Leo XIII led a retrieval and reconstruction of the teachings of Thomas Aquinas and the Thomist tradition to reform modern Catholicism, so Abraham Kuyper helped revive and retrieve the best teachings of John Calvin and the Reformed tradition to reform modern Protestantism. Much as Leo used natural law and subsidiarity theory to build a new "social teachings" movement for modern Catholic engagement with the world, so Kuyper used theories of creation order, common grace, and sphere sovereignty to build a comparable political theology for the Protestant world. Much as Leo understood the need for the "development of doctrine" to keep Catholicism as a vital and valuable alternative to secular forms of liberalism and socialism in his day, so Kuyper urged an ethic of *semper reformanda*, a constant openness to reform the Reformed tradition in light of new insights from Scripture and the Spirit, and new challenges of his religious pluralistic and rapidly secularizing world.[5]

(Grand Rapids: Eerdmans, 2000); James E. McGoldrick, *God's Renaissance Man: The Life and Work of Abraham Kuyper* (Auburn, MA: Evangelical Press, 2000); Cornelius van der Kooi and Jan de Bruijn, eds., *Kuyper Reconsidered: Aspects of His Life and Works* (Amsterdam: VU Uitgeverei, 1999); and Peter S. Heslam, *Creating a Christian Worldview: Abraham Kuyper's Lectures on Calvinism* (Grand Rapids: Eerdmans, 1998). Articles and dissertations: see, for instance, the excellent essays assembled in the *Kuyper Center Review*, 5 vols. (2011–15). See further periodicals listed in *AKB*, 729–44.

5. See, for instance, Jordan J. Ballor, ed., *Makers of Modern Christian Social Thought: Leo XIII and Abraham Kuyper on the Social Question* (Grand Rapids: Acton Institute, 2016); Symposium, "A Century of Christian Social Teaching: The Legacy of Leo XIII and Abraham Kuyper," *Journal of Markets & Morality* 5 (2002): 1–304; David VanDrunen, *Natural Law and the Two Kingdoms: A Study in the Development of Reformed Social Thought* (Grand Rapids: Eerdmans, 2010), 276–315; Russell Hittinger, "Pope Leo XIII,"

The main topics that occupy Kuyper in this volume *On Charity and Justice*—family, property, labor, welfare, democracy, sovereignty, and liberty—have been of cardinal importance to the Calvinist tradition since the sixteenth century, with deeper roots of reflection at hand in the Bible and earlier classical and Christian traditions. Most of these topics remain critical and sometimes controversial today, as Matthew Tuininga relates in his brilliant editorial introduction herein as well in as his own recent masterwork on Calvinist political theology.[6] On some of these topics, Kuyper largely stuck to the tradition, convinced by the enduring cogency of his forebearer's views, and content to make only modest reforms in light of new challenges. On other topics, he was transformative, urging reforms of thought and practice that still remain relevant. Allow me just two main illustrations.

Kuyper's discussion of the family or "The Family, Society, and the State" illustrates his more traditional side. The family was one of the first institutions that sixteenth-century Protestants had reformed root and branch.[7] John Calvin in particular replaced medieval Catholic teachings that marriage is a sacrament under the canon law authority of the church with the idea of marriage as a covenant under the spiritual guidance of the church and the legal governance of the Christian state. The Christian family was created by God as a two-in-one-flesh union of "male and female" called to "be fruitful and multiply" (Gen 1:27-28; 2:24). Couples were to court properly, and marriages were to be formed with mutual consent of the couple, parental consent on both sides, two or more witnesses, public state registration, and consecration and celebration in a church wedding. Both husbands and wives were called to respect the other's sexual bodies and needs and to abstain from sex only temporarily and by mutual consent (1 Cor 7:2-5). Spouses had to love, respect, and sacrifice for each other, although wives were to "submit in everything to their husbands" as Eve was made subject

---

in John Witte Jr. and Frank S. Alexander, eds., *Modern Christian Teachings on Law, Politics, and Human Nature* (New York: Columbia University Press, 2005), 39-73; Nicholas P. Wolterstorff, "Abraham Kuyper (1837-1920)," in Witte and Alexander, *Modern Christian Teachings*, 288-327.

6. See Matthew J. Tuininga, *Calvin's Political Theology and the Public Engagement of the Church: Christ's Two Kingdoms* (Cambridge: Cambridge University Press, 2017), esp. 1-22, 355-78.

7. See John Witte Jr., *From Sacrament to Contract: Marriage, Religion, and Law in the Western Tradition*, 2nd ed. (Louisville, KY: Westminster John Knox, 2012), 113-286.

to Adam after the fall, and the church "submits to Christ" (Gen 3:16; Eph 5:21–33). God hates divorce (Mal 2:16) and discourages remarriage (Matt 19:9; Rom 7:2–3), but allows it in cases of serious fault, such as adultery or desertion (Matt 19:9; 1 Cor 7:15), much as Yahweh himself threatened to "divorce" his beloved metaphorical bride Israel when she "played the whore" in violation of the covenant (Ezek 16; Jer 3:7–8; Isa 50:1). Both fathers and mothers were to nurture, educate, and discipline their children in loving preparation for their own vocations, marriages, and lives as adults. Adult children were to honor and obey their parents (Exod 20:12), and to care for them in their old age in exchange for presumptive inheritance. Church, state, school, and community alike were to support the family but without encroaching on its inner workings or liberties, or subjecting it to the "covetous" privations of neighbors. Calvin and his protégé Theodore Beza had built an intricate theology, law, and practice of the covenant family for sixteenth-century Geneva, and this early example was echoed and elaborated in numerous Calvinist communities thereafter in Continental Europe, Great Britain, North America, the Caribbean, southern Africa, and colonial India and Indonesia.[8]

This Calvinist family heritage was still part of Dutch Reformed theology and culture in Kuyper's day. But Napoleon's legal reforms after the French Revolution had catalyzed strong new efforts for reduced church involvement in marriage; greater sexual liberty and expression; enhancement of women's suffrage, education, and public access; joint marital property; easier divorce; joint child custody after marriage; and more.[9] Kuyper had rather little sympathy with such domestic reforms, and he used the pulpit, press, and political platform to push hard against them. For he regarded the traditional family to be an essential cornerstone of ordered liberty and a properly organized society.

Kuyper also recognized, however, that urbanization, industrialization, and international commodities trade were rapidly separating work and home, parents and children, managers and workers, rich and poor, and yielding many more industrial injuries, disabilities, and deaths, a trend

---

8. See sources and discussion in John Witte Jr. and Robert M. Kingdon, *Sex, Marriage and Family in John Calvin's Geneva*, 2 vols. (Grand Rapids: Eerdmans, 2005, 2020).

9. For a contemporaneous account, see L. J. van Apeldoorn, *Geschiedenis van het nederlandsche huwelijksrecht voor de invoering van de fransche wetsgeving* (Amsterdam: Uitgeversmaatschappij, 1925).

further exacerbated by destructive military campaigns and a scourge of natural disasters in his day. In response, he advocated stronger protections for workers; a more generous system of worker's insurance, compensation, and pension; and new forms and forums of social welfare for the "deserving poor." Kuyper defended private property and enterprise, market capitalism, and free trade, and he warned against socialist campaigns designed to foment "class struggle." But in his writing and policy making, he remained deeply concerned for "widows and orphans," the poor and the homeless, the sick and maimed, and other *personae miserabiles*. Jesus said, "As you did not do it to one of the least of these, you did not do it to me" (Matt 25:45), encouraging his followers to adopt an ethic of love and care of all neighbors.[10] Kuyper translated this teaching into a robust system of charity, welfare, and a "preferential option" for the deserving poor or involuntarily disadvantaged. His preferred system of caring and sharing was still rooted in family and kin altruism and in the church diaconate and private charity, but now amply supplemented with auxiliary state welfare.[11]

Kuyper offered a robust and revisionist account of democracy and liberty, laying some of the foundations for modern forms of Christian liberalism and Christian democracy in the Netherlands and well beyond. In this volume and in several other writings, Kuyper rejected the "secular narrative"—already popular in his day and pervasive in our own—that democracy and human rights were modern products of Enlightenment liberalism, individualism, and contractarianism, and dependent on the new secular trinity of *liberté, égalité, et fraternité* born of the French Revolution. In line with some other historians of his day, Kuyper argued that it was Calvinist theology, not Enlightenment liberalism, that laid many of the

---

10. For earlier views, see, for example, Jeannine E. Olson, *Calvin and Social Welfare: Deacons and the Bourse Française* (London: Associated University Presses, 1989); and Elsie Anne McKee, *Diakonia in the Classic Reformed Tradition and Today* (Grand Rapids: Eerdmans, 1989), with updates in Elsie Anne McKee, *The Pastoral Ministry and Worship in Calvin's Geneva* (Geneva: Librairie Droz, 2016).

11. See "Christ and the Needy," "The Family, Society, and the State," and "You Shall Not Covet," herein and more fully Abraham Kuyper, "Christ's Kingship and the Family," in *PR* 2.III.1–18, pp. 299–462. See further James D. Bratt, "Abraham Kuyper," in *Christianity and Family Law: An Introduction*, ed. John Witte Jr. and Gary S. Hauk (Cambridge: Cambridge University Press, 2017), 291–306; and Bratt, *Abraham Kuyper*, 221–28.

foundations for Western forms of constitutional democracy, limited government, enumerated rights, and rule of law.[12]

Calvinism, Kuyper writes, was not only a spiritual movement but also "a political movement which has guaranteed the liberty of nations in constitutional statesmanship; first in Holland, then in England [and Scotland], and since the close of the last century in the United States." It was Calvinists who first "lifted up freedom of conscience" and insisted that "the magistrate has nothing to do with a person's innermost beliefs ... or with a person's domestic life or friendships." It was Calvinists who first "reached the conclusions that follow from this liberty of conscience, for the liberty of speech, and the liberty of worship ... and the free expression of thought ... and ideas." It was Calvinists who "first developed the principle of separation of church and state," and the constitutional recognition that "the Church derives its authority directly from God, not mediately through the state or through the community." It was Calvinists who first effectively "protest[ed] against State-omnicompetence; against the horrible conception that no right exists above and beyond existing [positive] laws; and against the pride of absolutism [which is] death to our civil liberties." It was Calvinists who first pressed classical theories of mixed government into constitutional principles of federalism and republicanism, separation of powers and checks and balances between them. And it was Calvinists who led the first democratic revolutions against tyrannical authorities in France, the Netherlands, Scotland, and England in the sixteenth and seventeenth centuries.[13]

Not only had Calvinists defined, defended, and died for many features of democratic constitutionalism well before the Enlightenment broke out, Kuyper continued. Calvinists also grounded their political teachings in sturdier theological propositions than the thinner derivative postulates of the

---

12. See, for example, George Jellinek, *Die Erklärung der Menschen- und Bürgerrechte: Ein Beitrag zur modernen Verfassungsgeschichte* (Leipzig: Duncker & Humblot, 1895); with distillation of later scholarship in Josef Bohatec, *England und die Geschichte der Menschen- und Bürgerrecht*, 3rd ed., ed. Otto Weber (Graz: Böhlau, 1956). The next several paragraphs are adapted in part and updated from John Witte Jr., *The Reformation of Rights: Law, Religion, and Human Rights in Early Modern Calvinism* (Cambridge: Cambridge University Press, 2007), 321-34.

13. Abraham Kuyper, *Dictaten Dogmatiek*, 2nd ed. (Kampen: Kok, 1910-13), vol. 5, *Locus de Magistratu*, 387-88, 415; Kuyper, *Lectures on Calvinism*, 105-9; Abraham Kuyper, "Calvinism: Source and Stronghold of Our Constitutional Liberties," in *AKCR*, 279-322.

later Enlightenment. Instead of postulating a mythical "state of nature," as the liberal *philosophes* did, Calvinists grounded their teachings in the orders of creation and the commandments of God. Instead of assuming that natural human life was lawlessly "brutish, nasty, and short," they emphasized the natural restraints of God's law written on all hearts and God's common grace, which "shines on all that's fair."[14] Instead of seeing natural rights as pathways to a self-interested pursuit of life, liberty, and property of the sovereign individual, they saw rights as opportunities to discharge divine duties set out in the Decalogue and other moral laws. Instead of seeing constitutions as social and government contracts between individuals designed to protect individual rights, they treated constitutions as divinely modeled covenants between the rulers, people, and God, designed to protect human and associational rights, to break up and bracket political power, and to encourage and celebrate godly values. Instead of seeing free speech, free exercise, or free assembly as individual rights limited only by the rights of others and the boundaries of treason, Calvinists saw them as constitutional expressions of the biblical teaching that all persons are called by Christ to be prophets, priests, and kings in the world, with duties to speak, serve, and rule with others in the creation and protection of a godly republic. Drawing on these and many other such dialectics, Kuyper hammered out a striking new history of Christianity, democracy, and human rights, and a sturdy new platform of Christian liberalism.[15]

In several chapters in this volume, and in other works, Kuyper emphasized robust freedom of speech and press.[16] This was a quite innovative teaching and still controversial in parts of his Calvinist world. Calvin's Geneva and later Reformed communities on both sides of the Atlantic had firm censorship and licensing rules in place, and outspoken dissenters and contrarian publishers quickly found themselves in the docket, and often

---

14. Richard J. Mouw, *He Shines in All That's Fair: Culture and Common Grace* (Grand Rapids: Eerdmans, 2002). See also Mouw, "Volume Introduction," in *CG* 1:xviii–xxx.

15. Kuyper, *Lectures on Calvinism*, 105–9; Kuyper, "Calvinism: Source and Stronghold," 279–322; Kuyper, *CG* 1.3–6, pp. 19–54; 1.11, pp. 92–101; 1.18–24, pp. 155–207; 1.34–36, pp. 297–323; Abraham Kuyper, "The Ordinances of God," in *Political Order and the Plural Structure of Society*, ed. James W. Skillen and Rockne M. McCarthy (Atlanta: Scholars Press, 1991), 242–57. See detailed sources and discussion in Witte, *Reformation of Rights*, passim.

16. See especially "Is Error a Punishable Offense?," "The Free Word," "Celebrating Twenty-Five Years of *De Standaard*," and "The Press as Apostle of Peace," in this volume.

on the next ride out of town, sometimes at sword point. An early Calvinist champion of freedom of speech and press was seventeenth-century English poet and philosopher John Milton (1608–74), whom Kuyper lauded.[17]

Milton emphasized that God's universal calling to be prophets, priests, and kings gave everyone the right and duty to speak, write, and debate in church and state, family and society, school and business at once. This was the real driving force of a *semper reformanda* ethic, Milton argued. This was the best way to pursue the truth of God and Scripture, reason and nature, all to be discovered by free and robust education and inquiry, experiment and debate, publication and conversation. Only when freed from the tyranny of prelates and monarchs, of ignorance and error, of censors and licensors, Milton believed, could divine, natural, and human truth finally be discovered and developed. Only when bad speech was countered by good speech in a free and open exchange would the public good ultimately be enhanced.[18]

Milton proved to be a lonely and neglected prophet in his day, and his ideas took another two centuries to penetrate deeply into Western thought. But Kuyper reflected some of these same Miltonian sentiments. As a journalist, he saw the free press as a vital "estate," even an independent "social sphere" in a well-ordered and accountable democratic society. The press was a necessary check on the excesses and abuses of all authorities, even an "apostle of peace" for a divided and tumultuous world, he writes. Furthermore, as an educator, Kuyper prized literacy and learning not only as a means for every person to read Scripture and train for their Christian vocation, as Protestants had long taught. Education was also a great leveler and elevator of human society. Proper education for all gave full voice to all, especially the "little people" (*kleine luyden*) too often shut out and shut down from public deliberation. Kuyper was not into American-style free-speech absolutism, nor was he an unqualified advocate of "an open marketplace of ideas" or popular sovereignty *über alles*. He called for civility, not "rudeness," in all speech and writing; constructive engagement, not crass materialist or prurient excess. He also had little sympathy for hate speech, insurrectionary rhetoric, or expressions of "class egoism." While sometimes slipping in his early writing and speeches, Kuyper at his best

---

17. See, for instance, Kuyper, "Calvinism: Source and Stronghold," 292–97.
18. See Witte, *Reformation of Rights*, 259–71, expanded in John Witte Jr., "Prophets, Priests, and Kings of Liberty: John Milton and the Reformation of Rights and Liberties in England," *Emory Law Journal* 57 (2008): 1527–1604.

calls for respectful discussion of and public engagement with Jews, Muslims, and other "peoples of God."[19]

Here and there in this volume, and more fully in other writings, Kuyper defends other democratic institutions and liberties, now often lauding the United States of his day as exemplary of the kind of system he advocated for the Netherlands and beyond.[20] "America lacks no single liberty for which in Europe we struggle," Kuyper writes. "In America there is absolute liberty of conscience," and "no citizen of the State may be compelled to remain in a church which his conscience forces him to leave." In America, there is "separation of church and state," which provides a "better guarantee [of] ... ecclesiastical liberty than anything that now prevails in Europe." The state does not establish or prescribe religious texts, beliefs, or practices. It does not interfere in matters of church polity, property, or personnel. Nor does it "subsidize the churches," or collect their tithes. "In America, Catholics, Lutherans, Calvinists, Baptists, and Methodists are equally respected," each part of the "multiform manifestation of the Church of Christ on earth."[21] Also respected are peaceable Jews, Muslims, and other "people of faith." Indeed, Kuyper argued, "all things within the forum of conscience and on

---

19. See "Democratic Reefs," "Free Word," and "Press as Apostle of Peace," herein and further sources and discussion in Bratt, *Abraham Kuyper*, 320–35.
20. See analysis of Kuyper's deep engagement with America in Bolt, *Free Church, a Holy Nation*.
21. Kuyper, *Locus de Magistratu*, 387–88, 444–45; Abraham Kuyper, *Varia Americana* (Amsterdam: Höveker and Wormser, 1897), 18–22, 52–54, 136–62; Kuyper, "Calvinism: Source and Stronghold," 279–322; *OP*, 351–63; Abraham Kuyper, *Encyclopaedie der heilige Godgeleerdheid* (Kampen: Kok, 1909), 3:614–24; Kuyper, *Lectures on Calvinism*, 106–9. Kuyper set out his church ideal briefly in Abraham Kuyper, *Our Worship*, trans. and ed. Harry Boonstra et al. (Grand Rapids: Eerdmans, 2011), and more fully in *On the Church*. In "Rooted and Grounded," he writes that "the requirement of liberation is threefold: Let the church be free from the state, free from the money purse, and free from the pressure of office. ... Because the church is an organism, the church possesses its own unique life and thus its unique principle of law. Therefore, whoever seeks to force the operation of our church law to conform to the requirements of civil law or the workings of public law [or funding] is confusing what in principle is distinct. They are surrendering the freedom and independence of the church" (in *On the Church*, 66). See especially *On the Church*, 377–437, for his views of state and church with discussion in Wood, *Going Dutch*, 142–75.

domestic and private life must be free—for the atheist as much as for the full devout ... indeed, for all sects."[22]

Kuyper also praises the American principle of associational liberty and social pluralism, seeing it as exemplary of his signature doctrine of sphere sovereignty. The long American tradition of voluntarism and fraternity, Kuyper writes, has led to ample legal protection not only of churches and religious organizations but also of a plurality of other social spheres—families, schools, unions, guilds, clubs, convents, corporations, and more. Each of these social spheres is amply protected by the provisions of state criminal law. Each is amply facilitated by the procedures of state private law. But none of these social spheres is ultimately dependent on the state for its existence or for its competence. The formation and maintenance of each social sphere depend on the voluntary association and activity of private parties. The competence and authority of each social sphere, furthermore, depends on "its innate norms," its "God-given liberty"—its "inherent sphere sovereignty."[23]

Sphere sovereignty does not render a social sphere "a law unto itself"—just as personal sovereignty does not make each person a law unto oneself. Instead, sphere sovereignty entails that each of these social spheres has the liberty to operate independently of the state in accordance with its own God-given norms, and in deference to the liberty interests of other social spheres and of all individuals. "There exists side-by-side with the personal sovereignty [of the individual conscience], the sovereignty of the [social] sphere." And the "rights and liberties of social life" exercised by and within these social spheres come "from the same source from which the high authority of government flows—even the absolute sovereignty of God. From this one source, in God, sovereignty in the individual sphere, in the family, and in every social circle, is just as directly derived as the

---

22. Kuyper, *Locus de Magistratu*, 415. See, for example, Abraham Kuyper, *Liberalisten en Joden* (Amsterdam: Wormser, 1878), and *On Islam*. In *On Islam* he writes: "Religion is and will always remain the marrow of the life of nations, the central lever of their life force. A religion, once pervasive, governs the *whole* of life, and its innate desire to promote itself never sleeps. Neither Buddhism nor the religion of Zoroaster can compare to the Gospel and Islam in comprehending all human life and sinking deep into it" (304). See further Andrew M. Harmon, "Common Grace and Pagan Virtue: Is Kuyperian Tolerance Possible?," *The Kuyper Center Review* 2 (2011): 302–14.

23. See "Sphere Sovereignty" herein; Kuyper, *Lectures on Calvinism*, 90–99; Kuyper, *Varia Americana*, 38–49; Kuyper, *Locus de Magistratu*, 73–186; Kuyper, *Encyclopaedie*, 3:322–30.

supremacy of state authority." A plurality of spheres of personal, ecclesiastical, social, and political liberty thus stand alongside each other—each ultimately created by and accountable to God. A plurality of offices and activities within each sphere of liberty also stand alongside each other—each designed to discharge some portion of God's special calling for that sphere. This understanding of associational liberty and social pluralism, which Kuyper found so well expressed in late-nineteenth-century America, was an essential plank of his own political platform in the Netherlands.[24] Kuyper's teaching on sphere sovereignty has proved to be one of his most enduring and pervasive contributions to contemporary discussion of social and legal pluralism, in both Europe and North America.[25]

Kuyper's robust reflections on the success of the American experiment in ordered liberty and orderly pluralism—though strangely silent on its many failings for women, children, African Americans, Native American Indians, abused workers, the poor, and various minorities of the day[26]—were flattering enough to his American audience. Even more flattering were his robust projections of the place and promise of the American experiment in the world in the twentieth century. In his famous Stone Lectures at Princeton in 1898, Kuyper predicted that America would soon inherit from Europe the leadership of the Western world: "Old Europe remains even now the bearer of a longer historical past, and therefore stands before us as a tree rooted more deeply, hiding between its leaves some matured fruits of life. You are yet in your Springtide—we are passing through our Fall."[27]

---

24. See sources in n29; Kuyper, *Lectures on Calvinism*, 95–96; *OP*, 16–22.

25. See illustrative texts in Skillen and McCarthy, *Political Order and the Plural Structure*, and a recent illustration in Kent A. VanTil, "Abraham Kuyper and Michael Walzer: The Justice of the Spheres," *Calvin Theological Journal* 40 (2005): 267–89. For two recent legal adaptions of Kuyperian sphere-sovereignty theory, see Johan D. van der Vyver, *Leuven Lectures on Religious Institutions, Religious Communities and Rights* (Leuven: Peeters, 2004); and Paul Horwitz, *First Amendment Institutions* (Cambridge: Harvard University Press, 2013).

26. I say "strangely" because Kuyper was hardly blind to these problems at home. See "Christ and the Needy" herein. In Kuyper, *Varia Americana*, 3–5, 9–12, he does criticize briefly the impoverishment and lynching of blacks, and the problems of alcoholism and poverty among the working classes.

27. Kuyper, *Lectures on Calvinism*, 9–10. In a follow-up lecture, Kuyper made an even grander prediction: "America is destined in the providence of God to become the most glorious and noble nation the world has ever seen. Someday its renown will eclipse the renown and splendor of Rome, Greece, and older races." Lecture on

The devastation of World Wars I and II was grim vindication of Kuyper's bleak prophecy.

Kuyper did not wax so grandly simply to flatter his American audience. He also came to warn them that these Calvinist and broader religious foundations of law, politics, and society were cracking in America, having already been shattered in much of Europe during and after the French Revolution. These foundations needed to be shored up if America was to live up to its high promise. Kuyper's concluding lecture at Princeton in 1898 had the tone of a wizened Dutch uncle gently admonishing his young American relatives to live up to their pedigree:

> Lo and behold, while you are thus enjoying the fruits of Calvinism, and while even outside of your borders the constitutional system of government as an outcome of Calvinist warfare, upholds the national honor, it is whispered abroad that all these [fruits] are to be accounted blessings of Humanism, and scarcely anyone still thinks of honoring in them the after-effects of Calvinism, the latter believed to lead a lingering life only in a few dogmatically petrified circles. What I demand ... is that this ungrateful ignoring of Calvinism shall come to an end. ... I contend in the second place, for an historical study of the principles of Calvinism ... [that cultivated] the tree of liberty. ... I [demand] in the third place the development of the principles of Calvinism in accordance with the needs of modern consciousness and their application to every department of life. ... Finally, I would add ... that those Churches which lay claim to professing the Reformed faith, shall cease being ashamed of this confession. ... I exalt multiformity and hail it in a higher stage of development. Even for the Church that has the purest confession, I would not dispense with the aid of other Churches in order that its inevitable one-sidedness may thus be complemented. But what ... one confesses to be the truth, one must also dare to practice in word, deed, and [the] whole manner of life.[28]

October 26, 1898, quoted in John Bolt, "The Holland-American Line of Liberty," *Journal of Markets & Morality* 1 (1998): 1.

28. Kuyper, *Lectures on Calvinism*, 194–95.

Kuyper's four "demands," while controversial, have not gone unanswered in America during the past century and more—or indeed in other parts of the world now, too. Calvinism is certainly not ignored today, either in various Christian institutions or in the broader secular world. The historical contributions of Calvinism and other faith traditions to Western law, politics, and culture are coming under increasingly close study. The expansion and adaptation of these contributions to modern American life have continued apace. Calvinism is proudly confessed in a number of churches today both in America and abroad.[29]

Since Kuyper threw down his avuncular gauntlet in 1898, a number of Calvinist scholars have also taken up his third demand: to work for "the development of the principles of Calvinism in accordance with the needs of modern consciousness and their application to every department of life"— not least the "departments" of law, politics, and society, where the issues of charity and justice featured in this volume are of central importance. In the past century, scores of sturdy Calvinists have developed important new theories of law, politics, and society building in part on the insights of the Calvinist and broader Christian tradition. They have made important contributions to our understanding of modern international, constitutional, and social rights, and with a special accent on the legal protection of churches, schools, and families, and enhancement of the individual rights of the poor, the prisoner, and racial, ethnic, and sexual minorities.[30] The publication of this volume, and the others in Abraham Kuyper Collected Works in Public Theology, ensures that this work of *semper reformanda* will long continue.

---

29. See, for example, Philip Benedict, *Christ's Church Purely Reformed: A Social History of Calvinism* (New Haven: Yale University Press, 2003); George Harinck and Hans Krabbendam, eds., *Breaches and Bridges: Reformed Subcultures in the Netherlands, Germany, and the United States* (Amsterdam: VU Uitgeverij, 2000); George Harinck and Hans Krabbendam, *Sharing the Reformed Tradition: The Dutch-North American Exchange, 1846-1996* (Amsterdam: VU Uitgeverij, 1996); James D. Bratt, *Dutch Calvinism in North America: A History of a Conservative Subculture* (Grand Rapids: Eerdmans, 1984); David F. Wells, ed., *Reformed Theology in America: A History of its Modern Development* (Grand Rapids: Baker, 1997).

30. See, for example, sources cited above and further discussion in John Witte Jr., *A New Reformation of Rights: Calvinist Contributions to Modern Human Rights* (forthcoming); Witte and Alexander, *Modern Christian Teachings*.

ABBREVIATIONS

AKB	*Abraham Kuyper: An Annotated Bibliography 1857–2010.* Tjitze Kuipers. Translated by Clifford Anderson and Dagmare Houniet. Brill's Series in Church History 55. Leiden: Brill, 2011
AKCR	*Abraham Kuyper: A Centennial Reader.* Edited by James D. Bratt. Grand Rapids: Eerdmans, 1998
ARP	Antirevolutionary Party
CG	Kuyper, Abraham. *Common Grace.* Edited by Jordan J. Ballor and Stephen J. Grabill. Translated by Nelson D. Kloosterman and Ed M. van der Maas. 3 vols. Bellingham, WA: Lexham Press, 2015–2020
ESV	English Standard Version
ET	English translation
NKJV	New King James Version
NRSV	New Revised Standard Version
OBE	Kuyper, Abraham. *On Business and Economics.* Edited and translated by Harry Van Dyke. Bellingham, WA: 2021
OP	Kuyper, Abraham. *Our Program: A Christian Political Manifesto.* Translated and edited by Harry Van Dyke. Bellingham, WA: Lexham Press, 2015
OT	Old Testament
PR	Kuyper, Abraham. *Pro Rege: Living under Christ's Kingship.* Edited by John Kok with Nelson D. Koosterman. Translated

by Albert Gootjes. 3 vols. Bellingham, WA: Lexham Press, 2016–2019

SV   *Statenvertaling* ("States translation," or Authorized Version of the Dutch Bible, 1637)

CHRIST AND THE NEEDY (1895)

TEXT INTRODUCTION

On the eve of the general election of 1894 in the Netherlands, Abraham Kuyper took up the question of the relationship between the gospel and material needs. Prompted by the challenges of his coreligionists as well as political opponents, Kuyper argued for the expansion of voting rights, supporting a bill sponsored by Tak van Poortvliet (1839–1904). At the same time, Kuyper grounded his support of the measure in a powerful account of Christ's mission and its implications for human poverty. In doing so Kuyper challenged and in turn was criticized by Alexander de Savornin Lohman (1845–1924), a prominent antirevolutionary and political ally. By taking this approach, Kuyper can be seen as working out the implications of the call for an "architectonic critique" of the social question as articulated in his 1891 speech at the opening of the First Christian Social Congress, published as "The Social Question and the Christian Religion," which appears in translation in *On Business and Economics*. In this present series of articles, Kuyper explores the fundamental democratic and (para)egalitarian dynamics of the gospel. This series of ten articles first appeared in the daily newspaper *De Standaard* from June 18 to July 9, 1894. He followed with a subsequent series on the dangers of such trends, "The Reefs of Democracy," also appearing in this present volume, with the two series appearing together in published form in 1895.

SOURCE: Abraham Kuyper, *De Christus en de Sociale nooden en Democratische Klippen* (Amsterdam: Wormser, 1895), 11–56. Translated by Herbert Donald Morton. Edited and annotated by Harry Van Dyke.

CHRIST AND THE NEEDY (1895)

I

On several occasions during the last election campaign the relationship between the rich and the poor was referred to, also by us apparently, without proper care. We have to accept that this is so, now that one of our warmest friends, who is also from a prominent family, has told us that our words had offended him on more than one occasion.[1] There is, of course, always the possibility that the offense was in part taken rather than given, but when a loyal brother tells us that he was "irritated and aggrieved," then we are inclined for our part to seek the responsibility for this in the thoughtlessness of our words, and to entreat the aggrieved and irritated brother not to hold this terminological bumbling against us.

---

1. Ahead of the election of 1894, which involved the question of expansion of the franchise, Kuyper wrote: "It is our firm conviction that the Savior, if he were still on earth, would again align himself with the oppressed and against the powerful of our age." While Kuyper was in favor of expanding the ranks of eligible voters, his longtime ally Alexander de Savornin Lohman (1845–1924) was among those who were opposed. See Harry Van Dyke, "Abraham Kuyper and the Continuing Social Question," *Journal of Markets & Morality* 14, no. 2 (Fall 2011): 641–46.

Happily, forgiveness is always easy among us Christians, and when issues arise there is always one authority to which we are prepared to surrender unconditionally from the outset: *the authority of our Lord and Savior*.

That being so, it seems to us desirable to examine the case in point somewhat more closely and to respond more thoroughly to the question concerning the position that Christ took regarding the contrast between the rich and the poor.

Even if some ill-considered words may have escaped my pen, in the main we endeavored to follow in the footsteps of him whose words and example are decisive in life and in death for all who love the Savior. Naturally, here, we too can go astray; we are obliged and prepared, also in this matter, to pay heed to the brotherly criticism of those who confess Christ with us. Yet even those brothers who declared themselves to be the most deeply aggrieved and terribly irritated will readily concede that we may not speak otherwise than according to the light that is given us by the spirit of Christ.

We value this reference to what Holy Scripture teaches us concerning the contrast between the poor and the rich all the more because from our first participation in public life and not just now for the first time, we have always expressed ourselves in the same spirit respecting the needy in society. Such is also the case in connection with the Franchise Bill.[2]

Yet we shall leave aside, for the moment at least, the question of electoral reform. What motives of the heart have moved many of our socially high-ranking Christians to adopt a different position in this matter from our own is not for us to judge. Only the Knower of hearts may be the judge here. Therefore, we will scrupulously avoid saying that any one of these brothers acted contrary to conscience in this matter.

The only thing that saddened us—and, if we may speak frankly, that aggrieved and irritated us in our turn—was that the attractiveness of this political logic drew many of our noble brothers, probably against their will, into a company in which to our mind, given their credentials of *spiritual* nobility, they did *not* belong. In this way, their influence at the time became a support for conservatism, and even though we gladly assume that they neither intended nor willed this, they did not, as we see it, take sufficiently into account the virtually undeniable fact that their influence had perforce

---

2. This bill, sponsored by Johannes Tak van Poortvliet (1839–1904), would expand suffrage and was the key point of dispute in the election of 1894.

to tip the balance in favor of the status quo. Yet for the moment this can all rest.

What we need above all as Christians is that we go to God's Word; that we kneel at the cross of Christ with quiet reverence; and that we endeavor to arrive at complete agreement regarding how—from what standpoint and in what light—Christ would have us consider the vexing problem of the fearful contrast between the rich and the poor.

Even if we could not allow ourselves to hope that this exposition would bear fruit in bringing people to judge our position in a more sympathetic and brotherly spirit, it can never be without benefit to the readers of our paper[3] that also with regard to this grave problem we counter the slogan of the *revolution* with the voice of the *gospel*.[4]

That being so, allow me, by way of introduction, to call attention to the crushing condemnation by Anatole Leroy Beaulieu in the March issue of *Revue des deux mondes* regarding the position adopted by Christians, contrary to the spirit of Christ, with respect to money and thus with respect to mammon.[5]

We may invoke this witness all the more because Leroy-Beaulieu harbors *no* democratic sympathies but, to the contrary, warns against them. He at least cannot be suspected, as people suspect us, of harboring democratic leanings and invoking the gospel more strongly than is proper and permissible as we oppose the sinful and heaven-defying inequality in our earthly lots. Beaulieu writes,

> No one, so said Christ, can serve two masters. You cannot serve God and mammon. Now, mammon is wealth. Yet this splendid word from the Sermon on the Mount is out of date today. Christians of our day have arranged everything quite differently. There are four hundred million persons who have been baptized in the name of Jesus, but how many of them

---

3. This text originally appeared as a series of articles in Kuyper's daily political newspaper, *De Standaard*, June 18 to July 9, 1894.
4. This is an allusion to the antirevolutionary slogan popularized by G. Groen van Prinsterer (1801–76): "Against the Revolution, the Gospel!" That is, oppose secularism with Christian principles.
5. Kuyper is referring to the first part of a multipart work by French scholar and writer Anatole Leroy-Beaulieu, "Le Règne de l'argent," *Revue des deux mondes* 122, 15 March 1894, 241–60, subtitled "Autrefois et Aujourd'hui." There were ultimately ten parts in the series appearing through January 15, 1898.

show the slightest hesitation about serving mammon? After eighteen hundred years, mammon has again become king of the world. Those who are the most pious divide their time between serving God and serving mammon; it is not concern about their eternal treasures that weighs most heavily on them and oppresses them. In truth, one might even imagine that it was said not of the rich but of the poor that a camel might more easily pass through the eye of a needle than that they should enter into the kingdom of heaven. For if Christians had truly understood and absorbed the ideas of their Savior, they would not be out to make money but would much rather be fearful of possessing too much of it.[6]

Thus, to counter anti-Semitism, he adds that Jews may have become slaves of money, but this was only possible because they noticed that one could get furthest ahead in Christian society with *money*, always *money*.

Now, our fellow confessors of Christ among the upper classes will want to keep in mind that Leroy-Beaulieu discerns and denounces this unholy desire for money not only among the wealthy. On the contrary, he observes quite correctly that the wild slogans voiced by the lower classes of society arise from precisely the same passion. It is not that they disapprove of the possession of too much money and property in itself as such, from idealistic motives. No, what stirs them mainly is that others *do* and they do *not* have this power at their disposal. Thus if the opportunity should arise for them to become a favorite of mammon, they would quickly burn incense at his altar. Sad experience teaches that but for a few favorable exceptions, men who rose from poverty to wealth quickly forgot their earlier democratic sympathies and acted, if anything, even more harshly than others against the socially disadvantaged.

The revolutionary principles of 1789 in the most shameful way caused the hope of a better fatherland to fade and stimulated peoples and nations to find within this brief earthly existence the ultimate purpose of man's efforts. That is why the regime of Louis Philippe in particular gave such

---

6. Leroy-Beaulieu, "Règne de l'argent," 245.

an impulse to the revolutionary development of the service of mammon.[7] He desired before everything else to be the *money* king, believing that only *money* can bestow power and influence. This sinful revolutionary motive appeared in those days in two streams. On the one side, wealthy owners drove free capital up in various ways, even by fiction, to unprecedented, all-crushing heights. On the other side, have-nots endeavored to become wealthy, or at least well off, by taking the money away from its owners, either by violence or by legal measures.

Thus, however idealistic social democracy may present itself, its striving remains focused, at bottom, on nothing other than acquiring more *financial* power. It calls for more material well-being but to the neglect of every other element. Additionally, the passion with which thousands upon thousands follow its banner is not the passion for a higher ideal but well-nigh exclusively the passion for greater material well-being.

Against this revolution on the terrain of mammon, in either form, we Christians must place the gospel of our Lord and Savior—his principle, his spirit, something of his divine love. To this end, we must enlist among the upper classes the support of the handful of well-to-do, pious Christians who, God be praised, are not so few in number and who curse mammon and bless their Savior, not only with the lips but from the heart. Therefore, we must likewise seek the support of the truly pious among the lower classes, relatively more numerous in our population than in other countries, who value their heavenly country far above all the pleasures of this world.

These elements, from above and below, must work together in our generation to proclaim gratitude, in the spirit of the gospel, amid the turbulent forces in society. Yet let it not be forgotten, as Leroy-Beaulieu emphatically states, that while the poor were content and lived peaceably, it was the classes that were better off that aroused in them the thirst for sensual pleasure and thus for money. "It is the rich," he says, "who preached the love of money to the poor and who gave them lessons in corrupting the nation and coveting material things."[8]

---

7. Louis Philippe, king of the French (1830–48), during whose reign French policy favored economic expansion and severely limited the franchise to the highest taxpayers only.
8. Leroy-Beaulieu, "Règne de l'argent," 260.

II

If you want to understand correctly the *weight* and *significance* to be attached to what our Lord and Savior said about social relationships, then you ought to know, at least to some extent, what these social relationships were. Otherwise, you will not know to what circumstances Jesus' words apply and what the circumstances were that he either *commended* or *denounced*.

This is all the more needful now that there are Christians who try to escape the urgency of Jesus' words by objecting "that these hard, cutting words were appropriate at that time but they have neither *meaning* nor *significance* for *our time*." At that time, they argue, pagan and Jewish conditions were ruled by inhuman cruelty, which is why Jesus had to perform such radical surgery. However, today everything is different. We now live in a Christian society over which the gospel sheds its softer luster. It is therefore the height of absurdity to want to apply these statements of Jesus to our circumstances today without softening or tempering them.

This argument is so dangerous because there is indeed *something* to it, and this grain of truth can easily serve to cover up the incorrectness and exaggeration of the popular image—dangerous not so much because it leads to deceiving oneself and others but still more because it captures our hearts and gives us the delusion that we are indeed letting ourselves be led by the spirit of Christ when in fact we are still constantly acting contrary to his spirit.

We shall not neglect therefore to take the trouble to give a brief description of the social conditions that Jesus addressed.

Naturally, a broad sketch of these conditions would fill a small volume. A daily newspaper cannot think of providing that. Yet in a few short strokes we can still give our readers a clear answer to the question whether the circumstances of those times were so *inferior* to those of our times that Jesus' critique relates to the circumstances of his contemporaries but has nothing to say to us today. Therefore, we take first a quick look at the circumstances in the world of that day, and then a word in particular about the circumstances in the land of Palestine.

Now, insofar as general social circumstances are concerned (thus writes an authoritative source), the first century of the Roman Empire belongs to the happiest period not only of Roman history but indeed of world history.[9]

---

9. *Note by the author:* Gerhard Uhlhorn, *Der Kampf des Christenthums mit dem Heidenthum: Bilder aus der Vergangenheid als Spiegelbilder für die Gegenwart* (Stuttgart: Meyer & Zeller, 1874), 94.

The storms of the civil wars had abated, and peace reigned throughout the conquered provinces. Far away, along the fringes, at the frontiers of this mighty empire, wars were still being waged, but these did not touch the lands washed by the Mediterranean Sea. Granted, the Julian emperors were guilty of many unbearably arbitrary acts, but this arbitrariness subsided and did not reach much farther than Rome and its immediate surroundings.

Many inscriptions that have been found show that in the provinces, even under emperors such as Nero, people led quiet and peaceful lives and felt happy. The administration of government was outstanding; the administration of justice, particularly in civil matters, was equally outstanding; and exploitation of the provinces, as in the days of the republic, no longer occurred, at least not with impunity. Taxes were moderate and distributed fairly. Imperial collectors levied direct taxes, and indirect taxes were sometimes leased. Yet the successors to the good emperors did what they could to oppose misuse, and trade and industry flourished. Roads were splendidly maintained; in general, security reigned on land and sea; and harbors were built, canals dug, and river traffic regulated. The coinage system was regularized. The commercial cities around the Mediterranean Sea flourished. Incredible treasures were funneled from the provinces into the capital city of Rome—but also from Rome back to the provinces to pay great sums of money for all manner of objects of oriental provenance. The arts and crafts thrived as never before or since. Agriculture was practiced in a rational way. Market gardens, orchards, and vineyards flourished then as they do today in our most civilized countries. Pliny's letters inform us of social conditions in the Po Valley of northern Italy in which there was no poverty worthy of mention. Throughout the eastern empire, where the trades and industry flourished, the social situation was no less favorable. Food for the population was provided in abundance, and if a great catastrophe occurred such as the inundation of Pompeii by rivers of lava from Vesuvius, government and private initiative vied with each other in coming to the aid of the victims.

The ratio between wages and the price of bread was also favorable. According to one inscription, in an inn a traveler paid 5 cents for bread and 10 cents for other food. Only meat, which even today in northern Italy is still eaten only by the higher classes, cost 75 cents per kilogram of mutton, 1.75 guilder per kilogram of pork, and 75 cents for a chicken. However, a worker who earned an ordinary wage was in a position at the time to earn enough in five days that he could buy food for a month, so that the head of a household of five, the young children included in proportion, could earn enough in twenty days to feed his family.

The gap between rich and poor was great at that time as well, yet the distinction in social position was far from what it is today. The richest and greatest fortune that we read about among the voters was 54 million guilders.[10] Such a capital was possessed only by the Lentuluses and the Narcissuses, and they were the Rothschilds of their day.[11]

What does this mean, then, compared with the Rothschilds now? In 1875, the latter's fortune already totaled 2,400 million guilders; since then, it has risen to 5,000 million, and it doubles again every fifteen years. Credit, the curse of our time, was unknown. People were paid in cash. Virtually all capital was invested in land and could therefore not, as today, foster so much poverty. Therefore, poverty in the sense of our pauperism did not exist. Individual cases of impoverishment were easily alleviated. After the Antonines,[12] outright pauperism did break out in the Roman Empire, and it hastened its decline; but in the days in which Jesus appeared and spoke there was simply no question of poverty as a general phenomenon in the sense in which we know it. Thus explains our authority, whom we have followed virtually word for word in order to avoid any appearance of depicting things more favorably than they actually were.

That social conditions under the first emperors are often portrayed in an entirely different light is due to the fact that people paid attention almost exclusively to social conditions in Rome itself. But the city of Rome occupied an entirely exceptional position. This one city ruled the world and imagined that the entire world must work for her so that she could enjoy the sweet life of *dolce far niente*, of doing nothing. That is why its population of over one and a half million inhabitants had become practically unaccustomed to doing any work at all. People rested on their laurels. Furthermore, the municipal government sometimes spent more than *seven* million in a single year just to feed the people. On festival occasions, meals set out on 20,000 tables were served to the people. On 135 of the 365 days of the year, the people had to be able to attend all manner of free theater and sporting events. On important government occasions, civil servants

---

10. A guilder at the time of publication would be equivalent to roughly $12 in 2015.
11. The Rothschilds were the wealthiest family in the world in Kuyper's time.
12. That is, the reigns of Antonius Pius, Marcus Aurelius, Lucius Verus, and Commodus, which ended in AD 192.

were not showered with ribbons and knighthoods, but gold was given to the people, such that on one occasion Septimius Severus distributed 420 guilders in cash to every family.[13]

In addition, Rome looked after its poor in various ways. There were training institutes for the helpless and for orphans. To ease the pressure on Rome, colonies were planted abroad. A patron generally paid his clients 70 cents per day. The so-called *collegia* levied a monthly contribution for poor members.[14] In the case of a disaster or setback, the wealthy competed for the spotlight by contributing lavish gifts.

Jesus' activities, however, had nothing to do with local conditions in Rome. He acted and spoke in an eastern Roman province. In this province, generally speaking, social conditions were not inferior to today's but remarkably better. In any case, in those lands pauperism, at least as we see it on the rise again today, was unknown at that time.

III

Our readers will appreciate our framing this series of articles somewhat more broadly. The importance of the matter demands that we do so. This is necessary because for so many years the preaching in our churches has neglected to proclaim Jesus' direct teaching about social relationships. It often seemed as if Jesus' direct teaching about social relationships had no significance for us today. To our embarrassment it must be said that it was unbelievers and not the redeemed of the Lord who first called attention to the fact that Holy Scripture, too, and particularly the actions of our Savior, say something authoritative and important about these pressing social needs. However, people in our circles, both high and low, are so estranged from Jesus' word and spirit on this point that a brief reminder is insufficient, and there is an urgent need to place this entire subject in a clear and, if possible, convincing light, so that in this matter, too, there may again be a Christian consensus.

Now, our previous article sketched the general social relationships as they were found in Jesus' day in the Roman provinces, of which the Holy Land was one. We did not describe these relationships ourselves but laid before our readers Uhlhorn's description, partly to avoid any semblance of

---

13. The Roman emperor Septimius Severus reigned from AD 193–211.
14. *Collegia* were legal associations created for a wide variety of civic, religious, and social purposes.

bias and partly because Uhlhorn supports every detail in his sketch with documentary evidence.[15] His sketch showed us that social relationships in Jesus' day were not at all less favorable, and, in many respects, were more favorable than they are in our day. Yet with that not enough has been said. Our Savior appeared in a Roman province that from a moral and social standpoint distinguished itself extremely *favorably* from the others. To Israel had been committed the oracles of God; its national history was launched by God himself with a social framework that excluded poverty in the form of pauperism as we know it; impoverishment, to the extent that it occurred also in this nation through one's own fault or as a result of falling on hard times, was both restricted in duration and eased by the spirit of mercy.

Do not misunderstand this. We are by no means claiming that the sublime spirit of love that must be the hallmark of every Christian community already obtained in ancient Israel. Yet while Uhlhorn calls the pagan world, despite its bearable social conditions, "a world without love," he grants that this cannot be said of social conditions in ancient Israel.[16]

Accordingly, nothing is more incorrect than the notion that the commandment that we should "love our neighbor as ourselves" came first from Jesus' lips. The same statement appears literally in the Old Testament, and even love for one's enemies is prescribed already in Proverbs 25 and elsewhere.

The compassion or mercy that flows from pity and love and that was fundamentally different from pagan charity (*caritas*) and largesse (*liberalitas*) was enjoined upon God's people in his name not first in the New Testament but just as firmly in the Old Testament. Look at Psalm 37:26; 41:1; 112:5, again, in Job 29:16, and again in Proverbs 12:10. In Isaiah 58:7, we read about the kind of fast that God preferred: "Is it not to share your bread with the hungry and bring the homeless poor into your house; when you see the naked, to cover him, and not to hide yourself from your own flesh?" All this is so that the commandment given to Israel in Leviticus 19:18 might be fulfilled: "You shall love your neighbor as yourself: I am the LORD."

The only difference between the ministry of mercy under Israel and the mercy of Jesus' word was that under Israel the *commandment* was the mainspring, while according to Jesus' demand it is the *impulse* of the heart out of

---

15. See Uhlhorn, *Kampf des Christenthums*.
16. Uhlhorn, *Kampf des Christenthums*, 153.

thankfulness that must induce love; further that under Israel the demonstration of love was regulated by set rules, while among us it is spiritually *free*. In Israel's days, a tithe was required; Christians, however, must each decide for themselves whether they can afford a tithe, or, indeed, whether a tithe is enough in their particular case.

Yet under Israel, precisely because of the legal provisions that governed conditions in the name of God, conditions were in many respects *healthier* than they are among us Christians, to whom it is left freely to define the limits of our charity. The very laws God gave for land tenure were of such a nature that the gap between rich and poor was tempered to a substantial degree. From the outset every Israelite was steward of a piece of land from his God, and no one was helpless. Moreover—and herein lies the glory of Israel's agrarian legislation—even if someone through his own fault or as a result of setbacks had lost his land and belongings, this did not rest as a curse *on his heirs*, but this impoverishment was always only *temporary*. God had set a fixed term after which every piece of land, no matter how it had been lost, reverted to its original owner.

The concept of property was accordingly an entirely different one under Israel than it was under Roman law. The idea that someone could dispose absolutely over his property was unknown to Israel. All property gave only relative rights. One who owned a field or a vineyard, a fig or olive grove, was not allowed to harvest it clean: something had to be left in the field and on the tree for the poor (Deut 24:19–21). One who passed through a cornfield might pluck some ears with his hand, though not cut into it with his sickle (Deut 23:25). In the Sabbath year, the *entire* yield of the soil was for the poor (Exod 23:11). Lending at exorbitant rates was forbidden. What was loaned had to be forgiven in the Sabbath year (Deut 15:2). Wages were to be paid before sunset (Deut 24:15). In short, the entire management of property stood under a higher law and higher control.

In addition to this, there was also the second tenth, which was for the benefit not of the Levites but especially of widows and orphans. There were the sacrificial repasts, to which the poor too had to be invited; the charitable alms had to be given openhandedly and generously. Above all, there was the brotherly understanding that people had to adopt toward those who were poor and lowly. Accordingly, the social gap between the rich and poor as we know it was *entirely* unknown in Israel. You can tell that from Jesus' parables. From the hedges and from the highways people were gathered to come and sit at the banquets of the rich.

It must be kept in mind, of course, that reality, for all that, by no means matched the spirit of the law, and that Israel too sinned against the compassion of the law. If, however, one consults the Apocryphal books of the Old Testament, which inform us of the situation as it had evolved between Malachi and John the Baptist, then we see that after social conditions had become less favorable, care for the poor appears more prominently in these writings. Already even then the false notion insinuated itself that the giving of alms possessed sin-discharging power. Thus Tobit 12:8–9 states, "It is better to give alms than to treasure up gold. For almsgiving delivers from death, and it will purge away every sin." In Ecclesiasticus [Sirach] 3:30 we read, "Water extinguishes a blazing fire: so almsgiving atones for sin." Even when the Pharisees set the tone, no one rebuked them for giving no alms or too few alms but only for doing so from the wrong principle.

Accordingly, what the New Testament teaches us about the social relationships of the time nowhere betrays the existence of pauperism as such. People's duty to share with the poor was not challenged from any quarter. Of large fortunes not a hint is to be found, and what primarily characterized the situation is that the poor and the rich interacted with each other on the basis *of personal intercourse*: the poor visited in the homes of those who were better off, and in oriental fashion, sanctified by the spirit of Israel's laws, they were admitted even to the tables of the rich. Dives and Lazarus may paint a shocking picture, but the fact that poor Lazarus had entree to the house of the rich man and might have eaten the crumbs that fell from his table betrays a level of intimacy between classes that is foreign to our Christian society.[17]

Pulling all this together, first with respect to the general condition of the eastern provinces that were under imperial administration at the time, and also with respect to the salutary influence exerted particularly in Palestine by the impact of Israel's law, we cannot escape the conclusion that social conditions of the time, as Jesus observed them around him, were not *un*favorable but much rather favorable when compared with present-day conditions.

---

17. The rich man was sometimes referred to by the Latin word for "rich" (*dives*) as a personal name. See Luke 16:19–31.

IV

Not new, but then also uncontested, is the observation from which we must proceed here, namely, that our Lord and Savior himself did not choose his place among the *upper* but among the *lower* classes of society.

In this respect, too, the words of Isaiah apply:

> For he grew up before him like a young plant,
>   and like a root out of dry ground;
> he had no form or majesty that we should look at him,
>   and no beauty that we should desire him.
> He was despised and rejected by men;
>   a man of sorrows, and acquainted with grief;
> and as one from whom men hide their faces he was despised,
>   and we esteemed him not. (Isa 53:2-3)

These are harsh words, which for a long time were construed to mean that our Savior had a hideous face but that are now rather generally understood as referring to Jesus' social position and to public opinion of the rabbi from Nazareth. Now those of us who with the Christian church believe in the eternal preexistence of the Mediator know and confess that this appearance of Jesus in the lower classes of society was not accidental, nor that it was imposed upon him by *force*, but that he opted for this himself: "Though he was rich, yet for your sake he became poor, so that you by his poverty might become rich" (2 Cor 8:9). Christ was thus perfectly aware of his social position, as is clear from his incisively beautiful statement: "Foxes have holes, and birds of the air have nests, but the Son of Man has nowhere to lay his head" (Luke 9:58).

The fact that Jesus chose or adopted this position (if we may put it that way) among the *lower* classes of society even formed part of the gospel proclaimed by the apostles. This is evident not only from what we just cited from the second epistle to the Corinthians, but likewise from Philippians 2:6-7, where the wording has it that Christ, being in the form of God, "did not count equality with God a thing to be grasped, but emptied himself, by taking the form of a servant." That is why the Gospels, and in particular the Gospel according to Luke, make a point of highlighting this social position of Jesus while he was on earth and to focus attention on it in every possible way.

It is true that God sent a herald to prepare the way for Jesus—a herald of priestly blood. Yet, the son of Zacharias does not keep company with the upper crust of Jerusalem: he breaks with them and, content with the simplest of clothing, lives on locusts and wild honey in the wilderness.

When the sacred story comes to the conception and birth of Christ himself, it does not shift to Jerusalem, Jericho, or Caesarea but to the little country towns of Nazareth and Bethlehem—the one so despised that Nathanael asks, "Can anything good come out of Nazareth?" [John 1:46] and the other so insignificant that there was only one inn, too small to house all who sought to stay at it.

Mary was undoubtedly of high lineage, even of royal blood, but her social situation did not place her with the rich and prominent but with the disesteemed. The man to whom she was betrothed was a carpenter in a hamlet called Nazareth. Together the two possessed so little that the wise men from the East had to bring gold to make their flight to Egypt possible. As a result, especially of her lofty descent, Mary was so deeply under the impression of her low social status that in her song of praise she sang, "My spirit rejoices in God my Savior, for he has looked on the humble estate of his servant. ... He has filled the hungry with good things, and the rich he has sent away empty" (Luke 1:47–48, 53).

However scanty the reports of Jesus' early years may be, it is clear nevertheless that our Savior spent all but three years of his life in forgotten Nazareth, and that even there he did not belong to the more prominent families or to those invested with authority but to the class of small craftsmen. Tradition would suggest that it is not improbable that Jesus worked in the trades himself.

What was true of Jesus' own social position was also true of his surroundings. The first to whom his coming was proclaimed were not the members of the Sanhedrin or the members of the royal house of Herod but poor shepherds who watched their flocks by night in the fields of Ephrathah. It cannot even be said of these men that the sheep they watched were their own property; they rather seem only to have been hired to watch the flocks during the night. At the presentation of Jesus in the temple, Joseph and Mary, despite the friendship of these shepherds, were still so impoverished that they could not afford a *lamb of the first year*, hence lacked *three* guilders, and therefore fulfilled the requirements of the sacrifice with *a pair of turtledoves* as was permitted *the poor* in Leviticus 12:8. A lamb was required, but someone *not able to bring a lamb* was permitted to bring instead a pair of turtledoves or two young pigeons, birds that were very common in Israel and therefore cost very little. If the shepherds had been the *owners* of their flock, Mary would surely have been able to secure a lamb. That she offered the sacrifice of the poor proves not only that she lacked the means herself but also that the shepherds in the fields of Ephrathah belonged to the poor class of keepers of sheep.

That all this was no sad necessity but God's ordinance, and therefore *willed by Jesus himself*, is shown by nothing so clearly as his choice of disciples. Later, Jesus also had a few friends among the prominent men of Jerusalem; but Nicodemus came to Jesus by night, and Joseph of Arimathea remained out of sight. The circle from which Jesus chose his disciples is thus not the circle of high officials, nor the circle of the prominent, nor the circle of the learned, but the circle of the "simple in the land"—people of the lower middle class, as are found today in Scheveningen and Katwijk, in Noordwijk and Egmond, on Marken and Urk, fishermen who personally carry out their vocation together with their families.[18] John and James worked on their father's little boat and had to mend their nets themselves. They were thus not even fishermen whom you could compare to the ship-owners of Scheveningen, for these do not sail themselves. Besides, the little boats on Gennesaret were far from comparable to our *pinken*, our modern one-masted fishing vessels.

Later, to be sure—first in the case of Matthew, who was "sitting at the tax booth" [Matt 9:9], and still later in the case of Paul—Jesus also called men of a somewhat higher social position, but this does not detract from the fact that Jesus chose men almost exclusively of *non*prominent rank and that during the three years of his sojourn on earth he associated mainly with people of this lower rank.

Naturally, this is not in the least to say that Jesus never spoke with men of a higher position. It is clear from the wedding in Cana, from his visit to Zacchaeus' house, from his sitting down to eat in the house of Simon, and ever so much more, that our Savior certainly did have relationships in other classes. Nevertheless, all this cannot undo the telling fact that Jesus deliberately and voluntarily chose his place among the lower classes; that he kept company mainly with the lesser folk in the land; and that it was preferably from the less prominent that he chose his faithful followers and the men on whom he vested hope for the future of his sacred mission.

---

18. The first four are fishing villages on the North Sea coast; the last two were islands in the former Zuyder Zee.

Moreover, the multitudes that followed him when he sailed on the Sea of Gennesaret do not give the impression of being what we today would call a "distinguished public." Carelessly, without a knapsack or provisions, they follow Jesus; and when he feeds the thousands, art and tradition still portray a scene of the least of the land sitting in groups around Jesus in quiet simplicity.

This eloquent fact—that our Savior adopted and assumed his social position not among the great of the earth but among the least—is so striking from every angle and in every way that no one has ever tried to contest the certainty of this detail. Rather, in hymns and homilies, the fact of Jesus' humble birth, his sober position in life, and his less impressive surroundings has been acknowledged from age to age, crowned with a sacred halo, and glorified, not without fervor, in the ideal sense. It is just that the importance of this fact *for our social relationships* has not been sufficiently felt. People called attention to it in order to honor Jesus' humility. They spiritualized his earthly smallness and used it to exhort to heavenly mindedness.

However laudable that may be, there is more to it. Jesus was able to choose. He could have taken up his position wherever he wished—in a palace, among the mighty of the earth, or among the little people—the lowly in the land. And *he chose the latter*.

This must, of course, have been for *a reason*. There must have been something that moved him to avoid the palaces and houses of the mighty in order to seek the quiet dwellings of the little folk in the land—something that spoke strongly to him because he was of David's lineage, of royal blood, even King in the kingdom of God. We shall not guess at this, for who can penetrate the secret thoughts of the Lord? Yet it is clear that also in Jesus' days there was a certain contrast between a *higher* and a *lower* position in society and that in Jesus' birth, living circumstances, and surroundings, the connection with the little people in the land was much closer than it was with the prominent and great of the earth. It is also clear that Jesus expected much more for the kingdom of heaven from the small than from the great, as can be seen from his choice of disciples.

V

To establish the correct chronological order of Jesus' various meetings and the different addresses he gave is far from easy. The Gospels do not present a chronicle or journal but draw a single powerful portrait from many angles. Yet, it is at least certain that Jesus' appearance in the synagogue at Nazareth and the Sermon on the Mount, as it is called, followed shortly after the temptation in the wilderness and thus stand at the beginning of Jesus' "revelation to Israel."

Now in this connection one's attention is immediately drawn to the fact that *hunger* is the first factor in the temptation; that afterwards, in the synagogue at Nazareth, the text is opened at Isaiah 61:1, which says that Christ is anointed to preach the gospel to the *poor*; and that soon, in the Sermon on the Mount, the first beatitude likewise applies to the *poor*.

Add to this that Jesus referred the disciples of John the Baptist for evidence of his divine mission not only to his words but to the fact that "the gospel was preached to *the poor*"; and it is further put beyond all doubt that in Jesus' appearances and in his addressing the crowds, the main feature that stands out is that he purposely, by preference and by virtue of his anointment and calling, turns in the first place to the poor and seeks the subjects for his kingdom mainly among them. However, with respect to both Isaiah 61:1 and the beatitude regarding the poor, a brief explanation is called for. An explanation is indispensable in the case of Isaiah 61:1 because in our translation[19] there is no mention of *the poor* but of preaching good tidings to the *the meek*. Similarly, some explanation is required in the case of the beatitude because the text of Luke 6:20 differs from that of Matthew 5:3. We must, therefore, request the attention of our readers for a moment for what is in itself a question of exegesis.

Respecting Isaiah 61:1, the matter is simple, and we can be content with a brief reference to Luke 4:16–21, where we read the following:

> And he came to Nazareth, where he had been brought up. And as was his custom, he went to the synagogue on the Sabbath day, and he stood up to read. And the scroll of the prophet Isaiah was given to him. He unrolled the scroll and found the place where it was written,
>
> "The Spirit of the Lord is upon me,
>> because he has anointed me
>> to proclaim good news to the poor.
> He has sent me to proclaim liberty to the captives
>> and recovering of sight to the blind,
>> to set at liberty those who are oppressed,
> to proclaim the year of the Lord's favor."

---

19. The reference is to the authorized Dutch Bible, the *Statenvertaling* of 1637.

> And he rolled up the scroll and gave it back to the attendant
> and sat down. And the eyes of all in the synagogue were fixed
> on him. And he began to say to them, "Today this Scripture has
> been fulfilled in your hearing."

Evidently, Jesus himself interpreted the words of Isaiah 61:1 to mean preaching the gospel *to the poor*, and this, of course, decides the matter for us.

Not so easily answered is the question whether in the case of the beatitude one is to think in the first place of *the poor in spirit* or the poor in the *social* sense. As everyone knows, Matthew 5:3 says, "Blessed are the poor in spirit, for theirs is the kingdom of heaven," while in Luke 6:20 we read, "Blessed are you who are poor, for yours is the kingdom of God." The question therefore arises: Should Luke 6:20 be regarded as an abbreviated manner of writing, and should his message thus be spiritualized? Or should Luke and Matthew be brought into harmony such that *both* social poverty and spiritual poverty, the latter as connected with the former, are done equal justice?

Once again, we shall not present our own explanation, because our testimony in this matter would in all probability be considered suspect. We appeal instead to two expositors, the one from earlier and the other from more recent times, whose names have authority even in high society—Calvin and Godet.

Calvin states,

> But as the words of Luke and those of Matthew must have
> the same meaning, there can be no doubt that the appellation
> poor is here given to those who are pressed and afflicted by
> adversity. The only difference is, that Matthew, by adding an
> epithet, confines the happiness to those only who, under the
> discipline of the cross, have learned to be humble.[20]

Thus Calvin understands the beatitude as a beatitude not of the spiritually vulnerable but definitely of the *socially poor or repressed*, but he restricts this pronouncement of blessedness, with a view to Matthew 5:3, quite correctly to the poor and oppressed who are quiet before God.

---

20. John Calvin, *Commentarii in Quatuor Euangelistas*, vol. 6, *Opera omnia* (Amsterdam: Joannem Jacobi Schipper, 1667), 64; ET: John Calvin, *Commentary on a Harmony of the Evangelists Matthew, Mark, and Luke*, trans. William Pringle (Edinburgh: Calvin Translation Society, 1845), 1:261.

If we consult Godet in his well-known commentary on the Gospel of Luke, we find entirely the same explanation.[21] Godet does not hesitate for a moment to declare that Luke provides us with the more original reading, which he infers particularly from this that in Luke the words are directed to the multitude themselves: "Blessed are you who are poor," "you who are hungry," and so forth; and he explains quite accurately how Matthew had to alter this when he transferred the beatitude from the second person (you) to the third person.

Transferred to the third person, the saying "blessed are *the poor*" would have become baseless. Or how could all of the poor, including the most mischievous among them, be blessed? This saying was only correct and true when Jesus spoke personally to his disciples and the circle of believing poor who stood around him: "Blessed are you who are poor," "you who are hungry," and so forth. When Matthew proceeded to turn this into the third person, "Blessed are *the* poor, blessed are *the* hungry, and so forth," so says Godet, then a spiritual element had to be added, and therefore Matthew wrote, "Blessed are the poor in spirit." Godet elaborated Calvin's thinking still further and arrived with him at the conclusion that Jesus did truly bless the *poor in the social sense* though with the reservation, of course, that social oppression should not lead to spiritual demoralization but to the fear of God.

That being so, one can hardly approve of the constant *spiritualization* of all these statements in today's preaching such that every connection with life is eliminated from them by ignoring the social meaning implicit in them. Even our marginalia fall far short on this score and in exegetical precision lag far behind Calvin on this point.[22]

Yet it all comes down to one's point of departure. Once one imagines that all such statements by Jesus apply only to the condition of the soul, one breaks the connection between *soul* and *body*, between our inner and outer life situation—a connection to which both Scripture and Jesus hold fast; and so one slides unnoticed onto the wrong track.

Now, by universal consensus it is certain that Jesus in his reply to John's disciples pointed to the fact, as a mark of his Messiah-worthiness, that he preached the gospel to *the poor*. Here the texts of Luke and Matthew agree, and Mark leaves out any added allusions to *spiritual*. The meaning of these words cannot be that Jesus, as if he were engaged in some sort of

---

21. F. L. Godet, *A Commentary on the Gospel of St. Luke*, trans. E. W. Shalders (Edinburgh: T&T Clark, 1875), 1:312–15.

22. The reference is to the marginal glosses in the *Statenvertaling*.

"inner-city mission," proclaims the gospel not only to the rich but also to the poor and that he thus does *not forget* the poor. Such a dull, tepid reading would simply be absurd. Or, how would the fact that he brought the Word of God not only to the rich but also to the poor ever have been a sign of his messiahship? Thus, this entire thoughtless and superficial exposition simply destroys itself.

No, the lofty and striking sense of this declaration of Jesus lies precisely in his claim, as the One sent by the Father, that he had taken the gospel *not* to the upper classes but in the first place to the *lower* classes of society. That is the hallmark of the Messiah. Virtually all other founders of religions began by approaching *the great of the earth*. Not so Jesus. To the contrary, he approaches instead what is small and despised. Therefore he now lets John know that he will proclaim salvation not in the first place to the powerful of Jerusalem but to the poor people of Galilee.

People sometimes say that Calvin entertained tendencies that were more aristocratic, appealing to a poor interpretation of a statement in the *Institutes*. If you really want to know how Calvin explained the gospel, then open his *Commentaries* to Matthew 11:5 and Luke 7:22 and listen to what you then hear. Calvin writes,

> This passage is purposely quoted by Christ, partly to teach all his followers the first lesson of humility, and partly to remove the offence which the flesh and sense might be apt to raise against his despicable flock. We are by nature proud, and scarcely anything is much valued by us, if it is not attended by a great degree of outward show. But the Church of Christ is composed of poor men [*ex pauperculis hominibus collecta sit*], and nothing could be farther removed from dazzling or imposing ornament. Hence many are led to despise the Gospel, because it is not embraced by many persons of eminent station and exalted rank. How perverse and unjust that opinion is, Christ shows from the very nature of the Gospel, since it was designed only for the poor and despised. Hence it follows, that it is no new occurrence, or one that ought to disturb our minds, if the Gospel is despised by all the great, who, puffed up with their wealth, have no room to spare for the grace of God.[23]

---

23. Calvin, *Commentarii in Quatuor Euangelistas*, 122; ET: Calvin, *Commentary on a Harmony*, 2:9–10.

Thus we have established that Jesus cited his approaching *the little people of this world* as a principal sign of his status as the Messiah. We have likewise established that at his first appearance in the synagogue at Nazareth he again stressed the fact that he went to *the poor* with his message of salvation. We have also established that he was introduced to the office of Messiah by first being personally exposed to the temptation *of hunger*. Having established all this, the Sermon on the Mount would not be the Sermon on the Mount if we did not find in it this same touch.

If we now read in Luke that Jesus addressed the multitude in the second person and said, "Blessed are *you* who are poor," and at the same time, "But woe to you who are rich, for you have received your consolation," then there can be no doubt that Jesus had a very keen eye for the *social* contrast between the poor and the rich; that he felt drawn much more to the former than to the latter; and that for the future of his kingdom he vested hope not in the mighty and great of the earth but much more in the little, silent folk in the land.

Furthermore, if people should ask, finally, whether *humbleness* and *humility*, which is to say, social and spiritual poverty, are not causally related, then with Calvin we reply in the affirmative. Power, prominence, wealth, honor, prosperity, and well-being seduce people much sooner to turning to themselves and putting their faith in the creature and thus to becoming proud and puffed up. That is why it is so difficult for the great of the earth to be genuinely "poor in spirit."

Oh, how different things would be in Christendom if Jesus' preaching on this point were also our preaching and if the basic principles of his kingdom were not cut off and alienated from our society by overspiritualization.

VI

We needed to dwell somewhat longer on the opening of the Sermon on the Mount because prolonged lopsided, spiritualizing preaching had made the meaning of Jesus' words unrecognizable.

Having done so, we are now in a position to go on to examine the other basic ideas in the Sermon on the Mount that pertain to differences in society. These basic ideas are four in number.

The first is this, that *money* on earth has become an unholy power opposed to God and that a curse therefore adheres to capital as such. Mammon was the name of an *idol* worshiped in Syria, on the borders of Palestine, an idol that was also known in Palestine. Mammon was the name of what we often call *Fortune*. This idol was served, incensed, and worshipped as a means to make a fortune, to become rich and, even if by less than honest means, to make one's purse overflow.

Furthermore, Jesus says, "No one can serve two masters, for either he will hate the one and love the other, or he will be devoted to the one and despise the other. You cannot serve God and money [mammon]" [Matt 6:24]. Thus, Jesus means that the aims and efforts of the children of men can be gathered under two heads, the service of Jehovah and the service of mammon; a service that makes one pledge his soul and strength to either Jehovah or mammon.

Jesus observed that there were more than a few who wanted to serve neither the one nor the other exclusively but who attempted to unite the service of both: on the Sabbath Jehovah and during the days of the week mammon; Jehovah on Zion and at the great feasts, but mammon in their vocation and life in society. Against this, Jesus protested. That is not possible, says your Savior; you cannot serve two masters. You must choose between Jehovah and mammon. You cannot serve God and mammon.

Jesus thereby took a stand. He branded the service of money and of capital, the pursuit of the favor of Fortune and dedication to the service of Money, as *sinful*, as not of God but of the Devil and as directly contrary to the service of our God—a crass and cutting statement that opposes both the priests of Fortune and the choirboys of socialism, spokesmen who are driven by virtually no other motive than to improve their own social position. However, no matter how it may be taken, Jesus' statement about mammon sets the tone and governs all his preaching. Jesus turns against Money the moment it tries to act as a power that does not stand in the service of the Lord.

The second basic idea, which goes together with the first and follows from it, is this:

> Do not lay up for yourselves treasures on earth, where moth and rust destroy and where thieves break in and steal, but lay up for yourselves treasures in heaven, where neither moth nor rust destroys and where thieves do not break in and steal. For where your treasure is, there your heart will be also. [Matt 6:19–21]

This saying touches *the goal* toward which our lives should always be directed, and, as such, it pertinently and squarely opposes the pursuits of the world, especially in this century.

Financial power, climbing higher, collecting treasures in stocks and precious metals, purchasing houses and landed properties, becoming the master of earthly goods—this, it may safely be said, is the main thought that exercises the heads and hearts and senses nowadays at the stock exchange and in the world of our young people.

Everything stalks money. Everything thirsts for money. Virtually all senses and thoughts are set on acquiring money. To gain control over money people will use cunning and guile; they will cheat and deceive each other; they will risk the goods of their wives and children, and sometimes even the goods of strangers that have been entrusted to them. Everything is measured by money. Whoever is rich is a celebrated and honored man.

This is just what Jesus does *not* want. He sets himself diametrically *against* it. He proclaims that a world or a people who aim at it and pursue it corrupt themselves spiritually in the process. Storing up all kinds of treasures in order to heap fortune upon fortune, and imitating the financial barons on a small scale, he regards as cursed.

He does not want and will not tolerate the laying up of such treasures. The soul's longing and the heart's desire must be focused on something entirely different—on spiritual goods, on heavenly goods, on the treasures that neither moth nor rust corrupt and where no thief can break through and steal.

Jesus says that gold makes your human heart materialistic, for, where your treasure is, there will your heart be also. The thirst for money results in money's assimilating and annexing your heart; in making you lose all that is human, lofty, noble; and in debasing yourself as a human being and creature of God.

Closely connected with this is the third basic idea about social relationships in the Sermon on the Mount, namely, that you should desire no other treasures than what you need for your *daily sustenance*. Jesus expresses this in two ways. First, there is the fourth petition of the Lord's Prayer, where all prayer for earthly needs is confined to the sober entreaty: "Give us this day our daily bread" [Matt 6:11].[24] Then there are those beautiful words—oft repeated yet seldom practiced and understood—about the birds of the air:

---

24. For Kuyper's exposition of this petition in his commentary on the Heidelberg Catechism, see "Give Us This Day Our Daily Bread," in *OBE*.

> Therefore I tell you, do not be anxious about your life, what you will eat or what you will drink, nor about your body, what you will put on. Is not life more than food, and the body more than clothing? Look at the birds of the air: they neither sow nor reap nor gather into barns, and yet your heavenly Father feeds them. Are you not of more value than they? And which of you by being anxious can add a single hour to his span of life? And why are you anxious about clothing? Consider the lilies of the field, how they grow: they neither toil nor spin, yet I tell you, even Solomon in all his glory was not arrayed like one of these. But if God so clothes the grass of the field, which today is alive and tomorrow is thrown into the oven, will he not much more clothe you, O you of little faith? Therefore do not be anxious, saying, "What shall we eat?" or "What shall we drink?" or "What shall we wear?" For the Gentiles seek after all these things, and your heavenly Father knows that you need them all. But seek first the kingdom of God and his righteousness, and all these things will be added to you.
>
> Therefore do not be anxious about tomorrow, for tomorrow will be anxious for itself. Sufficient for the day is its own trouble. [Matt 6:25-34]

This is the weapon against all the temptation inherent in money and goods. Your *desire* dominates you. Money and goods are a temptation because physically and socially we have all sorts of needs and all sorts of wants. We must eat and drink; we must cover our nakedness; we need a place to live; and ever so much more. The desire to acquire provisions for our everyday needs is legitimate in itself, but it is precisely at this point that temptation slips in, for the moment we make our needs *too great* we are in the enemy's power.

Against that Jesus puts a threefold weapon in our hands: first, that we moderate our desires; second, that we vest our hopes not in the creature but in our God; and third, that we place the needs of our soul higher than our bodily needs. If your heart yearns for luxuries and delicacies, then the prayer "Give me my daily bread" has no meaning for you. Then it is a lie upon your lips. You pray the Lord's Prayer truthfully, that is, from the heart, only when your desire is for nothing other than the *morsel of bread*, only when you receive and value everything else as a free additional gift from your God.

This is Jesus' appeal for simplicity, moderation, and soberness of life. Free yourselves by limiting your desires. Become spiritually strong by hardening yourself in material respects. This is a basic idea of Jesus, which is thus diametrically opposed to our century's propensity constantly to increase our income and surround ourselves with luxuries and so intensify the power and influence of gold on our hearts.

A certain Reverend Barnett reports that he recently traveled through Japan and found, to our shame as Christians, that social relationships in that country are today much better than they are in ours.[25] This is what he writes,

> Rural life is well loved in Japan, and the majority of the people have absolutely no desire for the titillation of sensations that the great cities offer. In Japan one also finds little outward display of luxury. The morals and habits of the different social classes bear a remarkable resemblance to each other, and the rich do not make the poor jealous with their fine carriages, proud dwellings and precious jewels. The wealthy do love to acquire beautiful and remarkable works of art, yet they act with a certain moderation in doing so. The population accordingly cannot reconcile itself to the great European houses that ministers and other high-ranking civil servants order to be built for themselves. Thus, wealth is not invested in matters of no general public use, but is more available than elsewhere for productive labor.

Remarkable, on this account, is the similarity of manners between the different classes of society. Rich and poor are polite and urbane. The employer and the employee cannot be told apart by their external behavior. Both are tidy and neat in their appearance, easy in their movements, moderate, and restrained. The child of the high civil servant attends the same school as that of the workman, and they sit beside each other. The upper classes know that their children will not pick up bad manners from their playmates. As a result of this relative equality, a friendly relationship obtains between the

---

25. Samuel A. Barnett, "The Poor of the World: India, Japan, and the United States," *Fortnightly Review* 54, no. 320, (1 August 1893): 207-22. This essay was reprinted in Samuel and Henrietta Barnett, *Practicable Socialism: Essays on Social Reform* (London: Longmans, Green, 1894), 30-51. Kuyper refers in particular to the account appearing on pp. 46-47.

rich and the poor that disposes the former to bestow largesse when needed and the latter to accept it with equanimity. Remarkable too is what he adds: namely, that the people of Japan, so much more than we, love the beauty of nature, pay attention to the birds of the air, and consider the lilies of the field. Yet Japan is not saturated with the spirit of Christ; it lives only off remnants of common grace.

Oh, how things could be different among us if only the confession of Christ raised social relations, like those that already exist in Japan, to a still higher level—if indeed, by restraining and limiting our needs and placing our trust more in God than in the creature, we freed ourselves from the anxious temptation that is inherent in Money for both the rich and the poor.

Alas, people read the Sermon on the Mount and find it beautiful, but they do not believe Jesus really meant it that way. They find it to be delightful poetry but spiritually too high for the prose of our lives. Even the best Christian always retains a small chapel for mammon.

VII

Of the four basic ideas that Christ expressed in his Sermon on the Mount concerning social relationships, our previous article looked at three. That leaves one still to be examined.

This last one is certainly not the least weighty, and it concerns *our possessions*. The first basic idea was that greed, as such, is unholy; it is a service of mammon that stands opposed to the service of God. The second was, "Do not lay up for yourselves treasures on earth" [Matt 6:19]; the treasure that really enriches lies in the spiritual domain. The third was to remain free in the face of mammon, limit your needs and do not put your trust in the creature but in your Creator. "Father, Give us this day our daily bread" [Matt 6:11].

These three, as you can see, are tightly knit together, and all three serve to confirm the beatitude "blessed are the poor." In the eyes of Jesus—in the Sermon on the Mount, and really throughout the Gospels—it is *not* the poor man who is pitiable. The one to be pitied is *the rich* man.

Of course, one additional basic idea now comes into play. Greed is an idol. The soul's treasure is not *gold* but *grace*. A morsel of bread should be enough for you. Yet, and here we have the last question: what in that case is one to do, how is one to act, with *property*, with what you call *yours*, with the *goods* and *gold* of which you are the master?

In the Sermon on the Mount we find three pertinent statements. First, do not insist too strictly on your property rights. Second, lend to one who appeals to you for help. Third, give alms.

Jesus does not preach community of goods. He assumes rather that for all manner of reasons the unequal distribution of property will persist. Least of all may it be argued that Jesus accepted only provisionally and temporarily the existing unequal distribution of property as he found it while he in fact aimed at equality of possessions. This latter position is impossible because Jesus in the Sermon on the Mount is describing the basis of the kingdom of heaven in its earthly order; he is telling us in this way how things will be until his coming again. This is definitely confirmed when he declares in Matthew 25 that in the day of judgment precisely those who clothed the naked and fed the hungry will enter eternal life—something that would have made no sense at all if indeed Jesus had intended that his disciples should set out directly to implement equality of possessions.

A great deal more could be said about this weighty point, for it is sad in the extreme that Christians understand and put into practice so little of Jesus' basic idea for social life. For now, however, we will not let ourselves be diverted too far but instead be content to have shown that our Savior never desired, let alone demanded, a theoretical equalization of possessions. Everywhere Christ assumes that the inequality of possessions will persist until his coming again.

Yet, we hasten to add, what Jesus does want, also in the matter of possessions, is that not *envy* but *love* should reign, and that this love should level the inequality as much as possible. Jesus does not say that all the money the rich spend on the enjoyment of life or on prestigious projects is wasted and that everything you do not need for your daily morsel of bread must be given away.

At the wedding in Cana, Jesus does not stand up to say that people should drink water instead of wine and give the money thus saved to the poor. The Lord also did not condemn as wasteful Mary's pouring out upon his head a pound of very costly ointment that was worth three hundred *denarii*. Judas did that, while Jesus replied that her deed did her honor.

Jesus does censure and rebuke the possession of money and goods if people behave with them like a dog that finds a pile of juicy bones and, although it cannot possibly devour them all itself, still growls and snarls if other dogs approach because they are hungry.

That is why Jesus' first rule is: "If anyone would sue you and take your tunic, let him have your cloak as well" [see Matt 5:40 and Luke 6:29]. An ordinary Jew wore two garments: on his bare body a woolen shirt, here called a *tunic*, and over it a square piece of cloth that he wrapped around himself as a travel blanket, here called the *cloak*. Thus Jesus' statement is as trenchant as possible. It is not about a dispute before a judge about a parcel of land or a lamb from the flock, much less about pearls or jewels; it is a lawsuit about an absolute necessity: the clothes a person wears on his back.

The ordinary tendency of our heart is to be offended and annoyed and to rise to the defense of our right to our property. However, this is so wrong and reprehensible in Jesus' eyes that he immediately sets as the rule from his side: "If someone wishes to dispute your rights, even to the clothes you wear, then do not growl like a dog over its bone, but yield, and grant him even more than he demands, so that through your entire deportment you may shame him and in this way arrest the injustice in his heart." It is not greed that must overcome greed, but forbearance and quiet sufferance that must triumph over injustice.

Jesus' second pertinent statement has to do with *lending. Lending* is different from giving *alms*. It is a *temporary* leveling of an excessive inequality in possessions. John the Baptist had already established the rule: "Whoever has two tunics is to share with him who has none, and whoever has food [that is, whoever has a *double* portion of food] is to do likewise" [Luke 3:11].

In actual fact, the situation in the world is always such that two people stand side by side, one of whom has two beds to sleep on, two garments to wear, and two portions of food for his hunger, while the other has no bed to lie on, no raiment to cover his nakedness, and no food to ease his hunger. This cries out to heaven. Jesus is not speaking of luxury goods, nor is John. There is mention only of the three things that people cannot do without. Now the gospel demands, by the mouth of Jesus' herald and by the mouth of Jesus himself, that a feeling of humanity and love square this imbalance. Such situations must not be tolerated. All such inequality among Christians, if it persists, is sinful in the sight of the Lord. It is in this sense that *lending* is to be understood. It is not that someone who has a thousand guilders must give three hundred guilders to just anybody who comes along with a request. That notion refutes itself. For then the man who gave the guilders could ask to have them back immediately, as a loan, and the other, given the same rule, would have to give them back right away.

No, the intention is that where need exists, but need caused by *tempo-rary* inconvenience such that alms would be out of place and yet help is needed, you should not withdraw your hand but instead help your brother in such a way that he is both helped and later, by paying back what he has received, is left free of debt. Lending is therefore never in order unless there is ground for expecting repayment. When this prospect is missing, one does not lend, one gives alms.

This brings us naturally to the third weapon that we shall wield against the inequality of property. *Alms* is a word derived from a Greek word that means *mercifulness* or *compassion*. It is therefore not alms if you give something in order to be rid of an annoying supplicant. It is not alms if you give something in order to gain honor. Even less is it alms if you provide assistance in order to earn your salvation. The giving of alms should be the fruit of a stirring of compassion in your heart. You see a need, a want, a pain, and the very sight should stir you as a human being. The inner stirring of your heart should arouse your compassion. If you are so moved in your soul that you are ready to give and feel you must give in order to relieve this need, this pain, this want, then, but only then, are you giving alms.

The fact that alms are regarded nowadays as a humiliation is our fault, because we Christians have helped to degrade alms to a sign of inferiority, thus insulting the poor. To receive alms is no more degrading than it is degrading to be rescued by someone when you fall into the water or to need someone to watch over you when you lie sick and helpless in bed.

That is precisely why Jesus insists so strongly that all outward show should be avoided—for everything that smacks of show is fatal to mercy, and thus to alms. The basic rule for alms is found in Matthew 9:13, "I desire mercy, and not sacrifice." It is a rule that holds for all Christians, hence first of all for the church, and it is not least of all the diaconate that has violated (and continues to violate) this lofty rule through their callous, chilly, often humiliating "distributions."

If we now pull all this together, then no doubt can remain that to some extent Christ definitely did desire a certain sort of equivalency, a *para-equality* of possessions.

This is not communism, which did not exist in the first Jerusalem congregation either, as is clear from Peter's saying to Ananias, "While it remained unsold, did it not remain your own? And after it was sold, was it not at your disposal?" [Acts 5:4]. Nevertheless, it is a certain *para-equality*, that is, a certain equalization insofar as the ordinary requirements of life are concerned. *Shelter, bed, clothing,* and the *daily morsel* must not be scanty and insufficient but such that these needs are met for all alike, and then for all alike not through coercion but through the power of charity and mercy.

This is the right that the poor have, for Christ's sake, with respect to those possessing more. Those who possess more but fall short in this matter are not only unmerciful but commit an injustice, and for that injustice they will suffer the punishment of eternal judgment in eternal pain.

Such, and not otherwise, are the four foundations that Christ has laid down in the Sermon on the Mount for the social relationships among his own people. No one should regard this as if it were a peripheral matter and as if it is merely mentioned in passing in the Sermon on the Mount and does not really touch the root of the matter, for as we already observed, Matthew 25 proves *exactly the opposite.* If it is true that Christ in the last judgment will judge first and foremost whether we have clothed the naked and fed the hungry, then it follows directly from this that these *basic* ideas of Jesus about social relationships are at the same time the *main* ideas in his teaching about the kingdom. Precisely for this reason, there is no deeper mark of disgrace on Christendom than the curse of pauperism, which has broken out so dreadfully precisely among the baptized nations. If there are any "practicing Christians" who live off their wealth year in, year out, constantly laying up treasures on earth while hunger and poverty continue to inflict suffering—let them see to it how they may still escape, upon reading and rereading Matthew 25, the terrible word of the Lord: "For I was hungry and you gave me no food, I was thirsty and you gave me no drink. ... Truly, I say to you, as you did not do it to one of the least of these, you did not do it to me. And these," so ends the word of Christ, "will go away into eternal punishment."

VIII

The four basic characteristics connected with social relationships that we found presented in the Sermon on the Mount were confirmed by Christ again and again in his ongoing ministry. Yet, one thing must never be forgotten; it is mainly with respect to this point that the social democrats have gotten Christ wrong, namely, that almost all Jesus' statements in the social area have to do with the *kingdom of heaven.*

This point is crucial because it sharply distinguishes our own efforts in the social area from comparable efforts by the men of the Revolution.

Among them, social need is regarded as something in itself, and discussion of it extends *exclusively* to relieving the *material* needs of the poor and giving them "a decent living." Of course they will add that such an improvement in their lot will at the same time have the effect of once again elevating the oppressed *morally* and *intellectually*. For the time being these are just so many words, and meanwhile they restrict people's horizon to existence in this life. No account is taken of people as transcending earthly life and called to eternal glory, with the result that man's true *higher* "decent living" is left out of consideration.

Of such striving one finds *nothing* at all in Christ. There is no doubt that Christ opposes the social dominance of money, that he seeks to temper sinful inequality, and that he aligns himself not with the great but with the little folk on earth—yet never otherwise than *in connection with the kingdom of heaven*.

The misery already suffered on earth certainly broke his heart at times and aroused in Jesus' bosom feelings of the most profound pity. Yet Jesus shrank back even more from the "eternal pain," from "hell," where "the worm does not die and the fire is not quenched" [Mark 9:48]. However much earthly suffering may bear down upon us, Jesus still regarded this as a blessing if it breaks the pride of our hearts and drives us to flee eternal perdition. His entire social thrust (if we may put it that way) lies in the incisive word: "For what does it profit a man to gain the whole world and forfeit his soul?" [Mark 8:36].

Social reformers of every stripe who appeal to Jesus and yet aim at nothing but relieving worldly burdens wholly misunderstand Jesus' intentions and are quite wrong to invoke his name; and as long as they do not turn personally to the Savior of the world, they will never be able to bridge the deep, broad chasm that separates them from the Redeemer of the world. The gospel is and remains that "God so loved the world that whoever believes in Jesus shall not perish but have eternal life" [see John 3:16].

For us too, as Calvinists, there will always be a gulf separating us from the socialists (as they are called today). We both commiserate with the suffering of the oppressed, we both endeavor to improve this situation, and in doing so we both oppose mammon. Nevertheless, what separates us inexorably is that they will never lift a finger to save people from eternal perdition, whereas we Calvinists, as confessors of Christ, do not for a moment wage even the struggle against social injustice otherwise than in connection with the kingdom of heaven. This is the wide gulf that separates

Calvinists and socialists and that Patrimonium has never forgotten.[26] That is why the spiritual element stands in the foreground even in Patrimonium's social program. If men should be found in our ranks who have lost sight of this unbreakable connection with the kingdom of heaven and who when reminded of this sin have not repented, then they do not belong in our midst but are evidently socialists, *not* Calvinists.

In these articles, we strongly emphasize not only the four basic ideas in the Sermon on the Mount but also this connection *of Jesus' social program* (if we may put it that way) with the kingdom of heaven.

On this point we may not give in. When papers such as the *Dagblad van 's Gravenhage*[27] and circles of prominent people attack us as if we were socialists because we hold firmly to the social program of Christ, they show only that they have shrugged off any respect for Jesus' word and grasp nothing of the meaning of the kingdom of heaven.

It is only from this standpoint that the proper light falls on Jesus' reply to the *rich young man*. This young man was from the wealthier class and already possessed many goods. Yet he was not a loafer or a layabout but a young man with a kind of legalistic religion and a certain fear of God in his heart. He was even personally pious in the sense that he felt attracted to Jesus, provided only that he could remain as he was and in a certain sense be an ornament for the cause of Christ precisely through his high social position.

"Good Teacher," he inquired, "what must I do to inherit eternal life?" This question is all too seldom heard among our own rich young men nowadays. Then came Jesus' answer: "You lack one thing: go, sell all that you have and give to the poor, and you will have treasure in heaven; and come, follow me."

However, at this he succumbed. For the story continues:

> Disheartened by the saying, he went away sorrowful, for he had great possessions. And Jesus ... said to his disciples, "How difficult it will be for those who have wealth to enter the kingdom of God!" Jesus said to them again, "... It is easier for a camel

---

26. Patrimonium is the name of the League of Christian Workingmen, founded in 1876. It served as a kind of fraternal association for Reformed laborers and, as Kuyper points out here, was animated by a different spirit from socialistic labor unions.
27. Kuyper is referring to a conservative daily newspaper published in The Hague.

to go through the eye of a needle than for a rich person to enter the kingdom of God."

That this was no exaggeration but was meant seriously may be inferred from what the disciples asked in response to this perplexing saying, and from what Jesus said in reply. "And they were exceedingly astonished, and said to him, 'Then who can be saved?' Jesus looked at them and said, 'With man it is impossible, but not with God. For all things are possible with God' " [see Matt 19:16–26; Mark 10:17–27; and Luke 18:18–27].

Do not pass over this too lightly. Jesus states very clearly here that the possession of money and goods, as soon as it acquires the character of wealth and luxury, is a hindrance, an obstacle, a stumbling block on the road that leads to the kingdom of heaven. The link between that kingdom and *the poor*, drawn so clearly in the Sermon on the Mount, is here not only denied and disputed when it concerns the rich of this world but even pronounced impossible without special, very special grace.

In this meeting with the rich young man the contrast between capitalism and the kingdom of heaven is absolute. Even a man of capital can be saved, but not unless God the Lord bestows miraculous grace on him and conveys the camel through the eye of the needle.

Entirely in the same vein, Christ accordingly depicts the disastrous end of the self-serving capitalist in this striking parable:

And he told them a parable, saying, "The land of a rich man produced plentifully, and he thought to himself, 'What shall I do, for I have nowhere to store my crops?' And he said, 'I will do this: I will tear down my barns and build larger ones, and there I will store all my grain and my goods. And I will say to my soul, "Soul, you have ample goods laid up for many years; relax, eat, drink, be merry." ' But God said to him, 'Fool! This night your soul is required of you, and the things you have prepared, whose will they be?' " [Luke 12:16–20].

After painting this true-to-life portrait, Jesus adds ever so earnestly, "So is the one who lays up treasure for himself and is not rich toward God"; while he prefaced the parable with these cutting words: "Take care, and be on your guard against all covetousness, for one's life does not consist in the abundance of his possessions."

It is therefore noteworthy that Jesus himself possessed nothing but the garments he wore around his body. As he hung on the cross and died for the sins of the world, his cloak and his coat were the only things he possessed, which under the prevailing law of executions could fall as spoils to his tormentors.

Jesus owned nothing more and nothing else. Even less than the foxes or the birds, he had no place to lay his head. During all those years with his companions, he lived on gifts of love, on charity.

Indeed, lest money should break the power of his kingdom, he expressly instructed his apostles that they should carry out their mission without possessions. When he first sent them out he said, "Acquire no gold or silver or copper for your belts, no bag for your journey ... or sandals or a staff" [Matt 10:9–10].

Thus one should certainly never say that social relationships were a side issue for Jesus. In the Gospels the issue comes up again and again. It is explained both theoretically and practically in every possible manner. It forms one of the salient points in the whole of Jesus' preaching. Anyone who denies or disputes this is lacking in respect for the Word of the Lord. Anyone who bows before this Word must stand on our side in this matter.

IX

In keeping with the principles explicated in the previous articles, our Savior chose the side of the little, silent folk in the land—so conspicuously, in fact, that he was reproached for having flattered and seduced the people and having incited them to riot. Some said openly, "No, he is leading the people astray" (John 7:12). This explains why the prominent in society, even when they believed in him, kept themselves more or less at a distance, while the multitude followed him warmly and endorsed him publicly. We have already called attention to the furtive deportment of Nicodemus and Joseph of Arimathea; yet it is eminently worth noting what John 12:42–43 says in this regard: that "many even of the authorities believed in him, but for fear of the Pharisees they did not confess it ... for they loved the glory that comes from man more than the glory that comes from God."

Compare that now to the bold, spirited love that the little folk bore our Savior as they thronged around him without hesitation, followed him along the way and when he entered Jerusalem even strewed palm branches in his path and sang *Hosanna* to him.

To be sure, some have noted, in opposition to this, that shortly afterward the people chose for Barabbas and called for a cross for Jesus. This objection, however, has no weight and in no way proves the fickleness of the multitude, as if they acclaimed him one day and demanded his crucifixion the next. Some interpret it that way; and so it has been brayed forth a hundred times in oratorical style, but it is not correct. For the multitude who strewed palm branches in Jesus' path were the little people from the countryside, probably from Galilee, who were making their way to Jerusalem for the feast of the Passover, while the screamers for Barabbas belonged to the lower classes of the more cultured and highly developed capital city.

And yet even viewed in this way, the angry cry of *Crucify him! Crucify him!* may not be charged to the account of the Jerusalem plebeians, for the Evangelist states expressly that it was the priests—we would say the preachers—who went about among the crowd advising them to choose Barabbas.

There is only one well-to-do citizen of Jerusalem of whom it is known that he honored and supported Jesus. We are referring to the man in whose upper room Jesus celebrated the Passover. Yet take note, this man too preferred anonymity. His name is not mentioned once, and Jesus does not refer to him by his name but by the ass standing tethered before his door.

To the simple in the land, by contrast, Jesus felt so strongly attracted personally that once, when the crowd pressed in upon him, his mother and brothers advised him to be careful. He did not fail to stretch his hands openly toward the multitude and to proclaim loudly that those people were "his mother, his brothers, and his sisters" if they followed him in truth [see Matt 12:50].

He thanked his Father, the Lord of heaven and earth, that he had hidden the mysteries of his kingdom "from the wise and understanding and revealed them to little children" [Matt 11:25].

Those little folk toiled and served and worked in the sweat of their brow; and Jesus observes *how the great of the earth exercise lordship over them*, yet also how the rules of living for his kingdom derive more from these little folk. *It shall not be among you as with the great of the earth.* For Jesus came to serve, not to rule; and whoever would be great among you must be a *servant* [see Matt 20:25-27; 23:11-12; Luke 22:24-27].

Among "employers" (as we would call them nowadays) there was one featured by Jesus who even as late as the ninth hour hired the "unemployed" who were standing idle in the marketplace and still paid them a full day's wages. Whoever had given to one of these little ones who believed in him even a cup of cold water, he or she would receive eternal recompense in Jesus' future.

Furthermore, what Jesus stresses above all else is that intimacy with our socially lower brothers should not get lost. Notice how often Jesus speaks of the well-off man who brings in people from "the streets and lanes," from "the highways and hedges," until his house is filled and allows them to sit at his table [Luke 14:21, 23]. Even if we concede that Jesus' parables owed this picture to oriental hospitality, still it is clear that he purposely took the good element in this hospitality and raised it to a principle. For in Luke 14:12–14, we read these most remarkable words:

> He said also to the man who had invited him, "When you give a dinner or a banquet, do not invite your friends or your brothers or your relatives or rich neighbors, lest they also invite you in return and you be repaid. But when you give a feast, invite the poor, the crippled, the lame, the blind, and you will be blessed, because they cannot repay you. For you will be repaid at the resurrection of the just."

Here Jesus speaks in a manner indicating that the feasts that do the rounds among the well-to-do, such that one invites the other and is invited back in return, do not have his sympathy. He admonishes us, rather, to invite the poor and needy to our table, so that they can enjoy the taste not only of a good meal but also of our fellowship and brotherly love. In Jesus' estimation, this is so far from being a side issue that he links it to a wage, an eternal wage, when the time comes for the resurrection of the dead.

Jesus, therefore, had nothing against the more well-to-do. They too receive his saving love. He also visited the home of the wealthy Zacchaeus. However—and this is telling—Zacchaeus was a man who gave not a tenth but *five* tenths to the poor—*half* of his wealth. *Half* of what he received annually Zacchaeus gave to the poor, and yet no special word of praise escapes Jesus' lips to commend him for that act. Jesus is flat-out silent about it.

Yet if you would like to know when Jesus' lips do praise alms, it is when he sees the poor widow cast her mites into the temple treasury, as told in Luke 21:1–4:

> Jesus looked up and saw the rich putting their gifts into the offering box, and he saw a poor widow put in two small copper coins. And he said, "Truly, I tell you, this poor widow has put in more than all of them. For they all contributed out of their abundance, but she out of her poverty put in all she had to live on."

"They all contributed out of their abundance, but she out of her poverty." If Jesus now sees from his heaven how our little folk in the land give for their church and school and the like, even beyond their capacity, while so many who live in abundance are stingy and cold, would his approval not rest, even today, on the generous among the little folk?

And so, we come to the closing scene in which our Savior immortalized and sealed his relationship to rich and poor for all times: his moving parable of Lazarus and the rich man.

> There was a rich man who was clothed in purple and fine linen and who feasted sumptuously every day. And at his gate was laid a poor man named Lazarus, covered with sores, who desired to be fed with what fell from the rich man's table. Moreover, even the dogs came and licked his sores. The poor man died and was carried by the angels to Abraham's side. The rich man also died and was buried, and in Hades, being in torment, he lifted up his eyes and saw Abraham far off and Lazarus at his side. And he called out, "Father Abraham, have mercy on me, and send Lazarus to dip the end of his finger in water and cool my tongue, for I am in anguish in this flame." But Abraham said, "Child, remember that you in your lifetime received your good things, and Lazarus in like manner bad things; but now he is comforted here, and you are in anguish. And besides all this, between us and you a great chasm has been fixed, in order that those who would pass from here to you may not be able, and none may cross from there to us." [Luke 16:19–26]

This is moving; this is breathtaking. It makes an end of all disputes about Jesus' view of the needy. The *sinful* inequality in people's lot in life offends Jesus, and his wrath is ignited at the hardness of those who have. Here everything is dreadfully serious. Lazarus is pronounced blessed, and the rich man, through his own fault, is the spoil and prey of eternal perdition.

X

No one can say anything against the preceding nine articles. They were simply taken from the gospel, and they pitted this *gospel* against the *revolution* that sin has brought about in the world of property and social relations. In fact, all we did was assemble the various passages in the Gospels that bear on social relationships, link them together, and let them speak for themselves.

That this seemed new can only be ascribed to the astounding way in which the preaching of the Word has failed to bring this part of the gospel before the church to explain it and to apply it. Preachers remain caught up in the spiritual. Stuck in the same circle of thought, they neglect to preach the full Christ, whose gospel shows so clearly that he also wanted to affect social life—that he judged it as it was and desired it to be more sanctified.

We do not want to reproach our current preachers too harshly for this, for they have only continued onward in the one-sided track of their predecessors. They were accustomed to it—so much so, in fact, that "the rich man and Lazarus" seemed to be treated properly only when the social element was eliminated from it and everything was applied *spiritually*. Have they not treated the good Samaritan in the same way? Was that parable not really concerned with the saving of our souls, and was the inn not the church and the innkeeper the minister of the Word? Still, a *gentle* reproach is not altogether out of place. Cries of distress were heard loudly on every side, and social abuses were growing more unbearable all the time. People are asking constantly what the church can do to calm the social unrest. Is it then not sad to see how seldom the preachers have felt what an incisive force the power of the Christian gospel is to draw the wealthy away from their capitalistic tendencies and the poor from their socialistic inclinations? Take heed, "lest the righteous stretch out their hands to do wrong," proclaims God's Word, testifying in this way that in this world the poor and the little man, too, remains sinful and can be tempted to sin by the provocation of luxury [Psa 125:3].

Therefore, our appeal goes out once again to the ministers of the gospel, not only among the *Gereformeerden* but also among the *Hervormden*,[28] that they should muster the courage to remain silent no longer about the Word of their Lord concerning the needy but to put the trumpet to their lips and proclaim his holy gospel also with a view to our earthly circumstances.

---

28. The *Gereformeerden* were members of the free Reformed Churches in the Netherlands, the group to which Kuyper and Lohman belonged. The *Hervormden* were members of the semi-established Dutch Reformed Church, from which the *Gereformeerden* seceded. In Lohman's soon-to-be-organized breakaway party (the *Free* Antirevolutionaries), the *Hervormden* were in the majority, as were the more affluent of the middle and upper classes.

Actually, it is shocking and outrageous the way that prevailing conditions and personal relationships in our Christian society blaspheme the person and word of our blessed Savior. After all, also on the paths of social life he has left us an example, so that we can walk in his footsteps. Of how many Christians among us can it be truly said that also in *social respects* they are followers of their Savior? We have not disguised the fact that in all probability our words during the elections were too strident, too thoughtless, too little in tune with the sacred melody that we had heard from Jesus' lips. However, where were the affluent and the prominent among our Christians who upon hearing our words called out to us:

> You are speaking too stridently; you should let your words be more loving; but we do thank you for reminding us once again of the basic idea of our Savior in the social field. It is indeed so true that whoever lets himself be led by the gospel, and whoever imitates Jesus, must stand on the side of the little people and the oppressed of the earth.

Alas, it was not to be. A rare Zacchaeus cheered us on, but the Nicodemuses and Josephs went into hiding. Others protested vociferously against us. This was a cause of profound grief to us. Can it be that the salt has lost its savor among us? Do people no longer bow and submit to the Word? Is the Christ of God no longer the sacred ideal that beckons to us all? Even the Rothschilds with their titanic capital have found defenders among us. This makes our heart weep, for it harms the honor of our confession and deadens the appeal of the gospel.

Against the Revolution, the gospel! To be sure; but woe unto you if you take just half the gospel of our Savior and admonish submission, while concealing the divine mercy of the Christ of God for the socially oppressed and for those who must bear a cross.

Let everyone personally face the Lord. We judge no one. Only this we pray, that people will permit us and leave us free to hold high the banner of the gospel also in the social field, so that the rich man see the danger and guard his soul, and the poor man renounce murmuring and greed.

We have testified, for a quarter-century, that our social relationships are *unchristian* and that a *sinful* inequality has supplanted the inequality desired by God. We have felt obliged and compelled to raise our Christian voice with boldness and passion and without respect of persons, asking men to resist the mammon of our century and to choose the side of the little folk in the land. We have never obscured the fact that according to Jesus' own word, and the word of his holy apostles and the voice of history, there will always be very few rich people among the children of God, and that the grace of God is drunk most deeply in the circles of the little folk from among whom Jesus preferred to choose his friends. Can anyone deny this? Dare anyone contradict this? Do people not see—in the capital city and the seat of government[29] as well as in our towns and villages—that it is indeed so and not otherwise?

When from the side of democratic socialism and anarchism an enticing, defiant call is targeted also at *our* working people and little folk, with the aim of making them forsake their God, stimulate their greed, and inflame their passions, is it then not our calling, our bounden duty, to make the voice of our Savior heard in reply to those cries out of the depths, and yes, to quell that greed but also to implant the spirit of mercy and the tone of holy sympathy in their hearts?

Of course, that many do not follow us in this matter and even judge us harshly does not only partly impair our strength but also calls forth excesses in words and deeds that we, too, find offensive.

Who among the mighty of the earth is blameless before his God if he condemns such excesses yet shuts his ears to the word we recalled earlier? Take heed, "lest the righteous stretch out their hands to do wrong" [Psa 125:3].

Therefore, we care little if people call out to us that we flatter and mislead the people. We *may* not, we *cannot*, we *will* not fail, in the name of Jesus, to raise this testimony in this generation. Even if people should leave us standing alone, we would continue to cry out as long as we were given breath.

We respect the notables among Christians; we thank God that even among those of high social rank he has plucked a few out of the fire; we value highly the blessing they can bring us. Thus precisely for this reason the voice may not be stifled that tries to persuade them to follow in Jesus' footsteps also in the social field. Even in the midst of social unrest they can be a credit to their Savior, but only if, like Jesus, they stretch their hands toward the multitude and say with undivided heart, "These are my mother, and my brothers, and my sisters," and so keep them from greed and iniquity.

---

29. That is, in Amsterdam and The Hague.

THE REEFS OF DEMOCRACY

(1895)

TEXT INTRODUCTION

Following the series of articles "Christ and the Needy," Abraham Kuyper explored some of the political and social implications for greater democratization of public life. The increasing involvement and interest in politics by the lower classes of society was not something to be resisted, but in fact was something to be respected as a natural and necessary historical development. But even as he emphasized the legitimacy of such democratization, including the extension of the franchise to include greater direct representation of the citizenry, Kuyper also recognized some of the dangers and pitfalls of populist and majoritarian movements. Rather than harking back to the ideals of a previous aristocratic or bourgeois age, Kuyper advocates for a robust engagement with democratic trends, which he hopes can save the Netherlands from the excesses of revolution. This series of nine articles first appeared in the daily newspaper *De Standaard* from 30 January to 20 February 1895.

SOURCE: Abraham Kuyper, *De Christus en de Sociale nooden en Democratische Klippen* (Amsterdam: Wormser, 1895), 57–95. Translated and annotated by Harry Van Dyke.

THE REEFS OF DEMOCRACY (1895)

I

This paper and its readers will henceforth understand each other well: whenever *De Standaard* spoke, and will speak, of "steering in a democratic direction" it does not mean aiming at democracy as a *form of government*, but working to make *Parliament* more democratic.

To make Parliament more democratic means to reform our popular representation in such a way that people *of every rank and station* can be involved in determining its makeup.

By "people" we do not mean "the masses," nor just the lower classes, and even less the propertied class as though they were the whole people. We use "people" as expressive of *the entire nation* as it exists in all its organic components.

This people has a right to defend, *before* the government and if need be *against* the government, those God-given liberties which it has received in its organic components. Note that I speak of its *right*. This is not a legal but a moral right, and on that ground alone it never stops in its quest for a political voice.

The power that a people must have in order to defend its liberties has always resided—and will always reside—in the money a government needs and which it can only acquire from the people over which God has placed it.

In countries of a certain size, whose populations number in the millions and whose national life has transitioned from simple beginnings to more complex forms, the people can no longer exercise that power as it used to, because it comes together as before but now only in order to elect representatives who assemble on its behalf in a parliament or house of representatives.

But that system of representation itself goes through a process of development in the measure that a people's political consciousness transitions from slumber to sober wakefulness. At first a people is politically awake only in its higher, cultured members, even as its middle layers and lower parts are still asleep. But in a nation such as ours, which came to maturity as a result of a significant historical event,[1] this political alertness gradually filters down also to the middle and lower classes, until at last the day arrives when political consciousness is awake throughout the entire body politic.

That is not by coincidence. It is the divinely ordained law that governs the development of national life. And a nation that does not arrive at this stage remains backward.

The way a representative body is made up should, if things are well, stay in step with this development of a nation's political consciousness.

So long as only the higher parts are awake, it is they alone who represent the entire nation to the government. But once the middle classes awake it is the nature of *their* life that regulates the composition of parliament, its hallmark being the census.[2]

However, when political awareness penetrates even deeper and lower, the moment arrives that the totality of a people at all its levels begins to participate in the composition of parliament. And this is called the *democratization* of parliament.

The whole process, therefore, takes place in three phases. There is first the aristocratic phase, when the representatives are recruited exclusively from the higher classes. This is followed by the bourgeois phase, when

---

1. Kuyper here refers to the Dutch Revolt and the struggle for independence, 1568–1648.
2. Under the census system, a citizen was eligible to vote if he paid a minimum amount of annual direct taxes on land, patents, and/or personnel (income and property taxes came later).

parliament is dominated by the middle class. Finally, there is the democratic phase, when the nation in every one of its ranks and stations begins to awaken politically and demands a composition of parliament that reflects the new situation.

Thus it is not a disaster, nor an accident, nor a setback, when the current of national life is leading into democratic channels. On the contrary, it is the inevitable destination where the political process of national life must end up, by divine ordinance.

Now then, Calvinism—that is, the Christian religion in its most ideal conception—has delayed this process in not a single country but instead has always accelerated it. God's Word awakens people; allowing a nation to doze off is the last thing it does.

Accordingly, countries where Calvinism has been strongest, and where God's word has therefore had free course—these countries are anything but lagging behind other nations in political wakefulness. They are in fact far ahead of them.

The Netherlands is one such nation. It has made great progress in political maturity, comparatively speaking. For this reason, those who wish to prevent our people from moving from the bourgeois to the democratic phase are running counter to the requirement of our national life, similar to those men who fifty years ago failed to understand our people nor helped it to advance when they tried to keep it from moving from the aristocratic to the bourgeois phase.[3]

Such resistance does not avail in any case. When a stream of this kind descends from the mountain it is irresistible.

As a tree trunk during its growth expands and splits every bond and obstacle, so the natural growth of a people bursts every shackle with which its development is being held back.

A development such as this, including the current toward democracy, harbors no evil whatsoever. Rather, it is a demand of life. And even if others were not pushing in this direction, we Calvinists should obey this law for national life and encourage it in our country.

To be awake is better than to be asleep, so he who loves his people ought to promote a development that causes wakefulness to penetrate the nation in all its ranks and stations. No clear insight or sense of calling, therefore,

---

3. Kuyper here refers to the opposition by conservatives to the constitution introduced by the liberals in 1848.

but only misconceptions or class interests can explain why people resist the transition to the democratic phase in a country such as ours at our stage of development.

The calling of the Christian certainly is to oppose and deflect any unholy and wrong elements that can mingle in people's minds with the transition from one phase to the next. But our calling can never be to turn against that transition itself.

When the transition from the aristocratic to the bourgeois phase took place, voices of protest, including those of Groen van Prinsterer and Van der Brugghen, were heard against the seal of mammon intrinsic to the census principle.[4] Yet these men welcomed the transition as such. Groen van Prinsterer was clear when he remarked that he did not wish to agitate against the transition from the aristocratic to the bourgeois phase: "I was sorry to notice during the debates that ideas are ascribed to us that we dislike. I can assure members that I still consider, as I did in 1840,[5] ample influence of the middle class to be a constitutional and truly national principle and that we do not desire a return of aristocracies."[6]

He only deplored the fact that a mammonistic-intellectualistic element was allowed to triumph during the transition.

> Neither at the national level nor in the provinces nor in the municipalities does the representation correspond with the nature and essence of what is said to be represented. Everywhere a segment of the inhabitants has been placed over the population as a whole by means of an arbitrary grab at financial ability and presumed political competency. This is a fiction, a fraction, a faction.[7]

This standpoint was the correct one. To go against the developmental law of national life is not our task. On the contrary, the task of each of us as

---

4. The Constitution of 1848 tied eligibility to vote to the level of one's education and annual payment in direct taxes. Guillaume Groen van Prinsterer (1801–76) was a conservative critic of the French Revolution, follower of the Réveil, and Kuyper's mentor. Justinus van der Brugghen (1804–63) was a onetime ally of Groen van Prinsterer.
5. See G. Groen van Prinsterer, *Adviezen in de Tweede Kamer der Staten-Generaal* (Leiden: Luchtmans, 1840), 128; speech on September 2, 1840.
6. G. Groen van Prinsterer, *Adviezen in de Tweede Kamer der Staten-Generaal* (Utrecht: Kemink en Zoon, 1856), 350; speech on May 12, 1850.
7. Groen van Prinsterer, *Adviezen in de Tweede Kamer*, 356; speech on May 13, 1850..

Christians is to foster that development and at the same time to guide it into proper channels. We are to steer in a democratic direction, not moaning or grumbling, but with courage, enthusiasm, and holy earnestness, while at the same time testing developments against our principles in order to make sure that at least for our part this democracy will allow the Christian element to function freely.

That is what our editor understood to be our calling since he first came out in 1869.[8] He still does so today, this time on the basis of a conviction that has since had time to send down deep roots.

And there is more.

To steer in a democratic direction would be the calling of Calvinists in the Netherlands even if there were no trace as yet of a transition to democracy in countries beyond our borders. But now that the *signs of the times* cry out to us in a penetrating voice that *all* nations are experiencing a political awakening and that the democratization of political representation is *the* sign that marks the transition from the nineteenth to the twentieth century, now it behooves us all the more to arm ourselves against the reproach that we had once again failed to read *"the signs of the times."*

II

Our first article has set forth—in somewhat sharp formulations, to head off any misunderstanding—what it means that the Anitrevolutionary Party is a *Christian democratic* party.[9]

We needed to do that because opponents and supporters, going by the sound of the words, repeatedly ascribe to us notions and intentions that are not ours.

One cannot defend oneself against this every time a dispute breaks out, but the present occasion called for a deliberate and trenchant formulation of our intent. No one, after reading our first article on "Democratic Reefs,"

---

8. Kuyper is here referring to himself as the editor-in-chief of the daily *De Standaard*, in which these articles first appeared. His mention of the year 1869 probably refers to his article "De kieswet" (The electoral law), published in the Sunday paper *De Heraut* on November 5, 1869, in which he pleaded for extending the franchise to enable minorities to participate in the political process.
9. The Anitrevolutionary Party (ARP) was the political expression of the Reformed social movement inaugurated by Prinsterer and Kuyper. For Kuyper's exposition of the platform of the ARP, including a description of its identity as antirevolutionary and Christian-historical, see *OP*, especially 1.I.5-7.

can continue to cast aspersions against our intentions or cause others to harbor suspicions against them, except from ignorance or unwillingness. Our intentions are now crystal clear, so we shall not repeat them. We move on.

As strongly as we welcome the transition of a nation's political consciousness from the bourgeois to the democratic phase, just as clearly ought we to warn against the grave dangers which this phase, politically speaking, will bring in its wake.

It is like a son in the family who grows up quietly and turns from a boy into a young man and from a young man into an adult with a mind of his own. How foolish of a narrow-minded father or a small-minded mother if they look upon this growing up with regret and inwardly harbor a grievance against the fact that the boy can no longer be treated like a child or the young man like a boy, and that as he matures in spirit and body he makes more demands ... and costs more. Rather, that process of growth, that development from phase to phase according to the law of growth, should be a cause for joy with parents who are in a right relationship with their children and with God. They do not resist it (also because it would not help anyway) but instead promote it through sound upbringing for the soul and solid food for the body. They steer the child to become a boy; soon they help the boy to grow into a young man; and then they guide the young man toward adulthood.

However—and this is what parents' eyes should be wide open to—every transition to a phase of broader development threatens the path of their child with bigger temptations and graver dangers.

For the child that is still at home these dangers and temptations are barely worth mentioning; but as a boy he already begins to notice some of them. However, it is especially in the phase of young manhood that these dangers really begin to take on a dangerous aspect and that these temptations can become almost hellish—so destructive for the rest of his life.

But does the real presence of these reefs justify the advice not to go out into the world but to stay at home? No serious thinker will contend this. The damaged fruit of this advice that one comes across once in a while in the person of a mama's boy who blushes when he has to mingle with company—that certainly is not suited to recommend this apron-strings method of upbringing! That is not the way to show respect for the development of your child. That child has a right to his development, a right that flows from God's law in nature.

But what does follow from this danger is that serious parents will attune their child-rearing to it and will in a timely manner arm their child against it. And when the child leaves the home they will accompany it with their concern and their prayers.

Now transfer all this to the development of a nation in a democratic direction, and you will understand at once what we mean by "democratic reefs."

In the case of your people as little as in the case of your own child, are you permitted to thwart the natural development from phase to phase, the divinely ordained transition from one stage to the next? Now that our people after many years stands poised to transition into the democratic age, you should rejoice over it, just as a father congratulates his child when it comes of age. But do not forget: you are to rejoice over it *with fear*. With a fear that in part stems from the love of your people, but also in part from a guilty conscience. A father can suffer from a guilty conscience, not because his boy has reached maturity, but because he has failed to prepare him for young manhood, a phase from which he fears the worst.

That fear, born of a guilty conscience, is today assaulting the hearts of the so-called fathers of our nation. For at least fifty years—or upwards of eighty years, if you reckon from 1813—they have been privileged to make our people ripe for sound principles of politics and solid views of civic life.[10] That would have prepared the nation for the democratic age. And if that century or half-century had been put to proper use, we would now all be able to rejoice *without fear*.

But, alas, this was not done.

The child—here the people—as it grew up, has seen so many bad things of its parents and has heard so many evil words from their mouths that consequently it has been corrupted by their less than noble example.

The child has learned everything about reading and writing and swinging on the parallel bars. No money was spared for that. The head, if anything, is overstimulated; but the development of the heart lags behind.

Education has been broad-based, to the point of exhaustion. It has also been very shallow. This did not matter all that much as long as the child was under the supervision of the parents. But woe the young man who

---

10. The year 1813 marked the liberation of the Netherlands from France and the founding of the Sovereign Principality of the United Netherlands, the predecessor to founding of the Kingdom of the Netherlands in 1815.

enters the world on his own. He has no axis to revolve around except his own self. He does not know any sacred principles. He is not fired up by any noble enthusiasm. He has *no God*.

Do not get me wrong. Our people has many pockets of piety. There is a core which is still dedicated to things sacred and still lives for what is holy. There is also a broad stream that comes along when the sacred banner is unfurled. But our people as a whole, alas, resembles that poorly educated adolescent who is now entering upon the adult stage of life—the most dangerous stage—yet is without enthusiasm, lacks any higher principle, no longer knows his God, and is chiefly bent on enjoying life's pleasures to his heart's content.

There lies the seriousness of our situation.

And yet, even if the political education of our people these last eighty years had been what it should have been, its entry upon the democratic stream would still be accompanied by the hazards of many reefs.

But today those hazards, to put it soberly, have at least doubled, owing to the guilt of those who have held power all these years. For they are the ones who in many respects have corrupted the Dutch people by their offensive example and their unwise pedagogy.

The situation is critical indeed.

If it were at all possible, one would have to cry out: Delay the process in your development. Try to postpone the transition to the democratic stage for another half-century. And meanwhile, you who have the power among our people, *do your duty!*

But this is *not* possible. As little as you can defer summer once spring has shed its blossoms, so little are you able to stop the rise of democratic life for which our nation too is simply ready.

For all that, our future looks grave and perilous. Wherever you look, at ebb tide the reefs on which the democratic vessel can founder stick out above the water. And many Christians in our country, instead of working together to prepare the lifeboats in the face of the imminent challenge, are bent on fighting each other rather than on fighting the wrath of the elements.

Poor people of the Netherlands.

May God yet be merciful to it, for the sake of the fathers.

III

What is the most dangerous reef on which a democratized parliament might founder? Is it that the people would thus acquire *power*?

Is this reef, so familiar to experienced mariners, popular *power*? And can an experienced pilot help us avoid that dangerous reef by guiding us into the safe harbor of popular *influence*?

That is how it has been put more than once as a lesson in navigation—put in eloquent language, of course, with nothing but good intentions and many correct observations. But does that make this navigational advice correct?

We believe it cannot not be correct, for the simple reason that it neglects to define clearly what is to be understood by people, power, and influence. Sometimes two or three different meanings of one or more of these terms have been used interchangeably in one and the same argument.

Indulge me, therefore, while I subject this proffered advice about popular power and popular influence to a calm and serious critique. The present series of articles about the "Reefs of Democracy" is meant to make up for a double omission in the past: first, by pointing more incisively to the other side of the democratic coin; and second, by explaining our position more clearly when earlier we were not sufficiently aware that we could be misunderstood. But this double purpose requires patience. Please do not find it annoying if we broaden our series somewhat and take up time and space to define three key terms.

People. The word *people* can have several meanings. One meaning of *people* is "the inhabitants of a country collectively." Another use of *people* in our language is to denote the lower classes. The former meaning contrasts the people with the government; the latter contrasts the people with the higher classes. When we call the members of Parliament *representatives of the people* we obviously have in mind the first meaning.

Power. When we speak of the power of Parliament we do not mean that it has *authority* but that it has a certain capability to *oblige* the government to abandon its plans when it wants to do the wrong thing.

Influence. The power of Parliament is more than just influence, for influence exerts pressure but cannot coerce. When I try to influence someone I run the risk that he will go his own way regardless of what I say. But I can wield power if I have the means at my disposal to back up what I say and compel a person even against his will.

Now if this is the meaning of these three terms, then the question arises: Does our people, according to divine and statutory law, have only influence on the government, or also power to coerce the government?

By statutory law only one answer is possible. Our people has the constitutional right by means of Parliament to wield a certain power in order to oblige the government.

Ultimately that power resides in the power of the purse.

Leaving aside the question how far the right of budgeting extends and whether it is properly regulated in the Constitution and properly made use of, it is enough to establish that the government needs money and that it cannot acquire this money except with consent from the people speaking through Parliament.

The same holds for the competency of Parliament to prevent the enactment of a piece of legislation. It also applies in part to Parliament's competency to take the initiative in introducing a legislative bill.

Without going into further detail, it is clear that by statutory law our people not only has influence but definitely also *power* to lend weight to its word by means of Parliament.

The fact that this power, by its very nature, had to be solely negative, *preventing or forbidding*, and never positive, *compelling*, does not detract one whit from the case. By the mere right of budgeting and the right to veto, our people possesses real power over against the government.

This is also how it is according to divine law. A people is there first, and a government is added to that people for the glory of God. When that people is still at a very low level of development and its government consequently still has few needs, it can usually pay for its expenses from its own land holdings or out of tribute from its conquered enemies. But once a people begins to develop and so increase the government's needs—and so also increase the danger that it will oppress the people instead of governing it—then the government can no longer do without *the people's money*. It cannot just *take* the money but must be *granted* it by the people. And so in a beautiful way the means is offered, as government expands, to curb the evil that can flow from government expansion.

Almost all political liberty has been won thanks to the demand for money. The people was prepared to give money provided it was given guarantees against arbitrary rule; and those guarantees became broader and more generous precisely because governments always needed more money.

Accordingly, our conclusion can be no other than that our people, too, possesses a certain power to oblige the government in a negative sense— and rightly possesses this power on the basis of the relationship between a people and its government.

That this can lead to abuse, and has done so, we do not dispute. It is no secret that we have advocated a different arrangement for the power of the purse.[11] But however this right is regulated, the right itself may not be eliminated. It must remain. With this right a people possesses a power over against its government that is in fact uncommonly great.

Thanks to this power a people also exerts *influence* on the government. It does so through the press, public opinion, associations, and assemblies, as well as through its calm or restless behavior, its sympathies or antipathies. But that influence runs along entirely different channels and does not compete with a people's *power*, let alone cancel it. The influence that a people wields simply stands alongside its power and reinforces it.

But one should always keep in mind that Parliament may use its influence only for getting the government to do something, and that it may use its veto, hence its power, only for getting government *not* to do something.

Of course, having finished discussing the question of the power of the people, we could now turn to discussing the power of *the people in the sense of the lower class* and ask whether it should be able to have power over the government or only influence.

So long, however, as we are raising this whole subject in connection with the makeup of Parliament, to make a contrast here makes little sense. Whenever we discuss, after all, whether the lower class, too, should be involved in the makeup of Parliament, we are discussing *power* only. Not a power that the lower class as such would exercise, but only its share in the power that the people as a whole possesses over against the government.

It is out of the question to have the lower class constitute a third chamber next to the existing two chambers[12] and to give certain competencies to this third chamber. We are talking only about its impact on the power possessed by the people as a whole.

---

11. See *OP*, ch. 10, "Budget Refusal."
12. The Dutch Parliament consisted of a First Chamber, elected indirectly by the provincial legislatures, and a Second Chamber, whose members were elected directly by the voters.

True, it might be objected that the impact of the lower class might grow out of all proportion. But then we are debating the possible preponderance that one class of the people will have over the other classes, not the power that this class by itself will have over the government.

The contrast then becomes not popular power or popular influence, but ascendancy of this or that sector of the people in the formation of the people's power. That kind of ascendancy has existed among us for years. A very influential but not very large class determines the composition of our Parliament without it ever entering anybody's head to refer to this power of the people as the power of one segment over the other.

Now then, the intention may be, when the lower class joins in forming the power of the Dutch people over against the government, to avoid any *preponderance* and to strive after *equilibrium*.[13] We would favor that too. Only, bear in mind that thus far there has never been any equilibrium of the kind. We have always lived under a system of ascendancy. To such a degree, in fact, that to this day only a relatively small sector of the people (by law, to be sure) has spoken on behalf of the entire Dutch people and has lent the weight of power to its word. And this portion, mind you, is not a higher, *organic* portion, which would have been as it should be, but purely a *numerical* portion, measured against financial means.

IV

Do not misunderstand us. When considering the makeup of Parliament our ideal is not the ascendancy of one class over another but equilibrium, the organic harmony that does justice to each segment of the people and each sphere in the nation in proportion to its place in the whole.

All we have done so far is to point out that this equilibrium has thus far not existed. Thus far we have lived under a form of absolute ascendancy. And much good time has been wasted that could have been used to prepare us for equilibrium.

All the same, we would have liked nothing better than to see the Constitution amended to allow for equilibrium. Even during the fierce battle last spring[14] we declared our support for a prior amendment to the

---

13. Kuyper uses a play on words to contrast *"overwicht"* (superior weight, preponderance, ascendancy) and *"evenwicht"* (equal weight, balance, equilibrium).

14. The fight over extending the franchise was the occasion for Kuyper's series of essays in this volume, "Christ and the Needy."

Constitution, and only when we learned after careful inquiry that this had not a ghost of a chance to succeed did we follow the rule that *"à l'impossible nul n'est tenu"*—no one can be expected to try the impossible. A recent statement by a leader of the Liberals, the group whose support for a constitutional amendment would have to be assured, proved again that our information gathered at the time was correct.

Thus, the means to steer clear of the reefs of democracy will now have to be sought after we are at sea, not before we put out to sea.

If next we are asked whether we are not underestimating the people's *influence* in favor of its *power*, then this is our reply: on the contrary, we are convinced that one of the causes of our present woes is precisely that the people as a whole as well as the lower classes have been deprived of much of their legitimate influence.

If the Liberals had not made the mistake through its authoritarian public education policy to weaken private initiative and dampen personal energy, our people would in all its parts have been much more mature politically.[15]

If, as in England, the labor movement had from the beginning been guided and supported by the men of influence, the free and independent organization of the working class in our country would have advanced much further.

Also, if we had without delay installed chambers of labor in 1878, when the call for them was first raised, the lower classes would have been given a training school worth its weight in gold and we would have been saved from much wrangling and quarreling about competing interests.[16] We therefore warmly applaud whatever may still be done in that area and will support it vigorously. Furthermore, we shall use organizations and the press to try to reinforce the influence of the people, including the lower classes.

But all such influence of the people is not opposed to its power, nor to its share in the makeup of a parliament that wields this power. That influence runs alongside it and supports it.

With this declaration we do not mean to counter or condemn the views of others, but merely to make public, along with arguments, what our view is about this contrast that some have raised.

---

15. For more on Kuyper's struggle against the Liberal policy of promoting secular public education, see *On Education*, particularly "Grievances against the School Law."
16. Kuyper refers here to the early years of advocacy for a code of labor, which was a hallmark theme of his political career.

The disagreement between *De Standaard* and its adversaries is not about whether the coming democratization should fill us with some very serious misgivings and may entail a real danger that in its democratic phase our ship of state will strike reef upon reef.

The most dangerous reef, in our estimation, is by no means the threat that a certain redistribution of financial means may take place—although if it is arbitrary and too drastic it may pose no small threat. But the gravest threat is that democratization could attack the fundamental principle of our political system.

The system that is expressed in the formula *universal suffrage* is firmly and squarely rejected by all who believe with all their heart in the sovereignty of God Almighty. That cannot be otherwise. After all, what characterizes this system is not that every citizen in the land is given a ballot. Not at all. It is very well possible that in a given country every citizen and every office of government confesses and upholds the sovereignty of God and yet that the manner of electing a parliament is so arranged that all citizens without exception contribute to its makeup. It is even conceivable that a country's form of government itself is democratic in such a way that *all* citizens are involved in electing those who will hold public office.

But *universal suffrage* is a formula that stands for an entirely different system. It is a system that opposes God's sovereignty with the proposition that governing authority resides in the latent will of the state, and that every inhabitant as a member of the body politic contributes toward expressing the will of the state. Then the state no longer depends on God but is self-sufficient, and the people acts politically on a foundation of atheism. The state then on principle denies God, even if it maintains freedom of religion as a private affair.

So if ever the Crown were to table a bill in which the preamble or the text recognized the principle of universal suffrage, we on our part would not hesitate a moment. Regardless of the consequences we would resist such a bill tooth and nail.

This is not the case, of course, if the bill contained nothing of the sort, or if a minister merely made a personal statement that resembled that system all too closely. When you vote for a bill you do not vote for every argument used by the minister in his oral or written defense. What decides your vote is the preamble and the text of the bill itself.[17] Thus it is based on

---

17. The Constitution, following the revision of 1887, stipulated that "suffrage is granted to all who can demonstrate ability and social well-being." The controversial bill of

a misconception and breeds muddled thinking when people say that any-one who raises his voice in favor of a franchise bill that seeks to extend the right to vote to all adult males has thereby given up on his protest against the atheistic *system* that comes to expression in the formula "universal suffrage."[18] A sharp and principled disavowal of the unhelpful commen-tary given by the minister at the time[19] would by no means have been in conflict with a simultaneous undertaking to help introduce an extension of the franchise as widely as the Constitution could possibly allow. It was a missed opportunity also on our part, as we worked hard for that cause, to have deemed a principled disavowal superfluous at that time. Thus we gave only a weak comment in response.

Even so, while we frankly admit this and now make up for it, we still flatly deny that *De Standaard* for even one moment accepted the system expressed in the formula "universal suffrage." We always opposed it with all our might. And we still oppose it with firm conviction. And we shall continue to oppose it so long as we have any strength left.

However, let us not forget, the driving force today behind the intro-duction of an almost universal franchise stems in no small measure from those quarters where God is denied and the state is declared self-sufficient. From those quarters where popular sovereignty in the worst sense of the word has become the beginning of wisdom. From quarters, again, where men base their right to contribute to the makeup of Parliament on their arbitrary will, not on the ordinances of God for the life of nations.

Here lies the most dangerous reef. For the more the right to vote is extended, the more the triumph of the godless theory will be pursued in an uncontrolled, passionate, intemperate manner.

It even harbors the danger that a few confessors of the Christ, instead of continuing to resist this disastrous system deep from the heart, thought-lessly start to give it quarter and gradually begin to see some truth in it—in

---

minister Johannes Tak van Poortvliet (1839–1904) would have extended the vote to all men who could read and write, had a fixed address, and were not on relief, thus raising the number of voters from approximately 300,000 to 800,000 or 75 percent of all male inhabitants.

18. This is what Kuyper was accused of by his more conservative opponents within the ARP.

19. Minister Tak had remarked in his defense of the bill that it was a step closer to the "ideal of universal suffrage." Kuyper wanted to limit the franchise to heads of house-holds, in recognition of the family as the basic building block of human society.

such a way, in fact, that it does not promote God's honor in public opinion but obscures it and at last eliminates it.

This is the first reef that we identify, because for us antirevolutionaries it is the most critical and the most dangerous of all.

Not just because it would cause us to do harm to our nation. Much worse. It would cause every Christian who is seduced by it to be guilty. Guilty because it would cause him to sin. Sin because it would cause him to deny his God.

V

Thus the very first reef on which the ship of state threatens to founder with the democratization of parliament is the triumph of the idea of popular sovereignty.

We are not suggesting that the idea of popular sovereignty does not arise until the democratic age. On the contrary, this pernicious idea has been the basis of the political systems of our conservatives, liberals, and radicals. For more than fifty years already, this perverse notion has been the dominant one among our educated men as well as among those of our less educated people who follow these cultured shepherds like sheared sheep.

A principled rejection of popular sovereignty through a joyful acknowledgment of the sovereignty of God you will find only among Calvinists, some orthodox Protestants, the faithful among the Roman Catholics, and a few of our Jewish citizens.

Just by reading Groen van Prinsterer no one could possibly think that we learned about the misguided belief in the sovereignty of the people only after the democratic keynote of the future had arrived. And anyone who took notice of the political systems that were being defended by professors and newspaper editors simply knew far in advance that it would be absurd to think so. Nevertheless, it is indisputable that the present transition to the democratic age only threatens to worsen this deep-rooted heresy.

Things can also go in the opposite direction. It is conceivable that the majority of the common people may actually reinforce the belief in the sovereignty of God.

But one cannot know this in advance.

It therefore behooves us, both for our nation and for our antirevolutionary constituency now that we are setting out on this journey, not to lose sight for a moment of this most dangerous of reefs.

The second reef that we need to pay serious attention to is the "materialization" of political life. The Dutch language does not know this word, simply because the phenomenon is un-Dutch. It runs counter to the whole spirit and history of the Dutch nation, which fought an eighty years' war for the cause of religion and owes its glory to its defense of freedom of conscience.

Does that mean that for this reason our political life needs no reform of social relationships?

On the contrary. The social democrat is right when he denounces the inequality in society, an inequality that we indeed believe is not in accordance with God's will. His error only begins when he wants to replace it with an equality that is no more in accordance with God's will. Allow us a quotation, one that we feel is necessary to provide, lest God-fearing Christians take ill of us what we concede in part to the social democrats. This is the quotation: "The socialists are not wrong in desiring a reform of society that would put an end to the offensive and heart-rending contrast of plenty and poverty, wantonness and want, luxury and misery."[20]

Notice that it does not say "would end" but "would put an end to."

And who was it that said the socialists were right, and who branded the existing inequality not as willed by God but as "offensive and heart-rending"?

Was it Klaas Kater, the man from the lower class?

Was it Dr. Kuyper, the man from the middle class?

Not at all. It was Groen van Prinsterer, the genteel aristocrat of high birth![21] And he held this view not in 1895, when the times are critical, but already in 1849, when a mere cloud like a man's hand loomed on the horizon.

Thus the second reef we mentioned in no way discourages the endeavor to make the distribution of happiness, insofar as it depends on government, less woefully egoistic, less shockingly merciless, and more ruled by the Christian spirit. This is a noble endeavor, provided its object is not, as with the socialists, to completely level that wicked inequality, but rather to reduce it. That object has our full sympathy, as readers know who have read our articles on "Christ and the Needy."

---

20. G. Groen van Prinsterer, *Grondwetherziening en Eensgezindheid* (Amsterdam: Johannes Müller, 1849), 190.
21. Klaas Kater (1836–1916), founder of Patrominum, Kuyper himself, and Groen van Prinsterer are used as exemplars of the tripartite class division of society.

Admittedly, those articles have come in for some severe criticism by a theologian,[22] but the exegetical contortions he has allowed himself cannot for one moment—as will be shown in due time—stand up to scientific scrutiny.

The articles in question, I grant, cast light on only one side of the issue. But this had to be done if our Christian people were to be called back with some force from the materialistic view of things to the antimaterialistic keynote of the gospel.

Yet even aside from this one-sidedness, we cannot imagine a child of God who would not grant us that the current relationships in society are to be condemned at least as strongly in 1895 as Groen condemned them a good fifty years ago. Those relationships and the spirit of Christ are glaringly at odds. When we call on government to withdraw the regulations and administrative practices that have fostered this evil, or beg government to improve conditions wherever they cross its path, we are not championing a socialist cause but identifying a Christian duty.

That Christians offer the wretched masses little more than pie in the sky is an untruth. More, that a person who is hungry prefers to call for bread first is something we can understand.

Yet in principle this is not the way it should be. The spiritual should always have priority over the material. We are not a body plus a soul, but a soul within a body. When this body perishes *we* stay because our soul stays; our body goes into the grave but *we* cross over into a higher world. That is why our body can exist in no other way than as Jesus put it: "Seek first the kingdom of God and his righteousness, and all these things will be added to you" [Matt 6:33].

That rule is always valid. Even when bitter hunger is your lot. For when you are in danger of dying of hunger, you *pray* first, and then bread comes.

If you invert the order of things, in defiance of our nature, of Christ's command, and of the moral character of politics, and push material interests so emphatically to the foreground that the spiritual aspect becomes a side issue, then you debase our life as human beings. Then you lower us to

---

22. Kuyper is referring to his series "Christ and the Needy" and has in mind the criticisms leveled by Rev. Dr. Hendrik Pierson (1834–1923), a Lutheran minister who had sided with Alexander de Savornin Lohman (1845–1924), Kuyper's opponent as regards the franchise question.

the level of the animals, which care for their physical needs only, and you materialize law and justice.

This in turn influences the spirit of the people who, weaned of all higher ideals, begins to cry: "Let us eat and drink, for tomorrow we die" [see 1 Cor 15:32].

And the end result will be that your whole nation and country grows slack morally and before long will be easy prey for the greed of other nations.

Experience elsewhere shows how, among peoples who in their democratic phase did not manage to steer clear of this reef, the lower classes once again, as in imperial Rome, focus all their passion on "bread and games"; that class interests fuel a political war of mutual extermination; that people will be bribed to vote for parties that hope to gain enormously from public office; and that at last avarice and greed corrupt even politicians of the first rank, so that we see distinguished gentlemen, decorated and knighted, being tried, convicted, and sent to prison—former ministers and parliamentarians who enriched themselves through blackmail or by taking bribes in canal or railway scandals.[23]

This reef too is deadly. The ship of state that strikes it is irretrievably lost.

That is why Patrimonium rightly resisted the pressure, however well intended yet at bottom pernicious, to reverse Christ's order in its social program,[24] as though the rule were: "Seek ye first the improvement of your material needs, and the spiritual goods will follow."

No, that was not to be the rule. If Patrimonium had reversed the order set by Christ it would have entered on the track of materialism. By putting the things of God's kingdom first and foremost it remained true to its principle, to its tradition, and to the banner of Jehovah.

VI

Our sixth article can be brief. It concerns the third reef that our ship of state can strike during the transition to democracy. That reef is class struggle.

It is not the case that the struggle between class and class was ever absent or will ever wear off. Social inequality is simply a condition ordained by

---

23. Kuyper is thinking in particular of the Panama scandal that had broken out in France two years earlier.
24. Soon after the first Christian Social Congress of 1891, the Christian Workingmen's League, Patrimonium, had adopted a social program to guide its future activity.

the Creator. Multiformity in his creatures is the hallmark of his majesty, the stamp impressed on all his works.

As well, the desire, the tendency to defend one's own territory at points where class collides with class is so deeply rooted in class consciousness that it could be pacified only if our human nature were eliminated.

In addition, that which flows from the creation ordinance and speaks from our nature with an irrepressible voice always and everywhere, even when there is no question of democratization, looks questionable because *sin* on both sides of the class division stimulates covetousness and pride. Whoever belongs to a higher class cannot abide that a person just below him climbs up to his level, even as he himself tries to overtake or push aside the person just above him.

This is the sin that stirs in rich and poor alike. Even among the nobility the younger members envy the older ones and the older members look down upon the upstart nobility. And conversely, among the rich the *parvenus*, or unknowns who suddenly become rich, are always the most unbearable, and the *nouveaux riches*, those that have only become wealthy during their lifetimes, are the most insufferable of all.

All of it is one great stirring of lust for property and money and power, thirst for riches and pleasure, a spur for pride and arrogance. The rich are no better than the poor, and the poor are no better than the rich. All are corrupt. All stand guilty before God. "No one does good, not even one" [Rom 3:12].

So that is not where the difference lies. The reef that threatens the democratic current is not formed by this common phenomenon that you find back in every age and among all peoples. This reef has its own distinctive shape. It is called *class struggle* because it tempts one class in society to avail itself of the state machine as a tool to break the neck of the other class.

A related phenomenon would sometimes occur in the aristocratic and the bourgeois period, but then in a different manner. We can learn from history how the nobility used to ride roughshod over the middle class and how much blood was shed before the bourgeoisie got out from under the bondage to the nobility. Likewise, under the dominance of the middle class, which is now coming to an end, a great many things were arranged and adjusted for the sake of protecting its privileges and keeping the lower class down. It is even true that a wage earner is usually looked down upon less by a member of the aristocracy than by people of middle-class background.

Nor do we deny that in both the aristocratic and the bourgeois period, men misused their legislative power and political weight to bolster their personal status and the status of their class. Yet this was still not a class struggle with banners unfurled. Even during such brief periods of turbulence both classes continued to regard the state as called to uphold the law and administer justice, and therefore as transcending the interests of either. It is not as though the law was not at times most unjust; but that was an unhappy departure from the ideal that all had in common. The ideal was and remained to honor government as a moral power for a higher purpose.

That is how things stayed in modern times, though not because those who held the power were nobler or holier than people from the lower class. No, things stayed that way in part because the influence of the Christian tradition was still too strong, and in part—note this especially—because the conquered nobility was too small in number and the oppressed lower class was too poor. Since the middle class could not acquire any plunder, either upwards or downwards, it tended to focus its energy on the best way to develop its strength and to profit from its craftiness. It was not entirely innocent of some appetite for exploitation, but that was a side issue.

Today, however, things are different.

The threat today is not just natural envy, which sinful passion has turned into an iniquity, but a regular war between two organized forces, a war in which segments of the population are drawn up in battle array and in which the poorer class eyes a foe that can yield plunder. However, it would be a prize that would only disappoint. For as soon as the war were to erupt, that treasure would shrink like a snail and once divided over the masses would prove too small to justify the raid. Yet the mere thought of spoils is a spur to action. Just look at the tribes in Africa. Each spring they go out to plunder a neighboring tribe and yet century after century they continue to live in dire poverty.

Thus a class war of this kind would not end in reforming society into a pattern approved by God, but would destroy all social harmony. The disruption of society would kill all national energy. Government would be debased to an instrument for promoting economic interests. The feverish pursuit of happiness would be disappointed and turn into rancor and resentment. Before long, what was once a Christian nation would collapse into disorderly masses governable only by the sword and the whim of a despot. Not just peace, tranquility, and true happiness would be done for; it would be goodbye to liberty.

Of course the democratic wave need not necessarily lead every nation to such a deplorable state. Nor does the existence of this reef have to lead to a decision to forget about setting out on the democratic current. A real sea dog does not stay ashore just because reefs are a menace: he puts out to sea and tries to steer clear of them.

If we still had a choice whether or not to go in the direction of democracy, we might consider still other responses. But we do not have that choice. This happens to be the course things are moving, according to a law beyond man's power to control.

All the more reason for us to pay attention to this reef, so that we can be prepared for it and from the start take every measure to steer clear of it. Or, if the ship does hit it anyway, we will not share the blame and can help prevent the total loss of the ship.

Accordingly, our Calvinistic people should prick up their ears, not in order to listen to the siren song of the socialists who desire such a class war, but to listen to the Word of their God, who abhors and condemns it. The allure of a class war must not get hold of our hearts, not even if we are goaded by the other side. But that will not be possible unless God's ordinances and not our desires and passions remain the rule for our lives and we, strong in those ordinances, just as fervently and enthusiastically as the socialists, act for the following two causes: (1) for a reform of social relations that removes whatever is contrary to God's ordinances; (2) for a shoring up of the pillars of society, not by the compass of sinful covetousness, but according to the rules God has ordained.

VII

When making parliament more democratic, another dangerous reef that threatens to break to the surface from the political waters is rudeness.

This is borne out by experience.

We do not deny that also in the parliaments of the aristocratic and bourgeois periods, here and elsewhere, sometimes rude speech was heard and bad scenes were witnessed. Nevertheless, history shows that parliamentary civility was proverbial thanks to the moderation in tone. The hottest debates were carried on for hours and days on end by the fiercest opponents in the British Parliament and in our States General, yet without anyone sinning against good manners. Members refrained from trading insults. The president intervened immediately if something even remotely resembled a taunt. One way to gain a hearing in the house was to speak in an appreciative tone and to pay compliments. Read and reread the parliamentary speeches by Groen van Prinsterer to be refreshed by his refined and gracious language.

And although we may complain that our present States General is no longer at that high level, still we can be proud that in general the debates remain within the bounds of courtesy and decorum.

But compare this to what has been seen and heard in Washington, where at last a pistol was drawn and one "honorable member" of Congress threatened point blank to kill another "honorable member." Think of the wild scenes in the French Assembly whereby France's representative body long forfeited its parliamentary prestige and squandered the moral strength of the nation. Recall what happened in Berlin when socialists and anti-Semites played their last trump against each other. And look at Belgium: after the socialists had barely won seats in Parliament, all refined forms were trodden underfoot, and pandemonium became the order of the day.

In view of these sad facts, is it unrealistic to fear that in the democratization of our States General courtesy and decorum will be drowned under rudeness and vulgarity? Granted, even in a more democratic parliament men of more cultured background will retain the majority for a long time, perhaps forever. But experience shows, alas, that this advantage avails little once raw passions are unleashed. Already, Mr. Woeste and Abbot Daens, members of the more civilized classes of society, were provoked by the bad example of the socialists to a verbal battle that was no longer a duel or a joust but resembled more of a crude verbal sparring.[25] In France as well, especially since the Boulangist movement,[26] it became apparent that men of breeding can quickly forget themselves the moment their emotions are unleashed by the parliamentary rudeness of lesser gods.

This too is only natural. A cultured man is still a sinful man and therefore by nature prone to bitterness and anger. His "fancy manners" that keep him from airing these passions do not come from his sinful nature but are a bridle applied to his sinful nature. He puts up with this bridle; he even values honoring it so long as the odds are even and self-control improves his chances of success—that is to say, so long as he has to deal with an opponent who honors the same forms of respect. But when this is

---

25. Charles Woeste (1837–1922) was a Roman Catholic parliamentarian in Belgium who opposed Adolf Daens (1839–1907) and the Christian Democratic party.

26. Boulangism was a short-lived French nationalist political movement in the Third Republic in the 1880s, associated with General Georges Boulanger (1837–91).

no longer the case and he is confronted by men who try to impress people with coarse language and menacing gestures, then the bridle becomes a hindrance and he lets go of the reins and releases the evil passions which he has in common with his rougher opponent.

This danger would certainly be less grave if the lower class were represented by Christian men only. The Christian religion in and of itself restrains coarseness of speech. In the meetings of Patrimonium, crude voices are never heard. Belief in Christ makes also the common man well-mannered and polite.

But this benefit is lost if in our highest assemblies men are given the floor who for years have won a reputation for upsetting and disrupting all kinds of town hall meetings. For them, coarse language is their preferred weapon to hold up the normal course of things; and even if parliamentary discipline succeeds in wearing down such loose cannon, still an incredible amount of time will be lost, with the result that the sluggish pace of politics is further slowed down and the vessel of state at last seems to stand still instead of moving forward.

Moreover, cruder forms in parliament will have repercussions for political life in general, particularly when elections are held. Even now in America, France, and Belgium, influential politicians of cultured backgrounds and delicate constitutions are retiring prematurely simply because those rough campaigns are too much for them; their nerves cannot bear the tensions of incivility, and they feel out of place where men unleash their tongues and raise their fists.

In this way the influence of parliament on the life of the nation threatens to become the opposite of what it used to be. The example of parliament used to invite emulation of the parliamentary style. In town hall meetings, for example, people would be ashamed not to conduct themselves civilly. But if parliament itself discards the finer forms and incivility gains the upper hand, then not only the good example of yesterday will be lost and replaced, but a bad example will have a demoralizing effect throughout the land.

The public school in particular escalates this menace.

If our government had not systematically put obstacles in the way of the Christian school and if the old way of providing a Christian education had been continued for the children of the lower class, then undoubtedly they would have been better trained in the fundamental principles of respect and modesty, also in speech. But now that the public school for many years has almost entirely cut out the Christian element from schooling and the free Christian school can have an effect on only a small segment of the population, we are confronted with the fact that by far the larger portion of the lower class grows up without the benefit of cultural refinement fostered by the Christian religion. The phrase "Christian and civic virtues" that was inscribed over its doors[27] has proved to be little more than a reminder of "the olden days."

To be sure, the public school has taught the children of our nation to be proficient in reading, writing, and arithmetic, but without reflecting that reading skills give access also to bad literature and that being good at figures sometimes differs but slightly from always figuring in one's favor. Our lower class is better educated today, to be sure, but disproportionately so, with more for the head than the heart. That lopsidedness makes it so top-heavy today.

Perhaps we can take for granted that we will steer clear also of this reef. The national character of the Dutch has neither the excitability of the Frenchman nor the forcefulness of the Anglo-Saxon. Even our most heated debates are not remotely comparable to the scenes in Paris or America. The temperature of our blood is always ten degrees lower than elsewhere. For the very reason that a Dutchman speaks a lot less fluently and has more trouble putting his thoughts into words we need not be overly afraid of the rough language that flows so abundantly in other countries.

As well, our nation for a large part still bears the stamp of the Christian religion, which does put limits on hatred and bitterness even when vented in hard words.

But this advantage of our national character is completely lost if from the outset we are not fully alive to the menace posed by rough forms. Our Christian people, also of the lower class, should be serious about its holy calling not to make these rough forms worse but to tone them down by example.

A French magazine reported the other day on the peculiar phenomenon that we antirevolutionaries open our meetings with prayer and consecrate them with the singing of a psalm. Of course the Frenchman understands

---

27. "Training in Christian and civic virtues" was the phrase used in every Education Act during the nineteenth century to define the mandate of public education in the Netherlands.

nothing of this. But we Calvinists are keenly aware that precisely these holy forms have enabled us to keep the rough forms at bay.

VIII

Two more reefs need to be pointed out before we are ready to determine the course that is safe.

The first is the dominance of the absolute word; the other is the dominance of class egoism.

Absolute is the opposite of relative. Here it means that the working classes lack the ability to discern finer nuances and therefore will not put up with vague promises. They prefer absolute statements made without reservations or escape clauses.

To be sure, absolute, clear, and unequivocal statements have their good side but also their bad side. They have their good side if they dismiss the equivocators and feature the forthright when we need to get down to fundamental principles and expose the guarded language of the timid. Clarity of language is also good when it inspires others not only to reach out across the walls that divide but also to break them down and join your forces, becoming one with you in heart and soul.

In that sense the democratization of our parliament will have a positive effect. It will force members to show their colors. Those who dilute their wine or contaminate it will no longer count. It will put an end to playing fast and loose with principles that men profess in the abstract but in every concrete case declare inapplicable. In short, the absolute character of life for our working classes will also bear fruit for parliament by replacing artificial politics with a more natural approach and making cosmopolitan, revolutionary notions give way to a more national approach in line with Netherlandic traditions.

But this good side does not take away from the real danger that our politics, instead of just deepening, will also broaden, and that toxic slogans and glittering generalities will sap our strength as well. Without considering how to carry them out and what consequences to anticipate, men at mass rallies and at the polls, under ringing slogans, will applaud the most general policies while failing to show how they apply to the existing situation. The press no doubt will follow the delusion of the day. Even government leaders—just look at France—will be influenced by the slogans, hollow though they are. And the sad result will be that in practice not more but even less than hitherto will be accomplished.

The last reef we mentioned was the menacing dominance of class egoism.

If our suggestion of 1878 had been followed up and our States General were split into two branches, the one representing particular *interests* and the other representing the different political *views* among the people, we would at least have had the prospect of a better balance in our parliamentary system.[28]

But our suggestion fell on deaf ears, and even our closest allies opposed it.

Very well, so be it. But the result is that we are now entering upon the democratic age without any balance whatsoever and under the very one-sided dominance of *interests*.

Classes are a reality, and leaving aside whether they may someday disappear, in the years for which we and our children bear responsibility they are not about to become extinct. Now then, these different classes have distinct customs, different needs, various views, often conflicting interests. In an ideal situation these differences do not matter, for "out of many, one," provided the parts are fitted well together. That is how social harmony is born.

But exactly that harmony is missing today. Everything has become unhinged. And the sad result is that a conflict over interests has erupted quite vehemently between the classes.

A parliamentary majority among other things also gives power to promote the interests of one's own class over those of another. That is how it was in the aristocratic period, when nobility and clergy discriminated against the middle class. In part it was like that also in the bourgeois period, when the middle class was keen on reinforcing its position through new legislation. What reason could there be why the same endeavor will not be made again, this time in favor of the lower class?

It may be an endeavor that will not necessarily pose a danger. It may even be beneficial, so long as its sole aim is the removal of existing inequities. But it might become dangerous the moment class egoism takes on bolder relief and one class once again tries to benefit itself at the cost of the others. Then the outcome would not only be new injustices but also a source of bitterness between classes, fracturing our unity as a nation and inflating the passions.

This danger is heightened by the fact, as shown by the sad examples in France and Italy, that class egoism demoralizes the people who enter the lists as the champions of the various classes.

---

28. See *OP*, 12.III.139–140.

All egoism, especially when it targets *money*, is contagious. Government has a say in so many things, including banks and large corporations. It is easy to employ small, seemingly insignificant legal clauses and so benefit oneself and one's friends and move millions from the pocket of the one into the pocket of the other.

To be sure, in democracies such as France and America the danger has not materialized that class egoism led to robbing the rich and enriching the poor. But what we *have seen* is the scandalous fact that prominent men have availed themselves of the tensions created by class egoism to line their own pockets or unjustly to plunder the public coffers or the coffers of large corporations for their own personal gain or that of their close friends. Even former ministers have been found guilty of this.

In this way men move ever further away from their ideal. Respect for government and the law diminishes. While men may not promote anarchism—in fact, they combat it and try to eradicate it—they do foster in men's minds the despair of anarchy.

This sort of egoism is so contagious because by nature it is in our blood. Whether one is rich or poor makes no difference. Egoism, selfishness, is a spiritual factor from the evil one, which can therefore only be tempered and mastered by the spiritual factor that proceeds from Christ.

In Patrimonium—let these men be given credit—class egoism is constantly combated. In Patrimonium no one dares to be so brazen as to speak up for narrow class interests. And also among antirevolutionaries from the higher classes the danger of class egoism has always been reined in. Our party has had its differences, to be sure, as much among our counts and barons as among the workingmen of Patrimonium; but the spirit of Christ has held both in check.

Thus, if not only the children from the lower class attending primary school, but also the younger generation of people of birth enrolled in secondary and tertiary institutions, had been able to get an education governed by Christian principles, the danger would be less threatening. But now that the primary school focuses only on the three R's and the secondary and tertiary schools dispense with all higher ideals, we can't help but fear that class egoism, and the personal egoism of those who represent the various classes, will exert its evil influence also in our country.

The fundamental mistake of the disastrous education policy of the liberals will not really come to light among the higher and lower classes of society until the advent of the democratic period. It is a threat through which God issues a call to all citizens of Christian faith to confront the school of egoism with the Christian school, not only at the primary level but no less at the secondary and tertiary levels.

It is a call for us to combat, among high and low, class egoism and personal selfishness with the weapon of the Word.

It is a call as well, if the blight of this double egoism (God forbid) should break out among us, for us to be the salt of the nation that can stem the spread of this corruption.

IX

De Standaard can now no longer be accused of showing only the bright side of democratic developments and hiding the shady side. We have shown the pros and cons of democracy without holding anything back. We would almost dare ask whether the dangers with which democratic developments threaten our political life have ever been exposed in any conservative paper as pointedly as we have done in this series of articles about the *reefs of democracy*.

Nevertheless, we did not decide to write these articles for the sole purpose of invalidating our opponents' allegations against us.

What induced us to point out those reefs was the strong belief that in our own circles those dangers are not seldom weighed too lightly, and that this less serious assessment of the situation threatens to weaken the strength of our position as antirevolutionaries as a result of creeping notions foreign to our basic principle.

We are not indicting Patrimonium. On the contrary, we admire the steadfastness with which it defends the true principles and the tact with which it has managed to untangle the occasional troublesome knot.

But we must not forget that particularly in certain regions of the country social distress has mounted and needs have risen high. Owing to their work environment our Christian workingmen rub shoulders, more than we do, with workers of a different mindset and thus are exposed to greater temptation. Especially do not forget that the leaders of our people from the higher classes have failed as yet to give our workingmen what their counterparts received from Marx and his followers: to wit, a scientifically constructed system that offered a solution to the question that will dominate the politics of the future.[29]

---

29. Karl Marx (1818–83) was the leading theorist of revolutionary socialism.

This last factor especially induced us to browse through the writings of our opponents, and all too often in debates it caused us to sound less than firm about our own position, which morally undermined the activities of Patrimonium. We often lost ourselves in material calculations and in reflections detached from God's Word, and in that evil hour contraband crept into our men too. Accordingly, for the benefit of both our higher and lower classes, greater emphasis had to be laid on a definition of Christian democracy that is ampler than was sketched in *Maranatha*[30]—provided we define it, not in the sense of philanthropy, but in the sense of a fundamental principle.

In word combinations such as *Christian democracy*, the adjective *Christian* does not in the least mean that certain softer feelings of sympathy with one another's distress should have primacy. Not at all. It means that the arrangement of our national life and the ordering of our mutual relations should be in harmony with those all-controlling principles that were introduced into the world in the name of Christ.

Christ did not just attempt to foster softer feelings, but both in his holy person and by his divine work and powerful word he laid bare life-principles from which the life of the state too should grow, principles which ought also to govern our economic relations and which in a Christian society must be the basis of justice.

He who thinks that Christ preached rules of conduct solely for the realm of grace is not in a position to speak of *Christian* democratic principles. The trend toward greater democracy has nothing to do with grace but moves entirely and exclusively on the terrain of the natural life.

The expression *Christian democracy* makes sense only for those who profess that Christ sounded a warning also for nature, that is, for our natural life both in society and the state, in opposition to the false principles of the world. With divine authority he placed his seal and shed further light on the principles that God caused to be revealed to Israel.

In this sense, then, not according to a philanthropic but a principled understanding of the Christian religion, we call on our adherents in both the higher and the lower classes to defend the *Christian* principles and,

---

30. *Maranatha* was the title of Kuyper's opening address to the delegates of the Anitrevolutionary voters' clubs at their preelection convention on May 12, 1891. See *AKCR*, 205–29.

given the development facing our political life, notably the Christian *democratic* principles, against the false theories of those outside Christ and therefore also against the false conception of democracy.

"To the teaching and to the testimony!" [Isa 8:20]. Let that continue to be our slogan. And if our Christian working class does not heed this Word, they too will not have light of dawn in our political struggle.

Our voice too must be raised in tender compassion for the needs of the suffering segment of our population, and our plea must remain unabated for the rights of our lower class. But in that plea, and in the struggle that comes with it, we are to lift high the banner of the Lord.

Never, never may a child of God be in doubt whether he has become—even if only to some degree—a social democrat, or whether he stands, morning and night, with both feet firmly planted on the ground of Christian democracy.

We should not call a lie what is true about the complaints of the socialists just because they said it first. But before we echo their complaints we should deduce them *from our own principles* and vindicate them before the tribunal of God's Word.

To what length our wishes will go is neither here nor there. It may well be that on this or that point our wishes go further than those of the socialists. Provided—and this condition must never be abandoned—it is crystal clear to ourselves and to our fellow Christians that all such wishes are grounded in God's ordinances.

We shall not stay in port because of the reefs that threaten. Nor shall we set sail unless the compass we take along functions properly.

And therefore we shall not palm the lower class off with the label "Christian," nor distract it with the single tag "democratic." Only in the combination of the two lies our strength.

To be a Christian democrat offers a rule and guideline that helps point the way also in the franchise question and no less in political collaboration.

In the franchise question. For if you are only "democratic" you demand a voice in affairs as a natural right that is owed you as a member of the community. And if you are only "Christian" you declare your ballot to be worthless, you put the realm of grace ahead of the natural life and flee into the tent of evangelism, free of scot and lot thanks to the banner of politicophobia.

But if you are a Christian democrat you demand a voice also for the lower class as a *moral* right. That right stems from the fact that under the individualistic franchise law in our country injustice is done to one segment of the nation because the other segment arrogates to itself the right to reserve all representative power for itself.

Meanwhile, the nation's government has declared[31] that there is no weighty objection to allowing the individualistic representation of the nation to come from *all* segments of the people. Thus to continue to keep the right to vote from the lower class is now a moral injustice, perpetrated by the other classes on their fellow citizens and countrymen.

Our men too protest against this injustice with all the strength they can muster. But they will never lend force to their protest except with the divinely sanctioned means that can pass the test of the Christian religion.

As for political collaboration, the man who is only "Christian" will not hear of any other cooperation than with the conservatives who in their personal life more or less keep up the Christian traditions.

The man who is only "democratic" will greet the socialists as his natural allies and imperceptibly will allow himself to be absorbed into their ranks.

By contrast, the Christian democratic party, according to the rule made public by us already in 1869 and followed ever since, will not hear of any fusion or melting with whomever. Our party will always seek its strength in its isolation, that is, in its separate and independent party formation. And it will collaborate by turns with any political party whatsoever—whether it be factually, without prior consultation, or by prior agreement—depending on whether such collaboration is demanded by the shared aim.

Sometimes we join Rome against all the liberal groups. At other times we vote with the Catholics and the radicals against the domination of minorities by the liberal clique. And also at times, if necessary, we work with all the parties together against the socialists, or, as most recently, against conservatism, with Schaepman's caucus and the radicals.[32]

---

31. Namely, in the constitutional revision of 1887, which provided for voting rights to be extended by law to all males who were literate and not on relief.
32. Herman Schaepman (1844–1903) was a Roman Catholic priest and leader of a Catholic political group that critically favored democratic trends. He was a leader of the later coalition with Kuyper's party that would enable Kuyper's rise to the office of prime minister in 1901.

NOT THE
LIBERTY TREE
BUT THE CROSS!

TEXT INTRODUCTION

It was in the centennial year of the French Revolution that party chairman Abraham Kuyper gave the opening address at the Tenth Meeting of Deputies of the Antirevolutionary electoral associations. The meeting was held in Utrecht on May 3, 1889, in advance of the provincial elections. These elections were critical because a win for the Christian parties would result in reversing the composition of the liberal-dominated First Chamber, which was elected by the provincial legislatures. Accordingly, Kuyper encouraged the deputies to work hard in the coming election campaign.

Fittingly, Kuyper had given his address the title *Not the Liberty Tree but the Cross!* No expostulation in neo-Calvinist literature is more contemptuous and more denunciatory of the political and social fallout of the great French Revolution than this address. Few historians will venture to endorse every indictment here launched at the event of 1789, but, looking over the hall filled with the party faithful, the speaker appears intent on driving home the message that a godless, secular approach to politics is ruinous. It is a truth that he supports not only from Scripture or theology but no less from history. This is the truth, he explains, that our party is firmly convinced of and why it will not allow the antirevolutionary and Christian-historical witness to be silenced and banned from the public square.

At the same time Kuyper prepared his audience for adjustments in policy recommendations based on practical considerations. One year earlier, in April 1888, a Christian coalition had succeeded in forming the government. This was the first Christian cabinet in modern Dutch history, inexperienced and therefore cautious and circumspect. Keenly aware that since politics is the art of the possible, Kuyper wanted to warn his audience not to put their hopes too high and expect all their desired policies to be realized at last. In fact, in the last portion of his speech he seems to be leaning backwards to defend the prudent performance of the sitting cabinet.

SOURCE: Abraham Kuyper, *Niet de vrijheidsboom maar het kruis. Toespraak ter opening van de tiende Deputatenvergadering in het eeuwfeest der Fransche Revolutie* (Amsterdam: Wormser, 1889). Translated and annotated by Harry Van Dyke.

NOT THE LIBERTY
TREE BUT THE CROSS!

Dear Friends,

Having been given the honor of chairing your tenth meeting of deputies, thanks to the trust that your electoral associations have put in me, I would mistake the demand of the moment if in this centennial of what Thorbecke[1] still cracked up as "the great Revolution" I did not take a moment to reflect with you on the *Revolution of 1789*.

The political party that concentrates its strength and displays its unity in your meeting of deputies calls itself the *Anitrevolutionary* Party.[2] Not as though it is opposed to each and every revolution. Revolutions cannot always be avoided. Sometimes they are visitations of divine judgment. How could our party be opposed to all revolutions when our first prince of

---

1. Johan Rudolf Thorbecke (1798–1872) was a leading liberal who served three times as prime minister. Kuyper comments in a footnote that the context of this quotation—a proposal to limit provincial autonomy—shows that on this question, too, Thorbecke chose the principles of the French Revolution as his guide. See J. R. Thorbecke, *Aanteekeningen op de Grondwet*, 2nd ed. (Amsterdam: Johannes Müller, 1843), 2:1.
2. The ARP grew out of a larger social movement that opposed the radical social changes represented in the French Revolution, but also understood itself as positively embodying a Christian-historical vision of social life. On this nomenclature, see *OP* 1.I.5–7.

Orange heroically supported the people's revolt against Philip II, when our William III played a prominent role in the Glorious Revolution in England, and when our first king of the house of Orange at the beginning of this century bound his fate to our uprising against Napoleon? No, our party took the name *Anitrevolutionary* because it opposed, and still opposes, the pestiferous and blasphemous principles which for a terrible hour triumphed in France's horrific revolution.

The Anitrevolutionary Party opposes those principles because, constrained by conviction and taught by experience, it wants to be *Christian-historical*. That is to say, it wants to be rooted in Christ as its first principle and take its place in the course of history as a dispensation ordained by God.

The city of Paris, still drunk from the blood of its noblest sons, in 1830, and again in 1848, and a scant eighteen years ago in the uprising of the Communards, revived on a smaller scale the ghastly scenes from the days of Robespierre.[3] In that same Paris, Girondins and Jacobins today are preparing themselves for a noisy and mindless commemoration of what was ventured in 1789.[4] The bonfires will be lit. Whatever blinds the eye and beclouds the mind will be brought together to regale the pleasure-seeking and splendor-loving caravan of Europe's and America's traveling nomads with exhibits during the day and Venetian revelries at night.

But am I wrong in thinking that if Mirabeau could rise from the grave and Rousseau could hear the rustle and bustle of this vanity fair, would not a bitter cry of disappointment escape from their breast at the ominous constellation under which virtually all Europe laughs at France's weakness and its unworkable revolutionary system?[5]

---

3. The Revolution of 1789 was the beginning of a series of uprisings and unrest in France in the nineteenth century, including the establishment of 1871 Paris Commune, whose members and supporters were called Communards. Maximilien Robespierre (1758-94) was one of the most infamous of the revolutionary leaders and one of the engineers of the Reign of Terror, during which an estimated 17,000 people were executed.
4. Kuyper refers here to various figures and groups associated with the French Revolution. The Jacobins were a political club during the French Revolution who defended values of republicanism, universal suffrage, popular education, and the separation of church and state. Girondins were a loose group who eventually opposed the more radical views of other revolutionaries.
5. Honoré Gabriel Riqueti, count of Mirabeau (1749-91) was a leading revolutionary moderate. Jean-Jacques Rousseau (1712-78) was one of the intellectual inspirations of the revolutionary movement.

Or is it not a divine critique of what was perpetrated in 1789 that out of all the states of Europe precisely France today presents the pitiful spectacle of internal division, national self-humiliation vis-à-vis her neighbor, and absolute moral impotence to raise herself from its shameful sunken state? Glorious France, thus prophesied the Voltaires and the Diderots, would someday direct all nations onto the path to unheard-of prosperity, and inimitable Paris would show our whole continent the way to a paradise of human happiness.[6] Paris would be "a city set on the hill"; the gospel of revolution would shine like "a light on the candlestick." And the fact that some guillotining would first be required, what else was that but the unavoidable throes of a new birth that would soon produce the ideal of earthly bliss for France and a glory that would make all peoples envy her utopia!

Has any prophecy ever been given the lie more bitterly? Is there any country which has been more cruelly ravaged by internal turmoil in the past century than France? And has any other country appeared to be the very embodiment of self-infatuation? France passed through every form of government and wore them out as quickly as possible. She threw away her liberty for Caesarism,[7] her parliamentary honor for Wilsonism,[8] and through her endlessly alternating governments she has caused constitutionalism to look ridiculous. France stands ready today to throw herself into the arms of a fortune-hunting general;[9] and as her last-ditch convulsion to avert this dangerous threat she has resorted to "extra-legal justice," precisely the weapon from the arsenal of the *ancien régime*. *Liberty* was the borrowed slogan that drew the crowds, and the border guards have witnessed one group after another fleeing the country. *Equality* was the magic word, and never has the gap been wider between the suffering masses and the

---

6. François-Marie Arouet (1694–1778), better known as Voltaire, and Denis Diderot (1713–84) were leading figures of the French Enlightenment and well-known critics of religion.
7. That is, rule by an emperor elected by plebiscite.
8. Daniel Wilson (1840–1919), son-in-law of the French president, had used his position in the palace to sell decorations and other favors. As a result, President Jules Grévy (1807–91) was forced out of office. Here Kuyper uses this to refer to a corrupt and decadent ruling class.
9. With widespread discontent throughout the French Republic, the popular general Georges Boulanger (1837–91) gained much support, including that of the army and the church, for his ambition to lead the country. He might have staged a successful coup in January of 1889 if at the last moment his courage had not failed him.

nabobs that roll in money. *Fraternity* was to unite all citizens, and was there ever a nation more like France today, wracked by internecine quarrels?

And what is the attitude of France's neighbors toward her shameful self-abuse? At the start, yes, almost every country lent its ear to the siren song issuing from Paris. They emulated France. The French Revolution infiltrated all states and empires. And even after the Restoration, following Leipzig and Waterloo,[10] installed its paper dam against the stream, the revolutionary current was so strong that at a signal from Paris, in 1830 and again in 1848, well-nigh all Europe rose up in feverish agitation. Yet how great the disillusion that has since ensued! Historians and philosophers have exposed the revolutionary and liberal theory as a joke. Who still picks up the constitutional monstrosity which for half a century bore the title of a "social contract"? Unlike the Restoration, which was hungry for reaction, nearly all countries of Europe for the last quarter-century have seen the triumph of a more sane and sound politics in place of liberalism.

Where today in Germany are the once so powerful National Liberals? And the Liberals in Austria, have they not long vacated the seats of power and honor? Indeed, wherever you look in Europe, just about everywhere antiquated liberalism has outlived its day of glory. There is no doubt that something of the divine laughter mentioned in Psalm 2 can be heard in the remarkable fact that in the centennial year of the French Revolution liberalism has been ousted from most governments of Europe—in England and Scandinavia, Belgium and the Netherlands, Germany and Austria. Our conclusion can be no other than that Paris is inviting everybody, as it were, to come to the *Champs de Mars*[11] and see for themselves how French genius still glitters, how French fingers continue to be skillful, how French love of pleasure is and remains resourceful; but also how her political theory has been a fiasco, how it has turned out to be a blunt tool, unwise, foolish, for governing a state and a country, and how her philosophers and statesmen were hothouse politicians. It's as if from the top of the Eiffel Tower the maid of France is calling out to all Europe: "Let Paris teach you, O nations, the art of living with taste and grace in sensual pleasure and luxury; but also, learn from my national shame and political self-abasement how *not* to constitute your state and how *not* to govern your people if you do not want to sink into misery like the misery of my deeply unhappy France."

---

10. Decisive battles in 1813 and 1815 that spelled the end of the Napoleonic empire.
11. A reference to the large park located near the Eiffel Tower.

And so the tree is known by its fruit,[12] and among the nations of Europe, including our own country, men are inclined to turn their backs on this treacherous liberty tree and go back to the quiet shade of the cross of Calvary.[13] For this is the incredible thing, my friends, that one hundred years after Voltaire defamed himself with his *"Ecrasez l'infâme!"*[14] the Christ, thus cursed, again became the object of veneration for the men of power and influence in Europe and America. Over in America they have a president who every morning reads his Bible and kneels. In Germany, an emperor humbles himself every night before his Savior. In Austria and Belgium, men in government worship (albeit according to the Catholic rite) the Crucified One of Golgotha. And, praise God, in our own country we have a cabinet named after Mackay and Keuchenius, men who only last year prayed with us here in the name of Jesus and who today, with a prayer for the help of God on their lips, are ministers of the Crown.[15]

This is altogether different from what the Restoration intended and at first achieved under the Bourbons of France and Metternich of Austria.[16] The Restoration wanted revenge. It struggled to recover what was irrevocably judged and condemned. The Restoration leaders did not hate the Revolution principle but the consequences of the Revolution. And provided they could regain their former power and privileges they were prepared to grow the new political order from the root of the Revolution. In our country, too, the power of the former regents[17] was all but swallowed up in the torrent that rolled in from France, and the regents' descendants were

---

12. This was the theme of Groen van Prinsterer's book *Ongeloof en Revolutie* (1847); ET: Guillaume Groen van Prinsterer, *Unbelief and Revolution*, ed. and trans. Harry Van Dyke (Bellingham, WA: Lexham Press, 2018). See also Matthew 7:15-20.
13. The Liberty Tree was adopted as a symbol of the Revolutionary government in 1792.
14. Literally "Crush the infamous," a notorious formula appearing in Voltaire's correspondence. Historians disagree whether by *l'Infâme* Voltaire meant the church or Christ.
15. In this section Kuyper quickly surveys the religiosity of leaders of various nations, including President Benjamin Harrison (1833-1901) of the United States, Kaiser Wilhelm II (1859-1941) of Germany, and in the Netherlands, the antirevolutionary parliamentarians Aeneas Mackay (1838-1909) and L. W. C. Keuchenius (1822-93).
16. The post-1815 era was marked by suppression of thought and the press throughout Europe, under the leadership of Prince Metternich of Austria (1773-1859), in the interest of preserving a stable order while nipping any sign of revolutionary propaganda in the bud.
17. The oligarchs that ruled the former Dutch Republic were known as *regents*. Their rule was overturned by the Napoleonic order instituted in 1806.

prepared not to object to the revolutionary system as long as it could restore their dominance under the guise of liberalism.

This is what ignited the opposition of men such as Chateaubriand and Stahl, in our country men such as Groen and Elout.[18] Awakened by their word, our spiritual kin increasingly and in ever-broader circles began to style themselves the *antirevolutionary* party. Our chief quarrel, after all, is not so much with the Revolution's *consequences* as with its *starting principle and ultimate objective*. God's order, not man's will, shall be supreme! Christ, not Voltaire, shall be the Messiah of the nations! As Groen put it in his immortal aphorism: *Against the Revolution the gospel!* Or if you want the same antithesis in pure Dutch terms, then say: *Not the liberty tree but the cross!*

From this it follows, friends, that we antirevolutionaries are anything but eulogists of the *ancien régime*. Rather, we condemn more strongly than the revolutionaries the state of affairs as it had become by 1789 both in Paris and in our country. Let me tell you how we got lost in that swamp. In Asia, despotism was of old indigenous, as a result of sin. The people existed for the ruler. The ruler was everything, the people nothing. But God, who is gracious, had made *us* hear the angel's song of freedom. First through Israel, where the whole people lived as one family and shared in the governance of land and state. Then in Greece, where he caused the power of personhood to open up. Next in Rome, where he placed the blessing of a free community under the guarantee of law and justice. And soon no less in the Germanic tribes, nations of free men who had never known the yoke of coercion. But in none of these nations was *political* liberty able to maintain itself, owing to lack of a *moral* emancipation. Israel approved in an even more frightful sense than the Jacobins the death penalty of its anointed King and today wanders dispersed among the nations like a people without a head. Greece sank away in skepticism and became ripe for the Caesarism of Alexander the Great and his epigones. In Rome, civil liberty succumbed to moral degeneracy, to kneel before a monster such as Nero while crying *Divus Augustus*—Hail Divine Majesty! And the Germanic peoples consumed

---

18. These are significant figures who either served as inspiration for or direct influence on the antirevolutionary movement in the Netherlands: in France, Francois-René de Chateaubriand (1768-1848); in Germany, Friedrich Julius Stahl (1802-61); and in the Netherlands G. Groen van Prinsterer (1801-76) and Pieter Jacob Elout van Soeterwoude (1805-93).

themselves for so long in feuds that the Roman legions were able to invade through that breach.

A divine lesson is transparent in this sad history. Asiatic despotism revealed to what state of self-abasement the sinner is doomed as long as no divine grace intervenes. Athens, Rome, and the Germanic tribes in their best days made visible some of the nobility that common grace can already restore to our human life. Equally visible in Israel's heart-rending demise, Athens' death, Germanic subjugation, and Rome's dishonoring Caesarism is the fact that no nation, so long as it wears liberty as a mere cloak, can maintain its political freedom if it does not have a point of support in the moral liberation of man. Freedom cannot descend upon man from the state; freedom must ascend to community life from liberated man. And then our Father who is in heaven out of divine pity gave his only begotten Son to the world, and that son, that only perfectly free man and therefore the Son of Man who was ever born of women, before he mounted Calvary, left behind, for all men but also for every nation that thirsts after freedom, this immortal, this humbling, this moving testament: *Not until the Son has made you free shall you be free indeed* [see John 8:36].

This testament contains the root and jumping-off point for all Christian-historical politics; and thanks to this testament a radical change went out from Golgotha, a transformation in political life that is a matter of historical record. Through this testament something seeped into the life of nations, something that transformed all existing conditions. It was the beginning of the Christian era. Freedom returned, but a freedom for the people and deliverance from despotism, as the sinner turned back to God to live in obedience to him. Men learned again to bow to God and to stop kneeling to men. Freedom was reborn, but this time grounded in a *moral rebirth*. First, the yoke of slavery to sin was cast off, enabling escape from the enslavement to the tyrant. The ruler would now exist for the people; the people would be subject to the ruler only for God's sake; and both ruler and subject, kneeling together before the Almighty, would be bound by his holy law.

But now listen to how the shameful situation arose that 1789 put an abrupt end to, yet also, as a judgment of God, in a deeply moving and stirring way. The waters of sin had once more risen; moral liberation declined and slavery to sin returned. And then unfree man was again overpowered by an unfree state, but this time in its most egregious, most offensive form. For despots rose up anew, at first among knights and clergy, and when their power was thwarted, in the royal courts. *"L'état, c'est moi!"* that is, "The state, it is I,"[19] proclaimed His Most Christian Majesty,[20] who never scorned the Christ more arrogantly than by this bluster in the manner of Rabshakeh.[21] The angel of freedom departed from us, and a despotism returned that reminded us of the days of the Belshazzars and the Pharaohs, but this time, still worse, a despotism labeled and adorned with the Christian name. That was how the divine right of government turned into a torment of the nations, and the divine authority of kings, hijacked for personal glory, became a farce. What the Stuarts perpetrated in London, the Bourbons in Paris, and our regents in Holland's towns was worse than treading on popular liberties: it was trampling underfoot the honor of our God.

This provocative and heaven-defying situation was terminated by the ordeal of 1789, in Paris and here at home. Looking at the French Revolution from that perspective, we bow our heads in anxious reverence even at the things that a revolutionary leader such as Robespierre was permitted to do. Everything cried out for vengeance. And that vengeance came. It came in a terrifying way. People fail to distinguish the divine judgment in the French Revolution from the principle that drove it onward. This perplexing mixture alone explains why homage and sympathy is extended to the French Revolution even by men such as Vinet and De Pressensé and their parrots in this country.[22]

Let this be a warning, friends. Always be on guard against mistaking such a mixture. Never say one word in praise of the height of ungodly despotism in which royalists and regents had entrenched themselves toward the close of the eighteenth century. And never overlook the righteous judgment of God which came down on this dehumanizing situation in the atrocities of the French Revolution. But also watch out that you never say, because of the judgment which God executed on Israel through Nebuchadnezzar, that Nebuchadnezzar had right on his side. Or, applied to 1789, never allow

---

19. This claim is most often attributed to French King Louis XIV (1638–1715).

20. This is the title first given to the French King Louis XI by Pope Paul II in 1469 to commemorate the conversion of Clovis, first king of the Franks during the transformation of the Roman Empire into the Christian Europe of the Middle Ages.

21. Louis XIV's blasphemous declaration is compared with that of the Assyrian commander Rabshakeh, as related in 2 Kings 18:28–35; Isaiah 36:4–20.

22. Alexandre Rodolphe Vinet (1797–1847) was a Swiss theologian, and Edmond de Pressensé (1824–1891) was a French Protestant clergyman, author of *L'Église et la Révolution française: Histoire des relations de l'Eglise et de l'état de 1789 à 1802* (Paris: Ch. Meyrueis, 1864): ET (abridged): Edmond de Pressensé, *Religion and the Reign of Terror*, trans. John P. Lacroix (New York: Carlton & Lanahan, 1869).

yourselves to be tempted to acquit Rousseau and Voltaire, Mirabeau and Sieyes, Robespierre and Napoleon just because *God used them as a scourge* to humble and punish monarchs and regents for the sin they committed on God's peoples and against God himself.[23]

Here, too, only one question is decisive: Did the French Revolution and the nations it inspired seek first to be delivered from the yoke of sin and in that way, by kneeling before God, to be delivered from their tyrants; or did both the Revolution and the nations spurred on by its example allow themselves to be driven by wild passion and enmity toward God? We admit that things could not stay that way. Baptized nations ought not to be subjected to blind tyranny. Judgment had to come. Yet here, too, no power on earth could undo the perpetual validity of Christ's testament. The nations could gain their freedom, but only if they let themselves be freed *by the Son*.

Yet this was precisely *not* what the nations desired, what their blind guides wanted. On the contrary, instead of realizing that deliverance from the yoke of tyrants can only be had among men at the price of submitting to God, their hearts embraced the satanic thought of *"ni Dieu ni maître,"* neither God nor master, and Europe fancied that the only sure means to attain true political freedom was to cast away the cords that tie us to God. To be sure, there is an excuse to be made for them. The rulers who as "most Christian kings" in the name of God put their feet on the necks of the people, as well as our regents who made a political issue out of public prayers for their majesty but at the same time domineered the people as an oligarchy— the rulers and regents are to blame that such a toxic idea found acceptance, a guilt that is shared by the church which, lacking all courage and spirit, failed to resist the tyranny and lead the people on the road to moral emancipation. And yet, all this does not remove what was sinful in the French Revolution, nor can it ever whitewash the false starting point in its godless system. For that, the antithesis between truth and falsehood is too absolute.

Every human being as a created, moral being ought to submit absolutely to the Triune God. Our sin is that since paradise we have withdrawn that submission to God. We incurred the punishment for that sin by losing our freedom as human beings, among other things by being downtrodden by

---

23. In addition to the other revolutionary figures listed here, Roman Catholic clergyman Emmanuel Joseph Sieyès (1748–1836) was one of the leading political theorists of the Revolution. The triumph of Napoleon Bonaparte (1769–1821) in the French Revolutionary Wars led to the establishment of the French Empire.

tyrants and despots. Thus it stands to reason that the nations cannot be delivered from that tyranny unless man personally returns to the acknowledgment of God's sovereignty. There is no political liberation except as a fruit of moral liberation. For that reason Christ is the Messiah also of the nations, because he alone breaks the works of the Devil in your heart. So says God's Word, so speaks the Christian conscience, and so testifies Christian-historical politics.

The French Revolution, however, turns this upside down and says that precisely by submitting to God mankind was enslaved and so became the cause of all tyranny among men. That is why the Revolution is on principle opposed to all religion, opposed to God and his Christ. It promises freedom to the citizen only at the price of being silent about Christ and his cross in the public realm.

At issue here is a struggle for power. Man has been granted three types of power of which our heart, our head, and our hands are the organs, in that order. From the heart are the issues of life, the head shapes the impulses of the heart into conscious form, and the hand takes this kindled power and directs it toward outward action. Commensurate with this, the Christian-historical mind maintains that freedom, too, is born in our heart; that only he who is set free in his heart can understand with the mind what freedom is—and then lawfully and with bold hands do battle for the honor of that freedom by pen or by sword—always, therefore, on a moral basis.

The French Revolution, however, failing to notice the significance of the human heart, skips the heart, neglects moral liberation, and throws itself solely, when civilized, on the power of the head, and when the uncivilized enter in, on the violence of the hand. Hence its spiritual fathers are not men of moral character but philosophers, seeking to base their power not in a moral ideal but, through sinful intellectualism, in academic learning and theorizing. And when it mattered most it raised its bloodstained hands, made the barricade its throne, and pressed on with raw violence. By contrast, ours is a Messiah who gives himself over unto death, denies himself for the sake of his enemies, and even in his dying on the cursed tree is great through the power of a divine love. But their Messiah is either a Voltaire who has a heart that is corrupt and who glitters only through the brilliant gifts of the head, or soon it will be a Robespierre who has the heart of a nonhuman, unmatched in heartless brutality.

And the outcome, my friends, shows how this falsely chosen means to make people free issued in cruel disappointment. History is again the final judgment. The Girondins freed France of the monarchists, only to be escorted to the guillotine by their spiritual sons, the Jacobins. King Louis XVI was rendered harmless on the scaffold, only to be succeeded by Danton and Marat.[24] And although moderation has since returned, what else did the Revolution, now moderated, accomplish but the exchange of one tyranny after another? It has destroyed the head of one dragon, only to generate seven other monsters from its maimed member. For, to be sure, the former despots have been disarmed: God's righteous judgment put a stop to their blind lust for power; but what has the Revolution bequeathed to us in her genetic spiral of pseudo-conservatism, liberalism, radicalism, socialism, and communism[25] other than velvet-gloved oppression, unbearable party despotism? This time it is not a despotism of the ruler over the people, but much worse, of one social class over another. Floral wreaths are draped around the slave's neck, but the yoke weighs no less heavy—this time not by means of *royal fiat* but, to add insult to injury, by means of the *law* which the sovereign people presumably makes for itself. The "general welfare," the "common good," "power to the people" are splendid phrases; but meanwhile the free citizen and freedom of conscience are in fact strangled by the silver cord of the Revolution, by the power of money.

If only the church of Christ at the close of the eighteenth century had better understood her calling instead of going whoring after royal favors and the goodwill of regents! If only she had, with the courage of an Ambrose,[26] stood up to the throne on behalf of the oppressed people and stuck up for the government to the people by appealing to their conscience! How many horrid scenes would not have been avoided; how much bloodshed, lawlessness, and savagery would not have been prevented; yea, how different would the course of history not have been! But for that, the church herself would have had to stand on a higher moral level, believe more fervently in the gospel she purported to be preaching, and recognize the secret of her

---

24. Georges Danton (1759–94) was an early leader of the French Revolution, eventually guillotined for alleged corruption. Jean-Paul Marat (1743–94) was a radical journalist and controversialist and who served as a rallying force for Jacobins.

25. From Kuyper's perspective, these are all kindred versions of secular politics based on the same fundamental principle of human autonomy. He traces the genealogy of atomistic individualism and socialistic collectivism in "Social Question and the Christian Religion," in *OBE*.

26. In AD 390, Bishop Ambrose of Milan (ca. 340–397) barred Emperor Theodosius (347–January 395) from attending Mass after he ordered a massacre in Thessalonica.

strength in the cross of Christ. This, alas, was not the condition the church was in. She suffered moral decline along with the nations. She had deprived the gospel of its soul through tepid and vapid rationalism. She had frozen her prayers in formalized ritual. She had cut the pith and marrow from her confession. Still worse, her clergy reasoned about Christ with cool heads instead of warm hearts aglow with holy love; her pastors shrunk back in false shame from the scandal of the cross of Golgotha. No fewer than two hundred and fifty clergy in the Estates General at Versailles supported the madness of the revolutionaries; nearly all Protestant pastors followed this reckless example.[27] In our country as well, ministers of the church danced around the liberty tree; and when the oath[28] was demanded from confessors of the gospel, it was Bilderdijk[29] who had to lead the way in offering manly resistance, opting for exile rather than dishonor and choosing principle over social position and livelihood.

Now join these factors together: the brutal tyranny by those in power, the moral decline of the tormented peoples, and the shameful failure of the church, and the result could be no other than what it became. It was bound to come, that terrible revolution which turned against throne and altar alike and soon unleashed a host of evil demons.

But, praise God, the situation did not stay that way. The church of Christ may fail, but she cannot fall, because she is the bearer of imperishable spiritual strength. No sooner had the scourge of Napoleon spent itself all over Europe than in all parts of the church and among all kinds of Christian groups a new life began to stir. And it is to that revival of the Christian life that our Anitrevolutionary Party owes its rise. After Leipzig and Waterloo, the task which lay on Christianity's path before 1789 and which she had shamefully neglected was taken up again. The report of this marvelous Réveil spread far and wide.[30] A spiritual movement throughout

---

27. Kuyper refers here to the support of Roman Catholic as well as Protestant clergy for the French Revolution.
28. After the revolutionary government was installed in the Netherlands in 1795, all public officials had to swear an oath of loyalty to the new regime.
29. Willem Bilderdijk (1756–1831), poet, historian, publicist, was also a barrister-at-law, in which capacity he too had to swear the new oath of loyalty, something he refused to do.
30. In the early nineteenth century the Netherlands experienced the revival movement spreading throughout Europe and the United States. In the Netherlands the Réveil took place largely within the Dutch Reformed Church, and it stressed individual piety and concern for the poor.

Christendom, not bound to any particular country or church denomination, brought about, almost unexpectedly, new fire in the faith, music in the spoken word, and in the realization of an immediate calling the prophecy of a rebirth of the nations.

The first tremor caused by that impulse was an as yet undefined Christian stimulus, ahistorical, far from antirevolutionary. It did cause the stream of Christian life to flow again, but in the naïve joy of its infancy it had not yet recovered the memory of its past. It hardly grasped that it was charged with a life-and-death struggle against the principle of the Revolution. Yet precisely this fact was a blessing: it kept the stream pure and undefiled. It needed time to mature and ripen, and meanwhile it kept the whims of the Restoration at bay. Soon, Christianity's calling was to proclaim this double credo among the nations: *first*, that there is no liberation of the nations without moral liberation from sin; and *second*, that the liberation from sin is found nowhere else than in Christ our Lord. But thanks to the blessed influence of the divinely naïve Réveil, Christian action, also in our country, began exactly where it must always begin: in the conversion of the hearts and the moral elevation of that which had sunk into sin. As yet, no one thought of political action, but enthusiasm was kindled for Jesus as the only Redeemer. A mighty crusade of evangelism went out to seek those who had drifted away, to call them back to Christ. Shelters for the homeless were provided. Unwed mothers were given a helping hand. Alcohol abuse was combated. The blind were comforted. Young people were brought together in better company. Tract after tract was handed out, the Bible was restored at the family altar, wholesome literature was distributed among the lower classes, and love was aroused for missions among the Jews and the pagans. In short, a spirit awoke which did not look out for itself but sought others, a spirit which did not want to dominate but to serve and which warmly invited all men to experience the mercy and compassion of God.

And this was the way! Back to Christ, to be liberated from the bonds of sin, in order thereafter to arrive at the political liberation of the nations.

People became antirevolutionary before they realized it, not from political calculation but in response to a bold manifesto: da Costa's *Grievances against the Spirit of the Age*.[31] This publication was the Christians' cry for help as they were increasingly vexed by the havoc that the Revolution fever had

---

31. Isaäc da Costa, *Bezwaren tegen de geest der eeuw* (Leyden: L. Herdingh, 1823). This "tract for the times" is often referred to as "the birth-cry of the Réveil."

caused in every societal relationship. And when the writer of this rather awkward and ungainly prose reached for the lyre and sang out his prophecy in the poem "*Zij zullen ons niet hebben, de goden onzer eeuw,*"[32] it was as if an electrifying shock passed through Christian Netherlands, and from that day forward the antirevolutionary nature of our struggle was established.

How could it be otherwise? We had to wake up from the sweet dream that it was possible to bring the gospel to people without coming into conflict with the spirit of the Revolution. The men of the Revolution were sure to see to that! And because people wanted to be Christian and not deny Christ his glory, they could not but be antirevolutionary, that is to say, they could not but clash with the spirit of the Revolution in every field of human endeavor.

This proved true most powerfully in our school struggle. In the field of education, too—there is no denying or minimizing it—the Spirit of Christ directly confronted the spirit of the Revolution. At stake were the baptized children of our nation—the seed of the church. At stake was the future of our entire nation. You see, the spirit of the Revolution demanded, true to its intellectualistic principle, that the head comes first and the heart only second, and that the coming generation should be inspired not by the name of Christ but by the glory of reason. And this the Spirit of Christ could not abide. The Savior of the world, who had died also for children and at whose command those children were baptized, he could not tolerate that moral education would take a backseat to intellectual instruction. The schoolchild, too, had to be seen before all else as a creature of God, and for all the value of preparing it for society it was never to be forgotten that the child was created for a higher life, called to an eternal existence. Therefore the child of Christian parents could not be permanently surrendered to the school of the Revolution, and the school of Christ had to face that school head-on.

And so it happened, not only in our country but throughout Europe, that the spirit that was to rule the school became the apple of discord and the bone of contention.

But precisely for the sake of the school we could not rest there, and so we advanced toward the political arena under the incomparable leadership of

---

32. The first stanza of this poem of 1844 reads, in free translation: "Possess it they shall never, / our good old Netherlands! / For all the woes we suffered / it still belongs to God! / Possess it they shall never, / the idols of the age! / God set our country free / not so we worship them."—"Set our country free": that is, liberate us from the agents of the revolution, namely, the invading "Patriots" of 1795 and the French occupiers of 1810–13.

Groen van Prinsterer. For it was particularly in the world of politics that the spirit of the Revolution had made its home. By means of the power of the public purse the Revolution ensconced itself in the quasi-neutral primary school. What else could have broken the Revolution's spell that bound our people other than challenging the Revolution's hegemony also in politics? Thus the political struggle could not be avoided. The state school was simply a manifestation of what had infiltrated our politics from the root of the French Revolution. And that, my friends, is how we antirevolutionaries became a political party—in spite of ourselves, in spite of the politicophobia in Christian circles, but under pressure from our principles.

* * *

The *principles* that we as a political party are to advocate and are to plant in the hearts of the people cannot be chosen at will. They are given in our very origin, in our view of life, in our quarrel with the French Revolution. All baptized nations have been given the grace to not have to bend under a yoke of despotism. The principal issue for us is and remains that Christ Jesus shall be glorified and that his gospel shall have free and untrammeled course in church, school, and press, and among all ranks and classes of the population. Political freedom is there for state and nation, on condition of complete submission to God. Hence our opposition to *l'état athée*, to the irreligious state. We believe that government has the authority to rule by the grace of God. Conversely, we resist every attempt at sacrificing to state omnipotence the sovereign freedom of the life of civil society.

At the same time these principles—free course for the gospel and acknowledgment by ruler and subject of God's supremacy—flow together for us in the sacred conclusion that all spiritual coercion is anathema. The gospel shall be embraced from free conviction, for Christ will not be loved except from voluntary love, and his offer of salvation is not to be accepted except in unforced gratitude. Our target of attack is compulsion and superior force, and our program is authority and freedom, linked by justice. The way our country is governed must reflect something of the divine majesty, and what better reflects that majesty but the *righteousness* that exalts a nation and the *compassion* that lifts a sunken people from its misery and distress.

These are the principles by which the Anitrevolutionary Party lives, and all Christians who confess the same basic principles therefore belong factually to us, even if for a while they oppose us for secondary reasons. To be sure, our party does have a program in which its principles are spelled out in more concrete terms,[33] but its content was never intended to be treated as *dogma*. A party must nurture a bond and maintain some form of discipline, but the stream of life cannot be tied down to this order. Whoever seeks to honor God in politics and defends the gospel and puts moral before intellectual formation is on our side and works in our favor. That keeps us from being narrow-minded and prompts us to open our ranks wide for whoever wants to collaborate with us in this critical struggle. Here, our persons are nothing, principles are everything. Dogmatism creates mechanical artifices; we boast in free organic life. This explains our growing influence, our ability to recruit young people.

The fact that for the time being not everyone is able to march in our ranks is due to the *historical* character which our party at first lacked, recovered when it was almost too late, and now that it has retrieved it can no longer turn its back on. The Réveil no more than the Restoration was rooted in history. Even Groen van Prinsterer at first did not link up with the historic tradition of our country. Not until his work for the *Archives* of the House of Orange[34] and his studies for the *Handbook of Dutch History*[35] was he led to embrace it. And when the Christian people in the land had awakened and joyfully applauded the activity of the Réveil, it was inevitable that the current of our antirevolutionary life had once again to turn Calvinist and therefore return to our national heritage.

Our Calvinist nation, more fortunate than Catholic and Lutheran ones, was privileged in the sixteenth century to graft political liberation into the trunk of the gospel. Calvin, who came after Luther, stands for an incredible step forward for politics that caused the political freedom of peoples to flower on the root of religion. The only sound solution of the problem that 1789 ignored and today is more and more aspired to by every Christian nation was anticipated by Calvinism already in the sixteenth century. It is unanimously agreed that it is to Calvin's brilliant solution not only in the

---

33. See *OP*.
34. See G. Groen van Prinsterer, *Archives ou Correspondance inédite de la Maison d'Orange-Nassau*, 1st series, 9 vols. (Leyden: Luchtmans, 1835-47); second series, 5 vols. (Utrecht: Kemink et fils, 1857-61).
35. See G. Groen van Prinsterer, *Handboek der Geschiedenis van het Vaderland*, 5 vols. (Leyden, 1841-46).

ecclesiastical and social but also political realm that our country owes its independence from Spain and its rule of law.

The Anitrevolutionary Party owes its considerable growth since 1869 especially to an increasing awareness of its historical and national character. Unfortunately, however, this renewed emphasis could not be adopted without at the same time temporarily estranging a portion of our brothers—for a reason that is obvious. It is no secret that a small group of esteemed brothers looked for Christian inspiration less from our national, historical confession than from, on the one hand, Schleiermacher, and on the other Vinet—from Schleiermacher, one of the noblest products of German Lutheranism, and from Vinet, the champion of French individualism.[36] This could only keep their followers from joining us. Schleiermacher could never inspire love for a free civil society independent of the state but only tempt nation and school and church to lean on the arm of the state. And Vinet could only foster among his followers the hybrid product that looks to the gospel for moral liberation but finds support for popular liberty in liberalism.

Let us not allow a root of bitterness to rise in our hearts as we see these brothers choose other paths. Their reasons are understandable, and what seemingly arises only from differences about the church actually has deeper roots in the sad fact that our Calvinism thirty years ago wore a veil over its face and as a result cleared the way for German and French influences.[37] Anyway, this fact will not hold up the process that has been set in motion. The backbone of the common people remains Calvinist, however strongly the higher classes undergo those foreign influences for a time. The pitiful fiasco suffered by their National Party in the elections of March 1888 was eloquent proof that our people are not fooled, something which their leader Buytendijk has openly and frankly conceded.[38]

---

36. Friedrich Schleiermacher (1768–1834) is often seen as the father of modern liberal theology.
37. Although the ARP was formally founded in 1879 with the publication of its party program, antirevolutionary political advocacy, including activity by Kuyper himself, had already begun in 1869 focused on the schools question.
38. Rev. S. H. Buytendijk (1822–1910), ethical-irenic (Modernist) pastor, resigned his membership in the ARP because it was supposedly "unfaithful to Groen van Prinsterer's principles." Together with like-minded pastors, in January 1888, he cofounded a Christian party, the National Party, that was conservative in outlook and failed to win any seats in the general elections.

Meanwhile, this should not prompt anyone to harbor the suspicion that we are *democratic* in the bad sense of the word. Our political party can never be democratic in the sense that the lower classes should dominate over the higher classes. We rejoice in seeing rich and poor seated at the same supper of the new covenant and we urge both to kneel with reverence before the exalted God. But when German influences wish to reinforce the state at the expense of civil society, then indeed our Calvinistic heart rises in protest against that un-Netherlandic idea, and we persist in awaiting the political liberation of our people from the influence of the gospel.

Such would be our view even if the social question had never been placed on the agenda. But we hold this view all the more now that one of the bitterest fruit of the French Revolution is the growing tension between the well-endowed classes and those who never eat their bread except by the sweat of their brow. In this situation, no Christian can, to speak with the apostle, be foreign to his own flesh [see Eph 5:29]. From every Christian's lips today, mercy should triumph over the harsh law of necessity. And the Anitrevolutionary Party, too, will not rest until a solution to the social question is found so that peace may return between rich and poor and citizen contentment may again work to bind together sons of the same fatherland.

In sum, friends, the progress of our movement has been unforced and healthy. When the terrible Revolution invaded our country in 1795, the church of Christ was at a low ebb. It lacked vibrant faith and remained silent. The most she hoped for was that she would be tolerated as the silent majority in the country. That lasted until the Réveil gave us back our faith in the power of the gospel. Da Costa, the great heir of Bilderdijk, sang his song against the idols of the age, and Groen van Prinsterer attacked them in the political arena. The reawakened Calvinist people before long put the historical and national stamp on this endeavor. In consequence, men of German and French sympathies chose other paths, and when the social question came on the agenda it was Christ who constrained us to stand up for what divine mercy offers also to suffering people.

And so our current position is the fruit of a natural and spontaneous movement, lacking all cool calculation and rigid mechanism. Thus far, our party has never had "diplomatic" statesmen, and probably never will. Whoever among us spoke up and acted, spoke up and acted in response to a higher impulse. No honor was to be had among us except by serving the brothers. And although we too paid toll to what was spoiled by sinful words and deeds, yet at this tenth meeting of deputies we may, thanks to the God of our fathers, glory in the fact that no political party anywhere in the world will easily assemble a group of men such as we have here—men who devote themselves tirelessly to the public well-being of their country and who almost never demand anything for themselves. An advantage that benefits us not because we are better than our opponents but solely because the gospel that guides us also bridles any rising passions and gives us freedom and independence from our most noteworthy leaders. This makes us invincible.

Liberals may thwart our plans, cross our intentions, repulse us on more than one issue, but that will not help them, because after every defeat we show up in larger numbers. Indeed, if the progress of the gospel could be stopped, our power too could be broken. But so long as this is impossible, no shoring up of the dikes will avail against the swelling stream of antirevolutionary life. The secret of our strength lies neither in talent nor organization, but solely in what the Man of Sorrows, whom the French Revolution sought to dethrone but who now reigns in glory at the right hand of the Father, and is working from heaven in the hearts of the children of our nation. The Revolution cries: "Knowledge alone is power, and to man be the glory!" But he lives and continues to testify from heaven: "All power in heaven and on earth, including the Netherlands, including the hearts of the Dutch people, is given unto me!" [see Matt 28:18]. And that triumphant cry, that victory call, *he will make good.*

***

All this explains the flexibility and pliability of our practical action, my friends. Dogmatic politics imposed on life is rigid in form and stiff in movement. It lives by a system, attempts to press the life of the people in a straitjacket, and so must consider her game lost as soon as the cords of this jacket snap. The liberals would like nothing better than to see us follow that path. We have a program, and we published a program of action. It would be worth a lot to the liberals if they could tempt us to bind every supporter to the letter of our program and every cabinet minister to all the articles in the program of action. For then we would duplicate their mistake and our party would become as fragile as a layer of ice underneath which the stream of life had flowed away. But fortunately, that is not how we are. Our strength does not lie in the rigid mechanism of theory, but in the guiding thought that resides in organic life. Because we have *faith* we do not rush things but work in a timely fashion.[39] Because *love* is active among us, our vanguard possesses the most inexhaustible patience to wait for our rear guard to catch up. And because *hope* can never leave us, disappointment sometimes galvanizes us more than success and triumph.

Moreover, the position in which the Revolutionaries forced us to join battle makes that flexibility a condition of life for us. We are bound, after all, by the Constitution and by the corresponding legislation which liberalism under Thorbecke's inspiration forced through now thirty years ago.[40] And since this erected state edifice has been completed as much as possible in the style of the French Revolution, we have been forced at the outset to make the best of this framework. It is a framework that is foreign to us, and the end goal of our action cannot be achieved until our ranks are so strong and so numerous that we can begin to think of a new gable for the old house. Groen van Prinsterer put it this way in 1874: "We are going for a wholesale revision of the Constitution!"[41] and when the latest revision offered us little more than a poor imitation of a reform bill, we certainly did not neglect to register our expectation that the real constitutional revision would be made in the future.[42] Thus for now all we can do is shape our conduct as best we can according to the current political structure, pending the better day that is coming. The Anitrevolutionary Party does not want to *force* anything. We are averse to coercion and wish to triumph only by changing public opinion. And although we have made significant progress in changing people's minds, the moment is still far off that the last vestige of the revolutionary theory is wiped off our constitutional arrangements.

---

39. Kuyper plays on the words of Isaiah 28:16: "Whoever believes will not be in haste."
40. Kuyper may be referring here to the legislative debates over the validity of teaching characteristically Christian doctrines in government schools. For more on this controversy, see Abraham Kuyper, "Teaching Immortality in the Public School," in *On Education*, 17–28.
41. See G. Groen van Prinsterer, *Nederlandsche Gedachten* (Amsterdam, 1874), 5:360 (10 February 1874). See also Groen to Kuyper, February 5 and 7, 1874, *Briefwisseling* (The Hague: Nijhoff and Instituut voor Nederlands Geschiedenis, 1992), 6:506–7.
42. The Christian parties gave up their blocking of the proposed constitutional revision of 1887 after the sitting prime minister stated publicly that granting public financial support for private schools was not necessarily unconstitutional. The revision which then passed also broadened the franchise, thereby more than doubling the electorate, which resulted in a majority for the Christian parties in the general elections of 1888 (55 of the 100 seats).

However, precisely because we know all too well that public opinion is formed not just by the medium of the printed word but even more so by existing laws and government policy, therefore we refuse to sit still and instead involve ourselves in the political issues of the day.

First and foremost, we oppose every form of *state orthodoxy* in the areas of religion, morality, and learning. The error in former days was a government which, bound as such to the Reformed confession, had to discriminate against dissenting citizens as pariahs and suppress them as serfs. The error of liberalism, and the just punishment for our former exclusivism, is again binding the state to a form of orthodoxy—this time to a "Christianity above sectarian differences," and to an autonomous morality and the pronouncements of a one-sided conception of learning and scholarship. Peace will not come to the divided children of our nation until the state leaves religion to its adherents, morality to people's conscience, and learning to its innate structure. The fact is that under God's dispensation our population of four million is split in three roughly equal segments: our country is shared by rationalist, Calvinist, and Catholic fellow-citizens. We accept this fact. And we stand by our conviction that the government of such a mixed population may not favor one group over another. All intellectual tyranny of the state is an insult to the noble status of intellectual life and a hateful and accursed offense against civil liberty.

I do not hesitate to say this openly, even though I know that it touches on the thorny church question. Precisely because of our fixed principle this question, too, does not embarrass us in the least. This would be the case if one group among us had the intention to force the situation at the expense of the other group. But to plan that would be to abandon our course of action and that was never our intention. Since the supporters of the free church and the state church are at this moment still carrying on their grave struggle in all our cities, towns, and villages,[43] we are enticed neither from the left nor the right by any other goal than to persuade each other of our position. Hopefully, inspired by the same ideal, we can still work together for reform in the political arena. The liberals, not knowing us, have grossly misjudged the church struggle. Now that we are divided in two halves, they expected us at election time to allow them the benefit of our splitting the vote. But that hope of malicious pleasure has ended in a bitter disappointment for them, and they found out last year—and they

---

43. The struggle chiefly concerned church lands and other property.

will find out again this year—that the men of 1816 and 1834 and 1886,[44] for all their ecclesiastical differences about the gospel of Jesus Christ, choose as one man to rally under the banner of that gospel whenever the struggle against liberalism, and in them against the French Revolution, beckons us.

The same holds for the franchise question. No doubt here too contrary sympathies arise. But however much the more democratic and the more aristocratic elements among us diverge, we are of one mind about this: that popular sovereignty is a sinful notion; that suffrage tied solely to financial qualifications is a mockery of our constitution; that the identical voter qualifications for our national Parliament, our provincial legislatures, and our city councils is totally at odds with the practical demands of life; and we all agree that our ideal will not be realized until each and every segment of the population can have a say in public affairs without the lower classes dominating the higher or the higher the lower classes.

We will not make a partisan issue of national defense. To be willing to sacrifice one's life for the freedom of one's country is an inborn impulse that is common to the Albanian and the Abyssinian, the Prussian and the Russian, the Japanese and the Javanese. What is to be done to repel an enemy and protect a country's territory is a question that is never decided by a party program but solely by the means of attack which the enemy has at its disposal. To the extent that the Anitrevolutionary Party has its own principle in regard to this issue, it is that it calls for free primary schools, in order that proper knowledge of our national history can stimulate patriotism; that it demands a sound diplomacy, in order that the struggle for right may prevent the struggle for might; that it wishes to see shining in our armed forces the mighty weapon of moral strength; that it protests against any organization of national defense that wants to make every son of our nation pay tribute to moral decadence and blasphemy by conscripting him for military service.[45]

Our ideal in the area of education at all levels remains that schooling and scholarship may one day grow proudly from its own root and as much as possible be free from influence by the state.

---

44. Here Kuyper refers to participants in major dissent and splits from the national church, as in 1816 those who protested the organization of the national church under government tutelage, in 1834 those who seceded from the national church (in the *Afscheiding*) to preserve orthodoxy, and in 1886 those who under Kuyper's leadership broke away from the national church (in the *Doleantie*) to preserve the church's integrity.

45. See *OP*, 18.II–III.229–36.

In the struggle between capital and labor we may not drop the demand that every citizen of good will in the Netherlands be assured of a decent, what is more, of a Christian, standard of living—provided it not come from government handouts which would eventually break the resilience of the working man—by also giving labor the legal right to organize, in order thus to reconcile through lawful struggle what may otherwise end in a struggle of might versus violence.

No dogma forces us to be in favor of *free trade* and no system compels us to be for *protectionism*. All we ask is that government not sacrifice the citizen to the foreigner or the farmer to the businessman, but instead follow a system whereby the Netherlands is strongest vis-à-vis the outside world and helps domestic industry, commerce, and agriculture flourish in their interconnectedness.

And finally, concerning the colonies, the gospel as our principle gives us no other command than that the free course of the gospel not be hindered; that the sin of the opium trade not reduce Christian missions to a hypocritical show of piety; that Dutchmen shall honor the men of Java and Timor as creatures of God and therefore not surrender them to exploitation by either by the government itself or by greedy private enterprise looking for easy profit. And finally, the gospel demands that the mother country realize she is accountable to God when he will one day ask her to give account of her colonial policy, saying: "O nation of Holland, O king of the Netherlands, what did you do with my beautiful Indies, what did you do for the thirty million souls living on my Malay archipelago?"

***

Now then, if it were the case that the Mackay-Keuchenius ministry[46] gave no evidence that it is one with us in steering in that direction, it could hardly inspire our love and expect our support. But that is what these men do want to do. Not of course as if they can already guide us into the land of promise in the space of one year or four years. They are aware, as much as we, that we are still wandering in the desert and will be able to go down

---

46. This cabinet had the support in Parliament of Catholics and Calvinists, representing, respectively, the League of Catholic Riding Associations and the riding associations or voters' clubs of the ARP. They were known as parties "of the Right," even though they contained both conservative and progressive politicians. Liberals and social democrats were known as the parties "of the Left."

to Jordan's banks only after meeting with vehement resistance. But that does not harm us so long as we move in a better direction. We ourselves as deputies of the party have to watch over our program of principles during elections, and our Anitrevolutionary caucus in the Second Chamber has to defend our program of action,[47] but both we and the caucus already have a reason to rejoice when a cabinet is composed of men who put a stop to the ongoing national corruption by liberal ministries.

In fact, we wonder how many voters would today want to exchange the present government for a liberal or more conservative cabinet. Consider, the king's council of ministers today stands out so favorably above its predecessors that it is not intent on harming and excluding its opponents and that at least it does not harbor a longing to coerce the people or domineer over them. There is something of a Christian, paternal, and civil element in its mode of operation. The slander that they are sitting still and doing nothing is simply ridiculous, especially from the lips of our liberal opponents who for years on end gave the impression that both government and Parliament avoided their responsibility by seeking refuge in a political work stoppage. To be sure, the present ministry is not an Anitrevolutionary cabinet, nor may it be touted as a *"cabinet de combat,"* a government of protest; but however moderate its proposals, however cautious its moves, our people have already felt again and again that these men love the gospel and hate the Revolution. Their administration means a respite for our people after our painful discrimination and scornful oppression. And we are even more aware not only that our people pray for the government but also that his Majesty's counselors, these advisors of the Crown, pray for the people.

It is only too bad that there is one critical stumbling block on their path which prevents them from acting decisively with the kind of energy that they themselves would want to wield for serving the national interest. That stumbling block is the First Chamber. I shall not now talk about its composition and constitutional position. You know how many of us would want to have a totally different upper house, not one that is a faint duplicate of the Second Chamber but one that has its own root and works out its own role as representative not of political views but of social interests. But that topic would lead us to digress. Yet it irritates us to see the woeful condition that the revolutionary system has brought about also in this respect, hampering

---

47. For the difference between these programs, see *OP*, xiv.

our progress as a nation.[48] It has meant a meaningless, atomistic method of electing the provincial legislatures, and in those legislatures a harmful mixture of political and provincial interests. Instead of organic regional governance it has installed a delegated national administration exercised by a department of the central government, an ascent from these legislatures through staggered elections to a First Chamber, and as the fruit of this system an upper house that lags behind the country like a convoy of turtles.

For the current composition of the First Chamber both we and our opponents are to blame: our opponents, for their refusal to help us reform it during the recent constitutional revision; we, for our low turnout in the last provincial elections. This time let us do better. Men of antirevolutionary confession, show yourself not unworthy of the extension of the franchise from 150,000 to 350,000. Do not feel obligated to reelect the stuffy members that were elected under the old electoral law. Even if he is the lord of your manor, a prominent citizen in your town or village, or your very own burgomaster, these men have been sent home, and it is now up to you to refresh the First Chamber with members who have their heart in the right place. Make use of the heightened interest in the provincial elections. In many districts, election fever has reached the boiling point. But steam is not enough. It needs to be directed to the cylinders, and the cylinders need to be connected to the wheels, and the wheels need to be set on the right track. You will be sorely disappointed on May 14 if you have underestimated your opponent or neglected to assure united action.

Not that I fear that Dr. Jonker's quotations will separate you from our allies.[49] Just remember, without that alliance the Mackay-Keuchenius cabinet could not survive for one minute. Anyone who lacks the practical sense not to honor this [Calvinist-Catholic] coalition in the provincial elections is thereby also choosing against the national cabinet. Allow me to add, in confidence, a personal experience, to be sure, but one that is of importance also for you. When I was elected in District Gouda in 1874, Groen van Prinsterer wrote me that he would now change from arguing for amending Article

---

48. For Kuyper's view of corporative representation, see *OP*, 12.II.135–38; 20.II.291.
49. This is a reference to an anti-Catholic pamphlet by A. J. Th. Jonker (1851–1928), an ethical-irenic (Modernist) pastor, titled *Kalvinistische ingenomenheid met Rome aan Kalvijn zelve getoetst* (Rotterdam: Bredée, 1889). In the printed version of the address, Kuyper spent a two-page-long footnote mocking the Rev. Dr. Jonker's erroneous translation of a Latin quotation from Calvin in which the Reformer purportedly lumped Roman Catholics with the Libertines of his day.

194 in the Constitution to insisting on a *general* revision of the Constitution, out of consideration that every stumbling block to cooperation with our Catholic countrymen had to be removed.[50] To be honest, that did not appeal to me. But when Groen impressed upon me that we could never hope to triumph over the Revolution and disarm liberalism unless we joined forces with our fellow citizens of the Catholic persuasion, I relented and since then have steered in that direction.[51] Not that I ever forgot the fundamental contrast between our view of *freedom of the word* and the system of Rome and the papal hierarchy. However, the speculation that this system could ever be restored in our free country might scare voters off at election time, but such fancies never persuaded anybody of sound mind, whether liberal or Catholic or Calvinist.

To conclude: One hundred years ago, my friends, the liberals invaded our country and with the help of the French planted that obscene liberty tree. And the people that had grown estranged from the blessing of the gospel lay down in the shadow of its branches. Today, in 1889, it so happens that almost on the very day that the Estates General met in Versailles, the Dutch people are called to vote for electoral colleges for the First Chamber of our States General. Very well, O people of the Netherlands, having learned from the sad experience of that long century, testify as one man that you have found the tree of liberty to be toxic and, converted to something better by the gospel, look for protection against the heat of the day under the better tree of Calvary. May your voice on the fourteenth of May reflect sincere penance for the sins committed by our fathers against the majesty of our God. Even as the liberals are privately hailing France's Revolution heroes but are kept from erecting bonfires on our soil from fear of falling out of favor with the public, may you, O Christian Netherlands, renew the covenant of our nation with the God of our fathers, and may the fervid vow rise from the depth of the national conscience: "As for us and our children, we shall not kneel to the idol of the French Revolution, and the God of our fathers shall again be our God!"

I thank you.

---

50. Catholics favored keeping Article 194 intact because it enabled them to have publicly funded schools with a Catholic tinge.
51. See Groen to Kuyper, January 30 and February 7, 1874; *Briefwisseling*, 6:501, 507. See also Groen to Kuyper, December 21, 1873; *Briefwisseling*, 6:484.

SPHERE
SOVEREIGNTY

TEXT INTRODUCTION

The Free University was at the heart of Kuyper's dreams. Here he could fulfill all his callings at once: scholar, institution-builder, leader, liberator, and guide of the common people. It is fitting, then, that the speech he gave to inaugurate the school captures so well the heart of his vision, from title to tone, in its substance and its unspoken assumptions.

Three years of meetings in the city of Amsterdam by a small consortium of private persons who supported Abraham Kuyper culminated in the fall of 1880 in the opening of the Free University. This private academy would be free of state and church and would base its instruction and research in accordance with what were called "the Reformed principles." The Association for Higher Education on a Reformed Foundation, which sponsored the new school, asked Kuyper, as chairman and visionary, to be the main speaker at the dedication ceremony. His oration on this occasion, dealing with the concept of sphere sovereignty, has come to be one of the chief sources of the pluralist approach to cultural engagement by Dutch Calvinists. It makes the threefold claim that the concept of sovereign spheres marks the character of the Dutch nation in its best days, forms the bedrock of all genuine scholarship, and constitutes the first principle of the Reformed view of life and the world.

The setting of the speech given October 20, 1880, was apt as well. Kuyper spoke in the New Church (in fact, centuries old) on Amsterdam's principal square, next to the royal palace—thus at the symbolic center of national life. The near-climax of Kuyper's speech comes at one of his most famous utterances: "There is not a square inch in the whole domain of our human existence over which Christ, who is sovereign over all, does not call out: 'Mine!' " The first half of that sentence sounds an equally vital conviction: "Not one segment of our intellectual world can be hermetically sealed off from the others."

Kuyper here was founding a university, but the comprehensive vision of the speech shows how education has implications for all of life. Higher education and advanced research were of enormous importance for Kuyper: religiously, for exploring and enhancing God's creation; strategically, for (re)shaping society and culture; socially, for raising the self-respect and life-chances of common people.

SOURCE: Abraham Kuyper, *Souvereiniteit in eigen kring; rede ter inwijding van de Vrije Universiteit, den 20sten October 1880 gehouden, in het koor der Nieuwe Kerk te Amsterdam* (Amsterdam: Kruyt, 1880). Introduced, newly translated, and annotated by Harry Van Dyke while consulting earlier translations by George Kamps, Harry der Nederlanden, Gordon Spykman, Wayne Kobes, and James D. Bratt. A translation with an introduction and annotations (adapted with permission for this present volume) by James D. Bratt appeared in *Abraham Kuyper: A Centennial Reader* (Grand Rapids: Eerdmans, 1998), 461–90.

SPHERE SOVEREIGNTY

Address at the Dedication of the Free University, delivered on 20
October 1880 in the Chancel of the Nieuwe Kerk in Amsterdam

Esteemed audience,[1]
Those who are in charge of this institution[2] have assigned me the honor
of dedicating[3] their school for higher education by publicly introducing
it to the authorities and the general public. For that task I ask your sympathetic ear and kindly indulgence. You will appreciate the earnestness

---

1. The oration opened with the customary salutations to those in attendance, whom
   Kuyper addressed in the following order: "Your Excellency minister of the Crown,
   lord mayor and city councilors of Amsterdam, president and secretary of the City
   University of Amsterdam, honored members of Parliament, other respectable officials and dignitaries, learned academics and university administrators, venerable
   ministers of the Word, esteemed board members of kindred organizations who
   with us combat the dechristianization of our nation, worthy university students,
   journalists, and members of the general public, ladies and gentlemen."
2. This is a reference to the Association for Higher Education on a Reformed Foundation,
   which was organized in 1878 for the purpose of establishing "a school for higher
   education based on the Reformed principles."
3. The consecration of the Free University had taken place the night before, in a prayer
   service led by Professor Ph. J. Hoedemaker (1839–1910). In a homily on the text in
   1 Samuel 13:19, "Now there was no blacksmith to be found throughout all the land
   of Israel," he had explained that with this university a training school was being
   erected for the adherents to historic Christianity in order to equip them for the
   ongoing struggle in church, state, and society.

of that request when you consider that I am not about to deliver a professor's inaugural address or a principal's annual report. No, the nature of my task bars me from the quiet retreat of scholarly research and drives me onto the slippery terrain of public life, where nettles burn on every path and thorns wound at every step. It is no secret, and none of us wish to hide it: we have not been driven to this work as patrons and benefactors in love with disinterested science. What impelled us to this risky, if not presumptuous, venture, rather, was a profound sense of duty that what we were doing *had to* be done—for Christ's sake, for the name of the Lord, for the sacred interests of our people and our nation. Thus our action is not all that innocuous. The public interest through good and ill report has prejudged this institution even before it received its charter,[4] and we are deeply convinced that today's interest in this opening ceremony does not concern our persons but stems solely from the public's impression that the Netherlands is witnessing an event that may well leave its mark on the future of our nation.

Would we have undertaken this task if a higher criterion could have induced us to acquiesce in the status quo? Our venture is a quiet protest against our current environment, along with the claim that there is a better option. This apparent presumption alone, which follows it like a shadow, makes us humble. It might offend, it might hurt, and so I hasten to reassure you—whether we look at the overwhelming power of learning, prestige, and money arrayed against us, or feel embarrassed about our own smallness and powerlessness—I hasten to reassure you that what we say here today with such confidence is not expressive of lofty conceit but only of quiet humility. We would rather have stayed in the background and enjoyed seeing others take the lead.[5] But now that this was *not* possible, we *had* to act. So we stepped forward. Although we are far from indifferent to people's antipathy or their goodwill, we nevertheless regulate our *line of*

---

4. The association was founded on December 5, 1878, and received royal assent on February 12, 1879.
5. This is a reference to the wider Reformed community, many of whose leaders at first participated in planning the Christian university but who backed away when it became apparent that it would have a decidedly Calvinist stamp. The issue is discussed in three of Kuyper's publications at this time: *De Leidsche professoren en de executeurs der Dordtsche nalatenschap* (Amsterdam: Kruyt, 1879); *Bede om een dubbel "corrigendum"* (Amsterdam: Kruyt, 1880); and *"Strikt genomen": het recht tot universiteitsstichting* (Amsterdam: Kruyt, 1880).

conduct exclusively according to what we believe is demanded by the honor of our God.

Your expectation is that I will tell you about the school we are introducing as it makes its appearance in our national culture: What is its mission? Why does it does it brandish the cap of liberty? And why does it pore so intently over the book of the Reformed religion?[6] Allow me to link together the answers to these three questions through the single idea of sphere sovereignty by pointing to that *sovereignty of the spheres* as the hallmark of our institution,

in its *national* significance,

its *scholarly* intention, and

its *Reformed* character.

I

Introducing our institution to you *in its national significance* is to be the first part of my address.

In our awesome century, ladies and gentlemen, our nation too is going through a profound crisis, a crisis which it shares with every nation of any importance, a crisis that pervades the whole world of thoughtful humanity.

At stake in any crisis is a way of life that is beset by a disease which either promises a new lease on life or predicts a decline unto death. So what is the "diseased way of life" that is now under assault? Just what is at stake in this crisis, also for our nation? Would anyone want to repeat the old answers: that the contest is between progress and conservatism, between uniformity and diversity, between idealism and realism, or even between rich and poor? It has become all too clear that each of these diagnoses is inadequate, distorted, superficial. Since then, the watchword has become *clericalism or liberalism!*—as though it were a contest between those who misuse religious influence and those who wish to purge it from public life. But this curtain too has been contemptuously shoved aside, and people have come to realize what was first grasped only by the prophets of our age but

---

6. This is an allusion to a sixteenth-century seal that featured the maid of Holland seated before an open Bible behind no more than a low hedge and brandishing a spear topped by a liberty cap. In the seal of the Free University, on the other hand, the defenseless maiden is seated in a fenced garden and raises her right hand to point to the Sun of Righteousness, in which the word YHWH appears; the conscription around the rim reads: *Auxilium Nostrum in Nomine Domini*, that is, "Our Help is in the Name of the Lord."

then by ever wider circles: namely, that the current world crisis is not about nuances, interests, rights, but about a *living person*—that the crisis revolves around the Man who once swore that he was King and who for the sake of this sovereign claim to kingship gave his life on the cross of Golgotha.

"The Nazarene: A noble example! An inspiring ideal! A religious genius!" So people exclaimed for a long time with great enthusiasm. But history has protested that all such praise is at odds with the Nazarene's own claims. The calm and crystal-clear self-identification coming from his divine-human consciousness was that he was no less than the *Messiah*, the Anointed One, hence the King of kings, possessing "all authority in heaven and on earth" [Matt 28:18]. The claim that was written and nailed to the cross, the crime for which he had to die, was not "hero of faith" or "glorious martyr," but *Melek, Rex, Basileus ton Ioudaion*, King of the Jews—that is, the Bearer of Sovereignty. As in the first three centuries so again today, a debate about that sovereignty—about the presence or absence of that authority in the man born of Mary—is at the center of the crisis in the intellectual world and among the ruling elites throughout the developed world. This debate is at the core of the burning question whether the *Basileus ton Ioudaion* is the saving truth to which all people say Amen, *or* ... the fundamental lie that all people must oppose. The question has demanded a decision ever since the life of the Nazarene and is once again causing a rift in our intellectual world, in our life as human beings, and in our existence as a nation.

What is sovereignty? Would you not agree with me that sovereignty is the authority that has the right, the duty, and the power to break and avenge any and all resistance to its will? And would you not also agree with the commonsense realization that original, absolute sovereignty cannot reside in any creature but can only be associated with the majesty of God? If you believe in him as the designer and creator of the world, the founder and director of all things, then your soul, too, must proclaim the Triune God as the only absolute sovereign. Provided—and this I would emphasize— provided you acknowledge at the same time that this exalted sovereign once delegated and still delegates his authority to human beings, so that on earth you actually never encounter God himself *directly*, in visible things, but you meet his sovereign authority in some office or other exercised by *a human being*.

Now, when God's sovereignty is vested in a human office, the crucial question arises: How does that delegation take place? Is the all-encompass-ing sovereignty of God transferred undivided onto a single person? Or does an earthly sovereign have the power to command obedience in a restricted orbit only, an orbit or sphere of action that borders on other spheres where someone else, not he, is sovereign?

The answer to this question will vary depending on whether you dwell in the atmosphere of revelation or outside it. For those whose minds had no room for revelation, the traditional answer for a long time was that supreme sovereignty is delegated "as far as possible *undivided*, but penetrating *all spheres!*" "As far as possible," because divine sovereignty over the things that are above falls beyond humanity's reach, over nature it exceeds humanity's power, and over fate it is beyond humanity's control. But for the rest, *in the absence of* sphere sovereignty, it was the state that was given unlimited power to command, disposing over persons, their lives, their rights, their consciences, even their religious beliefs. There were many gods in antiquity, so as a result, thanks to *vis unita fortior*,[7] the single unrestricted state seemed more imposing and more majestic than the divided power of the gods. Eventually the state itself, embodied in Caesar, became god—the divine state that could tolerate no other "states" beside itself. Hence the passion for *world* domination, under *divus Augustus*, the god-emperor, with Caesar worship as its religion. A deeply sinful notion, not worked out in a theory until eighteen centuries later in Hegel's system of the state as "the immanent God."[8]

By contrast, Jehovah proclaimed to Israel through the voices of messianic prophecy: "Sovereignty shall be delegated, not as far as possible, but in an absolute sense, undivided and unbroken!" And that Sovereign, the man-Messiah, did appear, with power in heaven and power over nature, with the claim to authority over all peoples, and to authority *in* all peoples, even over their conscience and their religious faith. The very bond between mother and child had to yield when challenged by his call to obedience. Thus it is an absolute sovereignty over all things visible and invisible, over both the spiritual and the material, and all of it placed in the hands of a Man. It refers not to one of the world's kingdoms, but to the absolute kingdom. *"For this purpose was I born and for this cause came I into the world. ...*

---

7. That is, united force yields greater strength.
8. The German philosopher G. W. F. Hegel (1770–1831) developed a complex philosophical system in which world history is the progressive self-realization of divine Reason that reaches one of its high points in the absolute. See Hegel, *The Philosophy of Right*, trans. Alan White (Indianapolis: Focus, 2002), part 3, third section, "The State."

Therefore all power is given unto me in heaven and on earth. ... One day all ene-mies shall be put under my feet and every knee shall bow to me" [see John 18:37; Matt 28:18; 1 Cor 15:25; Rom 14:11]. Such is the sovereignty of the Messiah which the prophet once announced, which the Nazarene claimed, which he began to demonstrate by doing miracles, which his apostles defined further, and which the church of Christ confesses on their authority: a sovereignty undivided but nonetheless by delegation—or rather, taken over by Christ in order to be given back again to God; for perfect harmony will one day break through when Messiah's sovereignty returns to God himself, who will then be *ta panta en pasin:* "all in all" [see 1 Cor 15:28].

But here is the glorious principle of liberty! This absolute sovereignty of the *sinless* Messiah at the same time directly denies and disputes all absolute sovereignty on earth among sinful men. The life of humankind is divided into *distinct spheres*, each with its own sovereignty.

Human life, with its visible material foreground and its invisible spir-itual background, appears neither simple nor uniform but constitutes an infinitely composite organism. It is structured in such a way that what is individual exists only in groups, and only in groups can the whole become manifest. Now call the component parts of this one great machine "cog-wheels," each propelled on its own axle by means of springs; or else call them "spheres," each animated by its own spirit. The name or image is not important, so long as you recognize that there are in life all kinds of spheres as numerous as constellations in the heavens, and that the circumference of each sphere is drawn with a fixed radius from a unique principle as its center or focal point, according to the apostolic *hekastos en to idio tagmati:* "each in its own order!" [see 1 Cor 15:23]. Just as we speak of a moral world, a world of science, a world of business, an art world, so we speak still more properly of a sphere of morality, a family sphere, a sphere of socioeconomic life, each having its own *domain*. And because each forms a distinct domain, each sphere has its own sovereign within the bounds of that domain.

There is, for instance, a domain of nature whose sovereign uses energy to work on physical matter according to fixed laws. Similarly, there are domains of personal, domestic, scientific, socioeconomic, and ecclesiastical life, each of which obeys its own laws and stands under its own supreme authority. There is a domain for thought where no other laws but those of logic may rule. There is a domain of the conscience where none but the Holy One may give sovereign commands. Finally, there is a domain of faith where the person alone is the sovereign who through faith consecrates himself in his innermost being.

Now then, all these spheres interlock like cogwheels, and precisely this mutual interaction and meshing of the spheres creates the rich and many-sided multiformity of human life. At the same time, however, life runs the risk of having one sphere bending its neighbor inward, causing a wheel to jerk and jolt, twisting and breaking cog after cog, and so disrupting the smooth operation of the whole. Hence the reason for the existence of still another sphere of authority, that of the state. The state is there to enable the various spheres, insofar as they manifest themselves visibly, to interact in a healthy way and to keep each of them within the confines of justice. And since one's personal life can be suppressed by the group in which one lives, the state is also there to shield the individual from overbearance by his own group. The state is the sovereign who, in Scripture's pithy expression, "builds up the land by justice" [see Prov 29:4], since without justice the nation will destroy itself and collapse.

Accordingly, as the power that protects the individual and defines the mutual relationships among the visible spheres, the sovereignty of the state rises high *above* them all by its right to pass laws and its right to enforce them. But *within* these spheres that does not hold. There another authority rules, an authority that descends directly from God, apart from the state, an authority that is not *conferred* but *acknowledged* by the state. And even in defining laws for the mutual relationships among the spheres, the state sovereign must not be guided by its own will or preference but is *bound* by the choice of a higher will as this comes to expression in the nature and purpose of the spheres. The state is to see to it that the cogwheels operate as they are meant to operate. Is that not what every state sovereign would want: not restricting life or limiting freedom, but making it possible for each of the spheres to live and move freely within its own domain?

Thus, two credos stand diametrically opposed to each other.

We who live in the atmosphere of revelation, and live in it consistently, can only confess that all sovereignty resides with God and can therefore emanate from him alone. We confess that this divine sovereignty was conferred integrally on the man-Messiah and that human freedom is safe under this Son of Man who was anointed sovereign. For, not only the state but also every other domain of life enjoys an authority that is derived from him—that is, possesses sovereignty within its own sphere.

By contrast, those who do not discern and therefore deny such a special revelation insist that the question of sovereignty be kept strictly separate from religious faith. They assert, accordingly, that no sovereignty is conceivable other than the sovereignty of the state, and so they work hard to see to it that the exalted idea of sovereignty be embodied ever more perfectly in state supremacy. Hence, they can grant the other spheres of life a measure of rights and liberties no more generous than the state *allows* them, out of its weakness, or *allots* them, by dint of its supremacy.

I call these two positions "credos" about sovereignty. They are life convictions, not theories. The gulf that separates them does not lie in a different arrangement of ideas, but in a recognition or negation of *facts of life*. For us who live by revelation, the Messiah lives, Christ works, and he is seated as sovereign on the throne of the power of God in a more real sense than you are sitting here on the tombstones in this chancel. Conversely, those who do not share this confession must oppose it as an inconvenient self-delusion that stands in the way of national development, a harmful dogma, a fanciful bit of nonsense! The two confessions, therefore, are flatly contradictory. To be sure, cowardly compromisers have time and again shoved them aside, to replace them with a broad range of hybrid systems, mixtures of more of this and less of that, or equal portions of each. In critical times, however, this unprincipled game is angrily interrupted by the two principled credos that impart some color even to these colorless systems. Representing the only true, mighty antithesis that divides life at its root, the two camps openly challenge each other to a battle of life and death, staking their lives on these credos even as they disturb the lives of others because of these credos.

Sphere sovereignty defending itself against state sovereignty: that in brief is the course of world history even before Messiah's sovereignty was proclaimed. The royal child of Bethlehem does indeed protect sphere sovereignty with his shield, but he did not create it. It existed of old. It lay embedded in the order of creation. It was part of the plan for human life. It was there before state sovereignty arose. But once the sovereign state arose, it realized that the sovereignty of the spheres of life constituted its chief rival, while those spheres themselves weakened their power to offer resistance by sinning against their own laws of life. Thus ancient history shows us the shameful spectacle among nations everywhere that after stubborn, at times valiant struggle the spheres lost their freedom, even as the power of the state gained ground and turned into Caesarism. Socrates drinking the poison cup, Brutus plunging the dagger into Caesar's heart, the Galileans whose blood Pilate mingled with their sacrifices—those were the savagely heroic convulsions of a free, organic way of life that finally collapsed under the iron fist of Caesarism. As antiquity drew to a close, freedom was no more. There were no independent nations, no sovereign spheres. It had all become one sphere, one world empire under one sovereign state. Only in a drunken stupor induced by decadent affluence did mankind, sunk in disgrace, manage to drive this infamy from its heart.

But then a man arose within that iron ring of monolithic power who by the supernatural power of *faith* reintroduced a distinct, free sphere, and in that sphere a free sovereignty. That man was Jesus of Nazareth. With God in his heart, one with God, himself God, he withstood Caesar, broke down the iron gates, and posited the sovereignty of faith as the deepest pivot on which all sphere sovereignty rests. Neither the Pharisee nor his disciples understood that his cry "It is finished!" entailed, besides the salvation of the elect, also a *sōtēria tou kosmou*, a salvation of the cosmos, a liberation of the world, a world of freedoms. But Jesus understood it. Hence that word *Basileus* above his head on the cross. Asserting himself as the sovereign, he contended with the "ruler of this world" [John 14:30], that usurper, for authority over that world. And no sooner do his followers form their own circle than they too run afoul of state sovereignty. They succumb. Their blood flows. But Jesus' sovereign principle of faith cannot be washed away even by *their* blood. *Christ is God!* or *Caesar is God!* becomes the shibboleth that will decide the fate of the world. Christ triumphs and Caesar topples. The nations, set free, emerge again, each with its own king, and in the realms of these kings separate spheres, and in these spheres distinct liberties. And only then did that glorious life begin, crowning itself with noble chivalry, exhibiting in an ever richer organism of guilds, orders, and free communities all the energy and all the glory that sphere sovereignty implies.

In our country this development was even stronger than elsewhere. Apparently, the country could more forcefully defend sphere sovereignty against state sovereignty when it was divided into separate polders rather than if they had all been one. That is what King Philip[9] discovered when the people who attended the proscribed worship services in the open fields

---

9. This is a reference to King Philip II of Spain (1527–98), heir to the Habsburg possessions in the Low Countries from 1555. His taxation policies and the introduction of the Inquisition ignited the Dutch Revolt.

and sang from a Protestant psalter collided, against their will, with the sovereignty of the state. That is what the Stuarts and the Bourbons discovered in the following century, when the immortal sea hero upon whose stately tomb we here gaze, our glorious De Ruyter, withstood the resurgent absolutism of kings such as Charles II and Louis XIV and opposed it on every sea and broke it on every shore.[10] The ineradicable passion for liberty which along with De Ruyter inspired the entire phalanx of our naval heroes was the saying: "I, next to God, skipper of my ship!" a seaman's term which they bore across the oceans as the regal claim which in legal language is called "sovereign within one's own proper sphere!"

But alas, before a century had passed our fatherland too fell into decline. Holland sank away in sin, and along with our republic so did the last bulwark of liberty remaining on the continent. The tide of royal absolutism rose. It began to tread upon the countries, to trample the peoples, to torment the nations, until at last in the most inflammable of the nations the fire of vengeance ignited. Passion flared, the Revolution of principle struck off the crowned head of the sovereign in order to crown the sovereign people. A horrific event! Born from a thirst for freedom but also from a hatred of the Messiah, it resulted only in oppressing liberty even more. For the sovereign that was put into power on election day was forced the very next day to submit to utter control by the electorate—first by the Jacobin club, next by Caesar Napoleon, then by the specious ideal of a constitutional state, hastily installed in France, soon advocated by Germany's philosophers as "right" and "rational."[11]

And so once again liberty lay prostrate in disgrace, and for the second time a single sovereignty threatened to swallow up all other sovereignties. And what arrived to save the day *then*? Not the restoration spirit of the

---

10. This is a reference to Michiel de Ruyter (1607–76), successful naval commander of the Dutch Republic in battles against England and France and their respective royal families, the Stuarts and the Bourbons.
11. This litany of political turmoil in France from 1789 to 1813 refers to the initial supremacy in government of the radical Jacobins, who were replaced by the dictatorial Napoleon, who in 1813 had to make room for King Louis de Bourbon, who "graciously deigned to grant" the nation a charter of guaranteed rights which basically restored divine right monarchy, thus undoing all claims to power by the "sovereign people."

Congress of Vienna;[12] not Haller's and De Maistre's idolization of princes;[13] not the Historical School whose physiological views smothered every higher principle;[14] nor yet the pseudo-constitutional system with its royal figurehead and its tyrannizing factions.[15] No, it was the Messiah, the Sovereign seated at God's right hand, who quietly sent out among the peoples a spirit of grace, prayer, and faith by means of the most beautiful revival that has ever revived nations.[16] This movement automatically gave birth to a distinct sphere that worshipped a sovereign other than some earthly power, a sphere that addressed the soul, that supported works of mercy, and that inspired our political bodies "not as politicians but as confessors of the gospel."[17] In this way a hope for the nations was born, not by political manipulation but by moral power from within the soul.

In our country, too, that part of the nation that honored the Messiah, the *pars Christiana*, the Christian part, became, despite itself, a national party. A party, not *for* ruling but *by* serving. A party, not a faction, not some artificial coalition; nor a fraction, a mere splinter group; but a *people's* party representing a distinct part of the people, a segment of the whole, a temporary

---

12. At the Congress of Vienna in 1815, Europe's leaders undid a quarter-century of revolutionary upheavals by reinstating the prerevolutionary heads of state and territorial boundaries.
13. Karl Ludwig von Haller (1768–1854), author of *Restauration der Staats-Wissenschaft*, 6 vols. (Winterthur: Steinerische Buchhandlung, 1816–34), and Joseph de Maistre (1753–1819), author of *Considérations sur la France* (London, 1797), both contested the ideology of the French Revolution and defended a form of divine-right monarchy.
14. The Historical School of Jurisprudence, dating from 1814, held that a nation's laws are the inviolable products of that folk's unique spirit as it develops in history.
15. These words represent Kuyper's appraisal of the reign of King Louis-Philippe, who called himself "king of the French" and whom others called the "citizen-king." His reign (1830–48) was marked by easier access for common citizens to His Majesty at his weekly audience, several assassination attempts, and intense factional discord in the Chamber of Deputies.
16. The Réveil movement or religious awakening swept Western Europe in the years 1815–60.
17. This is an allusion to a celebrated word from Dutch parliamentarian G. Groen van Prinsterer (1801–76), who during the election campaign of 1864 asked voters to support him "not as a politician, but as a confessor of the gospel." Groen van Prinsterer was the father of the antirevolutionary movement in the Netherlands and became Kuyper's mentor and friend. Kuyper succeeded him as leader of the movement and in 1879 organized its political manifestation, some twenty antirevolutionary voters' clubs from electoral districts throughout the country, into the ARP.

self-imposed isolation[18] for the purpose of inspiring once again, if possible, one nation indivisible, wonderfully united for higher ideals. Bilderdijk drew the circumference of that segment when he cut the roots of popular sovereignty with the axe of his poetry; da Costa sounded the keynote with his hymn to the Sovereign Messiah; and Groen van Prinsterer finally wrote the political credo with his telling formula, "sovereignty within its own proper sphere."[19] And for the past thirty years, by virtue of that principle which has come down from God himself, people have wrestled on their knees, sought out the lost, evangelized with all the passion of their souls. For the sake of that principle our country has been adorned with one institution after another, as homes of mercy. For the sake of that principle people have suffered abuse, given up their peace, sacrificed their financial resources. For that principle people have labored among the common people, petitioned the throne, pleaded in the council chambers.[20] What kept this band of brothers together, which would otherwise have stayed divided, was the slogan "Sovereignty within its own proper sphere, under the supreme sovereignty of Jesus!" Hence those relentless efforts that steeled the little strength we have, that rowing against the current that boosted our courage, a case of *pressa uberior*, growth under pressure which invariably caused the depressed spring to bounce back. And so we gradually and spontaneously outdistanced our fellow countrymen, to whose superiority in so many other fields we humbly pay our respect.

---

18. This is an allusion to a famous motto of Groen van Prinsterer: "In our isolation lies our strength," by which he meant: our strength lies in being an independent party with our own set of nonnegotiable principles and beholden to no other group, standing alone if necessary.
19. The exact phrase is not found in Groen's oeuvre, but in much the same sense he used the expression "independence within one's own sphere"; see his *Ongeloof en Revolutie*, 2nd ed. (Amsterdam: H. Höveker, 1868), 43n**; ET: Groen van Prinsterer, *Unbelief and Revolution*, 23. Willem Bilderdijk (1756–1831) was among other things a famed poet, as was Isaäc da Costa (1798–1860). Both served as inspirations for the Réveil as well as the antirevolutionary movement. Kuyper outlines their significance in "Not the Liberty Tree but the Cross!" in this volume.
20. These sentences describe the antirevolutionary movement until that time in its actions for social justice, works of mercy, and Christian day schools, in the name of the kingship of Christ, or as Kuyper calls it in the next sentence: "under the supreme sovereignty of Jesus." For a further sketch of the origins and development of the antirevolutionary movement through the first three decades of its political advocacy and social action, see "Not the Liberty Tree but the Cross!" in this volume.

Thus we fought[21] for the indivisibility of sovereign authority[22]—for a parliament *alongside* and *opposite*, not *in* or *under*, the government. Thus we did not defend a theory of deterrence but upheld divine vengeance on those who dare to shed human blood. Thus we protested the compulsory vaccination of our children with contaminated needles. Thus we prophesied that the church would be disestablished.[23] And thus at last we focused our entire struggle on the struggle for the primary school when the public school threatened alike the sovereignty of conscience, of the family, of pedagogy, and of the church.

Now then, once a principle has sown its peculiar seeds it will not stop until it has germinated all its seeds into a scientifically ordered, coherent whole. Thus, once a people champions such a principle it cannot rest until it has also learned to grow from the root of its faith the fruit of scholarship. Such all-round learning cannot be cultivated except in a school at the university level. With iron necessity therefore, and from an inner vital force, the day had to arrive, as it now has, that we would launch this vessel, small and unseaworthy, but chartered under the sovereignty of King Jesus and with a mission to fly at every port of knowledge the flag of sphere sovereignty!

II

You may also expect sphere sovereignty to be the hallmark of our *scholarly intentions*. This too I take to be practical. We intend no abstract and arid scholasticism, but firmness of principle, depth of insight, clarity of judgment—in a word, sanctified intellectual power, a power to resist whatever would restrict freedom in our lives.

---

21. This paragraph enumerates some of the more prominent planks in the platform of the ARP as outlined in Kuyper's book of the previous year, *Ons Program* (Amsterdam, 1879). Note that for Kuyper a primary school is not a sphere, but a symbiosis of four spheres; see *OP*, §§162–65.
22. Antirevolutionaries espoused the constitutional principle of dualism: namely, that in a constitutional monarchy the government—the Crown, that is, king and cabinet—is the sole bearer of political sovereignty, a power in which Parliament does not share, although it has the right to be consulted, to voice critique or disapproval, to initiate legislative bills, and to check government by having to approve budgets and money bills. See *OP*, §§85–87.
23. For this prophecy, Kuyper could point to his very first publication: *Wat moeten wij doen, het stemrecht aan onszelven houden of den kerkraad machtigen?* (Culemborg: Blom, 1867).

Let's not forget, any state tends to look upon liberty with a wary eye. The various spheres of life cannot do without the sphere of the state, for just as one space can limit another, so one sphere can limit another unless the state regulates their boundaries. Thus the state is *the sphere of spheres* which alone among all the other spheres covers externally the whole of human life. The state is therefore mindful to strengthen its arm in the noble sense of the word (thus not for itself but in the interest of all the other spheres) in order to resist and try to break any attempt on the part of a sphere to expand and enlarge its orbit. So it is again today. Observe the signs of the times. Did Mommsen, in the bold portrait he painted of Caesar, not suggest a return to the imperialistic policy once followed by that Caesar as the ground rule of political wisdom for our time?[24] Does Germany's chancellor look like a freedom-loving statesman to you?[25] Or was it perhaps the man who was so profoundly humiliated at Sedan by that chancellor?[26] Freedom-loving or authoritarian: What is your impression of the people's tribune in Paris who has now replaced the man of Sedan in popularity?[27]

This was inevitable, both as a discipline and as a medicine for the craven and emasculated nations who by the atrophy of their moral energy had made this bridling of their liberty possible. The state after all is the supreme power on earth. There is no earthly power above the state that can compel the sovereign to do justice. Thus every state, either from a base lust for *power* or a noble concern for the *common good*, will by its very nature draw the iron hoops around the staves as tightly as the spring of those staves allows. In the final analysis, therefore, it depends on the spheres themselves whether they will flourish in freedom or groan under state coercion. If they have moral resilience they cannot be cramped, they will

---

24. In his works on Roman history and Roman law, Theodor Mommsen (1817-1903) wrote favorably about the early emperors whose strong arms had established the power of Rome. See Theodor Mommsen, *Römische Geschichte*, 3 vols. (Leipzig: Reimer & Hirzel, 1854-56); Mommsen, *Römisches Staatsrecht*, 3 vols. (Leipzig: S. Hirzel, 1871-76).
25. Otto von Bismarck (1815-98), prime minister of Germany, was renowned in the 1870s for his discriminatory laws against the Catholic church and repressive measures against the socialists.
26. Bismarck provoked France in 1870 to declare war on Germany, leading to the defeat of Emperor Napoleon III (1808-73) at the Battle of Sedan and the dissolution of the French Second Empire.
27. Following its disastrous war with Prussia, France's political leaders campaigned for re-establishing the French Republic under the leadership of the popular, charismatic, and strong-willed Léon Gambetta (1838-82).

not submit to being crushed; but if they are servile they lack even the right to complain when pressed into the shackles of slavery.

But exactly here lies the problem. *Sin* threatens freedom inside each sphere just as much as state power at the margin. When a cooper wants to draw hoops tight around the staves, he lights a fire inside the circle of staves, and that fire on the inside, more than the blows of his hammer from the outside, causes the staves to bend and shrink. So it is with our liberties. At the heart of every sphere burns a fire, a flame of passion from which the sparks of sin fly upward, and this unholy fire undermines moral strength, weakens resilience, and in the end bends the strongest staves. In any successful attack on freedom the state can only be an accomplice; the *chief* offender is the citizen who neglects his duty and whose sins and sensual pleasures sap his moral fiber and rob him of the power to take initiative. In a nation that is healthy at its core and whose people continue to guard the health of the various spheres, no state can remove the proper landmarks without encountering the people's moral resistance with the help of God. Not until all self-discipline had vanished and affluence had crept in and sin had turned brazen was the theory[28] able to bend what had grown slack and was Napoleon in a position to trample what had moldered away. And if God had not time and again, in part through oppression, poured fresh energy into those lifeless spheres so as to transform atoms into dynamos (as the latest philosophy of nature would have it),[29] the last sovereign sphere would long since have broken down and nothing would have been left of our freedom but an inscription on its tomb: *sic transit gloria mundi*, thus passes the glory of the world.

Now then, one of the means, a most prominent means, with which God has endowed more cultured nations for defending their freedoms is higher learning, science, scholarship. Among the spokesmen of the Holy Spirit was

---

28. By "the theory" Kuyper means the ideology of the eighteenth-century Age of Reason and Enlightenment, which weakened the intermediate bodies of civil society and so prepared the democratically supported tyranny of the French Revolution and the despotism of the populist Napoleon, who developed into the dictator of a highly regimented nation.

29. Here Kuyper uses the dynamo, a technology invented in the nineteenth century, as an image of God's common grace. A dynamo uses magnetism to convert kinetic energy into an electrical current. He may also be referring more specifically to contemporary theories concerning the nature of physics, particularly as they were manifest in German scholarship in the nineteenth century, concerning magnetism and electricity.

a highly educated man from Tarsus; and was it not from the intellectual gifts of Paul, rather than from the pensive John or the practical James, that Luther laid hold of the freedom of the Reformation? I am well aware that higher learning too can betray liberty and has more than once done just that, but that was despite its sacred mission, not by dint of it. Taken in its authentic form, God sent it to us as an angel of light.

For what robs a lunatic, a psychopath, a drunkard of their human dignity? Is it not precisely the lack of a *clear mind*? And to acquire a clear mind, not only about ourselves but also about that which exists outside ourselves, is that not exactly what science is all about: thinking God's thoughts after him, grasping what he has thought prior to us and about us and in us, what he infuses into the consciousness not just of a single person but of all mankind across the ages! This ability to grasp what exists, and to capture in our reason what is reflected in our consciousness, is an honor that God has bestowed on humanity. To possess wisdom is a divine trait in our being. Indeed, the power of wisdom and knowledge has grown to such an extent that the course of things mostly does not run according to reality but according to how people conceive of reality. How can people say that ideas are not important? Ideas shape public opinion; public opinion shapes the public's sense of what is right; and that sense either thaws or chills the currents of intellectual life. That is the reason why anyone who wants his principles to have influence cannot stick with woolly sentiments; he will make no headway by appealing to the imagination and will get only halfway by professing his beliefs. He will not gain hold of the public mind until he attains to authority in the intellectual world and succeeds in transferring his intuition—the *Deus in nobis*, the "God in us"—from what he *senses* to what he *knows*.

Provided—and I adhere strictly to this—provided scholarship remains "sovereign in its own sphere" and does not compromise its character under the guardianship of church or state. Scholarship too forms a distinct sphere of its own. Here truth is sovereign. Under no circumstance can a violation of science's law of life be tolerated. That would not only dishonor science but also be sin before God. Our consciousness is like a mirror in us, reflecting images from three worlds: from the world *around* us, from the world of *our own being*, and from the invisible, *spiritual* world. Reason therefore demands (1) that we allow each of these worlds to reflect these images according to their distinct nature, or *aisthesis*, that is, by observation as well as apperception; (2) that we apprehend those images with a clear eye, or *noesis*, that is, with our cognition or understanding; and (3) that we gather what has been apprehended into a harmonious coherence, or *gnosis*, that is, by comprehending the images as necessary and beautiful. In other words, reason requires mirror images, reflection, not speculation. Truth brings knowledge that makes wise, that draws from life to benefit life, and that ends in adoration of the only wise God!

A scholar such as Spinoza understood the sovereignty of the sphere of science, whence we admire his character as high as we esteem the faint-heartedness of Erasmus low.[30] To be sure, Spinoza's method, and therefore his observations, were deficient; hence his conclusions could only be erroneous. Yet, given what he saw and how he saw it, he steadfastly refused to lend himself to an infringement of the sovereignty of science. That is something no Reformed person finds fault with; rather, the Reformed place it high above the unsteady wavering that has seduced more than one person (who now knows what Spinoza never knew) to endorse unprincipled compromises. We must therefore resist tooth and nail any attempt by the church of Christ to impose her lofty position on science. At the very real risk of suffering harm at the hands of science, the church should herself urge scholars never to allow themselves to be enslaved but to maintain the sovereignty due to them within their sphere and to live by the grace of God. There is, to be sure, the satanic danger that some scholars will degenerate into devils of pride and tempt science to arrogate to itself what lies outside its domain. But, to begin with, one can't climb a tall steeple without at the same time running the risk of a steep fall; and, in the second place, what we discovered just now about the tyranny of the state applies equally to the tyranny of science: it cannot arise unless the church is in decline. But it is also true that after going through a spiritual revival the church will address the science that came to chastise her in the name of God and push it back inside its proper boundaries.

Almost the same can be said of the state. I say "almost" because the state remains the *exousia architektonike*, the architectonic power that was given the authority to define the legal boundary also for science the moment science manifests itself as a visible organism in schools. Only, before it crosses

---

30. Baruch Spinoza (1632–77) was expelled from the Portuguese synagogue in Amsterdam for his rationalist criticism of the OT, which he refused to recant. Erasmus of Rotterdam (1466–1536) began by endorsing Luther's criticism of the church, but when Luther was excommunicated Erasmus reaffirmed his loyalty to Rome.

that boundary to enter the domain of science, the state must respectfully remove its sandals and renounce any sovereignty that would be out of place in that domain. Scholarly learning in the service of the state, such as the Ghibellines and the Guelfs played off against each other,[31] as France's bureaucracy employed to control its populace,[32] as German reaction tried to do in the shame of Göttingen[33]—is a self-demeaning prostitution that forfeits any valid claim to moral influence. But even if, as in our jurisdictions, the state is animated by a nobler disposition, and even if scholars, as in our country, are too proud to bend, still it will benefit and do credit to our academic life if the universities reaffirm their own root and grow and develop their own distinct life and so outgrow the guardianship of the state. That is how the schools of the prophets in Israel and the wisdom schools in Jerusalem held their own: they stood in the heart of the nation, free and independent. That was the free activity of the ancient philosophers in Greece and their imitators in Rome, and that was the independence enjoyed by the scholars of the early church. That was the liberty enjoyed by the medieval universities of Bologna and Paris: not as training schools for civil servants, to pour knowledge into their heads, but as centers of learning that carved out a place for themselves amid society. It was in that free form that the university was able to contribute to the liberating movement of the Reformation, and it was not until the close of the eighteenth century, when that free framework was transformed as if by magic into a "branch of the civil service," that the new-fangled university as an institution of higher learning allowed itself to be riveted to the state.

This did not come about as a result of someone's personal decision but because of the press of circumstances and the general exhaustion of the peoples. Today it would border on the absurd to demand that the state should suddenly withdraw from the world of the university. At present the

---

31. In late medieval Italy, the Ghibellines championed the Holy Roman Emperor, while the party of the Guelfs supported the pope in Rome. Each party combated the other with what scholars knew at the time about rival claims of pope and emperor dating back to the late Roman Empire.

32. Successive governments of France asserted control over the universities both before, during, and after the Revolution in order to be able to censor any thought hostile to the regime.

33. The "shame of Göttingen" refers to the dismissal in 1837 of seven professors from the university there after they had protested the new king of Hanover's abrogation of the constitution.

public shows too little enthusiasm for higher learning, the well-to-do too little generosity, and alumni too little energy to hazard the attempt. For now, the state simply has no choice but to continue its support, provided—and this we must insist upon—provided efforts are directed at emancipating the university and seeing science itself embrace again sphere sovereignty as its ideal.

Is it then "unscholarly" that our school should venture a first timid step in this direction? At the public universities so many drawbacks encumber the scales of equity. Money, it cannot be said often enough, creates power *for* the one who gives and power *over* the one who receives. That is the reason why the arts (with the exception of music), because they rely on funding, were never able to raise the emancipation of the masses to higher levels. Who shall calculate the influence that state funds have had on our country's future and its academic development by the single appointment of a Thorbecke, or a Scholten, or an Opzoomer?[34] Where is the intellectual-spiritual criterion that can guide the state when making such influential choices for these higher, crucial disciplines? Moreover, to force Jews and Catholics to help pay for theology departments that are in fact and by law Protestant—does that not grate somewhat upon your sense of justice? So when the law of the land recognizes our right to establish a school and, as we just heard,[35] the Crown grants a charter to our institution which is not encumbered with those drawbacks, does then the founding of a university supported by the common people not prophesy a bright future for higher learning and our national life?

For here is a group who less than thirty years ago were called obscurantists and who now wear themselves out in pursuit of an academic goal. The least esteemed from the "nonthinking" segment of the population[36] have come running from behind their plows and their kneading troughs in order to collect the pennies for starting a university. Elsewhere, people

---

34. Earlier in the century, Crown appointments in the University of Leiden had gone to J. R. Thorbecke (1798–1872), who worked out a liberal constitution for the country, and to rationalist J. H. Scholten (1811–85), who introduced orthodox students (including young Abraham Kuyper) to Modernist theology. Positivist C. W. Opzoomer (1821–92) was appointed to a philosophy chair in the State University of Utrecht, where he developed into an influential philosophical atheist.
35. Earlier in the ceremony, Willem Hovy (1840–1910), chairman of the board of directors, had read the official documents establishing the university.
36. This epithet was a description of the common people by the liberal elite.

work for progress from *above*; they want to bring higher learning *down* to the people. But surely this is better: a segment of the population willing to do with less so that an academy may flourish! Is there a solution more practical than this for the problem of establishing a bond between higher learning and everyday life? Are scholars who live off the common people's money not obliged to nurture a closer bond with them and to develop an aversion to dry and abstract knowledge? Besides, is *giving* itself not a power for good? Is the ability to part with your money not a moral asset? Who will estimate the moral capital that will accrue to our nation through this costly venture? People complain about dearth of character, but what can be more helpful in forming character than such free initiative on the part of engaged citizens? And if other universities are able to operate ever so smoothly thanks to the coercive power of the tax collectors and the readiness of the paymasters, of that too we are not envious. We may be facing a "struggle for life," but that very struggle brings out the power of the most glorious devotion. The monies entrusted to us conceal a higher value than their weight in gold: they are bathed in prayer, are offered with love, and represent the earnings of hard work.

III

We have seen how sphere sovereignty is the stimulus that has given birth to our institution. We have frankly avowed that for us, too, sphere sovereignty is the prime condition for any science that would flourish. It now remains for me to defend our disputed claim that sphere sovereignty also be granted as our *principle*—I mean our *Reformed* principle. In using that name I hasten to correct any chronic misunderstanding and dispel any suspicion as though by "Reformed" we mean anything other or anything less than the pure, authentic Christian religion. Just as the merchant speaks of *net* weight, the minter of *pure* gold, the silversmith of *sterling* quality, and the Scriptures of *precious* nard, and a certain newspaper in the city on the Spaarne River calls itself the *Oprechte*,[37] so we too, if we wanted to play the eccentric, could speak of "net" Christianity, of a "precise" Christianity, a "pure" Christianity, an "authentic" Christianity, and, not incorrectly, of a "sterling" Christianity. But we prefer to do without such strange terms and according to usage and the demands of history speak of "Reformed

---

37. Reference to *De Opregte Haarlemsche Courant* (the Genuine Harlem Paper), Holland's longest-running newspaper (1656–1942).

Christianity," in order to sharply distinguish all counterfeit, compromised, or condensed forms of the Christian religion from the Christian religion that is according to God's Word.

The lone adjective "Christian" says very little. That could also refer to Roman Catholicism or the Remonstrance, and there is as yet not one Modernist theologian who has given up on the name "Christian." Has it not been observed in Parliament that men who consider it an honor to deny the existence of God nevertheless pin the false label of "Christian" on the dechristianized public school? Thus something needs to be added; we cannot escape the confusion of tongues at a lesser cost. And since also the spiritual realm enjoys sphere sovereignty, and since it is not up to the individual to name and define principles but that this belongs to a sphere's authoritative organ that is the bearer of its tradition, so therefore it is not for us to choose any other name for ourselves. Nor do we have the right to profess our principle in an arbitrary way. We simply must present ourselves as belonging to the Reformed religion, of which we are the historical bearers as sons of the Dutch Reformation, and to understand by that name not what pleases us but what the church has lawfully decided, namely, the bold and unconditional confession of the Canons of Dort.[38] In so doing we do not reject our Lutheran brothers. To look down on other Christians would make us blameworthy. All we ask is that we not be forced to exchange what is finer in our eyes for what is less fine, and that we be allowed to build again in the unadulterated Reformed style the Reformed temple that has fallen into ruin.

This has been my aim also in the present address. And so, as demanded by Scripture and modeled by Calvin, I have placed in the foreground the *sovereignty of God*, because it alone stimulates life at the root and helps overcome all fear of men, even of Satan himself. And if anyone wonders whether sphere sovereignty is really derived from the heart of Scripture and the treasury of Reformed life, I ask him, first of all, to consider that Scripture's *principle of faith* runs very deep, and then to note the decision of the tribes at Hebron to crown David king, to note Elijah's resistance to Ahab's tyranny, the disciples' refusal to submit to a police ordinance in Jerusalem, and, not least, the word their Lord laid down about what is

---

38. The Canons of Dort (1618–19), born out of controversy with the Remonstrance and the theology of Jacobus Arminius (1560–1609), comprise one of the three main confessional standards of the historic Reformed churches.

God's and what is Caesar's. As to Reformed practice, have you never heard of Calvin's *"magistratus inferiores"*?[39] Is not sphere sovereignty the basis of the entire Presbyterian church order? Did not virtually all Reformed countries lean toward a confederative form of government? Do civil liberties not flourish best in Calvinist nations? And can it be denied that domestic peace, decentralization, and local autonomy are, still today, guaranteed most securely in the lands of Calvin's heirs?[40]

It is entirely in line with the Reformed spirit, therefore, that we insist on sovereignty for our Reformed principle in our pursuit of science and scholarship as well. We cannot enter into a pact of neutrality and participate in a university together with those who live from another principle. I do not deny that among non-Christian governments there still is found a fear of God and his justice, a fear that Calvin honored even among pagan tyrants. Nevertheless, such a pious trait is little more than a foundation bearing at most a section of wall but lacking a roof or windows. Or if you would like a still better metaphor, what use a tower that lacks a steeple, hence a carillon, a clock, and a weathervane—in short, everything for which it was erected? If we were meant to participate in an existing university, a different proposal would be more acceptable, namely, a large state university for which the government would furnish only lecture halls and laboratories, with the right for every scholar to teach there and the right for every social group to install scholars there. It would be a sort of scientific "central station" where all lines converge but each with its own philosophy and its own administration.

Yet even then the right of each principle to enjoy "sovereignty in its own proper sphere" would still be infringed on both sides. Does not history show that the scholarship practiced by every social group with a distinct principle ends up looking quite different? There was once a form of Greek, of Arabic, of Scholastic learning, forms that may not speak to us yet were thoughtfully developed by giant intellects in whose shadow none of us could stand. Likewise, after the Middle Ages learning looked rather different in Catholic and non-Catholic universities. The succession of philosophers who have

---

39. That is, the "lesser magistrates," who may lead the people in revolt against a tyrant. See *Inst.* 4.20.31, where the defenders of popular liberties are called *"magistratus populares."*
40. For Kuyper's earlier development of these claims, see "Calvinism: Source and Stronghold," 279–322.

been active since Kant have produced schools of thought that are mutually exclusive, depending on whether they stress the subject or the object. How would you wed a monist to an atomist? Indeed, so compelling and so dominant is the strength of a principle that Hegel's intellectual power, everyone concedes, generated a wholly distinct system in the fields of theology, law, physics, in fact in every field, so that anyone studying criminal law in Hegel's school and civil law in the school of Herbart[41] will inevitably find his conception of justice totally confused.

If it is clear that weaving the same cloth together is impossible when there is a difference in *intellectual* principles, how much more is sphere sovereignty imperative when different *life* principles are involved! As the example of Fichte has shown, if a merely intellectual principle is involved it is always possible to return to what was initially rejected.[42] But that is not possible in the case of a life principle. A life principle is rooted in *facts*. Or stronger still, in the case of the Christian principle it is rooted in a *living person*—in a person whose coming precipitated a crisis in the midst of the world, at the center of world history, in the heart also of the intellectual world. Just ask this living person, ask Christ, ask his authorized spokesmen, and what do you learn? Does the rabbi from Nazareth declare that his knowledge is wedded to the knowledge of earthly sages? Do his apostles tell you that continuing your studies in Jerusalem or in Athens will gradually and automatically lead you to the higher knowledge that is his? The exact opposite! That rabbi will impress upon you that his treasure of wisdom is hidden from the wise and the prudent and revealed unto babes. And the academically trained Paul draws a wide gulf between the knowledge formerly acquired by him and the life principle now implanted in him, a gulf so wide, so deep, so impassible, that he contrasts the *foolish* mind of the one with the *wise* life of the other [see 1 Cor 3:18–19].

Shall we then pretend that we can build together on the selfsame basis what according to the express pronouncement of Jesus' divine self-consciousness is built on entirely different foundations? We shall not venture it, ladies and gentlemen! Considering that a principle marks a starting point

41. Johann Friedrich Herbart (1776–1841) was a philosopher and educational theorist who attacked German idealism, notably in Hegel's philosophy of right.
42. Johann Gottlieb Fichte (1762–1814), a German philosopher, at first ranked inner-worldly morality over transcendental religion but later reversed the order and taught a form of pantheism as the basis of human society.

and that a distinct principle therefore marks the start of something distinct, we shall defend sovereignty for our principle as well as for the principle of our opponents throughout the sphere of thought. That is to say, just as they employ *their* principle and its corresponding method to erect a house of knowledge that shines brilliantly (though it does not entice us), so we too from *our* principle and *our* method will grow our own plant whose stems, leaves, and blossoms are nourished with its own sap. We happen to claim that we perceive and observe something that our opponents label self-deception. So be it; we cannot but pass as fools for that reason, just as we cannot refrain from quoting the proverb that "the godless also in our days do not understand knowledge" [see Prov 29:7]. Not because they are inferior to us in knowledge—they may well be our superiors—but because they say that it is *not* a fact what is for us an assured fact in Christ, and because they declare that they have *not* found in their soul what we consciously grasp in our soul. Belief in the Word of God, objectively infallible in the Scriptures and subjectively offered to us by the Holy Spirit: there you have the line that separates. Not as though the knowledge of others rests on intellectual certainty and ours merely on faith. All knowledge proceeds from faith, of whatever kind. A person relies on God or he proceeds from his inner self or he holds fast to his ideal. The person who believes nothing does not exist. At least, he who has nothing that he accepts as self-evident would not be able to find a starting point even for his thinking; and how would a person whose thought lacks a starting point ever be able to investigate anything *scientifically*?

Thus our intention indeed is to build next to what others have built, with nothing in common except the terrain outside and the view from the window, with a printing press to maintain, like a mail carrier, the exchange of ideas. For we do agree that a battle of ideas back and forth is possible and necessary, but only about points of departure and schools of thought. For once a school of thought is defined and your point of departure is fixed, when these are consistently followed the direction of your research is set; and in the measure that you stand at the left or are found on the right, everything appears different to you and every objection argued against your position lacks the power to persuade. Anyone who thinks organically is therefore right to scoff at the individualistic pretension that everybody, growing up, must personally think through all systems, search through every confession, and then opt for the one he considers the best. No one can do that, and no one does. No one has that kind of time or that mental energy at his disposal. Only a naïve person, one who does not yet understand what higher learning entails, can fancy that he has done so, or may think that others have done so. That so-called sampling of any and all systems merely fosters superficiality, destroys clear thinking, corrupts character, and renders the brain unfit for more solid work. Believe me, one does not enhance one's knowledge of building construction by nosing about in house after house, but only by a careful study of one well-built structure, basement to attic.

Accordingly, our scholarship will not be "free" in the sense of "detached from its principle." That would be the freedom of the fish on dry land, of a potted plant uprooted from its soil, or if you will, of a day laborer taken from his hamlet on the moors and suddenly plunked down on Broadway or Times Square. We bind ourselves in our own house strictly and inexorably to a fixed regimen, convinced as we are that a household thrives best under set rules. The most generous academic freedom is found only in the rule that whoever wants to leave should find the door open, plus the rule that no outsider may enter your house to lord it over you; but also, that others are just as free to build on the foundation of *their* principle, in the style of *their* method, displaying the results of *their own* research.

Finally, if you ask whether we desire such separate development not only for theology but for all the disciplines, and if you find it hard to suppress a smile when you hear scoffing references to "Christian medicine" and "Christian logic"—then hear our reply to that objection.

Given that we have professed God's revelation—reformed, after its deformation—as the starting point of our project, do you really think that we would have only theologians drink from this fountain and for the rest spurn this source for the study of law and medicine and philology? Do you view the world of science, properly so called, as separated into rigid compartments?

What do people mean when speaking of a *medical* faculty? They are not sick mammals that medical science seeks to benefit, but human beings created in the image of God. Judge for yourselves, then, whether it makes a difference if you view man as a moral agent with a higher destiny for soul *and body* and as a creature bound to God's Word. Should a medical doctor tell a dying man of his approaching death, or should he keep it from him? Should he recommend anesthesia for a woman in labor, or advise against it? Insist on vaccination, or leave it to free choice? Urge young men to practice self-control or indulgence in his passions? Join Malthus and curse a mother's fertility,[43] or join Scripture in calling her blessed? Treat the mental-health patient psychically by counseling him, or physically by drugging him? Or, to name no more, condone cremation, permit vivisection without restriction, and halt the spread of syphilis by the most detestable of medical examinations at the cost of degrading public authority and disgracing human dignity?[44]

What shall I say about the law faculty? Does it not make a difference if I view man as a self-improving product of nature rather than as a condemned sinner—if I view the law itself as a functionally developing organism of nature rather than as a jewel that comes down from God himself and is bound to his Word? Will that not determine the purpose of criminal law and afford a guideline for international law? When the Christian conscience, quite apart from the science of law, rises in protest against the dominant school of political economy, against prevailing business practices, against the predatory relationships among the social classes— when in civil society all our Christian people are urging a return to decentralization by way of sphere sovereignty and under current law are establishing separate Christian schools at a rate of three to one[45]—then can you name me one chair in the law faculty that is not affected by the contrast in starting principles?

As for our natural scientists, I grant that if they strictly confined themselves to what can be weighed and measured, the wedge of starting principle would not be able to penetrate their field. But who operates that way? What scientist works without hypotheses? Who does not pursue his science as a human being and not as an impersonal measuring instrument? Who does not see what he sees through subjective lenses, and who does not extrapolate beyond what he can see, always according to his subjective opinion? Can someone properly assess the value of your printed book,

---

43. Thomas Malthus (1766–1834) advocated lowering the birth rate by means of abstinence or birth control because he calculated that the world's population would sooner or later outstrip the world's food supply.

44. Under the system of regulated prostitution, in conjunction with laws against the spread of contagious diseases, prostitutes had to register with the police and submit to periodic medical examinations against syphilis. Their customers were spared such humiliating measures.

45. Kuyper here calls attention to the fact that in 1880 separate, privately funded Christian primary schools were proliferating at triple the rate of new starts of religiously neutral, publicly funded schools.

pamphlet, hymnal, who only figures out the cost of paper and ink required to print them? Is the value of the finest embroidery exhausted by the cost of thread and fabric? Or better still, is not all of creation before the eyes of the natural scientist like one grand painting, and is then the value and beauty of that work of art really to be judged by the gilded frame around it, the yards of linen underneath it, and the pounds of paint upon it?

Why go on to speak to you about the faculty of letters? Of course, learning how to read words and conjugate verbs has nothing to do with being for or against the Messiah. But if I take you further and unlock Hellas's palace of art[46] or enter Rome's world of power, does it then not make a difference if I resurrect the spirit of those ancients for the purpose of banishing the spirit of Christ or instead for subordinating that spirit to the spirit of Christ in accordance with both human and divine standards? Does the study of Semitic languages not change depending on whether I regard Israel as the people of *absolute* revelation or at most as a people with a genius for religion? Does philosophy stay the same if it continues to pursue "Ideal Being" or instead joins us in confessing Christ as the ideal "incarnate"? Will the study of world history arrive at the same result no matter whether it brackets the cross with the cup of Socrates or instead regards the cross as the center of world history? And to name no more, will the history of our fatherland kindle the same fire in the heart of young people, regardless whether it is unfolded in all its heroic beauty by a Fruin, a Nuyens, or instead by a Groen van Prinsterer (och, that he were still alive)?[47]

Ladies and gentlemen, how could it be otherwise? Man, be he a fallen sinner or an evolving product of nature, shows up in every department and every discipline as "the subject that thinks" or "the object that invites thought." Not one segment of our intellectual world can be hermetically sealed off from the others, and there is not a square inch in the whole domain of our human existence over which Christ, who is sovereign over all, does not call out: "Mine!"

We declare that we too have heard this call and it was only in response to that call that we made preparations to take on this great task—a task that is really far too big for us. But we had heard the plaints of our brothers

---

46. By the words "Hellas's palace of art" Kuyper means the art of classical Greece.
47. Robert J. Fruin (1823-99), W. J. F. Nuyens (1823-94), and G. Groen van Prinsterer (1801-76) were prominent historians representing, respectively, a liberal, Catholic, and Protestant interpretation of Dutch history.

about their tragic impotence when their knowledge proved inadequate for defending their principle with the kind of force that does justice to it. We had listened to the sighs of our Christian people who in their humiliating embarrassment had learned again to pray for leaders to lead them, for pastors to feed them, for prophets to motivate them. We realized: the honor of Christ cannot be allowed to remain like this, trampled under taunts and sneers. As surely as we loved him with the love of our soul, we had to *build* again in his name. And it mattered not if we compared our weakness to the strength of those who opposed us, nor considered the absurdity of undertaking so bold a venture: the fire kept on burning in our bones. There was one mightier than we who spurred us on. We could not remain idle. In spite of ourselves we had to go forward. That some of our brothers advised against erecting a structure of our own at this time and preferred to stay under the roof of humanism was a very painful cause of disappointment for us. But it merely reinforced that inner urge, seeing how the future of our life-principle appeared even more precarious, now that men such as these wavered.

And so our little school was born, embarrassed to the point of blushing with the very name *university*. Poor in financial resources, most frugally supplied with scholarly manpower, and more lacking than luxuriating in public sympathy. What will be its course, how long its life? Oh, the thousand questions that arise in connection with its future, they cannot crowd your skeptical minds more than they have raged in my heart! Only by keeping constantly in mind our sacred principle every time the waves crashed over us did we bravely raise our weary heads again. If this cause were not from the Mighty One of Jacob, how could it stand? For I am not exaggerating: for us to dare establish this school is to set ourselves against all that is called great; it is to challenge a universe of scholars, to row against the current of an entire century, a century of such enormous attraction.

Look down then, as freely as your conscience permits, on our persons, our strength, and our academic significance. The Calvinist credo, to consider God all and man nothing, gives you the full right to do so. One thing only I beg of you: even if you are our fiercest opponent, do not withhold your respect for the *enthusiasm* that inspires us. After all, the confession we have dusted off was once the heart-cry of our downtrodden nation; the Scriptures, before whose authority we bow, once comforted as God's infallible witness the sorrowing among your own people; the Christ, whose name we honor in this institution, was he not the inspiration, the one and only, the adored one of your own forebears? Even if we suppose, in line with your credo and in accordance with what has already been written in the studies of the scholars and echoed in the halls of the steel mills, that the Scriptures have done and Christianity is outmoded, even then I still ask: Has Christianity not been, also in your eyes, a historical phenomenon too imposing, too majestic, too sacred to come to a humiliating end and fall without honor? Or does *noblesse oblige* no longer exist? Could we allow a banner such as we carried off from Golgotha—could we allow it to fall into the hands of the enemy so long as we had not attempted our utmost, so long as one last arrow remained in our quiver, and so long as our country still had a bodyguard, however small, for the One who was crowned by Golgotha?

To that question—and with that I close, ladies and gentlemen—to that question our soul responded with a resounding: "By God, never that!" Out of that "never" our association was born. And upon that "never," as an oath of allegiance to a higher principle, I ask for an echo—may it be an Amen—from every patriotic heart!

* * *

What remains for me to do, before this ceremony is concluded with thanksgiving to God, is to say a special word to each of the spheres assembled in this auditorium.[48]

First of all, it is my privilege of addressing Your Excellency, minister of the king, with sincere gratitude for the honor of your august presence and with humble solicitation of your favor for the association which was begun by a gracious act of the government of this country. In 1876 our revered king wrote in his law the right of the people, recognized already in 1848, to freedom also of higher education.[49] May it please His Majesty, may it please Your Excellency, that within a mere four years this law does not appear superfluous and that the people are availing themselves of that

---

48. Our translation omits most of the obligatory forms of address used by Kuyper in speaking to each distinct group. For example, when turning to the pastors and theologians present, he says: "Weleerwaarde Zeergeleerde Heeren, Bedienaren des Woords, Hooggeachte Broederen!" (that is: reverend sirs, learned gentlemen, ministers of the Word, highly esteemed brethren).

49. The Higher Education Act that received royal assent in 1876 clarified that the freedom of education clause in the 1848 Constitution applied not only to primary but also to secondary and higher education.

freedom. At the time, on March 11, 1876, the king's minister defending the law stated: "If Amsterdam acquires for its university *ius promovendi* with *effectus civilis*,[50] then the problem will inevitably arise that others too will demand equal rights and then it will only be reasonable to grant them the same right." Very well, allow me the privilege of concluding my tribute to you with the prayer that if we should someday earn our spurs, no less fairness than is expressed in those words shall be found with the ministers of the Crown.[51]

Lord Burgomaster, esteemed aldermen and clerk of this city! To you too I owe my respectful homage. In particular you, mayor of this city! To greet a former professor as mayor is too rare a privilege for the dedicator of a school for higher learning not to hope for the best. Next to the costly acquisition of the older school with which Pallas Athena gifted your predecessor,[52] to now gain, without money and without price, a younger daughter of Minerva for your beloved Amsterdam can only be welcome to our burgher father, as we are fond of calling you. Our historic Amsterdam, we thought, was the obvious city for such a historic institution.[53] May City Hall in future not withhold from us the affection which it has already shown us thus far as a welcome surprise, also by favoring this event with its presence.

Learned sir, rector magnificus and secretary of the university of this city! The republic of letters has traditionally not suffered very much from rivalry in rank and status, I do not say among the professors but certainly among the universities. Otherwise, as rector of this small, younger school, how I would dread facing you, the illustrious regent of the older school! You

---

50. *Ius promovendi* is the right to grant doctoral degrees. *Effectus civilis* is legal effect or licensed competence to practice law and other designated professions.

51. Ironically, what the minister at the time meant as a warning is turned by Kuyper into a promise. His own Higher Education Act of 1905 would finally grant these rights to the Free University.

52. By a law of 1877, the Athenaeum Illustre of Amsterdam, founded in 1632, was converted into a degree-granting institution funded by the city and named Municipal University of Amsterdam. Kuyper contrasts this school as the gift of the Greek goddess Athena and his own school with the Roman analog, Minerva.

53. The executive of the association, after briefly toying with the idea of erecting their school in Prussia or Belgium, turned to their own country and considered a location "somewhere in the provinces" (rejected because "not very educational surroundings"), Utrecht ("too wishy-washy"), Leiden ("harmful influence of the academic environment"), The Hague ("too frivolous"), to finally settle on Amsterdam as the location of choice.

know that, many years ago already, voices were raised, also in your senate, calling for a "Free University." Could Professor Moll ever have guessed that it would arise *alongside* the Municipal University in the same Amsterdam, on a foundation chosen by *our group*?[54] And arise, indeed, without evoking jealousy? Our size does not warrant it.[55] The more so since your mission is more local whereas ours is to serve the whole country. May the honor of the classically educated always sustain among us the desired relationship, and may we continue to share love of truth and love of learning, even if we live out of different principles.

From government and government bodies I turn in the second place to society's spokesmen in Parliament, associations, and the press.

Honorable members of Parliament! The school now founded is in part a fruit of your indefatigable labor. You have never stopped speaking up for our popular liberties, especially in the area of education. Rather, you have unremittingly championed the freedom of universities. Your popular tribunate, relying on the tribunate of the Son of God, brought a turning point in our politics and our society that is already palpable. For that our association thanks you. For that our people spell your names with sincere affection. May you find a rich reward, as you sit here among the people you serve, in the grateful tribute that all of us extend to you for so much loyal dedication.

Esteemed board members of Christian associations! Our association invited you to our founding day because you are one with us in the cause of combating the dechristianization of our country. We greatly appreciate the courtesy, even more the demonstration of your love, that is expressed in your attendance. We do not all have the same view of the conflict, but we have all sworn the oath of enlistment to the Messiah under one and the same banner of the cross. As we humbly and devotedly serve, each in his own way, our dear fatherland, our nation, and in that nation *Christus Consolator*, let our battle be for the honor of his name!

---

54. The Rector Magnificus at the University of Amsterdam for the 1880–81 school year was Cornelis Pijnacker Hordijk (1847–1908), a professor of law and politician. Kuyper may be referring here to Gerrit Moll (1785–1838), a famed Dutch polymath and native of Amsterdam.
55. At the time of its conversion, the Municipal University had 8 professors serving some 250 students. The Free University at its start had 5 professors serving 8 students.

Representatives of the press! In your hands rests a power which our old academies did not know but which the younger university wants to reckon with from the outset. Thus I do not depart from my traditions if as a disciple of Groen van Prinsterer I honor also the press as a force in the nation.[56] Where Groen was the first to break with custom and take up his place in your midst, should I not count it an honor that I entered your ranks as one of yours? As rector of this school, but also as an old comrade-in-arms, I ask for this newborn institution the salute of your word.

***

Highly esteemed directors of this school! If I now retreat to a narrower circle and come at last to you who are bound up with this institution in a more personal way, allow me, first of all, to offer you the gratitude of a brother's heart. It was always a point of honor for the merchant class of Amsterdam to live, work, and sacrifice for science and scholarship, including the kind that honored Christ.[57] To see that class, now in league with brothers throughout the country as provincial directors and provincial secretaries—to see you involved in the governance of such a school, that surely is a comforting, inspiring, uplifting thought. May God's favor and people's responsiveness lighten the heavy load resting on your shoulders, and may it be given me to serve you as professor and rector in such a way that your trust is not put to shame and that you will never regret having appointed me.

With that same prayer I come to you, gentlemen curators, highly esteemed brothers! I feel deeply what it has meant for you as men of science to take on the academic oversight of a school whose charter has come from Dort. That you did not shrink from it and that you put up with the obloquy is therefore worth more than an honorary diploma: it is a patent of noble courage and moral dedication for which I thank you, for which this school honors you, and for which our people love you. May the search for the personnel you require be the answer to prayer through grace from on high.

---

56. In addition to his numerous pamphlets, especially during election campaigns, Groen van Prinsterer also wrote the political editorials in the daily newspaper *De Nederlander* from 1850-55.
57. Half of the legally required financial assets of the new university were contributed by a beer brewer and a stockbroker, both residents of Amsterdam.

An answer to prayer: may that be true as well of all our scholarship, highly esteemed colleagues, beloved brothers! We are privileged to lay the first stone for this structure. So much will depend on what you and I produce, for this field was plowed for the purpose of harvesting the products of our labor. We tremble sometimes at the thought of the enormously difficult task we have accepted. And yet who of us would want to back out? You too know the urgency, the impulse of a higher necessity. Moreover, we can boast, can we not, of one thing: among us the danger of rivalry, that plague of faculties, has once for all been cut off because everyone's subjective thoughts have been brought into captivity to the majesty of the objective, historical, authorized and empowered, officially spoken Word!

To you, friends and brothers who came to us from abroad! On behalf of the entire association, I offer you our thanks for such unexpected fraternal fidelity.[58] To receive tokens of sympathy from Scotland, from Germany, even from as far away as America, that too reminded us of Dort, where the whole Reformed family once gathered.[59] The Reformed confession no more than science recognizes national boundaries. And so receive our word of welcome in our midst and from this circle take home to your brothers our best wishes for peace, prosperity, and happiness.

Ministers of the Word! To see you present here in such large numbers adds considerably to the joy of this festive day. As you know, we are not *from* a church nor *for* a church. Academic life forms for us a sphere with its own sovereignty, hence an independent life. What will become of his purified and still more to be purified churches in our country will be decided by the King of the church, not by us. Blindly obedient, we await the outcome. Even so, we honor your station, we are refreshed by your bold confession, and we place a very high value on your public affection. After all, you are also theologians, also leaders of the multitude, also priests that pray for the people. Minister to us, then, as theologians by supporting us, as popular

---

58. The October 24, 1880, issue of the weekly *De Heraut* reported that present in person had been the Revs. P. Geyser (1824–82) and H. Calaminus (1842–1922), pastors of Reformed churches just across the German border, in Elberfeld, Wuppertal (North Rhine-Westphalia).

59. Notices of the event had appeared in the Reformed church papers in North America, while congratulatory telegrams had been received from M. Proches and J. R. Meille of the School of Theology in Florence; from Prof. Geymonet, Prof. A. Revel, and court chaplain A. Stoecker, of Berlin; from E. Staehelin and W. Arnold of the Evangelical Seminary in Basel, Switzerland; and from Robert Smith in Scotland.

leaders by recommending us, as priestly intercessors by praying for our association in the public worship services.

Last, I turn to you, founders, members, donors, district heads, or city wardens, you who were willing to offer your money, your time, your effort for our association, beloved brothers in our Lord Jesus Christ! Humanly speaking our fate lies in your hands, the provisions for this journey, the very possibility of growth. As you know, we are not nearly there yet. At the very least, the number of professors must increase threefold. That means that your love and dedication will have to increase threefold as well, otherwise our school will never become what it is supposed to become by law.[60] Nonetheless, we dare to hope that it will be completed, however bold this may seem to you now. We have hope because of what we have seen already. Because of the priceless faithfulness with which so many brothers have already surprised us. Not least, because of the enthusiasm for this sacred cause that I have seen shining in the eyes of our women. And then ... because of something else as well! Because of the presence in our midst of your cofounder, Groen's bosom friend—I mean you, Mr. Elout, noble elder, with your penetrating but always friendly eyes. What a period of history is not the span of your life! What a succession of kings have you not served! What storms have not raged over your now weary head![61] And that you then still wanted to be here with us! That you brought us your gift[62] and spoke a word of fatherly blessing to us young ones—oh, how that word would have stolen the hearts of this people if it had not already, before this institution was ever dreamed of, thanked God for giving you to us. But allow me at least to tell you openly how much the Reformed people cherish it when great men associate with us commoners; to tell you how our Reformed people feel attached to those historic persons who, like yourself, evoke for us two generations who have already passed on; to tell you above all how our people, who became great by the Bible and who wish to die with the

---

60. By law, the new university would not only have to have at least three departments at the start but would also have to add two more within fifty years of its founding.
61. Jonkheer Pieter Jacob Elout van Soeterwoude (1805-93), an early member of the Réveil circle in The Hague, developed into a prominent supporter of the anti-revolutionary movement.
62. Earlier that afternoon Elout had given a speech on behalf of the founding committee, at the conclusion of which he presented the association with the gift of 100,000 guilders as starting capital.

Bible, rejoice and praise their covenant God for the humble profession of faithfulness to the Holy Word of Scripture by a man of your position, your wisdom, your years. And since for you all things begin with prayer and end with thanksgiving, your soul will join me in prayer, as the quiet utterance of my word ascends to the Almighty in a doxology of praise.

To thank you, Our Father who is in heaven, fountain of all truth, wellspring of all true knowledge and source of all wisdom! The creature that strays from you finds nothing but darkness, nothing but weariness, nothing but bondage of the soul. But near unto you, immersed in your life, light envelops us, energy sparkles through our veins, and the freedom of the Christian unfurls in heavenly rapture. Adored Eternal Majesty, look down in favor upon this institution. May its resources, its strength, all its wisdom be as from you. May it never swear by any lesser, by any other power than by your Holy Word. And you who tries our reins, O Judge also of our nation and Inspector also of our schools of learning, will you yourself break down the walls of this university and destroy it from before your face if it should ever intend, if it should ever desire, to do anything other than boast in that sovereign free grace which there is in the cross of the Son of your most tender love!

Lord, Lord God! Let our help be in your name alone, let all our help be in your name! Amen.

* * *

And herewith I declare this ceremony concluded and the Free University opened!

Thank you.

IS ERROR A PUNISHABLE OFFENSE?

TEXT INTRODUCTION

"Is Error a Punishable Offense?" [*Is Dwaling Strafbaar?*] was published as a series of sixteen leading articles in Kuyper's daily *De Standaard* from May 25 through June 18, 1874. They mostly appeared on consecutive days and were never reprinted. The publication occurred simultaneously with that of "Calvinism: Source and Stronghold of Our Constitutional Liberties," a public lecture he had been giving in various settings since November 1873; the preface dates from May 20, and the brochure appeared in June. In both discourses he develops an alternative theory about the origin of the fundamental liberties: not the French Revolution, but early modern Calvinism was the birthplace of all modern freedoms. The content of the new series is in keeping with the former, with a notable difference: "Calvinism" is now completely absent. The term *antirevolutionary* is used instead, coined by Groen van Prinsterer (1801–76), with whom Kuyper still maintains close contact; it also serves Kuyper's political aims better with the readers he addresses here. Kuyper was elected to the Second Chamber in January 1874, and the series can be partially read as a political manifesto. It can also be seen as an answer to John Stuart Mill's *On Liberty* (1859); Mill's individualism (denounced by Kuyper in the Second Chamber) excludes any positive appreciation. Kuyper does quote extensively from James Fitzjames Stephen, *Liberty, Equality, Fraternity* (London, 1873), which contains an extensive criticism of Mill's position. Kuyper's own antirevolutionary hero is John

Milton, and especially his *Areopagitica* (1644), whom Kuyper encountered while reading the collected work of Edmund Burke in 1873.

SOURCE: Abraham Kuyper, "Is Dwaling Strafbaar?," *De Standaard*, no. 660, May 25/26, 1874–no. 680, June 18, 1874. Translated by John Kok. Edited and annotated by Johan Snel.

IS ERROR A PUNISHABLE OFFENSE?

I

Is one free to err as long as it does not result in culpable activities? May the strong arm of the state counter erroneous ideas only when they give rise to actual infractions? Are false notions, as long as they remain just thoughts and words, inviolable and not to be infringed on; such that only whenever they are acted upon, those activities, but never these false notions themselves, can be prosecuted in court?

Many communists teach that "property is robbery." That teaching is erroneous. But people preach, teach, and propagate it nevertheless. The respect that many have for property rights shrinks as a result, which leads in turn to burglary, theft, forgery, fraudulent bankruptcies, the abuse of trust, and swindle.

Is one free to propagate that false doctrine? Must the state watch, with the sword of justice in its sheath, and wait for the bitter fruit that this pernicious seed may engender before prosecuting and punishing the theft or racket that results—pursuing the misguided children rather than the spiritual father of these crimes?

Or how about a different claim: "The people are sovereign, given the rights of man," say some.

That declaration is not true. This mistaken notion undermines people's respect for the legitimate authority of the government, which, in turn, gives rise to resistance, mutiny, and rebellion. It is at that level that this fundamental fallacy bears its fruit. So where do we go from here? Are people free to spread this false notion without hindrance, forcing the criminal courts to stand idly by until the toxic fruits of this absurd doctrine manifest themselves in public rebellion and an uproar on the streets?

We deliberately choose two exclusively political examples. Disseminating or suppressing these false claims is less an issue within the church as it is beyond it; but propaganda for both positions is currently distributed everywhere with impunity.

Nevertheless, it must be said from the outset that similar dynamics are at play when it comes to deviations within the church regarding what it teaches.

To teach that "there is no God," that "original sin is a fiction," that "there will be no judgment day," that "the state of perdition is an invention of priestly cunning," that "the Bible is a book like any other book," that "morality and, hence, one's conscience are independent of faith" are equally instances of peddling utterly alarming fallacies, which warp the crossbeams of the social order, call into question the moral makeup of life, and are the underlying cause of the crimes and injustices that break out among the people.

The claims that "property is theft" and that "the people are sovereign" are merely derived convictions. The root also of these erroneous notions lies in the denial of God and his commandments. In fact, these misconceptions are innocent compared to the fundamental fallacy, which became the mother of all sins and whose formulation cannot take place anywhere other than at the level of the church.

The question whether one may hold to erroneous ideas as long as they do not transition into punishable offences holds therefore also for religious fallacies as well. It is a matter of principle, and thus to be extended to every area of life in which the power of thoughts and the influence of words sway the temperament of the human heart and human relationships.

Whether one answers this question positively or negatively changes what you hold to be the case regarding: the church itself; the relationship between church and state; the limits of the state's power; the freedom of the press; the freedom of conscience and worship; the freedom of expression and association; yes indeed, regarding all the duties and activities of the state. The importance of this question is undeniable. Only if those with whom you engage give you an unequivocal answer to that question will you know where they are coming from.

The weight of this question is not merely limited to the state and society; it reaches *to beyond the grave.*

One might remember the question raised by Macaulay in his essay "Gladstone on Church and State" [1839]:

> All the reasons which lead us to think that parents are pecu-liarly fitted to conduct the education of their children, and that education is a principal end of the parental relation, lead us to think, that parents ought to be allowed to use punishment, if necessary, for the purpose of forcing children, who are incapa-ble of judging for themselves, to receive religious instruction and to attend religious worship. Why, then, is this prerogative of punishment, so eminently paternal, to be withheld from a paternal government? ... What reason can [Gladstone] give for hanging a murderer, and suffering a heresiarch to escape without even a pecuniary mulct? Is the heresiarch a less per-nicious member of society than the murderer? *Is not the loss of* **one soul** *a greater evil than the extinction of many lives?*[1]

If the Son of God expressly assures us: "He who does not believe the Son shall not see life" [John 3:36 NKJV], may a Christian society then tolerate that the next generation—unharmed and with impunity—will be against every belief in Jesus?

We are not putting this side of the problem in the foreground. We would prefer to stick to its political import. We only want to point out that the question—whose solution we will want to test—is not limited to matters of the state but has to do with the whole person; not only with his timebound existence, but also with his eternal being.

---

1. *Note by the author*: Thomas Babington Macaulay, *Critical and Historical Essays Contributed to the Edinburgh Review* (Leipzig: Bernh. Tauchnitz Jun., 1850), 3:278. [*Ed. note*: Emphases added by Kuyper. Otherwise the text above has been adapted to conform to the published version of Leipzig edition. William Gladstone (1809–98) was a leading liberal politician and prime minister in Victorian England.]

Those, including some of our contemporaries, who have wandered so far away that they cannot even imagine the possibility of a judgment day will not be interested in what we have to say.

We, on the other hand, who cannot imagine that there would *not* be a judgment, and who definitely reckon with the reality of "eternal salvation," may not close our eyes to that side of the question either. The government, too, is God's servant. It does not lie outside God's plan for the salvation of sinners but serves as an instrument to that end.

II

The enlightened circles of our century do not pay much heed to deviations and consider them sooner as useful than as pernicious. They do not even know error in other than a metaphorical sense. That false notions are punishable offenses is out the question.

This should not surprise us. For someone to stray presupposes *that there is a way*, a clearly marked trail; that there is a discernable *truth* from which one deviates; and that immediately returning to *the true way* is what justice requires and what self-preservation demands of those who wander from it. How could our century, which denies that there is such a way and dismisses the pretense of absolute truth as madness, ever condemn something as erroneous? Without a path there is no straying from it; without absolute truth there are no absolute errors opposed to it.

People can err with sums, confuse dates in history, mishandle a commercial transaction, make mistakes in calculating weighable and measurable data; but these sorts of mistakes, miscues, and identifiable corrigenda have nothing in common with the moral concept "to err."

To err does not refer to the world we can inch and pinch but has to do with things unseen. Only when one seeks to penetrate behind what is visible to that which lies hidden in the heart of man, in his affections and will, or attempts to think through the coherence that connects the finite and the infinite, does one come to the spiritual motives and factors—to those principles in everyone's life- and worldview—of which it can be said that they are erroneous.

At that level, "error" in its strict sense is not recognized by the prophets of the age. When everyone is searching and none have found, no one path can be identified and, hence, no one can be said to have strayed from that path. People make assumptions, construct systems, and have their opinions about most everything, but no matter how these opinions may differ, each has its relative right. Some may complain about a lack of clarity, about internal inconsistencies, or at least about being one-sided or backward, but will avoid the conclusion that something is "erroneous." Every aberrant idea is honored as a new angle on the prism's spectrum; having to go through all these phases is good for the healthy development of our knowledge; there is nothing more that we can do. When the fixed touchstone was left to the side, gold could no longer be proved to be either fake or real.

People allow themselves only one exception to that rule: they know for sure that "scriptural faith" is *undoubtedly* erroneous. That we, who still hold fast to the Christ of Scripture, err, is certain. That our standpoint is untenable is a certainty. Room can be found for most anything, except for fanatical narrow-mindedness. Everything must be tolerated, except for us. People see in the age-old faith of Christianity an extremely harmful aberration of which those coming of age today are not worthy and that, in the moral opinion of the world, is a strike against those who are afflicted by it.

That is just the way it is.

In the chorus of seekers, the only unbearable dissonance is the voice of "Eureka!" If the only truths you know are *relative*, those who speak of *the* truth strike you as arrogant and conceited. That error is not tolerated because it undermines the very logic of purely relative truths.

For the rest, everyone's convictions are respected; and not just those whose convictions they are, nor only the forthrightness with which those convictions are professed, but those convictions themselves. Even stirring up such points of contention is considered out of place. Let everyone think about the issues of life as they will. They need to figure that out for themselves. If people are civilized, decent, and agreeable in their manners, they may think and believe what they want.

We strongly reject this view.

To err is a moral evil, because our agreeing with or denial of a truth—not the arguments derived from it, but what it holds to be the case in principle—depends entirely on the moral character of our environment and of our heart.

To deny this is a direct denial of the fact that God has revealed himself.

To do so, one sets a different framework over against God's revelation, which upends comprehensive concepts, changes the prevailing way of thinking, changes one's notions of duty and calling, rearranges the moral organization of domestic and social life, and ultimately arrives in a *modern* world, which, being the opposite of what the Christian world should be, calls the good evil and the evil good.

From that vantage point, to err is indeed entirely culpable.

The counterargument, that one cannot improve matters if one does not see it otherwise, does not make sense. The same holds as well for crime. At the moment, neglected upbringing, deficient education, poor environment, one's own past, the harassment of others, and mental confusion all contribute to crime. Nevertheless, people consider crime a punishable offense.

The only difference here is that the power of those entitled to condemn error is different from those called on to adjudicate crimes.

Error and crime are both subject to God's punishment. Already now he is punishing both in one's conscience and in life's experiences; both will be disciplined when all things are brought to judgment. "Whoever does not obey the Son shall not see life, but the wrath of God remains on him" [John 3:36]. There is reconciliation, also for error, through a high priest who "can deal gently with the ignorant and wayward" (Heb 5:2); but this atonement presupposes the guilt.

Persistent deviance is liable to be punished in every ethically minded, principles-based corporation—so also in the church. Whoever strays from what a church confesses may not be left to do as they please. A permanent place in its midst is contingent on their returning to the moral principles of the community.

A father ought not to put up with error in this sense of waywardness in his children; they must be chastened. On the other hand, those who allow the root of evil to grow unhindered will lose the right to be angry with the deeds this waywardness generates.

The same holds for everyday life, for the academy, for the power of words; one may not let error persist. Those who allow error to fester make plain that they themselves lack a defined perspective and are hence unable to venture labelling anything as erroneous.

So, does the state also have the right and duty to chasten error and to counteract its influence?

Rome has said as much, and European governments have followed suit. The Reformers did—in part—as well.

The idea is not as absurd as some suggest. If error could be eradicated in this way, who would consider the sacrifice too great? If Rome's claim was true, that an infallible authority can always identify the truth, also in its derived applications, for all countries and peoples, why would one wince? Error is the cause of moral evil and of all our grief and misery. If, then, by dealing effectively and with unrelenting rigor with one generation, the error, crime, and misery of all subsequent generations could be averted, who would object to that firm hand?

If ... but if that infallible oracle is missing, if eradicating error in this way never succeeds, if, in contrast, doing so only generates more erroneous convictions, stimulates an increase in crime, multiplies the misery ... then of course not.

And yet, is that not what history teaches us?

III

If the state was indeed able to avoid the danger of making mistakes in effectively eradicating erroneous ideas, this would be its duty. Think of Israel. Eliminating idolatry and image worship, to rail against blasphemy, to prevent foreign influence, was in Israel undoubtedly the task of government. For kings not to fulfill that task was a dereliction of duty, a sign of unfaithfulness. The best kings were those who were vigilant in opposing error.

There was nothing wrong with this. The inexhaustible vitality that Israel owed to that strict policy is evident from the outcome; and the conditions were such that this course of action could lead to the goal without breaking the law.

These conditions were (1) they knew what to honor as truth, knew the false teachings to be averted, and—in the Urim and Thummim as well as in the prophets—had a means to obtain certainty in dubious cases; (2) the inner lives of the people remained free, while the truth that Israel confessed was worshipped richly in public; (3) Israel's religion was a state religion and, at the same time, the religion of the entire nation. And finally: Israel's state was only provisional in nature.

That we may not incorporate such an approach in today's world, unless meeting these same conditions is a real possibility, is self-evident. If God commands leviratical marriage, on the condition that it exclude private land ownership, one acts *against* God's will—and not *according* to it—by maintaining this arrangement when there is no communal family property.

In answer to the question whether European governments were correct when, following in Israel's footsteps, they included eradicating false teaching in the state's program, one need only examine whether the said conditions were present—not only a few of them, but all four in their mutual relationship. Was there an oracle that infallibly indicated the error for what it was? Did the error reveal itself in ways they could perceive? Was it something that the *people* believed? Did the situation prove to be temporary?

Rome believed that it was possible to answer these questions in the affirmative. In the absence of the Urim and Thummin as well as prophetism, it created its own infallible oracle in the "vicar of Christ, who sat on the chair of Peter."

The worship service of the Christian church was of the same cast as Israel's and defined with precision in all its forms, customs, and formulas. Not counting the schismatic East and small divergent groups here or there, that all the nations of Europe followed its confession was an undeniable fact.

Soo too, Rome also assumed that the situation was a temporary one. The yet unrestrained roughness of the Germans, the aftereffects of pagan and Muslim influence, and the incomplete infrastructure of its own organism had allowed weeds to take root. These issues could soon be eliminated. Then came the great era of a Roman Catholic Europe.

This regime fit together well. It was thought through and consistent. Its power was attractive. The only question is: Are the factors that make up this institution inwardly true, or were they intentionally crafted to fit into the system?

Our firm conviction is that the latter is the case.

There is no infallible authority in the sense that Rome ascribes this to the pope.

The well-crafted externality of the worship service, within which Rome developed, is a work of art.

The nations were Roman Catholic only insofar as they were just outgrowing their childish ways and had not yet come of age.

The situation in which this institution arose was not a provisional one but would remain as it was. Instances of differentiation would not diminish, but they were initially timid in proceeding.

The Reformers too, and even the Puritans in America, cannot be acquitted of the suspicion that they were attracted to this arrangement as well.

John Calvin rejected the attempt to choose Israel's situation as a permanent criterion as "false and foolish," but the Reformers did not entirely escape the Roman Catholic view of the state.[2]

---

2. See *Inst.* 4.20.14.

They did reject the authority of the pope but believed that the synodical structure was a safe guide to distinguish between truth and error.

Although they rejected Rome's ways of worship, they found solace in a no less detailed description, breakdown, and definition of doctrine.

The illusion of the Reformation period was that all the nations of Europe would soon together embrace the single confession of a purified Christianity.

That the Reformers regarded the situation as a temporary one can be forgiven.

Nonetheless, our Reformers were in principle opposed to this endeavor. Practice would reveal this difference, and with the first spiritual movement that followed this change in practice, an opposite course of action very consciously had to be chosen.

That practice made its way into our country. It was John Milton who articulated the new principle.[3] Since then, the two perspectives stood over against each other.

On the one hand, the Roman Catholic approach: the state must use its strong arm to resist error. This framework came into vogue with degrees of difference in its application in all of Europe, except for England. Its thesis was contested by the French Revolution, but actually imitated in its own practices. Renewal under the motto of an all-powerful state becomes hegemony, only with this difference: previously, everything but Christianity was excluded, but today everything is tolerated except Christianity. *False notions* are now described as *truth* used to be.

On the other hand, there is the approach rooted in the life of the Reformed and first expressed by Milton. It gradually came to stand out in England and America, and, as far as everyday practice is concerned, is also followed in our country; namely, that the state as such can only punish erroneous ideas when they are interpreted in specific actions.

Both approaches deserve closer scrutiny.

IV

As we saw, there are two diametrically opposed answers to the question: Are erroneous ideas a punishable offense?

For the state to impair and attack error for what it was is the Roman Catholic position.

---

3. John Milton (1608–74), the English poet and intellectual, published an influential treatise on liberty, the *Areopagitica* (1644).

For the government to leave erroneous ideas alone until people act on them is the other. This is what Milton called for and, with an ever-milder spirit, was granted in Britain and America.

We are not interested in the Roman Catholic Church as such here, but only with what its doctrine teaches regarding the state. We hardly need to be reminded that Rome also is authorized and obligated to discipline—and when necessary to excommunicate—those of its members who oppose its principle of life. But that lies beyond our scope. We are interested in what it holds regarding the state.

We ask our readers to carefully think through Rome's approach, which *could not help but* end with the Inquisition.

There is a government. The government is God's servant, called to carry out his will; which means that it must know what God's will is. God grants knowledge of his will through the organ of his church, which, if it is to offer an unshakeable foundation for public law, must provide more than an opinion but rather a firm pronouncement, a statement that is not open to debate but is infallible—and respected by everyone as infallible. For if the government is to have the moral support of the nation, the foundation on which it rests must also be true and holy in the eyes of the people. To admit and disseminate the view that the church's doctrine is fallible breaks open a gulf between the government and the people that will undermine its authority and raze the state.

If there was indeed such an infallible doctrine, nothing could counter this syllogistic argument.

From that point of view, it would even be incongruous to tolerate another form of public worship.

To allow a segment within the nation to oppose the infallibility of that teaching would undermine the security of the state.

To tolerate the dissemination of dissimilar insights amounts to intentionally fostering mutiny and resistance.

From that perspective, censoring the printed word is the state's duty, as controlled by the church.

The freedom of the press, of expression, of speech, and of association can never be reconciled with this arrangement.

Faced with infallible church doctrine, freedom of conscience amounts to letting go of the erring conscience, and is hence loveless and dubious at the same time.

Restraining the printed word and the right to assemble are not enough from this point of view. Erroneous ideas can also be spread via conversations, letters, and derisive comments. In fact, errant persons are by their very presence an embodied protest against the legal authorities. The error persists as long as they are alive and well. As a result, inquests into suspected false teachings, in light of their malicious persistence, require the state—for its own self-preservation—to remove or eliminate the persons in question.

The fact that Philip II preferred to murder thousands of his subjects than to tolerate those confessing what he took to be errant was not randomness on his part.[4] The loathing he incited was likewise not because of his alleged wantonness. It was a result of a revulsion for the hardness of his heart, which, even in light of such inhumane consequences, did not recognize the unsustainability of the system.[5]

That the Roman Catholic authorities no longer apply this system with rigor is due to three reasons: (1) there are no longer any Roman Catholic governments in the strict sense of the word; though possibly still in South America; (2) the resistance to Rome has also been so strong in Roman Catholic countries that it cannot be contained or tamed by force; (3) applying the system is bound to fail because the greater part of the people in Europe are not on the same page in this regard.

The Peace of Münster was from the side of Roman Catholic governments grounds for putting the system on nonactive.[6]

The impossibility they found themselves in, trying to apply the system they confessed, was the most serious blow that the Reformation inflicted on Rome's view of the state.

The establishment of the *state church*, which then had emerged, shared in the hatred of the principle, but lacked—owing to half-heartedness—its strength.

---

4. Philip II (1556–98) was king of Spain during an especially intense period of the Inquisition as well as Spanish rule over the Netherlands.
5. That is, the system of ecclesiastical jurisdiction that Spain had received from the Vatican in prosecuting the Inquisition.
6. The Peace of Münster (1648) marked the end of the Eighty Years' War and the independence of the Netherlands from Spanish rule.

The system of state churches as it took shape after and through the Reformation is based on the difference between the majority of *regular inhabitants* and *others*. Only that main element of regular inhabitants makes up the actual nation, the national family, or household. That major portion of the nation confesses one religion and are members of one denomination. Only that part of the nation counts; it is they who exercise influence on the administration and can fill posts and occupy offices. The others are merely guests. They may be there, but nothing more than that. They do not participate in the administration of the country, nor do they have any influence regarding the future of the nation. They are not part of the family and are only tolerated to the extent that they respect the habits and rights of the regular inhabitants.

That is what the state church was like originally in all countries. It was the only thing that made sense from a constitutional point of view. Anything that deviated from this practice would be arbitrary and negate the system in principle. A resident is at the mercy of the landlord.

This system afforded people little joy. Where it still seemed to hold sway, as it did in Italy and Sweden for a while, they had actually returned to the strict Roman Catholic system. The landlord did not welcome—or showed the door to—those who did not please him.

On the other hand, in countries where the system of distinguishing regular inhabitants from guests was absolutely followed, experience everywhere taught that the guests provoked the inhabitants and spoiled family traditions. That is how things were in Germany, in England, and in our country. You are not protected from an infectious disease by sending the sick to a backroom of the house. Those who are infected will remain a threat to you as long as you allow them to stay. The only adequate measure is to *remove them from your home.*

People came no further with these hesitations. Another system had to be adopted; either that or return to Rome's approach. Mind you, I am talking here about the state, and not about the church.

Milton suggested this other system. In other words, an antirevolutionary, and not a liberalist, was its first advocate. You will find it set forth in his *Areopagitica.*[7] Its main ideas are found in [scriptural] statements such as these:

---

7. John Milton, *Areopagitica; A speech of Mr. John Milton For the Liberty of Unlicenc'd Printing* (London, 1644).

No human being can tame the tongue. It is a restless evil [Jas 3:8].

Do not be overcome by evil, but overcome evil with good [Rom 12:21].

Not by might, nor by power, but by my Spirit, says the LORD of hosts [Zech 4:6].

"Do you want us to go and gather [these weeds]?" But [Jesus] said, "No, lest in gathering the weeds you root up the wheat along with them" [Matt 13:28-29].

"Teacher, we saw someone casting out demons in your name, and we tried to stop him, because he was not following us." But Jesus said, "Do not stop him" [Mark 9:38-39].

Woe to the world for temptations to sin! For it is necessary that temptations come [Matt 18:7].

V

Milton's approach is outlined in his *Areopagitica*, which was published in 1644. It is honored by experts, even more than his *Tractate on Education*, as the masterpiece among his prose writings.[8] Understood well, it is merely an elaboration of the words of Paul: "There must be factions among you in order that those who are genuine among you may be recognized" (1 Cor 11:19); which in turn echo the more well-known verse: Christ is "a sign that is opposed ... so that thoughts from many hearts may be revealed" [Luke 2:34-35].

Milton's key themes can be summarized as follows:

1. In combating error, the government's calling is to give the truth as much room as possible.

2. This occurs:

    a) if the truth can be expressed unhindered;

---

8. John Milton, *Of Education* (1644).

b) if those professing the truth are seriously pushed to defend it when error clearly emerges;

c) when the prospect of error's claiming a martyr's crown is removed.

3. Consequently, the state must see to it that words and thoughts must be left free; not because man naturally chooses the truth, but because God, whose truth it is, lives and maintains it through spiritual means.

4. The only exceptions are Roman Catholic doctrine and atheism.

Regarding this last point he says literally:

> I mean not tolerated Popery, and open superstition, which as it extirpats all religions and civil supremacies, so itself should be extirpat, provided first that all charitable and compassionate means be us'd to win and regain the weak and misled; that also which is impious or evil absolutely either against faith or manners, no law can possibly permit, that intends not to unlaw it self.[9]

Apparently, the effect of Milton's writings was minimal. His only triumph was that Gilbert Mabot, someone charged with the licensing of books to be printed, requested on May 22, 1649, that he be discharged on the grounds that the state's inspection of printed documents was "unjust and illegal."[10] Even at the beginning of King William III's reign, Parliament issued another bill that threatened severe punishment for any "who assert, or maintain, that there are more Gods than one, or deny the Christian religion to be true, or the holy scriptures of the Old and New Testament to be of divine authority."[11] It was not until 1694 that Milton's approach was incorporated into English law, when Parliament refused to reauthorize the government's

---

9. Milton, *Areopagatica*, 37.

10. Gilbert Mabbot (1622–ca. 1670) served as the official licenser of the press from 1647–49 during the English Civil War. Mabbot was himself an influential publisher and journalist, and he reportedly resigned his post as censor out of conscientious objection to the office, citing arguments from Milton's *Areopagitica*.

11. This is related in James Fitzjames Stephen, *Liberty, Equality, Fraternity* (London: Smith, Elder, 1873), 75n*.

control over the printed word.[12] As a result of the measures pushed through by Charles Fox in 1792 and William Pitt in 1798, the restraints were lifted, such that unlimited freedom could also occasion libel.[13]

The same approach was defended by Edmund Burke—also an antirevolutionary—in his defense of the Irish and the Methodists.[14] He therefore differs with Milton regarding Roman Catholics, extending freedom to them as well, while retaining Milton's exclusion of atheism.

Given the above, the fact that thanks are due to England, and not to the French Revolution, for the freedoms of conscience and of expression needs no further explanation.

That the French National Convention [1792–95] also adopted the notion of the freedom of conscience in its program is known. But we also know:

a) that the French revolutionaries vehemently persecuted clergy who refused to take the oath of allegiance to the French Republic;

b) that Jean-Paul Marat, Georges Danton, and Maximilien de Robespierre merely pushed the limits of what was—without exception—the rule for all the governments of the revolution, namely, to use incarceration and the guillotine to silence every opinion that was not sanctioned by the government;[15] and

---

12. *Note by the author*: Stephen, *Liberty, Equality, Fraternity*, 75; and Friedrich Julius Stahl, *Die Philosophie des Rechts*, 3rd ed. (Heidelberg: Mohr, 1856), 2:497.

13. See Stahl, *Die Philosophie des Rechts*, 497–98. William Pitt the Younger (1759–1806) was a prominent Tory politician and prime minister of Great Britain (1783–1801) and the United Kingdom (1804–6). Charles Fox (1746–1806) was a leading Whig politician and opponent of William Pitt the Younger.

14. Edmund Burke (1729–97) was a longtime member of Parliament and political philosopher. He is perhaps most famous for his sharp criticisms of the French Revolution, and his support for church establishment was tempered by consistent and long-standing calls for extension of toleration of those outside the establishment. See Michael W. McConnell, "Establishment and Toleration in Edmund Burke's Constitution of Freedom," *Supreme Court Review* (1995): 393–462.

15. Jean-Paul Marat (1743–94) was a radical journalist and controversialist and who served as a rallying force for Jacobins. Georges Danton (1759–94) was an early leader of the French Revolution, eventually guillotined for alleged corruption. Maximilien Robespierre (1758–94) was one of the most infamous of the Revolutionary leaders and one of the engineers of the Reign of Terror, during which an estimated 17,000 people were executed.

c) that the printing presses have never been more stringently suppressed than under the thoroughly revolutionary regime of Napoleon.[16]

The fact that the freedom of the press in particular was not the result of the French Revolution or of Britain's national character but owing to Milton's efforts—and thus grew from antirevolutionary roots—stands out all the more clearly when one takes into account the fact that prior to his involvement censorship of the press was nowhere more pressing and tyrannical than in England. Just think of the Court of Star Chamber![17]

Rome's way of doing things and Milton's have often been characterized as being the one preventive and the other repressive. The preventive approach is said to prevent the publication and distribution of erroneous books, whereas the repressive approach punishes the writer or publisher of a published work that proves to be inappropriate. Friedrich Stahl, however, rightly observes that this distinction is not accurate because the second approach also prevents—once the published work is confiscated—further dissemination.[18] The pertinent question is not whether one works preventatively or repressively, but whether oversight of the press is given to the police or to the courts.

But even then, the scope of the issue is understood too narrowly.

People can be punished directly, but also indirectly. The state can privilege my opponent through provisions in the law, via the treasury, or by using its influence to confer accolades and offices. That preferential treatment happens at my expense. By being disadvantaged in this way, the state is punishing my convictions because it finds them inappropriate or erroneous.

James Fitzjames Stephen has quite rightly said: "The difference between ... paying a single shilling of public money to a single school in

---

16. The triumph of Napoleon Bonaparte (1769-1821) in the French Revolutionary Wars led to the establishment of the French Empire.

17. This "supreme" court evolved from meetings of the King's Council but became a political weapon during the reign (1509-47) of Henry VIII (1491-1547), under the leadership of Cardinal Thomas Wolsey (ca. 1473-1530) and Thomas Cranmer (1489-1556). Charles I (1600-49) used the court to prosecute dissenters. Its jurisdiction (and control of the press) collapsed around 1641.

18. See Stahl, *Die Philosophie des Rechts*, 499-500.

which any opinion is taught of which any single taxpayer disapproves, and the maintenance of the Spanish Inquisition, is a question of degree."[19]

So, we must investigate three things:

1. What are grounds on which Milton's approach rests?

2. What can be inferred from those grounds for the policy of the state?

3. To what an extent is state policy in the Netherlands contrary to this principle?

Yes, that last point as well.

After all, one must be certain that one's opposing the claim that erroneous beliefs are a punishable offense does not turn into favorable and preferential treatment of those ideas, and, under the rallying cry of the freedom of expression, leads to veiled animosity on the part of the state toward the Christian truth.

VI THE GROUNDS ON WHICH MILTON'S SYSTEM RESTS (1)

As was already clear from the tone of our first article about whether error is a punishable offense, we are not about to underestimate the danger that error poses. The watchword of our contemporaries as commonly understood, that "all convictions have a right to respect," evinces, also in our view, inexcusable thoughtlessness. The issue is not about cutting through the thread of life that binds the life of our mind and of our heart together for the sake of a zeal for the freedom of thought. Intellectual and moral well-being are inseparable. Because the ethos of our century has weaned itself from faith in the truth, it also lacks any sense of earnestness in the face of error.

Those who ask that errant teachings be punished by the state as well can in no way blame us that we are inclined to gloss over erroneous ideas or are driven by a surreptitious incredulity toward absolute truth. That may be the case for a liberalist, but not for an antirevolutionary.

That the attempt has been made, the possibility explored, to vanquish error through coercion, we entirely comprehend. One does not automatically dislodge a mindset, the likes of which even Plato was a zealous

---

19. Stephen, *Liberty, Equality, Fraternity*, 53.

advocate,[20] by merely charging it with incongruity. Only experience can unequivocally demonstrate that an erroneous mindset is untenable. It will only fall if the proving of it fails.

But that is exactly what happened to this formidable attempt to violently subdue error. It did not simply remain a model in theory but was put into practice. It was not introduced as holding merely for a few but was applied in every country over the course of many centuries. It has been used as a weapon by various authorities, many with very diverse objectives. It has been introduced, modified, revised, and stripped of questionable concoctions in all kinds of ways, such that no one will deny that its application has been both exhaustive and universal, protracted and conclusive.

And it is precisely in the trial by fire that practice provides that this seemingly timeless, venerable model definitively gave way, without even the possibility of appealing the verdict, to the court of justice and fairness.

It did not collapse because it was met with the whip and noose, with the rack and woodpile; if this argument held, then punishing the criminal would also have to be rejected. Rather, it collapsed because it served error instead of exorcizing it, held back the triumph of the truth, and enlisted the guilty to oppress the innocent. The mine, however well-intended originally, invariably proved destroy its own fortifications instead of the enemy's ramparts. Seeking to suppress error with error, they gave truth a weapon with which it could not rescue a soul but only maim its own more noble parts.

Found to be ineffective is the heaviest blow that this system, by venturing out on black ice, has inflicted on itself.

Ineffective: despite the unbelievably coldblooded callousness with which Roman emperors sought to exterminate what they believed was the error of the Christian faith, that "error" has prevailed! Ineffective: even though what the Argus eyes[21] of the inquisitors of the Roman Curia found to be erroneous in the teachings of the Waldensians, of Wycliff, Hus, and Jerome

---

20. Plato famously argued for the responsibility of the government to suppress artistic expressions judged to elicit immorality, evil, and corruption. See Plato, *The Republic of Plato*, trans. John Llewelyn Davies and David James Vaughan (Cambridge: Macmillan, 1852), book 3, p. 107, 401b: "Ought we to confine ourselves to superintending our poets, and compelling them to impress on their productions the likeness of a good moral character, on pain of not composing among us; or ought we to extend our superintendence to the professors of every other craft as well, and forbid them to impress those signs of an evil nature, of dissoluteness, of meanness, and of ungracefulness?"
21. This refers to Argus Panoptes, the many-eyed, all-seeing giant of Greek mythology.

of Prague and then sought to cut out of the hearts of the people—cost what it might—their "errors" were compelling and ended up alienating half of Europe from Rome.[22] Ineffective: even if all the Protestant governments inundate their files with prohibitive ordinances, the fragmentation among believers has run its course, heresy has erupted after heresy, and that precisely is why the most stubborn and fiercely contested errors remain defiantly standing in the room.

That said, it did sometimes *seem* as though these kinds of efforts were hitting their target. In Spain and Italy, the overwhelming zeal for coercive measures was so devastating and reckless that it at least *appeared* that the opposition had indeed been stifled. But this too should not mislead us. Their goal was to preserve the truth, and not to eradicate error; but see what Rome's teaching was able to achieve in Spain, now purified of the Protestant leaven; see how it worked out in Cartagena for the Spanish Empire; or ask what it gained in Italy when the popes became "the prisoners in the Vatican!"[23]

This result—this judgment of history—so straightforward and unequivocal, is one very rarely offered us. Nowhere ever, however you look at it, has the seemingly so commendable strategy to promote the triumph of the truth through the violent suppression of error yielded a different outcome from that error gained ground and the truth suffered loss.

This is true of the direct coercion as well as the indirect constraints they employed. Even when people were horrified by the use of torture, saw the inquisitor as inhumane, and could not even tolerate the word *inquisition*, and they nevertheless endeavored to weaken the power of error by excluding people from offices and positions, by using the weapon of privilege and the state church, fiscal taunts, and keeping a tight rein on free movement, the outcome invariably brought the policy of coercion to naught, exposed the powerlessness of compulsory means, and hurt the truth.

Nonetheless, even while fully acknowledging this condemning report, one needs to be fair. *That approach was itself an erroneous idea;* one whose inner perversity and deceit could only show itself through its being granted

---

22. All of those referred to here were found to be heretical and suppressed by various means by the pre-Reformation Roman Catholic Church.

23. Kuyper is referring to the papal response after 1870, when Italy's king Vittorio Emanuele II (1820–78) proclaimed Rome to be the capital of Italy, shearing the papacy of political sovereignty over the "holy" city and the "Romangna" (the former Papal States), and making Pope Pius IX (1792–1878) the "prisoner in the Vatican."

free reign. That Cato wanted to ban Greek literature,[24] that Plato sought to suppress free artistic expression, that our fathers sought refuge in local ordinances and the closed appointment of offices, is no reason for us to pat ourselves on the back. Had we lived when they did, we might well have done the same. After all, they lacked what we know today and what their coercive agenda brought to light. The law that governs the spiritual relationship between truth and error would still belong to the realm of mysteries were it not for the price of such a nameless atrocity that truth's natural maxim was discovered: "Invincible! ... provided that it has never been disputed."

The historical argument that we referred to is for Milton simply the root from which his means of proof arise like so many shoots. The historical proof is the decisive factor; the rest only helps to measure the force that lies in this result of history.

VII THE GROUNDS ON WHICH MILTON'S SYSTEM RESTS (2)

History shows that the strategy of seeking to "vanquish error through coercion" failed the test. That failure was owing to four causes: the strategy was (1) impracticable and (2) unprofitable, and it went (3) against nature and (4) against the Christian faith. Milton shows this from the constraints laid on the printed word because the printing press, even though its reach was less than it is today, stood out already at the time; and is still today the most powerful vehicle for errant ideas. "The meeting," which currently rivals the press's influence on the mind of the public, was not yet part of the panoply in Milton's day.

The strategy is impracticable.

Traveling through the air would certainly be preferable to traveling by land and sea, provided that ways were found to control the erratic gusting of the wind. Without that, air travel is impractical. Now, the approach that Milton combated faced a similar kind of challenge. For the state to counter error with coercion, three things are essential, without which this tactic cannot be put into practice.

These three conditions speak for themselves. The state must know what is erroneous and what is true; it must have agents who can make judgments

---

24. Roman statesman Cato the Elder (234–149 BC) was a well-known critic of Greek culture and science.

on its behalf given these criteria; and, for justice to be just, the evidence of error must be bona fide—mere suspicion will not do.

The entire project is doomed if the first of these three—there must be a standard—is not met.

How does the government decide what is true? To leave this question to the church apparently worked as long as there was only one church, but since the number of churches has increased that is completely impossible. What would then lead the state in choosing between one church and another? A person can make such a choice, but how can the state do that? Especially in a state in which those who serve on the crown's behalf are always changing? To defer to God's Word solves little in this regard. Scripture as such—without interpretation—is seldom definitive. Doesn't every heretic have his own favorite chapters and verses?[25] Will the state choose between one interpretation or the next? Or do you trust the state to interpret the text on its own? Appealing to reason, likewise, brings us no further. That two statesmen, both rational thinkers, often come to opposing conclusions is not uncommon. Who is right? Moreover, choosing reason as the determining factor would require the prosecution of every revealed religion. Were reason the standard, then only philosophers would see aright, and error would be the lot of every Christian.

This approach also cannot satisfy the second requirement. Authorized judges who are qualified to make such decisions cannot be found.

Remember that, according to this tactic, the state must appoint enough sufficiently skilled, strictly honest men who will search for error everywhere and clearly and correctly distinguish and mark it for what it is. Rash scoffers, serious thinkers, and penny-a-liner journalists, as well as professors, historians, and poets, will all be subject to their assessment. Who is competent enough to evaluate these things? The state would need to choose the most brilliant and skillful minds, without exception, to carry out this commission. Just imagine the intellectual development that would be lost if the country's best thinkers would have to waste their time and energy on the mind-numbing task of reading everything that is printed and to do so in such a way as to be sure of also finding burgeoning erroneous ideas. And yet, when the state lacks staff of this caliber, it subjects talent to the

---

25. Here Kuyper invokes the popular observation that every heretic (Dutch: *ketter*) has his own favorite scriptural text (*letter*).

critique of stupidity, genius to the lowbrow guise of everyday life, and the roles are reversed, allowing incompetent folks to evaluate the experts.

This approach is equally flawed when it comes to the third requirement: providing sound proof is not feasible.

Although this might be possible were this condition limited to prosecuting erroneous notions distributed via the printed word, but that is hardly thorough enough. As Milton rightly says, this would be like closing the eastern city gate, only to allow the enemy free access via the western gate.[26] Error nestles within a person, in the disposition of his heart, and for that very reason belongs to those hidden recesses about which guesses are conceivable, but about which certainty is beyond the reach of third parties.

You do not implement air travel unless the air listens to the yoke, the air resistance forces are known, and the speed remains within the margins of safety. But as long as these three criteria are not met, one may not take on passengers. Continuing to build railway embankments and steamships is the best option. Your project might be impressive, but it is impracticable.

This strategy is unprofitable as well.

After all, in the uncertainty regarding what to eradicate as error and what to retain as the truth there is obviously always the danger that the state will be mistaken time and again. People will in good faith take for true what is erroneous, and label as erroneous what will later prove to be true. In brief, lacking a fixed standard, the state will despite itself do the opposite of what the strategy intends and by prosecuting the truth not suppress error but stimulate its spreading.

That is not an empty assumption, but the sad reality. Despite what this strategy intends, history shows that it is invariably truth itself, and seldom error, that is persecuted, suppressed, and bound.

Turn to whichever century you wish in *Book of Martyrs* and you will find the model of coercion hounding not error but the truth.[27]

---

26. See Milton, *Areopagitica*, 16: "For if the fell upon one kind of strictnesse, unlesse their care were equall to regulat all other things of like aptness to corrupt the mind, that single endeavor they knew would be but a fond labour; to shut and fortifie one gate against corruption, and be necessitated to leave others round about wide open."
27. Kuyper provided an introduction to a new edition of Adriaan van Haemstede's *History of Martyrs* (1559), appearing as *Geschiedenis der Martelaren* (Doesburg: Van Schenk Brill, 1883).

That is not all, however. Milton exclaims, "The State shall be my governours, but not my criticks."[28] But the state does level critiques. When the state takes on being the inspector, the government is also implicitly sanctioning what it does not censor. What eludes its censorship is then current, endorsed with the great seal and recommended to the public as honorable and harmless. If one takes the impossibility of applying this assurance with rigor and the thus understandable sloppiness with which this system is always implemented, then here too one arrives at the opposite of what was intended. Erroneous notions were to be branded, but instead they are acknowledged.

The fable about the man who closed the gate to his garden to keep the crows away from his cherry trees applies here as well. Error exploits every aspect of the multifaceted wealth of human life. It uses pen and ink, but also whispered conversations; it catches the eye, and mixes in with the banter, play, entertainment, yes, even in the clothing and finery of everyday. Must all of this be assessed? Does the state have Argus eyes and ears? Is the state a god then, spying on everything that moves, divining the message of every thought? And if not, what do you gain if you raise the drawbridge to defend your castle, if the hostility of false ideas takes to swimming the moat or tunneling under your walls or perching on the ramparts of your fortress?

There is a cordon to every coercive effort; it is all about keeping error out. But how will that happen as long as Europe—indeed, the entire world—is not administered by a single state? What do you gain by suppressing erroneous ideas on your own if they are continually imported from afar? Citizens cross the border year after year and return home contaminated. Or will one also have to break up the market for foreign literature and ban traveling abroad?

And even if you could, where would you start when it came to the trove of literature from the past? There is not a single Latin or Greek writer who did not go wrong. Should we also ban the classics and quell all classical development in order to have the thinking mind starve and waste away on state-implemented rations?

Even those who opposed the freedom of expression most fiercely did not go that far. They could do no more than close the garden gate, and in the meantime the crows feasted on the beautiful cherry trees.

But is a scheme that turned out to be so unprofitable not ridiculous?

---

28. Milton, *Areopagitica*, 22.

So too, it failed to take the human heart into account, which comes into the world with the germ of error. Suffering from the evils of Pelagianism, it forgot what Milton reminds us of so clearly: "Assuredly we bring not innocence into the world, we bring impurity much rather; that which purifies us is triall, and triall is by what is contrary."[29]

VIII THE GROUNDS ON WHICH MILTON'S SYSTEM RESTS (3)

To maintain the truth through the coercive repression of false teachings is, it turns out, impracticable and unprofitable, but also, as we seek now to demonstrate, contrary to nature and to the faith.

Contrary to nature: that is to say, contrary both to the nature of truth and the nature of error. Coercion does not eradicate error. The truth does not benefit from material support, but it does suffer unquestionable damage with every strong-armed intervention on its behalf.

We are talking here about coercion; coercion exercised by the state, and hence exclusively about the circumstances and relationships of this earthly life. Our claim is a fact that no one can deny: error is just as indispensable to bring out the truth—to make it strong and triumphant—as the radiance of light cannot be imaged without the contrast of darkness.

We know that these circumstances are only provisional, that there is another world in which this contrast falls away, but we may not take this into account when it comes to political life. The political realm must focus on the circumstances that exist in this dispensation.

Judge then if there is anything conclusive to submit to counter these three givens: (1) no one arrives at the truth without having first been prey to a greater or lesser degree of error; (2) truth does not become a moral power without first having overcome error in a legitimate struggle; and (3) in all further development of the truth, the new that is found is initially mixed with error.

These three have altogether nothing in common with the interpretation currently in vogue, as though error is a necessary process that the truth must go through as does a child through the years of innocence. *Error and truth are incompatible.* The one does not develop from the other. A reciprocally persistent and restless combat is their calling. Truth does not triumph until it sees error vanquished at its feet.

---

29. Milton, *Areopagitica*, 13.

Having established that no one is by nature—of themselves—without error, it follows that a policy of coercion can only breed hypocrisy and pretense, giving voice to words that the heart opposes, countermanding people into giving the confession of truth a false sense of triumph.

If it cannot be denied that a truth that has not first proved its soundness by enduring spiritual struggle lacks an audacious sense of resilience, then it also follows that one dishonors the truth if one brings its opponent bound into the arena. This was done to please the Roman emperors, for example, who themselves craving the laurels of the arena had defenseless gladiators put to the sword. But all those in Rome with the heart of a warrior also detested the cowardice that avoided bona fide combat and yet sought the honor of victory. This also holds for the truth. If it is to command respect, to inspire awe, to fell error, and to rule one's life, then that monster must first be set free to confront it in the arena. Only in such a struggle does it become aware of its grandeur, unfurling its hidden powers and revealing itself as a divine power that impresses one with its royal appearance.

Christian theology expresses this meaningfully through its confession that Christ should not crush Satan but must conquer him according to the rules of justice. These hold for Satan as well, and therein specifically lies his reproach and Christ's honor; namely, that, despite the fullness of the rights granted him, he nevertheless succumbs.

In the administration of justice, a similar conviction prevailed. Even the most gruesome criminal is represented by a defense attorney. If he does not choose one, he is assigned one. Why? Simply because the eminence of the law does not tolerate that even the criminal should succumb unless it be shown beyond doubt that his actions were unwarranted.

According to the testimony of history, this also holds for the truth. As often as those who confess the truth are forced by error-driven opponents to whet their spiritual sword and defend themselves, the truth has shone in all its splendor, has proved to be a living power, and has adorned itself with heavenly laurels. On the other hand, when shielded by the strong arm of the law, the confession of the truth has changed as if into stone, losing its reputation by becoming literalistic and formulaic in its worship, losing the moral courage that it needs to be a blessing to the heart and in society.

Finally, as things developed further, the fact that the newly found truth was always mixed with error argues adamantly against every system of coercion. So too, in seeking to reverse error, every new development of the truth is also cut off. People stick to what was once found good and nip in the bud every new form in which the truth wants to show itself to us. That is why even Marcus Aurelius persecuted Christianity[30] and why Rome, given its fraudulent position, could not allow Luther's word to lead European society down new paths. A good deal of antagonism toward the academic disciplines takes root for similar reasons, and the recurrent longing for repristination is grounded in the same error.

This point of view evidences a lack of faith. Milton points this out as well. Using coercion to suppress error is contrary to the faith—and that in three ways.

It deprives the Christian church of its most beautiful task in life, betrays mistrust in its power, infringes on its rights, and is hence the cause of its degradation and decay. A church that is protected by means of coercion is as little able to move freely as a healthy person whom you would ask to use two crutches. A church that accepts that kind of safeguard retreats from the open air to the back of the house, becoming anemic and sick.

So too, leaning on coercion does not take God into account either. If people, among themselves, had to fight the case between truth and error to the end, the venture would be foolhardy, and truth's plight be irrevocably lost. But the Christian faith disputes this—confessing, as it does, that God himself maintains his truth and that we serve only as his instruments.

Finally, the destiny of divine truth is not to triumph visibly in the here and now. The current dispensation is actually characterized by the ever-increasing service of physical forces to the power of error. We know in the light of prophecy that the apparent triumph of error will become even more dreadful than it is today. And yet that era will come to an end, and Christ will return. Only then will we experience the ultimate outcome of the irrec-oncilable struggle being waged today between the light and the darkness.

Until then, the cross of Christ remains the law of life; and his words to the impetuous disciple—"Put your sword into its sheath" [John 18:11]—hold for us as well. The twelve legions of angels above stand at the ready but are held back out of respect for the truth. "If my kingdom were from this world, my servants would have been fighting. ... But my kingdom is not from the world" [John 18:36].

---

30. Marcus Aurelius (121–180) was a Roman emperor and Stoic philosopher famed for his wisdom and temperance.

IX WHICH STATE-LEVEL POLICIES FIT WITH THE "FREEDOM OF CONSCIENCE"? (1)

Without neglecting in the least the serious danger with which error threatens moral life and the well-being of society, we came to the conclusion that every coercive approach should be rejected unconditionally.

Error can never be in a worse situation—and truth never in a better state—than under the rule of freedom.

> Who ever knew Truth put to the worse in a free and open encounter? Her confuting is the best and surest suppressing. ... For who knows not that Truth is strong, next to the Almighty; she needs no policies, nor stratagems, nor licensings to make her victorious; those are the shifts and the defenses that error uses against her power: give her but room, and do not bind her when she sleeps.[31]

That is not the language of nineteenth-century revolutionaries, but of an antirevolutionary in 1644.

What is the state's duty in this regard?

The government, too, is the servant of God. It, too, is called to place its power and influence, and the talents entrusted to it, in the service of truth and righteousness. If we, like our fathers, summarize the many faces of error, for the sake of brevity, under the term "idolatry," then we believe that the state, too, is called on "remove and prevent all idolatry and false worship."[32] The power that is granted to the government is misused if it is not set up and exercised in such a way as is required by the interests and the triumph of the truth.

If the cause of the truth requires the government to intervene on its behalf, then its sword should be drawn.

If, however, it appears that the interests and triumph of the truth take exception to any form of coercion, then the government must comply with that protest and police the state accordingly.

That service is the humbler of the two.

At the old tournaments, while the knights jousted, the judge sat in the seat of honor and the herald of arms at the entrance to the park. The judge awarded the winning warrior the palm of honor; the herald of arms only

---

31. Milton, *Areopagitica*, 35–36.
32. Belgic Confession, Art. 36.

had to see to it that the appropriate rules were adhered to. To be appointed tournament judge was a great honor; the position of herald was less so.

What role does the government play in the tournament between the truth and error?

Until then, they thought: the judge. The government chose. The government decided. The government awarded the prize.

Therein lay the mistake. The government cannot sit in the tribunal for this spiritual tournament. Its task in this regard is to be the herald of arms, the gatekeeper at the entrance to the arena. It engages police supervision to prevent "vile tricks" and sees to it that everyone, irrespective of persons, has an equal chance. It has a heart for the truth but would fall short of honoring it by interfering. The most that the government may do is to always maintain the inviolability of the law. The state does not preside as judge, but *God Almighty himself*; the government, his servant, waits at the gate.

From this it follows that the calling of the state is to keep the arena open and free for the spiritual struggle, doing so through legislation, dispensing justice, and governmental policy.

This presupposes the freedoms of conscience and confession, of expression in speech and in the printed word, of association and assembly, of education and nurturing.

The freedom of conscience. One's conscience is fallible. Whoever denies this does not know himself. The conscience need not be respected for *what* it says, but *that* it is speaking. The conscience is the free person's final refuge, the innermost of his personality, the direct contact of his heart with the order of a higher world. Warp one's conscience and one's freedom, and moral resilience and personal independence are done for. That is why statutory laws, whenever possible, must avoid any conflict with people's conscience; the laws' strength will be enhanced, should it come to that, by avoiding the matter and not following through.

For example: a state that maintains people's freedom of conscience and, consequently, exempts some one hundred Mennonites from military service will be the stronger for it than another country that pays no heed to conscience and requires every last person to serve in the military.

But one must distinguish between *doing* and *allowing*. To force someone *to do what his conscience forbids* him is tyranny. On the other hand, by *allowing* people to do everything that their conscience often demands would lead to the state's demise. Forcing a government official, against his conscience, to work on Sunday is an abuse of power; but for the state to tolerate nudists walking about in public would be a dereliction of duty. We do not undertake the defense of *conscientious* objections; we always found that they went against the grain. In those cases, we insist that the government thinks three times before it accepts it when someone claims: *God forbids me to* ...

X TO WHICH STATE-LEVEL POLICIES DOES THE "FREEDOM OF CONSCIENCE" GIVE RISE? (2)

Freedom of conscience does not make sense without freedom of *confession*, which in turn coincides with *freedom of speech* and *freedom of the press*.

Every conviction aims for expansion. Whoever is simply satisfied, provided that they may believe for themselves what pleases them, does not believe wholly, lacks conviction, and lacks the satisfaction they profess. A conviction is like a ray of light that, except when obstructed, penetrates everywhere, or is like the air that presses against everything and does not rest until it has filled every accessible space. The longing to promulgate is the mark of authentic conviction. Dissemination is how it exhales. Without the passion to persuade others, your conviction is dead.

Words are the means to disseminating one's convictions; whether they are whispered in personal conversations or proclaimed loudly to the crowds, be they written, published, or conveyed with pen and ink. The state should, therefore, leave these words entirely free; neither espionage nor censorship are to be tolerated.

The distribution of the printed word may not be hindered (indirectly) by excessive taxation or postal rates. To put even minimal strictures on the printed word in general because some weeklies are filled with lampoons and satire would be to pay magazines of that sort far too much regard. That they may instigate malice must simply be accepted. It is not the case that the public always rejects what is misguided. But walking on frozen canals cannot be prohibited just because the ice claims its casualties every winter. So too here: because freedom has its dark side is no grounds for doing away with freedom.

Even the oft-repeated demand that every author be required to include his name must be rejected. Many splendid literary talents would never have seen the light of day if anonymity had been a punishable offense. Moreover, as writers oftentimes act as the organ of a movement, their signature does not say much. The author of some published pieces is not a particular individual, but a collaborative group of writers to whom "the author" lends his voice.

What does remain is the responsibility for the spoken, written, or printed word. People must be able to find a preferable defense against slander and insult. Likewise, what violates public morality must be disabused. Not that the proliferation of immoral writings or illustrations could be prevented, but by restricting their distribution to covert channels much can be achieved. The hawking and open display of what infringes on what is proper must be regarded as an offense. Likewise, even the bawdy singing of shamefully indecent songs on the street should be averted by policing. Free speech has nothing in common with the dissipation of wanton lewdness.

Likewise, the freedoms of *association* and *assembly* may not be withheld from citizens by the state. The strength of a concord that embodies an idea and propagates it in subsequent generations first arises from groups of like-minded people networking together. As this happens, individual tones combine and come to resonate in full harmony. No single person can grasp a notion completely. A particular facet of a truth makes a stronger impression on the one than on the other. Only by merging the different insights regarding the same truth does that truth come to exercise its essential force. It is like the front line on the battlefield. Ten thousand troops flying the same flag will inevitably be defeated by an opposing force of five thousand whose corps and frontline troops know how to work in a coordinated fashion, in a way that the larger force does not.

Prohibiting people from associating is not a viable option. By forbidding the establishment of associations, one merely exchanges covert conspiracies for free associations.

The above, however, addresses only a portion of what freedom entails. Though not to be dismissed, much more is required if there is to be "fair play" between truth and error. Do not forget that the struggle between the truth and error is a matter of the knight fighting against the robber, who unscrupulously and without hesitation lays claim to what the former defends with knightly honor.

That is why one must take careful note to ensure that the freedom proclaimed to you with the right hand is not skillfully taken from you with the other.

The "herald of arms" may not underhandedly assist error in the tussle. The "herald" must be impartial—because he cannot recognize the face of those jousting behind their closed visor—and is disingenuous if he secretly conspires with error.

As we pointed out before, the state can be enticed to surreptitiously give error preferential treatment if it gets involved with what lies outside its sphere, places its bullion in the balance, or violates its impartiality in its laws or executive orders.

This is grounded in the requirement that the government remain the *government* and not preempt the responsibilities of its citizens. That is why, except when other initiatives fail, the government should not take charge of education or prescribe an official science or what counts as legitimate art.

This is based on the requirement of *decentralization*. The freedom of expression lacks its natural basis when the smaller spheres of life—home, town, city, region—are not independent. The state then becomes monolithic, thinking and acting for all.

This is based on the requirement for an *independent parliament*. When a choice of the States General is decided based on the influence of civil servants, that is, arbitrary legal provisions or gerrymandering, that prevents the ideas that are at work in the life of the nation from exercising their rightful influence.

Finally, this is based on the requirement *to facilitate constitutional revision*. To obstruct changes to constitutional institutions is a prerogative of the dominant notions of an often very turbulent era; a barrier to purer thoughts breaking through; an obstacle placed in the middle of the fray, which makes sword flailing difficult.

Liberation from and disestablishment of the church is the final consequence, to which we now turn.

XI TO WHICH STATE-LEVEL POLICIES DOES THE "FREEDOM OF CONSCIENCE" GIVE RISE? (3)

The all-important question concerning the relationship between church and state is also clearly involved in the dispute regarding the use of coercive measures to counter error.

Pagan Rome persecuted the Christian church, having decided that it propagated falsehoods, that its teachings were erroneous.

Medieval states severely chastised anyone who deviated from the Roman Church's doctrine, judging that anyone who did so was guilty of a punishable offense.

Every state church is based on the conviction that, when compared to the confessions of the chosen church, the preaching of any other church is more or less flawed.

Even the financial support, found throughout Europe, that was promised for various denominations implicitly included the promise to suppress those who did not follow what the "true church" taught.

In each of these cases, the assumption—which we have shown to be unacceptable—was *that support extended by the strong arm of the state would benefit the truth.*

This assumption, and the policies that follow from it, may not be perpetuated.

The spiritual nature of the truth stands opposed to this untenable system. Experience repudiates it. It is gradually colliding ever more seriously with the principle of the freedom of conscience, which, despite our doctrinalists and our reactionaries, is increasingly gaining ground.

In its nature, the church is *militant*. It is and remains—on earth—a church *equipped for struggle*, called in every century to combat error as it manifests itself in that century.

Having an *open arena* as well as complete *freedom of movement* within that arena is indispensable to the church in that struggle. It does not ask for support from the state, but shuns it. The only influence it desires is the conviction of its members. As long as people respect its independence, it can take care of itself.

This requirement can be translated concisely and intelligibly in the formula: *the separation of church and state.*

Do note that this is *not* a separation between the church and the *nation*, but a matter of being separate from *the state*.

We are not talking about a divorce here, where the church is expelled with contempt as being unworthy, but of one who, having matured and taken leave of parental supervision, is going to act independently.

It is not a division, as though the functioning state had nothing further to with the fanatical cult of the Nazarene. They are related but distinct, because a state without a powerful church will perish, and the church cannot come into its own without that separation.

Therefore, being separate is, *for the sake of each*, highly desired.

Being separate is desired by the church because she knows that she can fulfill her calling to the Lord, to the souls entrusted to her, and also to the state only on the basis of complete freedom.

It is also desired by the state, which, when venturing into matters of the church, is like a blind person playing around with colors, and easily susceptible to jeopardizing its principle of "equal rights for all."

Being separate is desirable for the church, which can maintain itself in our society and rouse itself out of its humiliation only when completely free.

But it is also desirable for the state, which, itself unfit to nurture the morality of the people, must seize every permissible means to, via the church, again inspire the nation with moral rectitude.

That said, they must also be completely separate.

Mutual trust is a necessary condition for a good relationship between state and church, and that reciprocal confidence is only possible in two scenarios: either when they are united entirely or when they are completely separate.

Given the nature of the case, an unresolved relationship will foster mistrust. As long as the boundary is not clearly delineated, uncharted areas remain susceptible to constant disputes. Uncertainty is the worst of all conditions.

That is also why the separation must be financial as well.

Although it would not be a waste of money for the state to make a few million of its budget available for the religious interests of the people, doing so would actually harm those interests.

If the church would benefit from money from the treasury, then we would maintain that, among all the interests of the people, religious resilience stands so clearly front and center and that a budget for the church, even more so than the budget for defense, should be given a vote of confidence without delay. Do not offer just a little less than four for ecclesiastical life, but if necessary twenty million. Defense only serves what might happen; divine worship addresses a situation that is always with us.

However, on the other hand, by consulting the past and by comparing the resilience of the free churches and given the nature of spiritual life, we see that state money does not promote but rather obstructs the religious development of the nation. In other words, precisely because the flourishing of the church is in the state's best interest, the state is called to free itself of any monetary ties to the church.

Likewise, those who do nothing more than disburse funds exercise influence; those who have influence benefit from it; and using the power that holds the purse strings disrupts the natural development of the life of the church.

The grounds on which the state nevertheless acknowledges God Almighty, requires an oath, prescribes Sabbath rest, and in the event of a national disaster can invite a day of prayer can only be shown later. For the time being, it is enough to point out that the recent coronation celebration[33] has in fact shown that the state of the Netherlands, in a very official way—through its king, its high-ranking officials, and its people—still expresses its acknowledgement of God and prays, albeit indirectly, to him.

We will see later how this has absolutely nothing to do with Thorbecke's "Christianity beyond religious division";[34] indeed, that it is actually the opposite of this untenable position. Here we need only protest against drawing the wrong conclusion.

One other clarification must be added here.

No one, in the name of the freedom of conscience, denies a father the right to punish his child for going astray. Likewise, no one thinks to challenge the right of societies and associations to posit a principle in their statutes that counters something that they take to be erroneous. In other words, parental authority and the freedom of association pose pivotal limits to *the freedom of conscience* that *the state* must respect.

This shows how ill-considered the assertions of some Modernists are who claim that freedom of conscience must also be the rule for denominations. It is just the other way around. If freedom of conscience can be safely maintained *in the state*, then it may not be tolerated in the church, which exercises in part a paternal authority and stands or falls in part with the indispensable character of every free association.

XII DUTCH STATE POLICY IN RELATION TO ERROR (1)

We have neither underestimated nor disguised the serious, extremely questionable character of erroneous ideas. Head and heart cannot be divided in the long run. The nature of one's convictions bears fruit in the quality of one's morality. There is a first-degree kinship between false notions and crime. Failing to combat error is equivalent to condoning crime. The thorny problem when it comes to error is not *whether* it will be opposed, but *who* ought to do that.

---

33. That is, the celebration of the "silver" anniversary of the reign of William III, May 12, 1874.
34. Liberal politician Johan Rudolph Thorbecke (1798–1872) affirmed the public recognition of "Christianity beyond religious division," which applied as well in schooling policy. This view had been one of Kuyper's main targets during the school struggle.

We have seen that it makes some sense that people, in the first instance, acting in good faith, thought that the state was called to combat false doctrine. That approach was a rather obvious choice. Only by putting it to the test would they know if it would fail. Untested, it remained the recommended route.

Rome has attached its name to that approach. Its declared infallibility made its application in all its severity possible. Rome introduced this system into the public laws of Europe, and still maintains it via the *syllabus of errors* and papal encyclicals.[35]

This was offset by the Reformed church's framework of the freedom of conscience (and thought). Though first introduced timidly and reluctantly, and more in theory than in practice, it gradually came to be embraced very consciously. Milton was an avid advocate.

People rejected the old ways and chose this new approach because the old one had failed the test, reached beyond its purpose, proved to be unenforceable, ran counter to the nature of spiritual life, and was found wanting by the faith.

Implementing this new approach to freedom had already been tested, little by little, especially in practice, in our Reformed Church, in Reformed England, and in the Reformed Church in America, when the French Revolution broke out.

In theory, the Revolution adopted Milton's approach, albeit on other grounds. But in practice it returned to Rome's system. What was erroneous in its eyes was left to the state to punish with banishment, edicts, and the guillotine.

From this arose the irregularity that the governments whose state policy revolved around the revolutionary principle claimed Milton's label, but remained disposed to spiritual tyranny. Despite an endless stream of newly fashioned phrases *promising* freedom, governments repeatedly fell short when it came to *granting* true freedom.

This holds without exception for all the revolutionary governments in France that, starting in 1791, followed each other at a tiresome pace. It also

---

35. Pope Piux IX (1792–1878) convened the First Vatical Council (1869–70), at which the doctrine of papal infallibility was decreed. He also promulgated documents including the encyclical *Quanta cura* (1864), which condemned a variety of modern errors and to which the *Syllabus of Errors* was annexed.

applies to other European governments that, although at a distance, sought to imitate France.

The difference between state policies before and after the Revolution consisted for most governments merely in that people *before* 1789 usually saw in Christianity *the truth that they had to protect*, whereas *after* 1789 they viewed that same Christianity *as the error that they had to eradicate*.

This led to a binary politics.

On the one hand, there were the *revolutionaries*. They wrote freedom into its program, but actually focused on fighting Christianity.

And then there were the *antirevolutionaries*. They took the government to be a servant of God and Christianity as his most eminent gift to humankind and sought to protect the Christianity that the revolutionaries opposed.

Both movements split into separate subgroups.

Among the revolutionaries, some quietly embraced a more veiled, almost unconscious opposition to Christianity, while others, throwing their masks to the wind, advocated open attacks on Christianity.

So too, antirevolutionaries in Roman Catholic and Lutheran countries called for state aid in protecting Christianity; whereas in Reformed countries they sought to protect Christianity through the fair application of established freedoms.

For purposes of clarification, see the *revolutionary fight against Christianity* in the radical parties of Belgium and Switzerland; in Belgium for covert opposition and in Switzerland for overt attacks. And likewise, for the antirevolutionary protection of Christianity that turned to state aid to combat error, see the right-wing French Legitimists, Ecuador's constitution, and the old Prussian Conservatives. For the fair implementation of freedoms, see America's Constitution, the Dissenters in England, and the Christian-historical movement here in the Netherlands.[36]

We will intentionally not delve into the nuances in the bosom of each of these groups. Even where there are pointed differences regarding principles, no channel can be dug between people without there also being a bridge over it. Given the nature of the case, opponents in borderline disputes are not so far apart from each other.

Although it is sometimes tempting to explain away this difference in principle, attempts to do so—which evidence gross superficiality—must be resisted.

---

36. For a later narrative of the different developments in Europe and the United States, see Abraham Kuyper, "State and Church," in *On the Church*.

A comparison, based on a difference in *nationality*, sheds light on this.

As our readers know well, the difference between Belgians and the Dutch is hardly noticeable in the southernmost villages of North Brabant and Limburg compared to the northernmost regions of Belgium. Likewise, the difference between Germans and the Dutch is minimal in border villages of Gelderland and Overijssel compared to places in westernmost Prussia. At many border points, it is almost impossible to make out, based on accent, lifestyle, or clothing, whether one is past the border or still within its limits. The more or less randomly placed boundary post is the only way to know the difference.

These observable phenomena, however, should not lead one to conclude that there is hence no essential difference between the German, Belgian, and Dutch nationalities. One need only travel with the intercity train from Amsterdam straight through to Berlin or to Brussels to disabuse themselves of that illusion.

This holds as well for the boundaries of political parties. One must place oneself not along the edges of a party but in the middle—in the heart—of each, in order to be able to judge its unique character. Having done so, the four groups we mentioned above can, for the sake of brevity, be roughly described as follows.

The first group of revolutionaries consider those who confess Christ as being too insignificant to engage; the second group sees them as too dangerous to not have them put in chains.

Of the antirevolutionaries, the former group considers Christianity to be too weak to keep its head above water without state support; the second group sees Christianity as too intricately organized to not lose the gold dust on its wings should the state become involved.

What do you think of Christ? remains the question that still governs Europe's politics, depending on *how the state* responds: *He does not concern me!* soon warped into: *Crush the infamous!* Or: *Without the state's help, those in his service will waste away*; or finally: *He is too exalted to need the state's help.*

What is the response of our government's policy?

XIII DUTCH STATE POLICY IN RELATION TO ERROR (2)

The Dutch government considers error to be a punishable offense. It sees it as the state's calling to combat error, if not directly, then indirectly. *Narrow-mindedness, fanaticism, and intolerance* must be countered; *development, scientific sensitivity, and tolerance* must be promoted.

In the struggle between these two powers, the state maintains that it must also choose between the one or the other. The state's policies, articulated in legislation and by the government, must seek to serve the fight against what is *narrow-minded, fanatical, and intolerant*.

The state cannot flourish unless its citizens are adequately *developed*, support *enlightened* ideas, and are inclined to be *tolerant*. Narrow-mindedness breeds backwardness; superstitious sensitivities feed clericalism; intolerance by nature leads to theological infighting and the hatred among sects. The state must therefore keep its citizens from embracing the latter and encourage them in the former.

This way of thinking is the credo of our leading circles. Nearly every cabinet minister echoed this commitment. Almost every debate of significance in the House aligned itself as well. It is warp and woof for our daily newspapers; in clubs and meetings, it is simply assumed as axiom; our writers and pamphleteers consider any other starting point unthinkable; and, robustly supported by public opinion, the state is openly stepping up to implement this program.

Our government, too, approves accordingly; taking sides in accepting as its duty if not to eradicate the root of *narrow-mindedness, fanaticism, and intolerance*, then to counteract their wanton increase. To do this, it must give an account of where that root lies and, after investigation, comes to the unwavering conviction that this root lies in Christianity.

Having said this, we are not playing with words, but mean instead to cut off the opponent's play on words.

Christianity is a historical phenomenon. It does not float in the air but is embodied in denominations. Christianity's ideas may, therefore, be sought—at least by a national government—only in the confession of those churches.

Testing the correctness of that confession, based on the documents and records of Christianity, may be the calling of the theologian, may be asked of the philosopher, and, in part, may even be expected of the members of the church, but it can never be the responsibility of a government, which, as such, cannot evaluate the documents of Christianity and lacks the wherewithal to have someone carry out theological studies in its name.

It is on this basis that we say that the state, as such, can only know Christianity as it has appeared historically, which is to say, as it expresses itself in the confession of the denominations that the government acknowledges and protects.

For half a century, a primarily covert but nevertheless stubborn and irreconcilable fight has been waged against *that* Christianity.

The standpoint on which the confession of all the denominations with-out exception places itself in its historical documents—the only ones that the government can assess and evaluate—is branded as backward and archaic, as one that fosters narrow-mindedness.

The churches' adherence to this standpoint is considered to amount to the deliberate endeavor to extinguish the light of science, to find solace in obscurantism, and to react to modern developments by reverting to earlier superstitious concepts.

People find it even more dangerous in that those who embrace historic Christianity, and hold fast to their own convictions, are not ashamed of the faith they profess and thereby—so it is suggested—provoke a division among sons of the same fatherland, incite sectarian passion, foster fanat-icism, and spark hatred back and forth.

On this basis, people consider themselves justified in branding this point of view, which is to say, the fundamental ideas of the Christian churches' historical confession, as the last word in impropriety, national degrada-tion, and matchless provocation; in short, as THE ERROR par excellence and, inevitably, that the state is to oppose it.

They appear to honor the "freedom of conscience," claim *not* to be par-tial, and adorn themselves with the honorary title of *neutrality*, but in fact only misuse this motto to be able—covered by the banner of neutrality—to strike more confidently. P. A. de Génestet expressed it with exceptionable accuracy: Tolerant of all, except of those who are intolerant![37]

This campaign against error, that is, against historic Christianity, was waged in Paris in 1793 and openly today in Switzerland—through direct attacks and passionate, fierce, and relentless interference.

---

37. Petrus Augustus de Génestet (1829-61) was a Dutch poet and theologian. One of his short poems, "Tolerance," can be read as expressing a sentiment similar to Kuyper's attribution here. See de Génestet, "XCII. Verdraagzaamheid," in *Dichtwerken*, ed. C. P. Tiele (Amsterdam: Kraay, 1869), 1:329. This idea is directly asserted by Jean-Jacques Rousseau, one of the philosophical fathers of the French Revolution. See Rousseau, *Letter to Beaumont, Letters Written from the Mountain, and Related Writings*, ed. Christopher Kelly and Eve Grace, trans. Christopher Kelly and Judith R. Bush (Hanover, NH: Dartmouth College, 2001), 157: "The Protestant Religion is tolerant by principle; it is tolerant essentially; it is as much so as it is possible to be, since the only dogma it does not tolerate is that of intolerance."

Our government seldom went so far. The opposition to the Seccession, when it first surfaced, was exceptional.[38] The error, that is, historic Christianity, was regularly opposed by our government but only in a veiled, indirect manner; dispassionately, virtually without design or hatred.

Four strategies, in particular, paved their way.

a) The state baptized its agenda, directed against historic Christianity, with the name *Christian*.

b) The state aligns itself with those who, though deeply involved within the denominations, are opposed to the historic confession.

c) The state uses the country's finances, influence, and offices to further its own agenda.

Finally,

d) The state weakens the opponent by depleting its financial resources and undercutting enthusiasm.

In other words, it is a regular siege of historic Christianity including scheming, rapport with some of those under siege, an overwhelming barrage of tactics, and cutting off supplies—all without a shot being fired—to force capitulation.

... similar to what happened in Metz.[39]

XIV "CHRISTIAN" AS A WEAPON AGAINST CHRISTIANITY

Dutch state policy maintains that *historic Christianity*, which addresses the state exclusively in the confession of the acknowledged denominations, is erroneous.

Its error is hardly an innocent one, for it is said to obstruct the nation's development, distort its enthusiasm, and threaten its unity.

---

38. Kuyper refers to the Secession (*Afscheiding*, called the Christian Reformed Church at the time of Kuyper), a group that had left the national church under the leadership of Hendrik de Cock (1801–42). Early on, at the hands of the government, this group suffered persecutions including fines, imprisonment, and disruption of their meetings.
39. Kuyper is referring to the end of Germany's two-month siege of Metz on October 27, 1870, by Prussian forces, when France's Marshal Bazaine (1811–88) surrendered his 160,000 troops because of starvation.

To defuse this danger the state engages legislative and administrative measures. It has yet to storm the breach here. Encircling the stronghold, which fatigues the enemy into wasting its resources, would seem more fruitful for the time being. No bayonet has been put on the rifle yet. It is still a clash from behind the gabions.

Those who confess the Christ but are blind to this situation, who remain blind to it—blind enough to dismiss the clarion call as "pessimistic agitation"—show that they do not understand the nature of an alarming development in European politics.

A misunderstanding is often the cause of this.

Some people understand our claim that the Netherlands' policy, influence, and administration are all opposing historic Christianity as erroneous to mean that we are attributing *the evil plan* to illicitly attack the very heart of historic Christianity to cabinet ministers, to the members of the Council of State, or to the States General.

That misunderstanding needs to stop. We never spoke in that way and would contest anyone who said otherwise. What we claimed was never said of particular people in the administration, but had to do with the prevailing spirit that makes people in political circles, usually unconsciously and in spite of themselves, into those who put its far-reaching will into practice.

So here too.

When the Dutch state claimed the name Christian for what it was up to with the formula *Christianity beyond religious division*, the spokespersons meant and the public heard that the intention was to maintain the Christian element that, as the fruit of a history going back almost ten centuries, had been woven into the fabric of who we are as a people.

The warm glow of that notion shines through Thorbecke's statements. When Beets opposed singling out this phrase from Article 23 of the School Act, he was expressing support for the same idea.[40] Preserving the

---

40. During the school struggle, Nicolaas Beets (1814–1903) was one of the leaders of efforts to retain the "Christian" identity of the government schools. Kuyper viewed this article as an imposition on rather than a protection of the freedom of conscience. Article 23 of the School Law of 1857: "The instruction in the school shall be made serviceable, while learning suitable and useful skills, to the development of the intellectual faculties of the children and to their training in all Christian and civic virtues. The teacher shall refrain from teaching, doing or permitting anything that is inconsistent with the respect due to the religious beliefs of those who think differently. Religious instruction is left to the church denominations. For this purpose

"Christian element" in the nation was important to him. We would add: we wish to top Thorbecke's spirited appreciation and to emulate Beets. That element is a sacred pledge that no one may take their hand to. In fact, we take issue with the misuse of "Christian" in this context *precisely with an eye to rescuing that Christian element in the nation.*

To make one's product more attractive, nothing is more common than imitating the labeling of a well-known brand with such nuance that only the connoisseur notices the difference.

Doing so yields a threefold advantage: one increases one's sales; proves to be detrimental to the competitor; and, by supplying a lower-grade product, damages the reputation of the better brand.

That is what has happened here as well.

Christianity was well-known. It supplied the spiritual market, well-nigh singlehandedly, with food and medicine. When it came to public opinion, it knew no competition—until the French Revolution.

How would the Revolution sell its wares? By a bull-headed dismissal of Christianity? They tried that in 1789, but it did not turn out well; losing much more than what they gained. It was then that they resorted to skill and cunning.

If they were to succeed, with what from their brewing kettles could they fill their jugs, now adorned a quasi-Christian label, such that former consumers would buy it?

Historically, there had been a shadow side to Christendom. Because Christianity was maintained by limited, fallible, sinful people, there was a lack of unity and it suffered from religious division. In addition, it was expensive. Distancing oneself from one's own wisdom, sensual pleasures, and self-satisfaction was the price one paid.

They could use that to their advantage.

"Check this out, O Christianity-loving nation! It is not anything new, oh no! It is just more refined. The aftertaste of 'religious division' is gone. And, for next to nothing! Thanks to a fortunate discovery, we have found a way to spare ourselves the cost of 'dogmatics!'"

Is someone exaggerating here?

Let the reader judge.

---

the school facilities can be made available outside of school hours for the pupils who attend the school."

That the label was an imitation, needs no argument. Thorbecke and Article 23 of the School Act are proof enough.

That people found the new brew clearly superior to the old is implicit to the adage "*beyond* religious division." Division is a deficiency, something ugly, the opposite of harmony. This shortcoming was silently blamed, in the formula itself, on the Christianity of the ages. That defect had now been *undone*. The Christianity of old had been overpowered by the new—*without* "religious division." The *churches* were free to do as they saw fit, but the *state* retained the monopoly on what was best; literally, on something *superior* to historic Christianity.

There is also nothing debatable about our last claim.

Christianity is *not* a law beyond Moses' law. Christ did not come to preach a higher moral law, but *to fulfill* the—misunderstood and misinterpreted—one *revealed already* long before.

The core, the summary, of Christian ethics: *Love God with all your heart and the neighbor as yourself* was not articulated first by Jesus Christ but had already been revealed to Israel. Simply see Deuteronomy 6:5 and Leviticus 19:18. That Mr. Godefroi, too, appreciates this teaching should come as no surprise.[41]

The heart of Christianity is not to be found in "Christian ethics" or in "Christian virtues" but in the *reconciliation* of the conscience of those who have been unsettled by these teachings and in the *regeneration* of hearts that know their inability to fulfill that law. It is not found in the requirement that the life of God must fill our soul, but in that the life of God comes to us in the *person of the Christ*.

On the other hand, "Christianity revisited" closes the eye to the person of the Christ, considers regeneration to be a meaningless formula, reconciliation to be evidence of an arid dogmatics, and chooses to look for Christianity only in what Israel and the Gentile world (in part) knew already: morality and virtue.

In doing so, they appropriate the name *Christian* for what essentially is not Christianity and hence necessarily situate themselves in a hostile position with respect to Christianity.

---

41. Michael H. Godefroi (1814-82) was a Dutch jurist, member of Parliament (1848-81), and the first Jew to fill a cabinet position in the Netherlands—minister of justice (1860-62).

On Charity & Justice

After all, historic Christianity confesses that we *cannot* lead a moral life or exhibit those virtues until reconciliation and regeneration first change us. This newfound Christianity, on the contrary, presupposes that with education and advice these things are within our reach.

"Christianity beyond religious division" claims to stand taller than historic Christianity. It inverts the heart of Christianity and places over against Scripture's understanding of who we are another view of man that is irreconcilably and diametrically opposed to it.

The name is the same and the label looks to be so as well, but goods delivered are entirely different. Under the guise of improving matters, this deception does nothing but undermine the Christian faith.

In casting itself as an advocate for this new kind of Christianity, the state rejects historic Christianity, finding it to be erroneous, and disputes its influence over the spirit of the nation.

XV RELATIONS WITH THE RENEGADES

The state disputes historic Christianity as "erroneous" by misusing the name Christian for a framework that is the opposite of Christian. That was our first grievance. We turn now to the second, which we prefer to describe as *relations with the renegades* and will support with some undeniable facts.

In the great struggle between the cross and the crescent moon, between Christianity and Islam, the Muslims and the Christians who fell away from the faith that they were born into were called "renegades." A Muslim who renounced the Qur'an, as well as a Christian who disavowed the twelve articles of the faith, was branded a "renegade" in the eyes of those who remained true to their colors. With this in mind, and for the sake of brevity, we will use this term to refer to those denominational members who, in the struggle between historic Christianity and the state's version of Christianity, renounced the former and pledged their allegiance to the latter and, without ever leaving their church, lived accordingly.

Every denomination has its standards. A church is a religious association, which fights for its principles. That is why a church that does not know, and does not let others know, which principles it stands for is hard to imagine. A church remains a fiction if it does not discover its coat of arms in a clearly formulated confession. Churches that did not do this have never had a future. The manifest with which they acted might have been brief or extensive; their manner of proclamation different; the road to revision encumbered or smooth—for whichever denomination it was, disclosing its principles always helped to elevate its banner, to justify its actions, to attract new recruits, to provide the moral means to develop its own strength. Someone "with no convictions" is contemptible; "a church without a confession" does not count.

Now, in every denomination it happens, without exception, that some of the members object to this, that, or another article of the denomination's manifest or program or confession. Sometimes they do so openly, at other times in secret; and depending on the position they occupy, via learned debate, practical opposition, or acrimonious, peevish jibes. Protestants were not the only ones to struggle here; Rome suffered from the same problem. And today, issues in the Old Catholic Church here in the Netherlands are proof of the same.[42]

These resistant, unfaithful, and renegade members pose a serious threat to the safety of the denominations: they live under the umbrella of the church; they enjoy relative influence and power within the church, are familiar firsthand with the inner workings of their church, and are nonetheless the natural allies of every power that opposes the church from without.

This is also happening now.

The basic tenor of our century is in irreconcilable conflict with the confession of the church regarding the Christ. The confession of the nineteenth century and the confession of the first century, to which the church holds, presuppose different principles, lead to a diametrically opposed worldview, and rely on a plainly opposite goal.

As a result, there is now in every church a group that throws out the church's principle, abandons its worldview, rejects its goal, and yet, nevertheless, remain as members, wreaking despair and havoc within the church, so as to hasten the triumph of the principle that the church of Christ opposes.

The opponents of historic Christianity are one with these groups; they understand what they are doing. In the siege operations that people have launched against the church, they are used as allies; used by the sensual natures, used by the mockers, by the so-called philosophers, and used *also by the state.*

---

42. The Old Catholic Church of the Netherlands, mother church of the Old Catholic churches worldwide, parted with Rome and established its own apostolic succession in 1723.

That is true for Switzerland, Austria, and Germany; and *also for the Netherlands*.

By way of illustration, we will turn to six initiatives on the part of the state in relation to the Reformed faith tradition.

1. The Decrees of 1816 and 1823

After the French entered the Netherlands in 1795, the complete separation of state and church—including the churches of Reformed persuasion—ensued. In 1816, the State of the Netherlands took the oversight of the newly designated "Netherlands Reformed Church" into its hands (although the churches had little voice in the matter), reorganized its administrative structure, and recast the churches into a form that, given the character of the Reformed mind, that is, in light of *the basic features of its confession*, is impossible to accept. The renegades in that church made it official, clipped the wings of the faithful believers' influence, and, finally, reduced the denomination into a corporation that lacks character, pith, and enthusiasm.

This revamp was completed with the decrees of 1819-23, when, due in part to an arbitrary action by the government, the administrative power to manage the Reformed Church was put in part into the hands of state officials and in part handed over to local plutocrats, who, in general, no longer thought about taking *the confession of the church* into account.

Finally, in 1852, after *the power of the confession* had successfully been broken, those of Reformed persuasion were consigned to the whim of an ecclesiastical organization that, banking on the rejection of the confession, made even faithful believers, when still allowed on various boards, dejected and less loyal owing to bureaucracy and routine.

2. The Appointment of Professors in Theology

To this point, the state had appointed those who were responsible for forming the teachers in the Reformed Church. Quite obviously, their having a heart for the church's confession was crucial. The professing church confesses. Its teachers must rouse and encourage the church to remain faithful to the principles it professes. To do that they must be inspired by professors for whom loyalty to these principles is what it is all about. Accepting another attitude is to play with truth and the good faith entrusted to them.

And yet, what did the state do?

It first installed an administrative board that made attending a state university obligatory for future teachers—thus ensuring that the church would remain in the hands of the state. The state then resolutely chooses known opponents of the church's confession from the circle of overt renegades as professors until such time as that appointing a few orthodox scholars could no longer save the church or harm the state. The state, quite incredibly, used public funds to promote, first, old liberalism, then the Groningen school, then the Scholten direction,[43] and finally Modernism. Leiden was considered by all to have the greatest repute. Her theology faculty likewise received the lion's share of resources, with four chairs. And to which theological direction were these allotted? Naturally, to the most brilliant of the renegades who pushed the limits, to those most loyal to the cohort who strive to make short work of the church.

3. The Secession of 1834

What gave rise to the Secession? The state's rather arbitrary decree of 1816, which set an ecclesiastical hierarchy against anyone who, for the sake of the confession, seriously objected to this decree. Who was the first to remove people from office? The church's board, which was established by the state. What was behind its pursuing them? What other than the cramped atmosphere in which the state had enclosed the church? Who penalized those who left? Was it not the judges, appointed by the state? Finally, who sent the dragoons out after them? Was it not the state's police forces?

4. The Gift of Six Thousand Florin for the General College of the Reformed Church

The circumstances of the case are recalled. Free management abounded. The synodal party sought by ruse to capture the freely managed congregations. However, funds were lacking. And behold, the minister of the state was ready at once to offer some gold from the government treasury to the old opponents of the historic church of Belgium. Had the Parliament not prevented it, the agreement would have been successful.[44]

---

43. J. H. Scholten (1811–85) was one of Kuyper's professors at the University of Leiden, a leading Modernist who rejected supernaturalism, divine revelation, and miracles like the virgin birth.
44. Kuyper provides more detail regarding the conflict between centralizing government-allied elements in the church and independent forces, including the church in Amsterdam, particularly concerning the formation of a "General College" (*Algemeene College*) in 1869, in Abraham Kuyper, *Het Conflict Gekomen* (Amsterdam: Kruyt, 1886), 2:20–21.

5. The Moerdijk Question

Our assessment of this matter is well-known, but that does not detract from the fact that the Minister of Finance, an arm of the state, has supported the anticonfessional officials of the provincial church administration and not the confessional part of the Moerdijk congregation, by paying the government stipend to the church officials even before the rial had begun.[45] And finally, ...

6. The Proposed Legislation for Higher Education

The bill proposes that the theology faculties at the university level should be cast entirely on the basis of the Modernist approach and that each year a sum of 27,000 florin be disbursed to a synod—which systematically suppresses the confessional voice within the church—to appoint, on its own authority, six professors of its choosing. "It's better to be the master than the servant," says a Dutch proverb. That is how it will be here as well.

As the state tampers with the renegades within the church, the process of ecclesiastical devastation continues with unrelenting consequence; in a manner different from in Switzerland and Germany, but probably more effective.

XVI THE STRONGHOLD UNDER SIEGE

By calling its non-Christian endeavor Christian, the state has dulled the prickles of the nation's conscience. Robbed of its force through the state's rapport with the non-Christian contingent within the Christian churches, the nation's sense of right and wrong became the fruit of its own organization. What remains to be demonstrated is how every option for the stronghold of historic Christianity to make a sortie are being removed. We will see that their hope is that exhaustion and fatigue will lead to a forced surrender and our demise, our vitality stifled by the threefold effects of cunning, treachery, and majority.

The four cases we will consider are primary education, academic chairs, the judiciary, and the legislative process.

---

45. This concerns the suspension of W. H. C. Kocken (1847–88), the Reformed minister of Moerdijk, in 1872 and removal from office the following year by the provincial church administration because of his refusal to baptize certain children. In December 1874 Kuyper also condemned the finance minister's interference with the Moerdijk question in the Second Chamber. See Kocken, *De Vraag: Wat is the Moerdijk geschied?* (Utrecht: J. Bijleveld, 1873).

(1) Primary education is the moving force of a nation's vitality. When it wanes, the nation grows faint. When it becomes more robust, the caliber of our nation's development rises as well. In the struggle between historic Christianity and the Christianity of philosophical invention, what is happening in our schools is, therefore, of primary importance.

Having judged historic Christianity to be erroneous, the state not only has to do what it takes to keep primary education from strengthening the vitality of that Christianity, but also has to find out whether the schools can be a means toward removing any attachment to historic Christianity from the heart of the nation's youth. If that proves successful, the eradication of this "erroneous teaching" would be assured.

That agenda is being put into practice in a calculated fashion.

Christian schools are not being banned from opening. To do so would stir up the nation before it was ready for the new ideas. Hence, there is freedom for the Christians as well, and yet, on the condition that it is also clear that the state is intent on stifling the network and management of Christian schools.

To this end, the jackscrew of money supports the process in three ways. First, tax policies expropriate from the wallets of Christians part of the funds that were to help pay for Christian schools, but the monies collected are not used to help build those schools. Second, by increasing the expenditures required to run these schools, Christians are not left with enough in their wallets to maintain their schools. And, third, by offering free education also to those who could afford to help pay for those schools, they lure the unthinking crowd away from the market of the Christian school.

The embargo laid on the teaching staff serves a similar purpose. Well-kept school buildings, attractive homes, higher salaries, pension plans, and the chance for promotion are all enticements to which young prospective (yet to be converted) teachers naturally succumb when choosing their life's path.

The state school can, in that regard, be choosy when hiring its teachers. Those who are not a good fit are rejected.

This makes finding teachers for Christian schools extremely difficult. Downtime is even more deadly for them than for their competitors. Administrators are—unwillingly—pretty much forced to hire those who apply, even though there might be deficiencies. This all undermines pedagogical integrity.

And—as though that were not enough—the state even narrows the viable options for those hoping to become teachers by offering them scholarships and excellent training schools, things that the Christian school, which lacks an overarching organization, cannot offer.

School inspections are, likewise, one-sided. In contrast to the state schools, which are well-unified, with inexhaustible funding, and staffed by the best intellects, the Christian school is left to struggle. Weakened by its dispersion, never-ending deficit, inadequate staffing, and other challenges, these schools, so unequal in every respect, are then also caught in the shackles of a program of school inspections that is infused almost entirely with an uncompromising zeal for the state school.

Nevertheless, the Christian school surprisingly endured.

Does the state have a remedy? Indeed. The pressure can be increased even more. Just take note of the Association for Public Education's program.[46] Efforts to suppress the Christian school must be expanded—putting the screws on until it collapses.

(2) Academic chairs are just as useful a weapon for inflicting wounds on historic Christianity.

Knowledge is power. Emperor Julian already recognized that seizing control of the nation's intellectual development, while keeping one's opponents less literate, was an ideal strategy for wearing down the power of "erroneous" positions.[47]

It goes without saying that "theoretically gifted" is the sole standard for determining who is qualified to fill a professorate. Once it has been decreed that holding to the old fables of historic Christianity is a definitive characteristic of someone who is *not* theoretically gifted or academically inclined, the sleight of hand is a done deal.

As a result, one fosters scientific and theoretical studies among one's supporters and represses these interests among one's opponents. In doing so, you cultivate in your own mind what in turn will be cultivated in the courts, administrators, and upper echelon of the nation. In the end, you are also luring the budding geniuses of the next generation to your side.

---

46. The Association for Public Education (*Vereniging voor Volksonderwijs*) was founded in 1866 in response to the School Act of 1857. For Kuyper's own vision, see Abraham Kuyper, "Ideas for a National Education System," in *On Education*, 135–63.

47. Emperor Julian (331/32–363) was known as "the Apostate" for his rejection of Christianity and promotion of Greek philosophy.

By combining the brute power of money and the refined power of erudition, there is no conceivable opponent whose back you cannot break.

(3) The judiciary achieves the same effect by making the powerful wheels of the state's administrative structure open to personal influence.

We know that we are governed by laws. But we also know: (1) that a substantial part of the administrative turf lies outside the law, (2) that every law leaves room for interpretation, and (3) that the influence of civil servants on society, especially in rural areas, that is, in two-thirds of the country, is not limited by anything.

People do not proceed in a biased fashion when choosing judges. Oh no. Just as parents are free to send their children to a Christian school and professors are granted academic freedom, so too, impartiality is front and center when granting civil servants their office.

The most suitable ones are chosen. But keep in mind that your devotion to historic Christianity brings with it the presumption that you are probably less than suitable, or at least that they will scrutinize you twice over—an investigation that seldom will work to your advantage. That was not their intention, but they were simply not confident enough to nominate you.

That said, cronyism has not yet been abolished when it comes to conferring positions. Only men of influence are able to facilitate that, most of whom were themselves seasoned by others in the judiciary. This creates an *esprit de corps*, and the influence of that corps becomes more and more hostile to you. There is no runoff election, but people prefer to stay with those within the guild.

Additionally, thanks to this influence, the routines of the judiciary are increasingly permeated with a spirit that finds those who hold to historic Christianity disgusting. Some even raise the question whether our footsteps should even be heard in the halls of justice. It is difficult to calculate the incredible power that the state possesses throughout the wide-ranging spectrum of government offices—especially at its lower levels—to eradicate the "error" that is supposed to have been discovered in historic Christianity.

(4) The final trench that we pointed to, which completes the enclosure of the stronghold, is legislation. Should there be those who dodge the efforts above, the option that is always available is to suddenly move the line of combat, making previous endeavors useless and their application in the future impossible. Thus, your efforts extend only to the point where the opponent discovers where they, due to short-sightedness, forgot to cut you

off. The Primary Education Act of 1857 *will* be revised, but following the rule: "My father disciplined you with whips, but I will discipline you with scorpions" [1 Kings 12:11].[48]

The laws of the land are against historic Christianity at every point:

- in electoral law, wherein the state plays into the hands of that part of the population where the eradication of "error"—historic Christianity—has already succeeded the best;

- in local and municipal law, which provides from top down the means to force smaller circles within society, where the "error" may still be nestled in the local organism, to abandon this obstinacy;

- in the law for primary education, which prescribes taxation that privileges the thinking part of the nation, which is no longer contaminated by "the error";

- in the law for secondary education, which offers diploma-granting privileges, to the detriment of institutions that operate without state livery; and

- in the proposed law for higher education, which pretty much excludes the possibility of independent university-level institutions.

Other laws also hinder or impede the efforts of Christians. Think of the Sunday-closing law, which is seldom enforced; the law for the militia, when applied; the reach of medical laws; the one-sided legal provisions on getting married; or the anxiety-ridden laws for the administration of the East Indies.

Is there reason to hope that, in the end, the annoying "error" of historic Christianity will succumb to such an all-around, comprehensive, and resolute assault? Don't we have to admit that a siege with such heavy guns cannot be broken? Can we not already count the years before their intentions will inevitably be realized?

Then, as Thorbecke advised, we will have to become, whether we like it or not, a "silent party"; so quiet that any stirring will have to avoided, every

---

48. That is, revisions to the School Law will be increasingly opposed to Christianity.

cry smothered; even the cry of grief when you will see the men of 1789 triumphing over the ruins of a society that once was Christian.

Whether it will come to this, only the Lord knows. What we do know is that even under *these* ruins the *faith in his name* will not be buried.

But vigilance is called for and, as a result, an attempt must be made to open the eyes of our partners in the faith to the seriousness of the situation.

Despised as "erroneous," branded as "specious," secretly chastised today as "fallacious," to be openly persecuted later on, historic Christianity persists nevertheless; revealing its noble character as the only one daring to proclaim and not begrudge freedom for all, even when moving into a territory that poses the utmost danger to her, namely that of *error*.

Not daring to do this is the hallmark of our liberalist direction. To differ from them in this is the distinguishing mark of the antirevolutionary party.

FREEDOM OF SPEECH AND FREEDOM OF THE PRESS

TEXT INTRODUCTION

"Freedom of Speech and Freedom of the Press" [Dutch: *Het vrije woord*] was written as a series of four leading articles for Kuyper's daily *De Standaard* in November 1895 and never reprinted. They appeared with the usual interval of two days (at November 8, 11, 13, 15) and were—as were all leaders—written on short notice and partly in response to other newspapers' opinions. Kuyper joined the board of the Dutch journalists' association NJK [*Nederlandsche Journalisten Kring*] earlier that year, and he served as chairman from 1898 until 1901. In comparison with earlier writings on free speech and public opinion, there is now a stress on the "higher calling" of journalists and the need for a vigorously independent press. Especially from 1895 to 1901, Kuyper was cast as a champion of the young profession, and his writings reflect this new role in some unconventional theorizing and specific comments; he also lectured on elementary mass communication at the Free University. Among his fellow journalists, Kuyper was the only one to reflect so elaborately on the profession, partly in line with his wider academic approach, but also showing his international orientation. Already in his 1880 speech "Sphere Sovereignty" had Kuyper hinted at an independent sphere [*kring*] for journalism, or what he otherwise describes as the "new powers" of journalism and public opinion. The idea of journalism as a sovereign sphere of its own—applying the specific term intermittently—colors his theorizing from this point onward.

SOURCE: Abraham Kuyper, "Het vrije woord," *De Standaard*, no. 7263, November 8, 1895–no. 7269, November 15, 1895. Translated by John Kok. Edited and annotated by Johan Snel.

FREEDOM OF SPEECH AND FREEDOM OF THE PRESS

I

A few months ago, the editors of *De Tijd* wrote, "We prefer to avoid polemics with newspapers we have befriended."[1] And, for our part, we did not hesitate for a minute to say the same.

When more than one editorial office "called us on the carpet" for doing so, as if we had betrayed not only the press but even the name Calvinist, we hoisted the white flag and asked for a truce.

In order to talk this out freely, we felt that this dispute could only be discussed objectively once the course of time had separated us from any specific incident.

This may stand as the beginning of that discussion.

Two points stand in the foreground: first, we are convinced that the press *has a calling* and, second, the press *cannot fulfill this calling without the freedom to report news or circulate opinion without censorship.*

---

1. *De Tijd* (1846–1974) was a Roman Catholic newspaper, based (like Kuyper's *De Standaard*) in Amsterdam.

The first point, of course, can only be touched on here. But because there are, curiously, so few fixed ideas about the calling of such a powerful phenomenon as the press, its calling deserves our attention.

Rendering the Gallicism that is hidden in *courant* as "news, tidings," people originally saw the bringing of news as the only reason for starting a newspaper. This is the guiding principle of "journalism."

We *ourselves* observe very few things in our own environs and live in our own city without knowing what is happening two blocks from home.

That does not satisfy us. We want to know what is going on in town, in the country, in the world—at all levels and in many different areas.

The diligence that the editors of a world-class newspaper evidence in gathering, classifying, and reporting this news should, therefore, not be underestimated in the least. Doing so is a matter of principle and is in no way a marginal matter. Nothing presses on smaller newspapers so painfully, and establishes the disproportionate dominance of world-class media outlets, as the tremendous costs associated with gathering these news items. A newspaper that cannot allocate three to four hundred thousand guilders per year[2] to that end simply does not count as a world-class publication. In journalism as well, the law is beginning to prevail that the tall trees block the sun from the park's plants and bushes, which soon die off.

Sending journalists out—to report on events such as the war in Japan, the war on Madagascar, the state of affairs in Constantinople and Trebizond, and so much more—demands incredible sums because these agents must also be expert observers and persons of influence. Even a paper such as *L'independance Belge* is dropping in rank.[3] In the end, only the leading newspapers from large countries can sustain themselves in the large-scale, competitive system.

In a country such as ours, even the largest newspapers can do little more than keep us informed based on what others are reporting, then supplement that with news from their own correspondents in the capitals of Europe, and concentrate their focus on domestic news and news from the markets and stock exchange.

But even this requires relatively large sacrifices, especially in a country such as ours where the public spirit unfortunately drags its feet when it

---

2. That is, roughly 4.7–6.2 million USD today.
3. Founded in Brussels as *L'Indépendant* in 1831, it was renamed *L'Indépendance Belge* in 1843 and ran through May 13, 1940.

comes to advertising. To get a large newspaper up and running takes hundreds of thousands of guilders. So too, even with the best of results, keeping your head above water remains a constant concern; and there is always the possibility that once you have hit your stride some new initiative will try to make cheese with the cream of your efforts.

Only those not in the know might be inclined to complain that *smaller* newspapers, like ours, cannot even begin to think of competing in this market. These days, you are either a large-scale paper or a small-scale one. And the lot of the latter simply does not allow you to gather all the news yourself.

The income from subscriptions hardly covers the cost of the newsprint and the printing process. Long-term, significant advertisers can only be found among those in commerce and shipping. And if there is not a financially liquid consortium that, when needed, is good for at least a million in credit, experience teaches that you will squander your smaller sources of income without ever reaching your goal.

Even in its basis as gazette or courant, that is, in fulfilling its role as newsgatherer, there is a *moral*—and hence *higher*—calling for the press. For even though it may seem to be a very simple task, like simply providing a mirror image of the situation, actually gathering, ordering, and communicating the news is in fact not so easy.

To begin with, so much depends on *who* is doing the perceiving, and on *how* he perceives it, and on the *manner* in which he conveys his message. Two may witness the same incident, and yet they may convey an entirely *contradictory* account of what they saw, even though they are both committed to telling the truth.

But what is worse is that so much is happening which those concerned want to keep *hidden*, the ins and outs of which are not easily found out and take a great deal of effort to track down.

For some, deliberately *mis*representing the facts or concealing the same is a matter of *self-interest*. This happens in family affairs and in financial transactions—just think of the Panama saga.[4] But it also happens in diplomatic affairs; for example, when complications are in the offing or when war threatens—the prime example of which is the edited dispatch that

---

4. Kuyper may be referring to the Panama Crisis of 1885, an international incident involving the United States and Chile in an insurgent rebellion against the Colombian government, which held sway over Panama at that time.

Bismarck sent to Ems.[5] So too, again today, both the Sultan and England want the Armenian question to be cast in a certain light.[6] Similar examples include issues relating to East Asia, Cuba, and recently Madagascar.

There is a subjective element to all our perceptions, and that subjective element makes us partisan. To offset our one-sided impressions, the other party needs perceptions to counter these.

When communicating the news, in transmitting messages, in organizing and describing what we have come to know, all kinds of errors, inaccuracies, and deceit can creep in. This gives rise to the *moral* calling of the press as the bringer of tidings.

Very often, however, the press falls far short of that high calling. Then it does not serve the *truth*, but a party, a statesman, or also some other private interest, if not itself. There are numerous examples of people who support a newspaper with their deep pockets in order to serve their career and position, or to oppose another. Think of how many partisan papers prefer to see nothing but evil and disgrace in what other parties or people of ill repute are up to. Likewise, of newspapers that deliberately lend themselves—for a fee—to further some financial enterprise by propagating messages of a certain color, which end up lining the pockets of a few magnates at the cost of the ewe lamb of those whom these messages deceive.

For a financially impoverished newspaper to courageously turn away from temptations such as these is a heroic deed. *A conscience* is manifest in a paper that is true to its high calling—simply communicating the news straightforwardly.

And although the public does not notice—because it does not understand anything about the inner workings of a large newspaper—it is undoubtedly the case that painful struggles ensue between publishers and editors,

---

5. On July 13, 1870, Otton von Bismarck (1815–98) received a telegram from King Wilhelm I of Prussia (1797–1888) recounting an informal and courteous exchange he had had in the resort town of Ems with the French ambassador to Prussia regarding France's insistence that no German prince should be allowed to ascend to the Spanish throne. Bismarck, having been given permission by the king to release an account of the events, took it upon himself to edit the report—sharpening the language and cutting out Wilhelm's conciliatory phrases—such that it suggested worsening relations with France. The edited telegram, which was published (with a not-insignificant translation error) in French newspapers on July 14, is often cited as precipitating France's declaring war on July 19—the Franco-Prussian War of 1870–71.
6. The status of Armenian subjects of the Ottoman Empire became an existentially significant political question after the Congress of Berlin in 1878.

which in the end demand significant sacrifices, not only of money, but also of mutual understanding and friendship.

To provide readers every morning again with *accurate* and *true* insight into what has happened, into what is pending, and into what is brewing is not only technically and financially an extremely strenuous task, but from a moral perspective also often a very difficult vocation. A world-class paper without a stalwart editor-in-chief will either sink under the weight of its high calling or simply cease to exist.

The press is often referred to as "the queen of the earth." But it is also true of this queen that anxious wrestling and bitter suffering at times fill the inner chambers of her palace, even though she never shows the people anything but a calm and serene face.

Because the influence of the major newspapers is so vast—in a way that our small papers simply are not—they can almost not make a move without flattering the one and slighting another.

They cannot afford to keep silent; they *must* say something. And what they say about concrete events involves all kinds of people with many different interests. They must probe behind what is on stage front and center to ensure that false appearances do not mislead the public.

Those who see their plans thwarted in this way often hold that against everyone involved and want to have them pay for it—to see whether the press can be reduced from queen to *slave*.

To weather those headwinds, not letting them knock you out of the field, and to continue, irrespective of persons, to serve the truth and via the truth to serve the public, requires a courage that dares take on the burden and to which no one who is less inspired is competent.

II

Over the course of time, the press provided more than a news bulletin; it became an organ. With that transition came its higher calling, which increased and complicated the difficulties with which it had to deal.

What does this mean, that the press—that significant newspapers— became an organ?

We know that events do not exist in and of themselves. Composing an epic is not a matter of photographing the facts but of portraying what happened. Especially with powerful, moving events, there is what we see, but there is also a myriad of factors that we do not see. There are powerful, spiritual forces at work in those events—unseen mystical powers. People feel and experience things that we do not see on the outside; realities that can only be perceived through an intimate sense of community with those who suffer or struggle or have prevailed.

The task of the *epic* poet is not only to paint the dry skeleton of the visible facts, but for us to understand what *really* happened, that is, to give us a felt sense of what was going on in the spiritual world and people's hearts.

The same holds on a small scale for all events that influence how situations develop, how powers are ranked, and how your country, your people, and the life of humankind in general are situated.

Facts as they materialize were preceded by labor pains. Everything is being prepared. What we see is the harvest. But prior to its being gathered in, the field was plowed, harrowed, sown, and weeded, the rain fell, and the sun's warm rays shone, or the cold wind shrieked.

Limiting ourselves to life of a nation, people's views and impressions, the ideas with which they are most comfortable, the conversations they have, the sympathies and antipathies that they hold dear, all exert an uncommon influence on the course of events.

The nation does not take things in while standing at a distance. She is part and parcel of those events. She lives *in* the action, helping to bring them to maturity. She pours her own waters into the stream.

This has been the case for centuries. Even in the most despotic countries, the sins and sensitivities of the people—think, for example, of Israel's history—made a difference.

But especially in our freer countries, in the age of publicity, now that public opinion has become a power to be reckoned with, every important event goes this way or that depending on whether the pervasive influence of the public spirit worked in this or that direction.

This means that the power of everyday conversations—the regular chatter around the office and with friends—falls short, and that the different currents that make up the public ethos need other means to express themselves and to exercise their influence.

Normal conversations are local and bound to a very limited environment. They cannot have the reach that the same current propels in the thoughts of many.

The only way to get beyond the confines of the local and to reach all those of a like mind is through song and the written word; and specifically, through those songs and words that can be reproduced so that they are the same everywhere and can reach the entire community.

But singers can sing their song only so many times. A newspaper, in contrast, can steadily, day after day, fulfill the task of being the permanent organ for such a community and for such a specific current among the people.

A newspaper can be an organ that expresses what that group experiences, thinks, and values, and in so doing give words to what is going on in the heart of that group. And yet, as such, therein lies no higher calling. A paper that chooses to be an organ in the narrow sense of the word, one that simply reports what is going on in the heart of a particular group, would be no more than a telephone—calling from afar and into the distance, augmenting the limitations of the human voice.

But a newspaper *cannot* help but do more than that. Even if the news it reports is nothing more than a review of what the other presses are covering, implicit to its choosing which to report on, and to the way in which it reports on them, is a predilection; and every proclivity is owing to a higher motive.

Anyone who wants to put into words what is going on in the hearts of many must possess a higher disposition—a talent—for doing so. For that reason alone, he cannot simply be a phonograph, which records voices and then plays them back again.

He must use his own judgment and know what he wants, which means that he must also have a yardstick with which to determine his choices.

Here too, his calling can never be other than to serve the truth—truth not taken in the merely formal sense, but as the expression of what will truly be a blessing to the fatherland and the people. That makes every organ of this nature a party organ. It cannot be otherwise.

It is one or the other: the editor either has no fixed, sharply defined convictions—that is, he is a skeptic—or he does.

If he does not have such convictions, he cannot be an organ, because what lives in the people arises from deep-seated, often historical principles. Fluctuating opinions, which are not based on a principle, have no lasting value. If he has these kinds of convictions, then they must be rooted in his own principles; and these principles, to which he holds from day to day, must be the same principles that are operative in the lives of those he will serve as its organ.

It is precisely around these principles that people gather—not as political groups or factions, but as parties. Hence, the man of conviction, unless he distances himself from public life, can never be other than the organ of such a group or circle, that is, a party organ.

This being so, the high calling of such an organ lies in the fact that what lives unconsciously in people must be brought to mind in so many words; that what is going on in such a circle be evaluated on the basis of its principles; that what is pure in that group be sifted from what is false; and that in this way the press helps make life in that circle stronger, nobler, and healthier.

But here too, temptation again lurks around the corner.

With every attempt to have the principles of such a group function with greater purity and potency, one cannot help but be vilified by those who have preferred to make a treaty with their principle and to persistently hang on to what is judged by it.

This creates reluctance, which turns those most annoyed to resentment. This resentment is aimed at putting you at a disadvantage such that you—hoping to avoid this umbrage—may compromise the truth.

The discontented ones are then joined by the peace lovers, who prefer to read "first pure and then peaceful" as if it were "*first* peaceful and then *pure*," as the continued momentum of your work is buffeted and made more difficult.

Then it comes down to whether you have the audacity not to cave in to the people but to serve your principle, and in your principle your God, and not deviate—neither to the right nor to the left—from the path that the strict requirement of your principle sets forth.

This choice is so difficult because it is precisely that tension that brings with it the danger that you are too one-sidedly focused on the principle and are too little aware of life, or that you too quickly identify your own understanding with what it is that the principle requires.

This battle returns, time and again, at every point of the road.

In this regard, even the perspective in which you place the facts is so important.

Everyone tries to arrange these facts in such a way that they best support one's interests and understanding—hence the constant attempt to group the facts differently. If one emphasizes what is not important, the key issue will be obscured.

In addition to the above is the very serious challenge of doing justice to the person of those involved. No matter how committed one is to leaving personal matters out of the picture, life remains a drama, and this drama is played out by people.

A fixed rule of thumb in this regard is that a newspaper that takes itself seriously will never print a word that assaults someone's character; and yet you cannot ignore public persons.

If you can praise such a person, you will win his sympathy; but likewise, if you must check and criticize him, you so easily rouse his indignation.

Nothing is sweeter than public praise; but likewise, nothing is penalized more than public disapproval.

That is why, as an organ, a newspaper requires a high degree of moral courage; but given that moral courage also a good degree of serious self-control is required.

The press is unmistakably a power, and those who put their pen to paper use a weapon that can have dangerous repercussions.

The press, when it is what it should be, cannot exist without a deep sense of personal responsibility. A Christian could express this by referring to the words of Scripture: that we will be called on to account to God for every word—also the vain and empty ones—that flowed from our pen.

III

For the press to carry out this high and difficult calling, it goes without saying that the freedom of speech is central to its task.

Since the days of Groen van Prinsterer, the Anitrevolutionary Party has always stood up for free speech whenever it was attacked.[7] In doing so it was fighting for *a Dutch way of thinking*,[8] for—as Professor Fruin[9] observed more than thirty years ago—nothing is so deeply lodged in the Dutch consciousness as the urge, the need, to speak freely and frankly and not to spare even the highest in the state in its critique. There was no other country in

---

7. G. Groen van Prinsterer (1801–76) was a Dutch statesman, political philosopher, and Kuyper's mentor in the antirevolutionary movement.
8. This was also the name of Groen van Prinsterer's series of pamphlets, *Nederlandsche Gedachten*, 1st series, 4 vols. (The Hague: Vervloet, 1829–32); 2nd series, 6 vols. (Amsterdam: Höveker, 1867–76).
9. Robert Fruin (1823–99) was a well-respected professor of Dutch national history at Leiden University—the first in that field and one of Kuyper's teachers there—from 1860–94 (who in 1850 debated as a "liberal" with the "antirevolutionary" Groen van Prinsterer about recent liberalizing changes in the Dutch constitution). Fruin championed the notion that "true impartiality seeks to do justice to all the participants, not necessarily to please them all."

the world where pamphleteering was freer. And even the origin of cartoons, which in precarious moments can say so much, is in part Dutch.

Especially since the rise of Calvinism, "free speech" has generally become commonplace here. Yet, Calvinism lost a good deal of its credibility when it sought to stifle free speech with a policy of strictly censoring books.

Still today, the tendency to say everything that comes to mind continues to be active in all kinds of circles among our people.

That is what often happens at meetings; people likewise wrangle with each other in all sorts of newsprint and magazines. It is almost comical to see how many reached for a pen when an influential movement arose in our good fatherland, and how all sorts of cogent as well as incredible ideas were bantered about, sometimes with a bravado that was downright surprising.

Yes, even the old, typically Dutch trait of using critique or a word of envy to take everyone down a notch who stuck out above the crowd, demonstrated talent, or presumed a higher position still prevails as before.

Yet despite this in many ways darker, shadow side, free speech is still held high among us. Having thrown off the medieval restraints, we embraced freedom and, in the end, found ourselves best suited with that generous, mild, and sometimes limitless sense of freedom.

This being the case, shortly after our first appearing, our editorial staff—in a wide-ranging series of articles under the title "Is Error a Punishable Offense?"—explained why we, with eyes wide open to the dangers associated with it, unequivocally and with masculine decisiveness supported the freedom of speech.[10]

One key reason for this stance is that when free speech is muzzled, that muzzle can only be imposed by those who are in power at the time and who can do no other than to maintain the status quo, to work against, in a truly conservative fashion, any new ideas that are emerging, and, in doing so, to find themselves doomed to halt the development of the world of thought.

Although free speech sows many evil seeds, that is precisely what motivates the sowers of good seed to be alert and to more diligent in sowing that better seed.

Even though the good may sometimes suffer defeat for a brief period, after not too many days the mind of the nation will return to its senses. History attests to the fact that the true element can develop its full strength and will win out for those who desire truth.

---

10. See Abraham Kuyper, "Is Error a Punishable Offense?," in this volume.

The mere suggestion that our editors had allowed themselves to be adopted by the guild of those who want to stifle free speech was therefore a complete misunderstanding of our purpose and of our past.

Our editors have always welcomed the launch of newspapers in our circles—providing more than one organ with counsel and advice. For example, not so long ago [in 1893], the founders of *De Nederlander* sought the advice of our editor-in-chief as to whether they could best establish a national paper in the capital or a paper with a more local focus in Rotterdam, they followed the advice we gave them to begin in Rotterdam, where the activity of our press was as yet undeveloped.

Likewise, the claim that our editors sought to restrict in any way the freedom of what some refer to as the "little newspapers" is, briefly put, in conflict with history.[11]

When an association of these Christian newspapers was set up, some initiatives were introduced to send the smaller papers in a specific direction, but that attempt did not come from our editor-in-chief.

Seeking not to exert pressure at the association's meetings, he hardly ever went to them. The few times that he did attend were occasioned by the Christian Social Congress,[12] but he did little more than offer the smaller presses assistance in obtaining the relevant literature and encouraging them to study these so that they would not find themselves unprepared or unarmed for the social struggle question that was coming.

That our editors occasionally countered an opinion voiced in these smaller papers was not a failure on their part but simply a way of honoring the freedom of expression. Others were speaking, and we were allowed to do so as well.

But we have never accused organs that held to an opinion that opposed ours of "parroting" others, nor have we described them as "puppets."

Every editorial team was responsible for what it published, and their independence had to be respected.

That the various organs nevertheless held the same line as we did for quite a few years is by no means inconsistent with this. The very same phenomenon

---

11. The *kleine pers* refers to all antirevolutionary papers (both dailies and weeklies) that followed the lead of *De Standaard*. In the early 1890s they formed an association called De Kleine Pers, governed by Anthony Brummelkamp Jr. (1839–1919), formerly of *De Standaard* but then editor-in-chief of the *Nieuwe Groningsche Courant*.

12. A reference to the First Christian Social Congress, held in Amsterdam in 1891. Kuyper provided the opening address, which appears as "Social Question and the Christian Religion," in *OBE*.

occurred in the organs of *all* political parties. Up to the critical moment when the social problem proved to be divisive in every party, the printed voice of nearly every party was for all practical purposes steady and unanimous.

The liberalist organs were of one mind when it came to protecting their principles as well as what concrete application of those principles should look like. So too, the Roman Catholic press held to a unified and steady course for years.

This phenomenon was not limited to our country but was also the case in all countries for a long time. The liberal newspapers in England always shared the same view of things; and the conservative press, availing themselves of almost identical arguments, opposed the liberal approach. That is how it was in Belgium, France, and Germany, and that is how it was in Austria. Everywhere the newspapers of the same party moved in the same direction, and always stood as one voice with respect to the other parties. There might have been some differences when it came to how things were presented, how detailed the arguments were, or how they were arranged, but in their choice of means and ends, in propagating their principles and ideas, each was of one mind.

In other words, there was nothing strange, out of the ordinary, or affected about the Anitrevolutionary Party in the Netherlands speaking with one voice in its various organs. It was not the outcome of an agreement or stipulated condition or the product of coercion or restraint, but the entirely natural result of a unity *in meaning and intent*. They shared the same voice because they based their lives on the *same principles*, had the *same* goal in mind, faced the *same* enemy, and had to defend the *same* interests.

That said, we have never lacked for opposing dailies and weeklies in our own circles. Think, for example, of the fierce opposition voiced by the former *Wageningse Weekblad*, the *Kroniek voor Waarheid en Vrede*, and in part also by the *Banier*. The same was true politically and in church matters and is still so among us.

That is the way things are, and our editors, on principle, always spoke up for this free speech. But even if they had wanted to do otherwise, what means would they have at their disposal to hinder it? Quite simply, none. Or what in the world could our editors say about the establishment of other organs? What power did it have to contain their dissenting opinions? Even if they had wanted to think up resentful attacks on free speech, what *could* our editors have done to accomplish this unholy purpose?

These straightforward questions show how absurd the suspicions made against us are.

Given that our editors, in contrast, have tried in various ways to promote the launch of other dailies and weeklies and never sought to publish a rejoinder or to impose any inappropriate or unauthorized pressure in the association of our Christian press, we will not be deprived of the honor of having always remained faithful to our position on the freedom of the press

Infidelity in this regard would have amounted to us denying a significant principle. Despite whatever loss we may have suffered, as far as we know we have never forsaken our loyalty to this principle during the nearly twenty-five years of our existence.

A very different question, however, is whether another newspaper can *force* you into a polemic that you consider either pointless or harmful, or whether you, as editorial staff, remain *free* in this regard.

IV

Curiously, two responses critiquing what was written above came our way about the same time. But, interestingly enough, they contradict each other directly.

On the one hand, they claimed that we *were restricting* free speech.

On the other hand, we were accused of *not* respecting the limits to which free speech *should* be subject. Speech and discussion, this voice argued, should not be free; and our editorial office's daring to talk about free speech as we did was a well-nigh inexcusable mistake—and that in two senses.

First, we should not have used free speech to criticize members of the States General. And second, it was inappropriate for us to direct our comments about free speech to a cabinet that we supported.

Mind you, they did not take us to task for what we said per se, but posited a theory that the press's calling is to support, and *not* to criticize, its own party caucus or a government that it supports. This theory was couched as follows: if Dr. Kuyper could be a permanent member of the Second Chamber, he should also be the leader in Parliament, and thus would certainly be willing to defend his position in *De Standaard*.

The person who wrote this, knowing that Dr. K. *could* not serve as a permanent member of the Chamber, nonetheless maintained that our editorial staff, for its part, was formally required to defend the leadership provided by the party caucus and its leaders in its pages. Hence, this theory not only cut off the free speech of critique, but also demanded that the press should *defend* what the party caucus via its leaders was doing.

Whether this was thought through, we will leave to others to decide. It is almost unbelievable. We can also only presume that whoever wrote this only had an eye for unified action and wanted to make everything else subordinate to it.

But whatever the case, we were censured for retaining the freedom of discussion also when it comes to discussing positions taken by members of Parliament. So too, we were taken to task for allowing ourselves to criticize the attitude of the Mackay cabinet after initially approaching it full of confidence and with cordial congeniality.[13] This too was not as it should have been; the assumption being that we were mistaken in raising the topic of free discussion.

***

At the same time, the exact opposite reproach was also made: that we wanted to stifle discussion because we did not see eye to eye with the opposition voiced by the *Prot. Noordbr.*[14] and that we found engaging that opposition to be ill-advised.

So, while some think there ought to be no discussion, others, on the other hand, accuse us of wanting to stifle free discussion. What is at issue here is clearly a difference of opinion regarding the press's calling.

Germany is familiar with its "reptilian" newspapers[15] and knows how, also in France, a good part of print journalism is "sold" financially. Fortunately, this is an unknown phenomenon in our country.

However, in some circles here, the misinformed opinion prevails that an organ of the press has no other or higher calling than to serve certain interests. Newspapers were never meant to be independent. Specific papers are set up with a particular goal in mind, given specific circumstances. That constitutes the paper's *calling*, beyond which it has nothing to add.

We have always disputed this opinion. According to our deep conviction, the press has a calling of its own, namely, the calling to bear witness based on principles—and as the case may be, by serving party interests only to the extent that they evidence or promote one's principles. Regarding the

---

13. Aeneas Mackay Jr. (1838–1909) was an antirevolutionary politician who served as prime minister from 1888–91.

14. That is, the *Protestantsche Noordbrabanter*, an antirevolutionary weekly originating from a largely Roman Catholic area of the Netherlands.

15. A reference to newspapers in the service of the government to combat secret enemies of the state—stemming from Bismarck's comparing these secret enemies of the state to "malicious reptiles" in 1869. See H. W. F. Bonte, ed., *Kramer's Algemeene Kunstwoordentolk*, 4th ed. (Gouda: Van Goor, 1886), 1066.

chamber and the cabinet, the press has, as we see it, not only the right, but also the very serious and often extremely difficult obligation to exercise *critique*.

A paper that does not carry out this duty contributes to turning its party into a coterie. Not the least of the causes that led to our political malaise is the sad fact that the liberal press, in the glory days of the liberal party, did not carry through on this obligation to the chamber and the cabinet, or did so very feebly—particularly as relates to social interests.

We may *not* give in on this point. That said, we are not blind to the fact that the way in which we discharged this duty in the past leaves room for improvement. But this is no reason to give up on doing what is called for. Seeking to muzzle the press regarding chamber and cabinet amounts to wanting to reduce it from acting as an independent power to *slavery*.

***

Our refusing to respond to the polemics of the *Prot. Noordbr.* did not in the least betray a desire to restrict free speech but was based on clear guidelines.

The first of these rules is that every newspaper should be free to discuss as it wants, and, on the other hand, that every other paper should remain free to decide whether it wants to or feels obligated to participate in that discussion. In this way, as well, we challenge any coercion that any one paper would want to exert on another one.

The second rule is that a discussion that degenerates into a polemic with befriended publications is not desirable except in exceptional cases. "Polemic" comes from ancient Greek (*polemikos*), meaning: *of or for war*. Now, war and friendship are mutually exclusive. Although a "playful" polemic about minor matters is possible between friends, as soon as it becomes an aggressive polemic that *seriously* attacks each other's position, then a polemic among friendly newspapers is, in our opinion, a contradiction in terms.

The third rule is that we make a distinction between a polemic that arises briefly but will soon pass and a polemic that a newspaper hammers at daily so as to unceasingly and systematically thwart you. Then one is dealing with a tendentious controversy, and it would be simply silly not to see the potential danger that such a polemic holds in store for the unity among kindred spirits. The outcome has again, as in the past, shown that such a polemic invariably leads to increasing bitterness and finally to a parting of ways.

The fourth rule is that a distinction must be made between what can and what cannot be brought up for public discussion. This does not only have to do with the personal character of the politicians, but also as concerns questions of the party's administration. So too, character flaws should not be discussed, other than among a close circle of friends. Administrative matters may also be discussed, if that happens in the central committee or at the meeting of the representatives of the political associations. One does not discuss such things in front of the enemy, as does the *Prot. Noordbr.*, unless you have already decided beforehand that if not everyone agrees with you, you will go your own way.

Our last rule is that those who work together on a common project and in the same capacity should not discuss issues among themselves in public.

For example, two people who are members of the same cabinet ought not confront each other by name in the press. Members of Parliament who voluntarily work together in a coalition ought not poster the public square with the disputes that have arisen within that coalition. Likewise, those who jointly control the actions of a party ought not argue in public about heated discussions that the leadership team must deal with. If they do so, the action is broken by that very act, and whoever continues down that road, if they understand what they are doing, does so intentionally and assumes responsibility for their actions.

Our conclusion, therefore, is that our editors, far from wanting to restrict free speech, have always stood up for the rights of free speech and maintained them also (when called for) among friends and kindred spirits.

Wanting to smother or to preclude a free discussion about principles would amount to undermining the vitality of the press—something of which we never hope never to be guilty. We always find room for occasional polemics among befriended colleagues. But if there is someone who seems to make polemicizing his reason for being, you should be free to judge for yourself how you should proceed, given the interests entrusted to you and with an eye to your personal and political relationship to him.

It is in this sense that we explained at the time why we neither could nor ought to engage in a polemic with the *Prot. Noordbr.* The outcome, unfortunately, has shown that our premonitions as to where this polemic would lead were not mistaken.

CELEBRATING TWENTY-FIVE YEARS OF *DE STANDAARD*

TEXT INTRODUCTION

When Kuyper's daily newspaper *De Standaard* was approaching its twenty-fifth anniversary, his friends and followers decided that the occasion warranted a festive celebration honoring its editor-in-chief. The venue rented for the gathering was the great hall of the *Paleis voor Volksvlijt*, Amsterdam's "Crystal Palace." On the evening of April 1, 1897, exactly twenty-five years after the first issue of *De Standaard* rolled off the presses, the hall was filled to overflowing as upwards of five thousand invited antirevolutionaries, passes in hand and guided by forty ushers, came to express their appreciation for their inspiring leader. The doors opened at 5:30, and at 6:30 the expectant throng was regaled to an hour-long organ impromptu. At last, Dr. and Mrs. Kuyper, led by the committee members, entered the podium and a brass band struck up the Genevan tune of Psalm 68, sometimes referred to as the "Huguenot Marseillaise," of which the masses sang two stanzas.

The text below is Kuyper's thank-you speech which he gave after the chair of the organizing committee, Theo Heemskerk (1852–1932), and festive orator Herman Bavinck (1854–1921), had delivered their respective celebratory messages. Heemskerk emphasized that honoring Kuyper as leader was especially motivated by the fact that "he taught our people in the political arena not only to fight *for the faith* but also to live *out of faith*." This speech was followed by the communal singing of two stanzas of Luther's hymn "A Mighty Fortress Is Our God." Bavinck then stepped to the rostrum and spoke for half an hour, commending Kuyper for using *De Standaard* to turn from the ruling elite to the common people, inspiring them with a unique combination of deep-probing analysis and inspiring prose. Its broad vision, historical sense, and never-flagging idealism, Bavinck remarked, had forged the Anitrevolutionary Party into a national force and had led it for a quarter-century in uncompromising opposition to "the politics of unbelief and opportunism." Communal singing following this speech gave a rendition of da Costa's song, "They shall not have our country / the idols of our time."

After being presented with a memorial statue, eighty centimeters in height, made of black marble and silver, Kuyper got up and delivered his speech. His causerie, which at times exhibits elements of an improvisation, shows him as both the gifted orator and the homespun populist who knows how to use the power of the word to speak to the hearts of a mixed audience that is united in a cause. He described his fundamental ideas about journalism, interspersed with autobiographical details about the "life struggle" that had brought him to this point in his life. He used the moment to explain his belief that the modern daily press was a gift from God to be treasured. It had made it possible for them to be bound together in a shared sense of consciousness and purpose, thus counteracting the equally modern tendency of individualism that was causing the disintegration of society.

Kuyper's speech was well received and several times interrupted by loud reactions from the audience. As soon as Kuyper had finished, the assembly rose to its feet and sang to him the blessing from Psalm 121: "The Lord will guard and keep thee."

SOURCE: *Gedenkboek. Opgedragen door het feestcomité aan Prof. Dr. A. Kuyper. Bij zijn vijf en twintigjarig jublileum als hoofdredacteur van "De Standaard"* (Amsterdam: Herdes, 1897), 59–77. Translated by John Kok. Annotated and edited by Johan Snel and Harry Van Dyke.

CELEBRATING TWENTY-FIVE YEARS OF *DE STANDAARD*

Dear Brothers!

The poet Isaäc da Costa once sang: "The sweet wine of human kindness is inebriating."[1] And right now, I am experiencing firsthand how it is that self-control is called for to remain sober as the plethora of your signs of love and support surrounds me. I knew of my bond with more than one among those who know God in the Netherlands, but I never could have guessed or suspected that so warm an expression of devotion would fall to my lot as I have experienced today.

And yet, now that God allows me to empty this cup of your love and loyalty, I now say to you: love is sweet, loyalty refreshes the heart, and I will draw new energy from that full, mild, rich draught of human love that you gave me to drink.

Initially I was afraid when I heard of the plan to gather with so many thousands here in this large hall. I had heard whispers of Kuypermania so often, even though I had never noticed any of that among you. But then I

---

1. Isaäc da Costa, "Een Gebed voor den 'Heraut,' " in *Da Costa's Kompleete Dichtwerken* (Haarlem: Kruseman, 1863), 3:395.

began to wonder: Is that evil spirit real after all? And will it make its apparition here in this grand exhibition hall? But when I received a copy of your program and saw that the intent was not to honor a man, but at every point to give thanks and veneration to God, that fear was lifted off my shoulders and I was delighted to accept your invitation to join you here today. I thought to myself: if Israel's priests were allowed to dedicate sheaves and lambs—the fruit of the field and the fold—on the altar of the Lord, why should the children of men not bring the sheaves that are reaped on the field for which God has laid the foundations in the human mind, to place them upon his altar and to kneel before him with thanks and jubilation:

> Hallelujah! Glory, honor,
> Praise and worship, wisdom, power,
> Rise to Thee on earth and heaven,
> Lord, for your abiding love.[2]

Everything that I am, as I stand before you here, still in good condition for a sixty-year-old, with my uninterrupted health, with a mind that can think, a hand that can write, a mouth that can speak, what else are they but his gifts and his work? He who created me, predestined me, and led me since my youth; he who, even though I had no inkling of it, guided me unawares to this position, to take a stand for his holy name; he alone it was who also opened your hearts to me. This was all *his* doing. And even if you ask me if there is nonetheless also a "self" behind every gift and talent, and whether that "self" is not a personality that fires and animates these gifts, my response is still: even that "self"—that personality—does not come from me but is gifted to me by God alone.

Because you have infused your celebration with that same spirit and I am allowed to share in that same spirit with you this evening, I open my arms and call out to you: feel free to cast your crowns and garlands in my direction, as long as you allow me to take them from my head and shoulders and, redirecting all the luster and glory away from me, lay them with deep respect at the foot of the throne of the Lamb. And so I now feel free, without a reproach from God in my conscience, to thank you as instruments in his hand for this beautiful evening, for your coming from all walks of life and positions and from all the provinces of our country; and not only

---

2. Kuyper quotes the hymn "Halleluja, eeuwig dank en ere" by Abraham Rutgers (1751–1809), number 96 in the collection *Evangelische Gezangen* (Amsterdam: Johannes Allart, 1806).

those men hardened in the political struggle, but also those women who understood the power of prayer *during* that struggle, and *after* the struggle, when her husband returns home scarred by battle, to soothe his wounds with the balm of love.

And so I thank you all for coming; not only you elders, matured by the years, but also you younger ones, the second generation, those who will pick up the mantle once we older ones have passed on. May your labors be crowned with even greater fortune and generous blessings than were reserved for us!

I thank you all, and not in the least those who took the initiative in planning and arranging for this happy and joyous evening.

I want to especially thank those who have just spoken. Their good words have convinced me that we still have thoughtful people in our midst who have fully understood my struggle and have grasped the deepest motivation of my aims.

Kuyper received a statue of the Dutch Maiden (personifying the Netherlands) holding a banner engraved with the words, "Our help is in the name of the Lord, who created heaven and earth." Image and description courtesy Jan de Bruijn, *Abraham Kuyper: A Pictorial Biography*, trans. Dagmare Houniet (Grand Rapids: Eerdmans, 2014), 226.

I thank you no less for the wonderful gift you have presented me. When it was unveiled my first thought was: it's true, then, Calvinists have once again learned to value art. (*Applause*) Its ornate form and beautiful symbolism are proof of the fact that the days are past when we disdained all things external and lacked all sense of artistic expression and any feeling for what it can do to enlighten our sight. So, accept my heartfelt thanks for this valuable gift, for the beautiful symbolism it expresses, and for its elegant form and execution. My thanks is all the warmer because I know that shining in that silver and marble is not only the gold of the well-to-do, but also the silver of the sober burgher, and even the copper, the small gifts, of the little man; because I know that what contributed to its value includes the sweat of hands and the exertion of hard work; and above all because I know that in that gift you have sought to express the poetry of heartfelt love.

I accept it with thanksgiving. It will have a special place in my home, not to prove your homage—no, forget about homage—but to *memorialize* God's faithfulness and no less to *commemorate* the love, loyalty, and affection that you have shown me this evening. And since God has afforded me the blessing of seeing my own convictions take root in a happy family, you can rest assured that your princely gift will stand for many years to come as a witness for my children, and may it be for my grandchildren, inviting them never to abandon what was celebrated and professed this evening as our sacred principle. May it resonate in my lineage until the Lord returns! (*Applause*)

What brings us together here is, of course, a *celebration of the daily press*. Allow me therefore to say at the outset that although many in our circles often spurned daily newspapers, dismissing them with the label *newsprint scribblings*, for me the daily press, already since my youth, has been neither a human invention nor even less an instrument of the Evil One, but a gift from God to our generation in the nineteenth century, a gift that I do not hesitate to place on a par with the invention of the printing press.

What is the daily press?

Our fathers had no knowledge of daily newspapers. When they disputed issues or argued a cause they did so with pamphlets. These were usually rough in form and tough to digest. In their free hours, which sometimes dragged on sooner than flying by, they occupied themselves with these long-winded, wordy pamphlets. But life today has become completely different.

Due to technological innovations during this past century, the speed with which people can communicate with each other has seen revolutionary changes. They can often experience in one hour more tremors, a buildup of more powerful sensations, or a greater flood of emotions than our forefathers experienced in half a day. This faster pace of life means that the focus of our lives lies less muted in the recesses of our hearts and that we want to be more conscious of what all is going on in the world. This desired clarity of mind, in turn, requires that what can be known about these things reaches us as quickly as possible.

The call for the daily press emerged from these developments. Daily news was the only way to meet that need. It was, therefore, the same God who quickened the pace of our whole lives through all sorts of technological inventions that called the *daily newspaper* into being to meet the needs arising from these innovations. Single-sheet newsletters were known in the past, yet not until this century were these courants elevated to the powerhouse in society—the "queen of the earth"—that the daily press is today.

Still another, higher purpose was also at work here. While too much freedom and independence began to drive our generation down the path of *individualism*, which in turn contributed to the dissolution of our communal bonds, it is in the newspaper that God provides us with the means to bring unity back into the sensations of our consciousness. After all, those who are reading a newspaper know that thousands of others in the country are reading the same words that same evening or the same morning and as a result are aroused by the same emotions, infused with the same thoughts, encouraged in the same convictions.

In the midst of our individualistically diverging lives, God the Lord gave us the newspaper as a means of restoring a *sense of community* in our consciousness.

The newspaper has also cultivated what is usually called *public spirit*, or what I prefer to call a return to the standpoint of the ancient prophets. In Israel, those prophets did not engage the pious merely with what was happening in their own town or village, but they also told them about the kings of Egypt, about the kingdoms of Babylon and Assyria, about Moab and Edom, about Persians and Greeks; and those selfsame prophets compelled the faithful in Israel to take stock of all of *world history* and to discern God's plan with the world—which is exactly what the daily newspaper must do in our age as well.

There are some among the children of men whose world is no larger than their own house and who have next to no sense of what is happening in their own village. The Lord God grants others a broader scope; they at least are involved in the affairs of their village or town. Then there are others whose focus moves on from their town or village to the far more important interests of their country. Still others look beyond their own borders to also take stock of the fortunes and struggles of people in Europe, Asia, America, and Africa. And so, at last, human interest comes to embrace all history, in which God performs his mighty work and brings to pass his counsel and plan. And is it not your daily that takes you beyond your home, that forces you to broaden your horizon, to be informed about what is going on in your city and your country and among the peoples of Europe and other parts of the world? Yes, it is the daily newspaper that pries you loose from your narrow-mindedness and petty obsessions and helps you to live in the light of the great and mighty deeds of God.

Finally, the daily press *leads and guides* the public spirit. All too often in centuries past, public opinion was like a wandering, rudderless child. The daily news media has the high and sacred calling, as ideas and viewpoints are developing, to set out the path along which they can move forward, so that our journey through life can be clearly marked out in our consciousness. Thanks to the daily newspaper none of us stands alone with his own personal ideas. Kindred spirits in the north come into contact with like-minded folks in the south before they realize it, as though they were connected by telephone. Heartfelt opinions here resonate with deep-seated opinions there and in so doing end up binding people together. From these relationships and connections power is born, making the principles dear to many into a force felt throughout the country. Is it not the daily press which as a God-given trumpet broadcasts principles among the people, rallies them around these principles, and soon induces them to draw up in battle array, to take up the cause of those principles with irresistible force?

As can be gleaned from the above, my conviction is that the daily press truly is not an invention of the Evil One but a gift of God to our generation. When I came to realize how that mighty weapon was being used to propagate all kinds of principles and to *counter* the faith of our fathers and to oppose what you hold dear, I said to myself: If that God-given weapon already exerts such power when it is turned *against* his people, why should God's people stand on the sidelines? Why should they not use that weapon themselves to fight for the honor of their God? With that my decision was made: Christians in the Netherlands must also have their own daily newspaper, one that gives expression to what lives in their hearts.

Now I know that there are those who turn the matter around and say: it was not the people who inspired your newspaper, but you worked on those who read your newspaper and made Calvinists of them. There are even those who attribute a hypnotic power to me and blame me for turning my readers into *puppets*, the strings of which I manipulate to make them dance and jump at will. But, my brothers, to those who attribute this to me my reply can be short: *try for yourselves whether you can make puppets of our Calvinists!* (*Loud laughter*)

No, brothers, that has never been the case. It was like this: What was alive in you, though not always with clear awareness, found clear and lucid expression in my *Standaard*. All I have been able to do was to try to articulate the convictions stirring in your own hearts and minds. And the only reason I have been able to do so was because your life was my life and the life-breath of my soul was one with yours. (*Lengthy applause*)

And now, this newspaper, what was in it for me?

Was it my aim to become its editor? Was I looking to make a career of it? You know better. It was nothing more than a part of a much broader calling. If I may put it this way, my *Standaard* has never been anything other than a steed that I rode to reach the finish line of the course more quickly; and my *life's goal* lay in that finish line.

What was that goal, the thought that has driven and guided my life? Briefly put, it is this: to make not just antirevolutionaries, but if possible *my entire nation and country*, happy again by inviting them to turn back to the only trustworthy paths of life, which, as I see it, lie marked out in *the ordinances of God*.

Allow me to explain briefly—historically-psychologically, if you will—how I came to reach for that goal in life. I have read and loved newspapers since I was a young lad. My dear father disapproved of my infatuation—that I was hooked on the daily paper already as a boy of ten or eleven—and finally forbade me to stick my nose in the paper again. But my passion for journalism was so strong then already that whenever I was able to get my hands on a newspaper (though I should not have, because doing so was disobedient), I would sneak it into the attic and there I would sit as a young boy, on a packing box, reading the *Opregte Haarlemmer*.[3]

No wonder, then, that before I went to university I was already a mini-*politician*. (*Loud laughter*)

---

3. The *Opregte Haarlemsche Courant* is the oldest Dutch newspaper. It first appeared in 1656 and continues still today, now under the title *Haarlems Dagblad*. In Kuyper's day it was still read throughout the country.

I remember it still, as though it was yesterday: It was 1853, the year of Thorbecke's fall! He who stands before you today was at the time the fiercest antipapist imaginable, and the April movement made me an anti-Thorbeckian of the fiercest sort.[4] After all, I had long been told and was raised believing that Thorbecke and his supporters sought to undermine the honor and authority of the House of Orange. I, in contrast, had loved the House of Orange since my youth. My devotion was so deeply entrenched that when word of his dismissal reached Leiden on the evening of April the twentieth, that was all it took for me—almost beside myself with joy—to fly down the stairs and into my father's study and, like someone drunk with joy, to blurt out: Father, Father, Thorbecke has fallen!

Later I went to Beesd, where in 1866 I heard about Keuchenius as a political culprit who once again, though for reasons other than Thorbecke's, dared assail the authority of the king.[5] Along with the newspaper I was subscribed to, *Dagblad van Zuid-Holland en 's-Gravenhage*, I vigorously took issue with Keuchenius,[6] siding with the father of our esteemed chairman.[7]

4. The Dutch constitution, revised in 1848, stipulated the separation of church and state and guaranteed religious freedom. When in March 1853 Pope Pius IX (1792–1878) decreed the reestablishment of the episcopal hierarchy in the Netherlands, the liberal government, led by Johan Rudolph Thorbecke (1798–1872), had no grounds to appeal or prohibit this initiative. Protestants, however, protested that the Netherlands was a Protestant country and loudly objected to the pope's involvement in Dutch affairs, igniting a veritable "no popery" movement in the country. They appealed to the king, and William III (1817–90), sympathetic to their cause, refused to underwrite his prime minister's assessment of the situation, with the result that the Thorbecke Cabinet tendered its resignation.

5. L. W. C. Keuchenius (1822–93) was a supporter of G. Groen van Prinsterer (1801–76) and a powerful advocate of Christian education and foreign missions in the colonies. From 1869 to 1879, he held high judicial and administrative posts in the Dutch East Indies. Upon his return to the Netherlands, he served two terms as a member of Parliament from 1866–68 and again from 1879 until his death, interrupted only from 1888 to 1890, when he served as minister of colonial affairs. In 1866 his notorious motion in the lower house of Parliament, which reprimanded the Cabinet for playing fast and loose with the appointment of a governor-general for the Indies, was strongly opposed by the Cabinet, which painted it as an assault on the prerogative of the king to make such appointments.

6. It is possible that an anonymous letter to the editor in this leading conservative daily around this time was penned by Kuyper.

7. Prominent antirevolutionary Theo Heemskerk (1852–1932), who was chairing the evening, was the son of conservative Jan Heemskerk (1818–97), who in 1866 was head of the Cabinet attacked by Keuchenius.

This lasted until a ray of light from above pierced my heart while living in the quiet of the village where I was pastor. From then on and in that light, everything, including my political views, saw a turnaround. After many conversations with the simple pious folk of that village and especially with the headmaster of the public school,[8] an amiable Christian, with whom I frequently discussed current affairs, I gradually came to realize that my earlier views had been wrong and that the names of Groen van Prinsterer and Keuchenius should guide me.

As a result, breaking with what was behind me, I threw myself into that new—now holy to me—stream.

Not so long thereafter, I received a call to Utrecht; which for me, at that time only remotely acquainted as I was with Dutch orthodoxy, felt like being called to Jerusalem. The idea that there I would meet the luminaries of the orthodox of the day made my moving to Utrecht like living out the songs of ascent. But alas, it did not take very long for me to be disabused of those dreams. There, in that same Utrecht, my youthful enthusiasm was soon doused with ice water.

I expected to find professorial brothers there for whom the Bible was *the* authoritative Word for our lives; men who, with *that Word* as weapon, stood ready to defend the fortress of Jerusalem in the Netherlands with spirited resilience; men who did not just stand on the ramparts to fend off attacks, but who ventured out beyond its gates to engage the enemy.

But what did I find? Everywhere an atmosphere of small-mindedness. The entire leadership, timidly holed up in the fortress, prepared for nothing more than a weak defense, waiting for a bomb to strike, and only then, should it come, somehow or other to return fire, all the while relinquishing one outer work after another to the enemy.

I found officers there as well as troops. The officers were the professors and pastors, and I call the members of the congregation the troops, but the relationship between officers and troops was not one of trust, but of misgiving. The former did not dare tell the congregation frankly how dangerous and precarious they assessed the situation and how they sensed that the line of defense would have to be abridged even further. There was

---

8. H. A. Kievits, an aged schoolteacher and author of a popular primer on writing, *Oefeningen in het zuiver schrijven der Nederduitsche taal* (Tiel: Wermeskerken, 1840), formed a small reading club which included Kuyper, where they read works by Groen van Prinsterer and others.

a complete lack of unity in the plan of defense; the one defender countered and envied the other. Confusion was pervasive, and other than for church and theology there were no ideals to inspire people to once again challenge the enemy when it came to sociopolitical life.

That position, that tactic, the whole situation in that bulwark bothered me.

I felt: that was no attitude for a community of believers that considers itself to be *the armies of the living God.*

My immediate response was that before anything else, and with the help of all the brothers, we had to reembrace our basis of operation, which I believed could only be God's Word, the holy scriptures as they were handed down to us from the fathers. So I approached the entire circle of those brothers, all of whom were held in high regard at the time, to work together and publish an extensive volume with an eye to once again standing up for that Word of God. And they promised to do so. I wrote up a brief statement and distributed it to them all in which I professed my faith in Scripture and my firm resolve, without a moment of hesitation or fear of critique, to completely submit myself to God's Word and to be bound by that Word. But, alas, once they had read it, all but two replied rather harshly that it was impossible for them to work with me.

That became the turning point in my life. I concluded that cooperation with these brothers was not going to work because there was a yawning gap between us from the very start and the authority of God's Word lay between us.

Although I was probably a bit overconfident, I then became a kind of guerrilla fighter, hazarding confrontation at my own risk. I was not content to just defend the fortress that was being attacked. I decided to sally forth. Finding an apologetic approach pointless, I decided to attack, lobbing one grenade after another among the opponents. First, your Modernism is a mirage.[9] Next, your modern life, as manifest in liberalism and conservatism,[10] labors under *the curse of conformity.*[11] Then, a lecture in the Restored

---

9. Abraham Kuyper, *Het modernisme een fata morgana op christelijk gebied* (Amsterdam: H. de Hoogh, 1871); ET: *Modernism: A Fata Morgana in the Christian Domain* (1871), in *AKCR*, 87–124.

10. Abraham Kuyper, *Conservatisme en orthodoxie* (Amsterdam: H. de Hoogh, 1870); ET: *Conservatism and Orthodoxy: False and True Preservation* (1870), in *AKCR*, 65–85.

11. Abraham Kuyper, *Eenvormigheid, de vloek van het moderne leven* (Amsterdam: H. de Hoogh, 1869); ET: *Uniformity: The Curse of Modern Life* (1869), in *AKCR*, 19–44.

Lutheran Church targeting the Society for the Common Good, a leading movement in the Netherlands at the time.[12] That is how I felt liberated; and rooted in the authority of God's Word, I courageously faced the coming struggle. I was where Luther had found himself when he exclaimed: "The Word they shall allow to stand."[13] I experienced days that were rich for heart and soul.

But I soon noticed that something was still missing. Germany is Lutheran, and the work that Luther completed in Germany was lofty and grand. Nevertheless, the termites of false philosophy had crept across our borders from that same Germany, in order to eat away, here too, at the timbers of the theological edifice.

As well, the *Word* without further definition, solely as the basis of the church's confession, provided comfort for the soul and certainty for the inner life, but the gulf that cut the Word of God off from the bustle of society, from the life of the nation and the domain of art and science remained. In this way the church remained Christian, but life itself remained *dechris-tianized*. The unity between working within the church and working among the people was lacking.

I carried on in this way until an unforgettable evening. It was May 18, 1869. I was in the consistory room of the Domkerk in Utrecht, when I for the first time met the man who by his first look and his first word at once took such a strong hold on me and so profoundly impressed me that from that hour I became his spiritual associate, nay more, his spiritual son. Shortly thereafter, two men came down from Amsterdam to see me— both of blessed memory, brave, devout, cheerful Christians. And after I had personally met Groen van Prinsterer and then talked with these two men, the glory of Calvinism began to dawn on me. Stahl[14] was a *Lutheran*, I am a *Calvinist*, said Groen van Prinsterer, and from Dibbetz and Bechthold[15] I

---

12. Abraham Kuyper, *De "Nuts"-Beweging* (Amsterdam: H. Höveker, 1869); ET: "The Society 'For the Common Good,'" in *On Education*, 6–13.

13. *Das Wort sie sollen lassen stahn*, a line from the original German version of "A Mighty Fortress," which had been sung earlier in the evening.

14. Friedrich Julius Stahl (1802–61) was a Lutheran scholar who taught a Christian philosophy of law and politics in the University of Berlin.

15. Henri Joan Dibbetz (1817–74) and J. Bechthold were prominent members of the society Vrienden der Waarheid [Friends of the Truth]. Dibbetz was a retired naval officer. Bechthold was one of the 42 elders whose suspension (along with that of 5 pastors and 33 deacons) led to the schism of 1886 known as the *Doleantie*.

began to understand that this meant that Holy Scripture serves not only to find justification through faith and to provide light for the path to eternity, but that this same Word of God also points to *the foundation of human life in its entirety*, the holy ordinances which are to govern the whole of human life in state and society and which alone are able to restore that life to health. Once I had discovered that, I came to know Calvin better. From historical study I also learned that while public life in Germany had remained pretty much the same and little had been done to further popular liberty, in countries influenced by Calvinism, in contrast, the fight for freedom had been productive. Human life had flourished richly, first among the Huguenots, then in Switzerland, later here, then in Scotland and England, and later in America. This made it possible to honor much more of what *God's Word* requires among a free people. That is when things opened up for me and I came to the all-controlling conviction that Holy Scripture is not just a word for our soul, but that both Scripture and nature show us *the ordinances of God for human life in its entirety*.

With that motto in mind I now entered the world, and irrespective of whom I was talking with or what field they represented—the academy, the arts, society, or the world of entertainment—I would always ask them the same question: Is your life, is your work, are the priorities of your heart, in accordance with *the ordinances of the Lord?*

I set about seeking out those ordinances, elucidating them afresh, explaining and clarifying them, impressing them upon people's hearts, not as some higher wisdom that *I* had and preached, but as taken from God's Word. I was convinced that the *conscious* knowledge of these ordinances and our living according to them from day to day was the only way for our people to come to know true freedom and to be truly happy again. That has been my ambition; that is the only, the great, the mighty idea that I have been trying to embody for twenty-five years, also in *De Standaard*. Everything else, whether it was work or time or some other effort not related to this one great purpose in life, seemed to me loss and waste.

I have now been allowed to work toward that end for a quarter of a century. And so, what do you say? Do I not have every reason to offer praise and thanksgiving for the happiness I have experienced, greater in our circle than anyone in my position has ever experienced?

Take Bilderdijk. What a fighter! He fought for more than twice twenty-five years. But toward the end of his life, did he not sit as a Prometheus chained to a rock, without the hint of a voice anywhere in the land echoing the words of his heart?[16]

And da Costa! He sang in two meters. People certainly admired him as a poet. To poets, artists that they are, the artistic circles readily burn their incense. But what did da Costa see as the fruit of his labor while he was still alive? Who was there to stand with him and to gather around him when his soul shed tears for his country?[17] Who would not agree that da Costa was not allowed on this side of the grave to gather the sheaves of his field into the barn?

And Groen! When I first met him on May 18, 1869, he was already eight years older than I am now, and yet, only four years later did the hour arrive that he, a statesman like few others, a man of high position and constitutional erudition, had to restrict his support of candidates for his Anitrevolutionary Party throughout the country to a mere trio, including a little-known pastor and a public schoolteacher.[18] That God allows me to witness and enjoy today what these men, high in rank and reputation, never knew, it is not because my work has been so much more or so much better, but only because I have been permitted to sow where they had tilled the soil and to reap the benefits of their labor.

That is why I am—let me say it—a happier man than many. Thanks be to God alone!

Now, if you were to ask me whether there is not another thought that tugs at my heartstrings tonight, whether my joy is not also mixed, then

16. Willem Bilderdijk (1756–1831) combated the secular spirit of the age in prose and especially in poetry, but throughout his life he had few followers and was subjected to much scorn and abuse for his counterrevolutionary publications.

17. Isaäc da Costa (1798–1861) became a disciple of Bilderdijk when he studied law in Leiden. He gained great notoriety when in 1823 he published his tract *Grievances against the Spirit of the Age*, sometimes called "the birth-cry of the Réveil." His occasional poems, written at critical periods in the country's history, stamp him as an uncrowned poet laureate. But despite his talents and erudition, he was denied a professorship or any public office.

18. The three men were Keuchenius, Kuyper, and M. D. van Otterloo (1810–80), headmaster of the public school in the country village of Valburg. Groen trusted them because, unlike many other self-styed antirevolutionaries who more than once had betrayed their election promises, these three men pledged to stand unreservedly for the antirevolutionary program once elected, particularly when it came to rescinding the law which mandated setting up state schools in every community, even when all the children there were attending a Christian school, thus obligating parents to pay for both school systems.

I would have to say: yes, indeed. There is also a shadow of grief for my heart. I miss so many here, and that makes me sad. Those who know me personally, up close, know how my heart is attuned to sympathy. This is so true that, had I been left to myself, I would have been sorely tempted more than once to drop a sliver of our principles just to maintain the communion with all our brothers. And had God not seen to it that I was always surrounded by brothers who disabused me of these inclinations during those perilous moments ... I truly cannot say that I would have kept to the straight and narrow. I might well have slipped along the way. It is just not true that my attitude is one of exclusion, that my aim is to alienate people or be off-putting. But when the bond of principles isn't there, then not even the warmest sympathy brings with it a bonding agent strong enough to create durable, solid ties.

Time and again, men from all walks of life chose different paths and sought out other ways. For many, that was their only option. But on this beautiful evening I cannot help but miss many of these men from our circles. Not only because I feel that they belong to us, but also because I know that the path we stand on tonight is, also for them, the only way to keep a steady course and the only way to ensure the dawn of a better future for Christian Netherlands.

Only the other day, Rev. Hulsman's publication showed how unstable the waters elsewhere have already become.[19] The authority of God's Word is absolute, and those who deviate ever so slightly from the straight and narrow run the grave risk of losing their way entirely. That is why I would like to cry out to the best of our absent brothers, with all my heart: do not stand afar off but return to the midst of the brothers and let us once again, under one banner, go up together for the glory of our God and for the salvation of his people.[20] (*Applause*)

I urge you all, brothers: do not let the prayer for such a beautiful outcome fall silent in your heart. Even if harsh words are leveled at us, even if you

---

19. Kuyper is probably referring to a brochure by the young ethical-irenic pastor Gerrit Hulsman (1867–1958). Titled *Moderne wetenschap of bijbelsche traditie?* (Utrecht: Kemink & Zoon, 1897), the work sketched the challenge posed by higher criticism but ultimately professed submission to the authority of Scripture.

20. This plea was one of the last invitations by Kuyper to his colleagues of the ethical-irenic school to unite with him on the basis of a public theology that would combat the secularizing drift of national life.

are cold-shouldered, persevere in prayer. And then may God grant that one day more of the Lord's people join the battle as one man.

Allow me to end with this. The work of twenty-five years in this fascinating area of national life lies behind me. Another twenty-five years will not be added to them. But the strength that the Lord may still grant me, it will remain devoted *to your cause* until the day I die, because your cause is the Lord's cause. (*Protracted applause*)

I know that folks whisper behind our backs that this won't make any difference anyway, since what we have accomplished depends on my person and therefore is something that will last only as long as I am alive; that once I die it will be buried with me. I shall not try to refute this false impression, because I know how bitterly disappointed those who speak this way will be once I am gone. Then they will notice that what they have seen during my lifetime is nothing compared to what will come once I have passed on. Was that also not the case for Groen van Prinsterer? As long as he was alive and spoke his word, he was not only misunderstood and maligned, but the cause dear to his heart saw little progress. But no sooner was Groen buried than accolades resounded from every corner of the country and the voice of Christendom was raised everywhere, to declare: Groen was the man who showed us the way forward; it is his word that we want to follow. I dare say something similar will happen after my death. We have plowed too deeply, fertilized too intensively, sown with such sound seed than that the Lord God would allow this work, begun in his name, to come to nothing just because one human being is now gone. After all, whether I *am* here or *not* does not really matter – *God remains!*

And if some people, half sneeringly, should call out: "Pray tell, just where is the man who will succeed you?" then for that too I have a ready answer. In 1869, Groen van Prinsterer was eight years older than I am now, and only then did he first meet the person whom he would later kindly name his successor.[21] Given that analogy, I still have eight years! (*Loud laughter*)

---

21. See Groen to Kuyper, January 6, 1874: "You write about the danger to my party if [you took a seat in Parliament and] *De Standaard* would have to be discontinued. *Our* party: to that I should have no objection. But as soon as we begin to specify, it is not my but your party that would be endangered. You were the leader after me, to my delight, but in your own right, needing neither my permission nor mandate." See *Groen van Prinsterer. Schriftelijke Nalatenschap*, ed. L. J. van Essen, vol. 7; *Briefwisseling*, vol. 6 (The Hague: Instituut voor Nederlandse Geschiedenis, 1992), 489. This vote of confidence in a private letter was made public by Groen in a pamphlet of March 19,

There is the only thing I ask of you, brothers and sisters: When my pen falls quiet and I no longer can hold up our *Standaard*, then don't let anyone among you retreat for a moment but instead close ranks, and may this then be the sacrifice of love that you will bring after my death: that you rally around the same banner even more faithfully as one man and that you convey to your sons and daughters something of the fire that you have felt glowing in your own heart in the midst of our struggle. (*Applause*)

Our gathering here this evening is quickly drawing to a close. It was a rich, wonderful, and unforgettable hour for me. To all those who contributed to it, once more my heartfelt thanks! And if you want my final word, then allow me to close with my own free rendering of da Costa's song:

> My life is ruled by but one passion,
> > one higher urge drives will and soul.
> My breath may stop before I ever
> > allow that sacred urge to fall.
> 'Tis to affirm God's holy statutes
> > in church and state, in home and school,
> despite the world's strong remonstrations,
> > to bless our people with his rule.
> 'Tis to engrave God's holy order,
> > heard in Creation and the Word,
> upon the nation's public conscience,
> > till God is once again its Lord.[22]

I thank you. (*Tumultuous applause*)

1874: "Leader of the people that loves me and in whose prayers lies my strength, was and is Dr. Kuyper, with me and after me, neither by appointment nor by inheritance but *jure suo*." See G. Groen van Prinsterer, *Nederlandsche Gedachten* (Amsterdam: Höveker, 1869–76), 5:399.

22. Kuyper uses his own free rendering of the final couplet of da Costa's song "Vrijheid" [Liberty] that was first published in 1822; the final eight lines are entirely his own. Translated by Harry Van Dyke.

THE PRESS AS
THE APOSTLE OF
PEACE

TEXT INTRODUCTION

"The Press as the Apostle of Peace" (*De pers als vredesapostel*) appeared in the first issue of a new yearbook for international relations and international law. Kuyper probably wrote it at the request of Henri Van der Mandere (1883-1959), a journalist and peace activist, who edited it and contributed a number of articles himself. Its theme, however—the interdependency between press and public opinion, especially in times of war—is Kuyper's own. Already during the Franco-Prussian war of 1870, some of his first forays into journalism for the (then) weekly *De Heraut* had pondered it. Even more intensely had he been contemplating the new powers of press and public opinion during his active years in the Dutch journalists' association (acting as a chairman 1898-1901). More recently he had presided (1908-12) over a Dutch peace committee for internationalism, lobbying for the foundation of an Academy for International Law in the Hague. In Kuyper's view, it should have provided an independent academic underpinning of the interstate activities at the international Peace Palace in The Hague that opened its doors in August 1913 (and he resigned when the lobby failed). In 1912, he had also been invited by Van der Mandere to join the peace movement of Vrede door Recht (Peace by Justice), which he did, with the proviso that he withheld his support for the mistaken principle of pacifism, a theme he also elaborates in his daily *De Standaard* in these years (as he does in this essay).

SOURCE: Abraham Kuyper, "De pers als vredesapostel," *Grotius: Internationaal Jaarboek* (June 1913): 54–65. Translated by John Kok. Edited and annotated by Johan Snel.

THE PRESS AS THE APOSTLE OF PEACE

Given the push to preserve international peace, not enough can be said about the importance of the press.

There are two reasons for this: on the one hand, the ever-growing influence that *public opinion* exerts on international relations; and on the other hand, the ever-increasing influence that the press has on public opinion.

Although most constitutions assign the right to declare war to the government, it is totally inconceivable at this point in time that the sovereign in most countries would go to war if the public opinion among the entirety of his people found such a war to be unnecessary or unacceptable.

Waging war increasingly requires extensive preparations on a large scale. The expenses that such a venture requires cannot be legally allocated without the cooperation of the parliament. Even if the monarch can ramp up his military forces, the millions that it costs to engage these forces would require the parliament's involvement. And even though it be forced to comply, volatility in the stock market owing to public opinion might not be able to generate the capital required. Such a tense relationship has become even more serious when—as has happened in more than one country—the social democrats, banking on the public opinion's refusal to support the war effort, then attempt to use this opposition to encourage resistance within the ranks of the army itself.

Recent events in Italy, for example, made plain that this need not be a factor when public opinion supports the government. The conquest (and eventual annexation) of Tripoli in 1911 was in no way an initiative that captured the heart of the Italian people, and yet the prospect of colonial possessions was strong enough to convince the public opinion in Italy to support the government, and to dismiss every attempt on the part of the socialists to oppose the same as unpatriotic and as a betrayal of the nation's honor.

It may safely be assumed then that, compared to a century ago, the decision between peace or going to war, even though it must still be at the government's discretion, has nevertheless become dependent on public opinion. To enter a major war without the explicit support of the people is, today, out of the question. Every war is bought with the price of the blood and bullion of the people, such that every government that wants to wage a war but fails to inspire the public's spirit for that war is powerless.

This being the case necessarily implies that the predominant influence regarding war and peace rests with the evermore powerful press, which continues to significantly shape—though certainly not entirely—public opinion. Here too, exaggeration misses the mark; the public's imagined kowtowing to the press, "the queen of the earth," is based on self-deception. The press is at least as heavily dependent on the public as public opinion is dependent on it. There is interaction here. If the press refuses to comply with public opinion, then it loses its influence; and vice versa, if a part of the public fails to reckon with the judgment of the press, then it forfeits its influence on the country's affairs. These checks and balance are pivotal.

The fact of the matter is that when it comes to public affairs the press operates as a power responsible to one in particular. The great leaders of the European press, who in no small part in effect make European politics, do not wait for anyone to appoint them, but choose to sit where they will and pen what they write as they see fit. The monitoring and supervision to which a responsible minister is subject—and which keeps him from many follies—is completely absent in the editor's office. If the scrutiny of the public also disappeared, peace would be surrendered to the most brutal arbitrariness, and the rule of a hegemonic press sally forth in an unrestricted and most irresponsible fashion.

As often as the influence of the press is highlighted, one must also factor in the people's influence to which the press itself is subject. Of course, by speculating about all sorts of misunderstandings among the masses and by inhaling its own egoism, the press can undermine the extent of its influence. Likewise, as many examples attest to even in our country, a newspaper can easily lose its political influence and contact with the soul of the people by catering to its advertisers.

On the other hand, when the press is well-connected to what is alive and thriving among the people, its influence—its ever-increasing sway—in highly cultured countries cannot easily be ignored. In former days of suffering and glory, when we emerged as a people, the press did not yet exist. There was a sense of national awareness, but public opinion was not a factor. The national spirit was influenced most prominently by the sermons preached in the churches; but pamphlets flourished as well. Small dailies and periodicals began to appear, but almost exclusively to distribute notices and announcements. They did not think in terms of what we call a lead article or "three-star" item.[1] This kind of contemplative and evaluative material first appeared in so-called *spectatorial* periodicals and was only then transferred to daily newsprint. From there newspapers grew technically and politically.[2]

In terms of technique, they gradually moved from the brief recounting of important events to the inclusion of photographs. These images captured and showcased (even minute) details quickly and clearly, so much so that articles in large foreign papers took on an almost cinematic character.

Entirely distinct from those developments is the political pulpit that major newspapers afford—not to mention their influence on the markets. That political opening provided room for editorial assessments and the critique of the opinions and actions of others. That these editorials took sides speaks for itself. They turned the wheel of fortune at the ballot box. Ministers whose exploits the press could not stomach fell, and they forced earthly princes to take their editorial opinions into account. They challenged those they found wanting, breaking down or bolstering people's reputations as they saw fit.

---

1. Kuyper's articles daily commentaries in *De Standaard*, a daily Dutch newspaper, were unsigned, but they were recognizable by three stars printed in the shape of a triangle above each of his pieces to distinguish them from his articles or leaders. Everyone at the time knew that these came from Kuyper's pen. A typical daily would open with a leading article by Kuyper, followed by a couple of "three-stars" or short commentaries. The term "three-star" connoted compulsory reading.
2. Kuyper is referring to the wave of eighteenth-century Dutch "spectatorial" periodicals, named after *The Spectator* in England, but leading their own lives.

The press was likewise increasingly successful in swaying international relations, in antagonizing nations, and in reconciling peoples. More than once, the press pushed countries into war; while at other times it castigated war and called for peace among the nations. What the press can do in a small country such as ours comes nowhere near to what newspapers have done, for better and for worse, in large European countries—all the more so because they soon lost their peculiarly independent character when they fell into the hands of prominent statesmen and party leaders, who seized newsprint as a powerful instrument to propagate their own insights and to promote purposes of their own choosing.

We deceive ourselves, therefore, if we imagine that the press can be greeted as the great apostle of peace. Nothing is further from the truth. Rather, it is the press that keeps the pro-war vibrations beating, even though it does so under the guise of pacifism. It may be admitted that the press that in key countries dilly-dallies with philosophical reflection does unanimously choose peace and continues to shy away from anything that comes close to war. Given this blatant reticence, one was more inclined to complain about the thoughtless irresponsibility that often prompted their virtually knee-jerk praise for pursuing the ideal of peace. Their effusive use beautiful words sought to bring out the stamp of peace.

The press is the great apologist of every peace conference, the admirer of our new Peace Palace in The Hague.[3] Any buzz about peace is like heavenly music to its ears; they greet every peace conference with applause. Sometimes they even make a point of speaking didactically about peace, filling the air with a drumbeat for peace. They are more than kind when it comes to peace. They even pitch their encomium for peace far too high, often trying to give the impression that every war is based on misunderstanding, as though every time peace, which was to be forever, is undone that it is owing to a simple mistake or to the whim of an overzealous statesman. Convinced that more is involved than mentioning every hygienic panacea they know of to counter the misery of disease, the press wants above all else to implant the conviction in those suffering in their sickbeds that they could be permanently healthy if they would only believingly hold fast to a steady state of well-being. The blind man's eyes need to be tended to and

---

3. Visits were already organized earlier in that year, although the official opening of the Peace Palace was in August 1913, six months after Kuyper wrote this essay and two months after it was published.

reading braille can enrich his mind, but in the homes of the blind it must also be said in so many words that the illness of one's eyes is an entirely unnecessary, invasive evil, and that if one so wills it, every last blind person among us would enjoy clear vision—even without eyepiece or glasses!

By proceeding in this way the press wears its readers down with an idealistic phraseology that mocks reality. It lacks the courage or the love of truth needed to point to the sin of individuals and peoples as the painful cause from which, after a longer or shorter period of relative peace, the dark clouds of war will once again gather. Whoever warns those who will listen during times of prosperity that we should all avoid everything that can bring about infirmity and misery does them a favor. On the other hand, those who shout from the portals of the infirmary that all sickness is self-deception and that the sooner the better that every pharmacy is boarded up, medical degrees burned, and every hospital torn down, are the phrasemongers who for all their idle talk are put to shame by every doctor who visits their patients and by every nurse who makes up their beds.

However, the influence of the larger European news media in the hallowed peace movement was damaged by the ambiguous nature of their contributions. They occasionally championed the cause of eternal peace with powerful language and greeted with sympathy every sensationalized publication that argued for peace. They gave broad coverage to all the congresses, meetings, and conferences sponsored by leagues, clubs, and associations that advocated for peace. Major speeches promoting peace were reprinted in their entirety in their columns. When trouble threatened, they applauded every attempt to keep the peace. The great work undertaken at the Russian tsar's initiative aroused their admiration, and they could not say enough about Carnegie's gift for the Peace Palace.[4] In short, whenever the opportunity presented itself, they immediately resumed their drumbeat for peace. This steady and tireless praising of peace was so dominant that its influence was even evident in the council chamber and the royal palace, where for almost ten years there has hardly been a monarch who spoke or hosted a gathering that did not end up championing peace-inflected

---

4. In 1898, the Russian tsar, Nicholas II (1868–1918), invited major nations to join an international conference on peace and disarmament, and proposed that the venue for this first peace conference (held in 1899) be The Hague. In 1904, advised by (among others) then–prime minister Kuyper, US industrialist Andrew Carnegie donated 1.5 million dollars (42 million adjusted for inflation) to build a "Temple of Peace" in The Hague.

feelings. To that extent it can also be said that the press constantly defended the cause of peace and within the span of less than a quarter-century had shaped public opinion.

There are no longer any of sound mind who do not readily resonate with the psalm of peace. But what can be found in the media today that counters this mentality? There are no less than two factors that actively promote war.

First are those who seek to incite the mood of the nation when any conflict threatens—and second, once war has been declared, the extensive exposure given to war-related facts. People saw the latter happen just recently in reports about the Balkan War.[5] Almost every leading newspaper from Paris, London, Berlin, or Vienna sent its war correspondent to the area where blood was going to flow. These journalists vied to telegraphically transmit their word pictures of the most terrible scenes that this war had to offer. Two days later these telegrams were embellished into epistles with even more color added. What was not gripping did not count—which is why the sharpest pen was called for. Correspondents whose brush lacked luster faded into the background—only those who made you shiver and shudder when reading their reports made a name and secured a future for themselves. Four weeks would go by when every morning and every evening Europe's leading newspapers filled column after column with nothing other than war rumors, the one more gripping than the next. They did their utmost to fill edition after edition, time and again, with Balkan news. And the public did not bat an eye at what it cost them. Every day thousands more copies were bought—and what the people bought, they devoured. Especially when a bloodcurdling description of a misery-laden sequence of events came in over the wires, the rotary presses could hardly keep up. The public was captivated by the massacres, which followed each other at an incredible clip. People talked and thought about nothing else. The conversations among those not preoccupied with the pressures of everyday returned everyday again to that horrible war.

Now, in and of itself, one might conclude that nothing is more conducive to reinforcing an aversion to war and to arousing the call for peace than people seeking to find their way through a swirling whirl of descriptions of blood and gore. But think now a moment about the excesses reported on the crimes page.

---

5. The First Balkan War between the Ottoman Empire and the Balkan League (Bulgaria, Serbia, Greece, and Montenegro) had begun in November 1912.

It is important, especially in newspapers of lower caliber, to fill column after column with detailed reports of all kinds of horrific misdeeds. When there has been another disturbing murder, these newspapers seize an extra opportunity. It is simply the case that the general public prefers to lose themselves in what stimulates their senses. The same thing is true in the theatre. For a theatre's artistic director to be successful, he needs to know which pieces will engage the emotions. A play about two ordinary lives in a quiet, happy marriage does not attract an audience. But when passions flame all the while immorality is flaunted and someone else's honor is disgraced and the culprit's triumphs are celebrated, only to end in divorce, murder, or manslaughter, then the house is sold out before noon already. The same can be said for novels. Oh, indeed, good novels are still being sold, though many fewer than fifty years ago. But when you listen to publishers to find out what kind of fare is preferred by young and old alike, you notice time and again that sensational, titillating, less than clean, criminal, yes, even foul books are the ones people are buying by the handful.

It is simply a matter of fact that the calm, tranquil flow of quietly steaming water does not fascinate, while the storm at sea, with mountains-high clouds thundering across the sky, can capture the imagination. Normal, completely ordinary, quiet things are not gripping and do not entice. Only what is vibrant and visceral and sets things on a collision course attracts our souls and senses.

This, in particular, explains what arouses in all circles the nosy interest in what happens on the battlefield. The press knows that. It complies with the inspiration that this knowledge instills within it. They do it also for the money it brings in, but even more so out of a sense of duty to portray all special events as part of life. But whatever its motives, the fact remains that, from the facts of everyday, the press serves up what the same public also looks for on the stage, in novels, and in the crimes of the day: *stimulated sensations*. Every criminal will agree that nothing promotes crime more than those lengthy reports in the press about what people abhor and makes them shudder. It is likewise no wonder that living through two or three months of war-related sensations leaves a void when the ravages of war cease. The soul becomes unruly. Likewise, many were, oh, so disappointed when the Bulgarians did not keep fighting. How cowardly of the Turks to retreat to Çatalca!

But that is not all. The press's sensationalist reports from the battlefield not only make it difficult for those working on finding the words to further the peace process, but also feed all too easily stoked warmongering tendencies as soon as the interests of one's own country seem to be threatened. Combine what the press services of Vienna and Budapest published against Serbia and this past November and December, and all further proof of what we are claiming is superfluous. Except for the Slavic press, all the other papers urged the government, almost daily, to cede nothing to Belgrade or Cetinje, to occupy the harbor at Durazzo, to demand Albanian autonomy, not to leave Skutari to Montenegro, and to keep the road to Thessaloniki open for Austria. And when the Triple Alliance was sealed again, and Austria could also count on Germany as a result, the rattling of sabers in Vienna's newspapers was incessant: to arms, activate the reserves, divide the fleet in the Adriatic, and issue orders for ambulances, even from the Balkans! Give in to nothing; do not draw back a step from anything. Serbia-Montenegro will surrender or fall apart. The Danube monarchy was altogether "war ready."

That is how it was in Vienna, notwithstanding the fact that Austria-Hungary displayed less a sense of national unity than any other country. But now going back to 1909, if you ask yourself what the mood was in the English, French, and even Belgian press, you will still remember clearly that the newspapers in these countries were all even fiercer. And even though they were repeatedly tempered, it can safely be said that if peace can be preserved, the national press should not expect to claim kudos at the Temple of Peace, unless it be in the sense that in doing their utmost to suggest that war was in the offing, and in so doing inciting war, they had helped to intimidate the enemy, scaring them away from armed engagement.

The press, however, is not being arbitrary here, nor does it speak with ill intent. A nation's fervor motivates the soul of its people, which in turn affects everything. It is a mystical power that is not only on a continuum with kindred, ethnic, and societal love, but one that goes far above and beyond these in energy and compelling force. Moved by this sense of national identity, one is more than willing to sacrifice one's life and that of his sons. Editors, too, cannot avoid this strange power. People would protest if they would contest this national zeal. And even if the people did not, the press themselves cannot help but be gripped by it. If that is true, then the ambivalence of the press's actions cannot be denied either. They preach peace, preferably even an everlasting peace—peace not only as an ideal, but as a guaranteed reality—and yet their own war reporting ruffles the feathers of the hawks and calls for war when their own country's well-being is in peril. They do so to bring home the threat of war, but also, should war break out, to have the sword determine who is in the right.

The leading papers of Europe can only provide leadership in the desired sense if they (re)evaluate themselves in three ways. They must first distinguish between what is ideal and utopia and not mesmerize their readers with the possibility of enjoying everlasting peace now already. Doing so only confuses matters and fails to provide leadership. Second, without compromising the requirements of national identity, in the case of international threats to one's own country, they should not assess the situation themselves but allow others to weigh its pros and cons in the balance. And third, once a war has commenced, they should know how to temper sensationalism, which inundates the general public with all too graphic portrayals of bloody war scenes.

In these matters, the influence of the press in smaller countries is minimal. Our voice is hardly noticed in the larger concert of Europe. That is why the press in our country is seldom guilty of hyperbole. It holds to a unilateral pacifism and consistently advocates for the ideal of peace. It unanimously supports whatever promotes peace. And even though it sometimes joined others in publishing graphic war stories, it continued to distinguish itself from yellow journalism. Even when compared to more than one Belgian newspaper, ours continued to leave a calm, serious impression. Likewise, there were one or two papers that tended to side with domestic partisan interests in the international row surrounding Vlissingen rather than emphatically underscoring the issue as a national priority.[6] And while we do not commend this aberration either, we can say that the press in the Netherlands has generally speaking been able to strike a healthy balance, and that in so doing has nurtured a deep-seated love for peace among the populace, which, however robust—should our country ever be threatened— would in no way detract from the intensity of our national defense.

Dr. A. Kuyper

The Hague, February 15, 1913

---

6. In 1908, the Netherlands joined the German-initiated North Sea Conference, whose participants guaranteed each other the inviolability of their territory. In the same period, the Netherlands, while maintaining its strict position of neutrality, began constructing coastal defenses at Vlissingen—clearly directed against possible enemies (the German empire) from the west, and also involving the Belgian harbor of Antwerp. Kuyper is referring to partisan criticism in 1912 by a liberal newspaper like *Het Vaderland* of the cabinet's decision, which he in turn had condemned in his own columns. Dutch neutrality, however, despite this pressure, did not suffer any damage.

THE FAMILY,
SOCIETY, AND
THE STATE

TEXT INTRODUCTION

This text is a translation of Kuyper's series of fifteen articles that appeared in his daily *De Standaard* between January 16 and February 20, 1880, and published that same year under the collective title *Antirevolutionair óók in uw huisgezin* (Antirevolutionary also in your household). Appended to the series was a sixteenth article titled "De School," first published in the paper on February 23, 1880. The text of this slim volume was later included in its entirety as a supplement in the work "Ons Program"—seemingly an odd combination, yet justified by the fact that the overriding theme of the articles on the household is the significance of the household for the life of the state.

As with so many of Kuyper's writings, these regular installments in his daily newspaper, apart from some rehearsal every now and then of points made in earlier installments, little betray their provenance as newspaper columns; the prose is attuned to a widely varied readership and is by turns prolix and terse. The term *huisgezin* is used in a broad sense, reflecting social patterns of the late nineteenth century in a middle-class home. Here it is rendered by turns as "household," "home," "family," "family household," or "home and family," depending on the context.

From his descriptions of family life readers may deduce that the author at times draws on personal experience. Abraham Kuyper came from a home of ten children: eight girls and two boys; "Bram" followed two sisters as the third child in the family. When he wrote the present work his own family numbered seven children: four boys and three girls, ranging in age from fifteen years to eighteen months.

One may enjoy and at times be amused by some of Kuyper's concrete examples and counsels as he sketches the God-ordained structure of family life. Yet to profit from his sometimes very dated ideas, one has to look beyond them, to focus on the sources from which he draws. His sources are clear scriptural injunctions and keen everyday observations. Readers will find it refreshing to see how these sources enable him to expose creeping secularism in the common understanding and conduct of family life among Christians. Kuyper manages to shed new, sober, but also inspiring light on the fundamental values that undergird a healthy home.

SOURCE: Abraham Kuyper, *Antirevolutionair óók in uw huisgezin* (Amsterdam: Kruyt, 1880). Translated and edited by Harry Van Dyke.

THE FAMILY, SOCIETY, AND THE STATE

I OUR POLITICAL LIFE IS ROOTED IN OUR HOMES

We have stated more than once that we favor giving the right to vote to households rather than to all adult males.

We do so on the basis of our unshakable conviction that the household is the root from which grows the entire state, not according to human invention but by divine dispensation.

The household is a beautiful artifact of the Supreme Artist. It is majestic especially in the inimitable simplicity with which the simplest relationships in the home give birth to the greatest relationships, to those that comprehend the state, society, and the world.

God the Lord has so ordained things that no longer is every human being created anew, as in the Garden of Eden, but that henceforth man would be born of a father and a mother.

That is all. That one simple thought contains the idea of the household.

And yet, God makes all of home life, all family bonds, almost the whole of society and even the institution of the state flow readily and imperceptibly from that one, almost naïvely simple, idea. These things flow forth so naturally that they happen almost imperceptibly and that one barely notices the nodes where something new is budding forth.

Indeed, anyone who has ever taken the trouble to trace the avenues leading through this one idea of the household to the treasures of life and peace and to the formative power that enriches this world as if by magic, his soul and lips will turn with reverend worship to a God who was able to invent such a miracle and create such a work of art.

The antirevolutionary view of the state is more and more inclined, quite rightly, to free its politics of abstract concepts and to plant it, in terms of origin and immediate relevance, in that rich, full, glorious life of the household.

When you hold forth about concepts such as sovereignty, social contract, rights and freedoms, the limits of power, a few scholars may follow you, but the great mass of people will stop listening and turn away from those abstractions in disappointment. But once you let go of these abstract notions and put the concrete household in the foreground, most people will sense at once that you are turning to their daily lives, that you are talking about relationships in which they are personally involved, and that you are leading them into a world of ideas that they can follow step by step.

And that settles it. That tells you that you are on the right track.

Not that we believe that knowledge and learning should become common, plain, and pedestrian, and that it is a mark of purity and nobility of intellect if you lock yourself up within the confines of the thought world of the workingman or the peasant. That would be impossible as well as absurd. On the contrary, every branch of knowledge, even that of the workingman in his trade and of the peasant as he makes his butter and cheese, surpasses the everyday knowledge that people ordinarily have. But we do contend that no knowledge, of whatever kind, if it really wants to have an influence on life, can ever flourish unless it succeeds in finding a point of contact with that immediate sense of life that everyone of sound mind can follow and understand.

That is why the antirevolutionary movement was never able to become popular so long as it stayed in the sphere of abstract theory. But it suddenly took root and shot up like a miraculous tree when the schools question floated down from those lofty heights to the world of our children and compelled parents to deal with the meaning of their children's baptism, and to pray with greater earnestness, and to decide what place the Bible should have in the school.[1]

Yet even so, antirevolutionary politics could never gain a position of influence in the long run, or at least not with any lasting influence, merely on the basis of the education question. For if it were eventually to succeed in resolving the schools question to our satisfaction, the reason for our struggle, our party's reason for existence, would have vanished.

But the education issue, crucial though it is, concerns only a tributary, not the riverbed itself. Conceivably, the church might have enough resources to take care of all education, and then the country's politics would carry on without the education system as a bone of contention. Yet would that nullify the difference between the revolutionary and the antirevolutionary approach to politics? Would that make the principles of 1789 any less baleful? Would it be any less offensive to rotate the wheel of life so that man comes on top and God Almighty at the bottom?

One senses that this cannot be. Even apart from the baptism, nurture, and education of our children and apart from the question whether their schooling should be with or without the Bible, there must be another, more deep-seated root in ordinary human life itself from which flows the vitality of a politics according to the ordinances of God.

Now then, people have gradually discovered this root, and discerned it with increasing clarity and deeper understanding. They have found it in *the family household.*

Maurice[2] did not do this and Le Play[3] did not do this. Our movement did. The only thing that Frederick Maurice in particular did was to present with intellectual rigor and powerful prose what had already been surmised in our broad circle of kindred spirits before he ever sat down and composed his lectures on *Social Morality*. The simplest tracts, the plainest speeches,

---

1. The occasion for the antirevolutionary movement to organize politically, and eventually to form the ARP, was the so-called school struggle over the legitimacy of Christian schooling in relation to government education policy. For more, in addition to the final section of this text, see *On Education*.
2. Frederick Denison Maurice (1805–72) was a leading member of the Christian Socialists in Britain, author of *Social Morality: Twenty-One Lectures Delivered in the University of Cambridge* (London: Macmillan, 1869).
3. Frédéric Le Play (1806–82) was an influential sociologist and economist, author of works such as *De la réforme sociale en France*, 2 vols. (Paris: Henri Plon, 1864), and *L'Organisation de la famille* (Paris: Téqui, 1871).

and the smallest weeklies in our country had been referring implicitly, over and over again, to an idea that showed clearly how our unlettered and uneducated people were well aware that ultimately the issue comes down to *home and family*.

In saying this we do not mean to indict the other writers of antirevolutionary politics and blame them for lack of insight. Leading spokesmen such as Haller, Leo, Burke, Stein, Stahl, Guizot, Groen—they all at one time or another sang the praises of home life and pointed to the connection between the family and the life of the state.[4] For that matter, does it belittle a Newton[5] to point out that an astronomer like our Kaiser[6] saw more and better than he did? Is there not progress in every branch of learning? To see more and better is precisely the wonderful privilege with which leaders equip their later followers. It hardly diminishes the reputation of a Burke or a Stahl if we make no secret of the fact that the tree they planted, precisely because they planted it so well, has put down deeper roots than ever before.

We can take courage from the fact that our small intellectual circle has advanced and that we are making progress. It is one of the finest triumphs of antirevolutionary thought that in the most recent phase of its development it has succeeded in putting its finger on that exquisite creation of God which we admire and honor in the mystery of *domestic life* and which serves as its basis and starting point.

This means that we have the inestimable advantage of knowing that the subject we want to explore is within everybody's reach.

It means that we have the benefit of being able to ground our starting point not in what humans have contrived, but in what God himself has made.

It means that we have the blessing of having chosen as the basis of our politics an element in our everyday life which, however much it proceeds from God and leads back to him, is nevertheless not exhausted in church life but is eminently of a civic, social, indeed tangible nature.

---

4. Here Kuyper lists leading antirevolutionary theorists and statesman, including Karl Ludwig von Haller (1768–1854), Heinrich Leo (1799–1878), Edmund Burke (1729–97), Heinrich F. K. Von Stein (1757–1831), Julius Stahl (1802–61), François Guizot (1787–1874), and G. Groen van Prinsterer (1801–76).
5. Isaac Newton (1642–1726/27) was a leading English astronomer and natural scientist.
6. Frederik Kaiser (1808–72) was a Dutch astronomer and director of the Leiden Observatory.

II CIVIC AWARENESS, SOCIAL CONTENTMENT, AND LOVE OF COUNTRY

The basic premise of our antirevolutionary politics is rooted in the family. To study the family is to vindicate the antirevolutionary principle. The family confirms the rootedness and soundness of our endeavor, not thanks to ready wit of argumentation but thanks to the strength, the reality, the facts of life.

Those people are wide of the mark who interpret our appeal to the household, as they often do, to mean something like the following: "First there are homes; these homes are linked together into families; that's how communities are formed; those communities give rise to regions; and from these regions, of course, *the state* is born."

Nor does it mean: "Domestic life fosters civic virtue; socialites are the mothers of immorality and bad behavior; hearth and home radiate the warmth that must animate and inspire the state."

Both these statements indeed reflect reality, but they hardly exhaust the wealth of moral strength and moral notions that is present in the divine artwork of the family for the purpose of generating and developing a healthy state.

No, what always compels we antirevolutionaries to invoke the family is something quite different, something much deeper and of much wider scope. It is that the family—quietly and spontaneously, praise be to the divine Wisdom—is the first to give shape to all the veins of the network along which the state sends out its life-blood to its widest circumference and back again to its center.

Consider: in all ages and all parts of the globe, a normal, fully developed household shelters the following five relationships: (1) parents and children, (2) husband and wife, (3) brothers and sisters, (4) masters and servants, and (5) members and strangers.[7] And if you take the trouble to pay somewhat closer attention to each of these relationships that are fundamental to every human society, you will discover that they offer everything you need for the internal structure of the state.

Take the first one: the relationship between parents and children. This one bond alone denotes a sixfold relationship. It makes quite a difference if I look at a child in relation to its father, its mother, or its parents in general. We also have to distinguish between the relation of children to their

---

7. *Note by the author:* Maurice also follows this division, but without working it out except in rough outline.

parents in comparison with the relation of parents to their children. In fact, to be complete, we also have to distinguish between sons and daughters here, because the relationship of a son to his mother, for instance, is quite different from the relationship of that same son to his father.

If we now ask what moral notion and what moral force is at the very outset instilled into us by the fact that we have parents *of whom we were born*, then this great fact obviously delivers a deathblow to the idea of man's free will.

You came to be, you were born, you are here—and you had no hand in it whatsoever! And whatever imagined triumphs your free will—your unbridled appetite for autonomy and self-gratification—may boast of during the rest of your life, this is one fact that all agree on: you had absolutely nothing to do with what was for you the most important event of all, the fact of your birth. You will have to swallow the fact that it came to pass without any contribution or consent on your part.

That says a lot. For even if you rule out suicide and assume that not one person objects to the *fact* that he came to be, was born, and exists—that still does not establish that every person is *content* about the manner and circumstances in which they were born.

Is it really of no consequence whether you were born a girl or a boy? Does that small difference not govern your place in life, your upbringing and education, your whole future? It is not all that rare to come across the more suppressed and dependent ones among us and to hear them sigh: "If only I was born a boy!" or "Ah, if I were just a man!"

Moreover, does it make so little difference with what body you were born: healthy or sickly, strong or weak, handsome or homely? And still more, with what aptitude you were born, with what temperament and personality, with what gifts and talents?

And just to add one more thing: Does not everything in your life depend on whether you first saw the light in a God-fearing or a godless home? In an attic in a slum, or in the cradle of a prince?

And if you now add up all those things: "It was decided and settled without my will that I would come into the world and that I would be either a man or a woman, healthy or sickly, good-looking or unattractive, clever or dull, gentle or quick-tempered, filthy rich or dirt poor, and that I would have a good or a poor upbringing"—then is it not true that all the main decisions of your life on earth were actually made and settled apart from your input, and that the little variation added later by your free will is barely worth counting, and that this is true for the vast majority of the children of men?

Moreover, do you really think that such an encompassing, life-determining fact does not create an *impression* on your mind, a certain *slant* in your outlook and a *habit* in your inner self? Just listen to the conversations that our young people are having, how time and again they engage that mystery and even as they are laughing about it are actually *rebelling* against the fact that they were not consulted about the great fact of their birth. And when you see that foolish talk die a natural death at a later age and hear every person of sound mind admit that wishing to tamper with that fact is folly itself, what else comes to light in this than the moral impression made on people by the fact of their *birth from parents*?

Well then, transposing this to our relation to the country and to the people among whom we live, it is indelibly imprinted on our consciousness that behind us lies a *history* whose outcome we have to accept just as we find it and whose influence necessarily governs our whole position in life. In short, we become aware (1) that we are citizens, (2) that we have a duty to be content with our place in life, and (3) that we have a calling as citizen to love our country.

Civic-mindedness is nothing but the realization that we are members of a larger whole, just as having parents reminds us that we are members of a family. It is the awareness that we belong to something that was there before we were and that exists apart from us. It deals a deathblow to the delusion that we exist only for ourselves and that we can do with our life as we wish.

Class contentment is the counterpoint to communism and socialism. It is to recognize that there is an endless diversity of circumstances and relationships in life and that on the one hand we feel the urge toward equality but on the other suppress this urge by the realization, learned from the fact of our birth, that the decision about the social class in which we were born was not ours but was made by a power outside us.

And finally, love of country, getting involved in the life of your people, loving the past of that people, proudly upholding the nation's honor as your own, and the opposite: experiencing an indignity inflicted on your nation as your own personal shame and defilement—can it be born from anything other than the love with which children learn to love their parents, those living monuments of a past that preceded their birth and with whom they identify?

Once your mind begins to fathom somewhat the treasures that are offered to a well-ordered state in those three indelible tendencies—civic awareness, class contentment, and love of country—you cannot help but be seized with amazement at the great result the Lord God accomplished through the simple fact that he caused us humans *to have parents*. You will realize the gold mine that the state has in the family, and you will instantly be able to assess the damage that loosening domestic bonds would inflict on a country and its people.

To come to know the ruinous character of communism and the harm done by the elevation of man's free will, one need only lay open the foundation of the family household.

III GOVERNMENT AND PARLIAMENT

To a child, "parents" are something quite different from father and mother. And so, having discussed his birth from parents, we are not yet finished examining the child's natural caregivers.

On the contrary, we do not really get to it until we look at father and mother separately. For a child, "my parents" is just a concept, an abstract term, a word that a child only gradually grows into. Just yesterday a child of eight asked his father: "Daddy, what are 'parents'?" But there is a big difference for a child between "father" and "mother." These he knows best. They are quite different and much better than a concept; they are living persons, the main persons in his little world, whom he sees in his dreams and whom he calls to mind when they are not there.

That is exactly why a child from the outset knows perfectly well the difference, the distinction, the nuances that give both father and mother their own personality. Not that a child could tell you what that difference consists in. Nor that it favors one above the other. If you ask it, "Who do you love more, Mommy or Daddy?" it will answer quite simply: "Both the same." But the child does make the distinction whether to go to father or mother when it wants to ask something or when it wants to get something done or find out what it wants to know.

In fact, the child generally differentiates so instinctively between father and mother that any discriminating philosopher can do no better than to study and observe childhood also from this angle.

And if we now for our part inquire what image a child has of its father and what lasting impression it has of its mother, then the answer must be: of father, respect for authority and a sense of justice; and of mother, the courage to be free and a feeling for tenderness—four strengths which each in its own way belongs to the most precious and indispensable elements for the life of the state.

The child senses that his father is someone *who stands above him*. A father does not ask his child: "Is this what you would like?" He commands. Those commands may be given in a kind tone of voice, but commands they are. They are the expression of a higher will that transcends the will of the child. In the figure of father there is a "power" in the home which decides how things have to be and an authority that the child is to obey.

As a result, a child will automatically come to ask, "Daddy, may I?" This "may I" expresses the respect and honor that is kindled in our hearts when we come face to face with persons of authority.

Both reactions, inquiring after father's will and submitting to it, are not at all strange for a child who has remained natural—that is, has not yet been spoiled in the public school or through bad company or godless literature. Both reactions are only natural for the child. Not that a child never rebels against that will; but when it does, it knows that it is in the wrong.

That is how it comes about that a father has his authority automatically imprinted on the child without having to do anything for it. The child knows that there is a higher authority to which it has to surrender its own will, an authority that gives it permission to act this way or that, and an authority for which it nurses feelings of respect and honor.

But there is more. A father impresses his child with a sense of justice. And not just the nonexisting, ideal father, the paragon of uprightness. No, but also the fathers that you meet in real life. The father, after all, is the person in the household who metes out punishment. The mother too punishes, as does the nanny and the maid. But the child learns very quickly that the latter only punish when father is absent, and only in his place, in accordance with his instructions, and only insofar as he would approve. They themselves teach this to the child by repeatedly saying "I shall have to tell your father!" or "It's a good thing your father doesn't know this!" or actually by taking the child who has been naughty to the father so that he can take care of the matter. Now, the child may think father's punishment is harsh and most unpleasant, and it may pout and protest, but deep down it admits that father is fair and that he has a right and a duty to punish. When a maid hands out punishment the child experiences it quite differently from when it is chastised by father. In this way the child learns that punishment is just and that there is justice in the vindication of justice, even if through punishment.

This is also how the child develops the impulse, when others punish it even when it has done nothing wrong, to turn to the father for setting things right. Later we will deal with squealing and tattling. But this is certain: the first thing a child thinks of when suffering an injustice is to go to father so that he can right the wrong. And a father who is keenly aware of his calling will agree with his wronged child against anyone, even mother, even himself. In so doing he instills in the child's heart an ineradicable faith in the majesty of justice, the pith of all life in the state.

Matters are quite different with mother.

Not that mother is the exemplar of the weak and powerless woman over against the strength of father. Those who think that are fantasizing or perhaps know the *childless woman*, but certainly not the *mother* blessed with children. On the contrary, as a rule mother is a much stronger force in the home than father. Father is mostly out; mother is almost always at home. Father knows the things of the home only in broad outline; mother knows them down to the smallest detail. As a result, mother automatically gains an influence in the household that would far surpass father's influence if his authority did not shine with the glory of its divine origin.

This induces mother, where her children are concerned, to keep an eye on father's exercise of his authority, to moderate it, to oppose it if need be with the courage of a lioness.

If our fathers were without sin, abuse of their authority would be unthinkable. Now that they are not, the abuse can be a daily occurrence. That is the reason why God has created in woman, who bends when it concerns her own person, the heroic courage to insert herself between her husband and her children whenever that abuse takes on aggravating proportions.

Mother is the born advocate before father's regal authority. When children want father to do something, they ask for it by way of mother. When they have done something wrong, they seek her out to try to get a reduced punishment or an outright pardon. Similarly, for any child that has been hurt as a result of an abuse of power, she is the "good and faithful parliament" that stands firm in defense of the rights of her people.

With father there is *justice*; with mother, *fairness*. It is far from the case that we owe our constitutional liberties to male valor. Rather, it is exclusively to the mother (we do not say the woman) that Europe and America owe their respect for civil rights and freedoms.

Father is king, but mother is a guard whom God has added to father for the purpose of tempering his authority where it might commit an injustice.

The desire for self-serving freedom produces nothing but a wretched parliament of the kind we have in our country, a parliament that thinks only of expanding its power and forgets that its honor lies in pleading for the people. But a mother who quietly endures anything touching herself but stands up for her children like a lioness—she, and she alone, is the true image of that nobler representative body which does not seek its own power or glory but watches over its people.

This relates to the last point that we indicated: mother defends the *more tender interests*. If a woman does not have the courage to put up with injustice from her husband where her own person is concerned, she disqualifies herself for her divine task, which is to fight for her children. But inversely, if she bears her cross and never pleads except for her children, that man is a rarity who will not be softened by so much nobility of soul.

Accordingly, a woman's right and duty to offer resistance should never be based on an attempt to put her authority next to or in place of her husband's. It should rest solely on the undeniable circumstance that in the tiny society of the household, and particularly in the world of children, one has to reckon with sacred and tender interests that might easily get hurt under father's heavy hand. Those more tender interests, which find their natural storehouse in the inner life of the woman—such as the more quiet side of piety, the sense of compassion, attentive love, desire for sharing, and so on—must be tended carefully in accordance with the different personalities of the little ones. Thus, whenever father has no eye for these more tender and holy things and threatens to inflict irreparable damage on the children—if he starts breaking the twigs that might have put forth beautiful branches with leaves and blossoms—then it is the glorious, almost heavenly task of the woman to shield those more tender interests and to oppose a misguided father, if need be by sacrificing herself.

Of course this can lead to conflicts. But they would be conflicts that would be formative for both husband and wife and would be a blessing for the family, provided the husband is not jealous of his personal will but rather of his God-given authority, and provided the mother is not trying to erect a little kingdom of her own next to her husband's but is only being an advocate for her offspring.

Now, if these things are true—if our relationship with father automatically fosters respect for an authority that stands above us and imprints on us respect for the maintenance of justice, while our relationship with mother impresses us with the advocacy of fairness and the maintenance of the more tender interests—if this is true, then we ask: Is there a richer source available to the state for it to flourish: a father who instills respect for political authority and a mother who stands up for the rights of mini-societies? Does that not lead toward the purest ideal of a healthy state with constitutional guarantees? And can it be denied that constitutional rights and liberties have developed most powerfully precisely in those countries where the mother was most held in esteem?

IV TRUST, ACCOMMODATION, AND HONOR

Different again from the bond that ties parents and children together is the relationship between husband and wife.

The three great benefits that the state derives from the relationship of these two are mutual trust, accommodation, and a shared sense of honor.

Not that other relationships in life do not accustom citizens to these feelings. Yet no other single relationship imprints these moral dispositions so indelibly as does the day-to-day interaction between husband and wife in marriage.

The education act of a certain country speaks of making the schools serviceable to "instruction in Christian and civic virtues."[8] As if a virtue can be parroted or prompted or pushed by means of school attendance! No, the school does not educate, but God does. And in that great work of education the school is only a small link, aimed at having the child acquire certain habits such as orderliness, and so on. But God's skillful work of educating the children of men is so little limited to the school that it rather encompasses *everything* and achieves at least as much through family life as by means of sitting in a desk at school.

For, quite apart from the salvation of souls, it is God's good pleasure that even in *this* life already, society should be covered with a certain varnish of humanity and that a sphere should exist in society where a life of virtue is possible. If God had not ordained this and allowed humankind to "keep

---

8. This is an allusion to the Primary Education Act of 1857 in the Netherlands, to which Kuyper's party was opposed.

house" according to their own natural impulses, then society would become, as Calvin said so correctly, a pigsty,[9] and all decency would be gone.

And since that cannot be allowed, and since it is God's pleasure nevertheless to bring people, internally degenerate and perverted though they are, to a "somewhat humane" society and a "common life in orderly states," therefore God had to *educate* humankind, that is to say, he had to implant in them habits, customs, and inclinations which they do not have by nature and to which their sinful hearts are not inclined.

To that end God employs the family in particular. Not so much in order constantly to have it preach "virtue." Far more, rather, to accustom us to better habits by means of the relationships that arise spontaneously in domestic life, to give a certain direction to our character through force of habit, and to put a certain stamp on our inclinations by means of a series of constantly repeated impressions.

That is how God works on us. We are not aware of it; we even go against it; and yet God gets it done. At long last the home completes its formative power, and then you *discover* those habits imprinted in people; and then people prosper, at least outwardly, thanks to those "civic virtues."

Still, they are no more than "civic" virtues. The Kappeynes and Sixes[10] of this world may assure you a thousand times of the opposite; that does not alter the fact that "Christian" and "civic" virtues denote two totally different kinds of virtues. Christian virtues are the fruits of being born again; they are workings of the Holy Spirit; they blossom because they are rooted in Christ. Civic virtues, on the other hand, are simply favorable customs that a person gets used to from habit and which can well become a power in his life even if his heart remains as hard as stone and not a single fiber of his soul is rooted in sacred soil. Thus one should never say: "Truth is a civic virtue, but patience is a Christian virtue." That is nonsense. If you habitually speak the truth because you have been so trained, then morally it is without value and remains a mere civic virtue; and if you resist the lying spirit within you because you love the Holy Spirit within you, then the same virtue is a Christian virtue.

---

9. See *Inst.* 4.13.15, p. 1270. See also Herman Bavinck, *The Christian Family*, trans. Nelson D. Kloosterman (Grand Rapids: Christian's Library Press, 2012), 97.

10. Joannes Kappeyne van de Coppello (1822-95) was a sponsor of the Primary Education Act of 1878, and Jonkheer Willem Six (1829-1908) was minister in charge of implementing the act. The act confirmed the earlier redaction which mandated the public school to provide instruction in "Christian and civic virtues."

We do not want to be misunderstood. We are not saying that households are not also important for the coming kingdom of Jesus. But here we are dealing with the purely external and earthly goals which the Supreme Architect achieves for the construction of a state. He uses the household as an instrument in order to imprint on people, against the nature of their sinful hearts, certain valuable traits and manners which *must* be theirs if a state is to flourish. And among those nobler inclinations are mutual trust, a willingness to be accommodating, and a shared sense of honor—inclinations which in our society are fostered by the bond that unites husband and wife in marriage.

A state must live on trust—trust in its commerce and industry, trust in its senior officials, trust in its civil servants, trust in its bureaucrats and tax officials. One can shore up conditions by means of rules and controls, but that is all one can do. What becomes of a country where trust has disappeared can be seen in states like Egypt and Uruguay, where you can find rulebooks ten times thicker than with us yet where everything breaks down and drowns in misery.

This is only natural. Trust does not apply to what is within your power, but to what you cannot coerce. In other words, you need trust as soon as you have to do with human beings and not with machines, in which case you must rely on their desires and inclinations. You cannot always be with them; you do not know what they do in private; their inner life escapes all inspection. That is why a society of human beings has to depend for nine-tenths on trust, all the more so when the people in question are more mature or sophisticated and have more secret aids at their disposal to dodge every kind of surveillance.

And that trust you do not cultivate with the best and costliest public school. You cannot inculcate it with the finest sermons. Neither do the most beautiful books instill it into people's hearts. That trust does not come until people are open to the noble quality that is inherent in the notion of trust.

"Being faithful to someone"—that is the virtue that gives birth, albeit unawares, to trust. And not until a citizen knows what it is to be "faithful to his king" and not until a civil servant knows what it is to be "faithful to his superior" and a soldier what it is to be "faithful to his commander" does the civic virtue of mutual trust link together the diverse parts of the state.

"Faithful to another person"—is that not the essence of marriage? Our language expresses it beautifully when it calls the act of getting married "betrothal." "To break faith" with one's spouse is the crime of crimes. Marital troth or faithfulness displays its beautiful blossoms when husband and wife "know everything about each other" and "trust each other in everything." It is precisely through this faithfulness that the husband, and equally the wife, learns to become trusting, a quality which when practiced outside the sphere of the home very quickly becomes the cement of the state.

"Faithfulness" undergirds the inviolability of our oaths, the sacredness of our promises, the truth of our word. Or if you will, in each of these three instances it is the dedication of our *whole person* to another. For that reason it is as indispensable for the state as it is attainable only through marriage.

Mutual confidence and loyal trust are virtues that bind person to person in a typically human way. Hence the incomparable value of these two virtues for the organic bond between persons that we call "the state."

Next, the natural fruit born of trust is an *accommodating* attitude.

What a beautiful thing it is: accommodation. Without that flexible attitude, your interests and mine would constantly clash. People would continually be at loggerheads, pushing and shoving each other, a situation with no room for tranquility or peace of mind. Life would begin to resemble a busy intersection in the city of London where carriages crash into each other and where you are in mortal fear when you take a chance to cross the street. Trust has flown out the window, with the result that mutual accommodation is in short supply.

To be accommodating is to be willing to do something for someone else because we understand that we need each other and are therefore better off if we put two wheels under one cart than if we cut one another off with our one-wheel carts. By accommodating each other we really enter into a kind of partnership so that we can do business together rather than compete with one another. Reciprocal accommodation is characterized by the *quid pro quo* or the *do ut des,* the "give and take" of human society. As the saying goes: "One good turn deserves another."

If this is so, do we need any further evidence that the life of husband and wife is the strongest factor in stamping this habit onto our basic attitude? After all, is marriage not the most tender partnership? Is it not putting on a single axle two wheels that at first ran on their own shaft? And indeed, whatever you may want to regulate by means of rules or agreements or instructions, the life of husband and wife is utterly incapable of improvement on that score. For them, accommodating each other is the only rule. God said, "Let these two be one," and since life again and again jeopardizes that unity, there mutual accommodation is nothing less than repeatedly seeking the unity that God has ordained.

If trust produces the practical fruit of mutual accommodation, its ideal blossom is a *shared sense of honor*. What we mean by this is that the husband makes much more of something done to his wife than anything done to himself because he knows she feels so much more deeply, while the wife in turn may be able to put up with a lot when she is personally offended but is deeply hurt when her husband's reputation is maligned.

When it comes to honor they are of one mind. They share each other's good name. To put it even more sharply: there is an exchange of honor between husband and wife. The husband defends his wife, the wife her husband.

Again, for our general attitude to acquire this characteristic, nothing is more effective than the married state. To guard each other's honor is also done by son and father, by employee and employer, by supervisor and subordinate, yet never as deeply and intimately as by the two who are husband and wife. With them that sense kicks in immediately when facing the outside world or when meeting strangers. And it is only in the company of very close friends (or very intrusive female friends) that husband or wife is sometimes in danger of talking along with such visitors about the lesser qualities of the other partner. But leaving aside those few exceptions, the life of every people in every age shows clearly that a husband will love the honor of his wife more than his own life, not because he is such an excellent man but because God has imprinted this on his soul.

And now you have only to imagine for a moment what would become of a household or a state in which trust were no longer found in the hearts of men; no longer an accommodating attitude that removes the thousand and one problems that no policing can resolve; and last but not least, no longer a shared sense of honor to foster the deepest respect for the majestic manner in which God the Lord, by creating marriage, brought these moral forces to development in sinful, unregenerate human beings.

Allow us to say in conclusion that it is especially for this reason that adultery, prostitution, and all unchastity constitute a direct threat to the welfare of the state. These sins will gradually produce a generation without any faithfulness or trust, without any sense of mutual accommodation, and without any sense of honor for the nation.

V PERSONAL CHARACTER

We all know that beautiful song of the psalmist:

> How good and pleasant is the sight
> when brethren make it their delight
> to dwell in blest accord.[11]

But we also know that this is taking fraternal ties in the ideal sense. You almost never come across it, except in novels, which we find so captivating at times because they help us get over the sorrow that real life often causes us.

Expressions such as "sons from the same household," and especially "children of the same mother," capture the third relationship in the family: fraternal ties or sibling relations. Next to the relationship of parents and offspring and husband and wife, this bond completes the threefold cord with which a higher Wisdom has bound the family together.

Of course we shall again discuss only the formative power that these fraternal ties exert on the life of state and society, leaving aside the finer, often so very beautiful gradations of older and younger brothers, brothers and sisters, and the like. What concerns us here is the attributes that the fraternal ties instill in people in general, the character traits they develop in our citizenry, the habits that are imprinted in the human soul by the fact of being a brother or sister and having siblings.

Now then, however strange it may sound, we know no better way to express the significance of fraternal ties than by saying: relations among siblings contain the principle of *civil litigation*.

Just try once to explain fraternal ties from the charming side, and you will see how pedestrian your prose becomes, constantly lapsing into trivial platitudes. But take them up from the *un*brotherly side, and the whole relationship of brother to brother will come alive for you. To which may be added that by placing the unloving side in the foreground you are connecting with reality. Whether you approve or disapprove, the fact is that as a rule the unloving side is the side that comes out among brothers and sisters, and the charming side of their relationship is constantly suppressed by the unloving side.

In almost every household you hear parents complaining that the children are always carping and squabbling. They constantly call on father or

---

11. A common Psalter rendering of Psalm 133:1.

mother to settle all kinds of quarrels. When parents hear their children carrying on again they automatically react with: "What is the matter this time?" Ask the nursemaid and the nanny sometimes what they are doing the livelong day, and they will tell you that from morning till evening they are busy keeping the children in a good mood, telling them not to do certain things and to be nice to each other. We even find among our very little ones that the youngest child seated on mother's lap will fight off the next-to-youngest who is clutching mother's apron strings.

If you do not see what this depends on, and fail to understand its relative necessity, you will in all likelihood totally spoil your children, either by covering it up with lame excuses or else—equally bad—by turning them into sentimental Gumals and Linas without pith or personality.[12]

Scripture depicts no Gumals and Linas, but Cain and Abel, Ham and Shem, Isaac and Ishmael, Esau and Jacob, Joseph and his brothers. In other words, Scripture, in tune with reality, places the *divisive element* in the fore-ground, for the purpose of displaying the power and strength of a bond which in retrospect ultimately overcomes being pulled in two directions.

The secret of this apparent contradiction lies in the difference between the feeling a child has with respect to its *father* and the feeling it has with respect to a *sibling*; or better: between two feelings that God has planted in his soul. Facing its father the child lowers its head; facing its sibling it raises its head high. Father is its superior; its sibling is its peer. Father has been placed over it, but it sees its sibling as its equal. And since every child (born in sin) is by nature more inclined to raise its head than to lower it, it follows that a child is likely to want to seek compensation for always having to bow to father by crossing the lines of equality with its brother or sister. This results in a struggle to restore balance to the broken equality, and if the struggle cannot be resolved by the siblings among themselves the result is an appeal to justice and to father's decision by means of in-house litigation.

Over against father and mother, children feel unequal; but among each other they feel as equals. It is this awareness that is the deepest thought behind the fraternal bond, imprinted on the child. Mothers, give one of your

---

12. Gumal and Lina were the names of two young African converts to Christianity in a German classic in children's literature marked by romantic sentimentalism. For an English translation, see Kaspar Friedrich Lossius, *Gumal and Lina; Or, An Instructive and Entertaining History Designed Chiefly for Use in the Religious Education of Young People*, trans. S. B. Moens, 2 vols. (London: Smallfield, 1817).

children a fancy coat and to another nothing, and see how quickly Joseph ends up in the pit. Or, to take a milder case: notice how you cannot make a special sandwich with sweets for one child but another child will at once insist on its *right* to receive the same treat. And no matter how often you reply, "Isn't mother free to give as she pleases?" it won't do any good. The child keeps saying—or if you order it to be quiet, it keeps thinking—"If sis can have it, I have to have it too, 'cause *we're equal!*"

But what is the reality? In contrast to the deeply ingrained sense of equality are the many inequalities in life that cause brothers and sisters to forget about sweet harmony. There is first of all the difference in age. Should a boy of six get the same as a lad of sixteen? Yes, says the younger child; but the older will say, Of course not. Are sisters and brothers equal, or is there something to the saying that "brothers have an advantage" or that "boys are allowed to do more than girls" and that sisters have to accept that their brothers are allowed more? Then again, you have the mistake of father and mother—the old sin of Jacob—coddling their little Benjamin. Add to that the tactlessness of maids and the partisanship of friends and visitors—ah, it all contributes to upsetting the ideal equality and breeding discontent among the children.

And yet even that does not put the finger on the main reason why that sense of equality simply must again and again be offended. The reason is the difference in personality and aptitude.

Father and mother are always inclined to make the children conform to themselves. But while the idiosyncrasies of husband and wife are subject to attrition so that the two are more and more becoming one, brothers and sisters are there in order to be different from anyone else in the family circle.

A brood of children who resemble seven drops of water from the same glass or seven leaves from the selfsame tree is a sign of spiritual poverty, of a deficient education, of a morbidly sentimental upbringing.

Children *must* differ from one another. Depending on their differences in gender, body length, tastes, mental ability, intelligence, and practical sense, every child must grow up to be different.

And these two factors—the deeply embedded sense of being equal to one another and the directly opposite urge to develop one's own character and personality—these are the two poles, or if you will, the centripetal and the centrifugal forces, which together govern sibling relations.

You should not be surprised, therefore, that children quarrel; it should rouse your suspicion if they never quarreled. But in these clashes fathers and mothers will need to apply all their wisdom in order to make justice triumph over arbitrariness, and they will have to solve every conflict in such a way that irritation and anger are removed.

And if you would like see the strength of sibling relations, very well, just observe two strange boys who come to blows in the street and compare them with the squabbles among your offspring. Those boys in the street, when they get angry, have no sense of making legal claims, of litigation in the home: they clench their fists and fight. The street knows no other right than the right of the strongest, symbolized not by the scales of justice but by the sword.

At home, on the other hand, however noisily the children may quarrel, they know that getting physical is a great sin and that they can always defend their rights by calling on father.

Getting physical must therefore always be followed by severe punishment. Cain and Abel are there as a warning at the dawn of the history of family life. When brother and sisters come to blows they are going "against their own blood" and so violate sibling ties in the most shocking manner.

And if we now put the three factors together: (1) the sense of equality, (2) the actual inequality, and (3) decisions through "litigation" instead of decisions through violence—then it will begin to make sense what we wrote at the outset: the significance of sibling relations for the state lies in the idea of *civil litigation*.

To enlarge on this will be the theme of our sixth installment.

VI LEGAL ACTION, NOT VIOLENCE

Nothing allows us to enter more deeply into the minds of siblings than noticing their absolute aversion with which they detest anything that even remotely resembles "tattling." The world of children can put up with almost anything; a child can even stand biting and teasing. But if one of them dares to tattle, he is finished. Then all the others turn as one against the informer. They do not trust him anymore. They practically expel the snitch from their intimate circle. The little brother who tells on them is as good as dead.

How to explain this deep-seated indignation?

For think of it: if a moment later those same siblings start to quarrel and one of them feels he is wronged, then not one of them thinks anything of it when the injured party goes straight to father to tell him everything in full detail and living colors (and if possible making it sound a bit worse than it really is).

Still, it is not impossible to find out why children, with all their abhorrence of the telltale, can put up with the one who goes looking for justice. After all, the child that feels wronged is *not always* allowed to go to father or mother. If something has happened that cannot be restored anyway, so that the complaint can only lead to *punishment*, the other children will take it very ill of the tattler. And as soon as one of them dares to go and complain about what does not directly concern the rights, interests, and possessions of the household members, then they immediately put the plaintiff under surveillance as a *potential* "squealer."

Clearly the facts indicate that demanding punishment is as deeply detested among children as demanding justice is thought fair.

Siblings do not need to go and do what father and mother are appointed to do. Father and mother are the ones charged by God to uphold justice, to safeguard their children's moral sense, and to protect the household goods and the family treasures. Thus if a child is deficient in reverence for God, if it tells lies, if it has been at the cookie jar, or if it ill-treats its clothes or is rambunctious and breaks a glass or a piece of china—then the other children will not protest if the guilty one is punished. Sometimes a child may leap up at father or mother to try and stop a brother or sister from being punished, but this occurs only when it does not understand the reason why punishment is meted out or else is still too young to grasp what was so wrong in what brother or sister did that it deserves punishment. But the other children, if they understand the reason why a brother or sister is being punished, will almost always think the punishment fair and will look on with awe and respect.

Yet as natural as children think it is that father takes care of justice in the home and that mother backs him up and that the maids sometimes act as detectives, so unnatural do they think it would be if one their siblings starts to spy on them and wants to become a kind of counsel for the prosecution. Children believe father and mother have no problem setting bounds to their little world, and that it is therefore cowardly, disloyal and holier-than-thou if one of them goes and "rats" on them.

Still, we should also differentiate between kinds of tattling. They are not always the same.

Parents harm their family as a rule if they lend their ears to a child that turns informer. That creates bitter feelings. It sows distrust. And it gives children the impression that father and mother lack the strength to find out for themselves whether a wrong was committed. To lend ear to a tattler is to betray weakness.

But there is "telling" and "telling."

If without father's knowledge things are being done among brothers and sisters that are dangerous or that seriously offend moral sensibility, and one of them risks informing father of it, then it usually does not harm his standing with the others. If they are playing with fire or with gunpowder, or if a child is risking its life, or if things occur that are shameful, then in a God-fearing home the fear of God will always prompt one of them to report it to father. Provided—and that makes all the difference—provided it is clearly evident that he is not doing so out of spite, but that he is moved by holy indignation.

Real tattling is almost always accompanied by and mingled with a certain cowardice of character. A spiteful informer is a spoil-sport who wants to ingratiate himself with father and who separates himself from his siblings in a kind of betrayal: he acts the little wiseacre who wants to be the "good boy" in the eyes of the grownups.

It will be important in child-rearing, therefore, to distinguish between motives. Informing because prompted by conscience must be encouraged. Informing because the informer is a smart aleck, or, if you will, acts unbrotherly, should never be accepted, should never even be listened to, but should be firmly dismissed, sometimes even punished.

Summarizing, it is clear that brothers and sisters want to see "criminal procedure" left to the in-house authority, but next to that they wish to reserve room in the household for *private* justice by developing the notion of legal action among each other or, if need be, legal action against each other.

When one child sits down in another's place; if they have been into each other's desk or closet; if a pencil is gone from someone's case, or if sister has pulled a favorite doll's arm out of its socket—these are the cases for "civil litigation" among children. And then the child goes to father, not to ask him to punish brother or sister, but to ask father to tell Tommy "to get off my chair" or Johnny "to leave my things alone" or Billy "to stop doing that," or to order sister to fix the doll's arm or else pay for a new one from her allowance.

Thus, restoration of rights and compensation for losses. No less. No more. And as they demand this the children will automatically develop that respect for the sacredness of justice that can only benefit the state.

The accused will insist that the plaintiff should tell father "when I'm there" and not "behind my back." No secret justice. Public proceedings. Furthermore, when the informer has finished the accused will insist on giving his side of the story. This is a right that children are usually so keen on that they almost always start interrupting each other for fear that father might get the wrong impression of what happened. Then they call on their witnesses, and most of the time the siblings will divide into two groups, forcing father to order the hot-tempered litigants to be quiet so that he can hear from the others "who were there" just what took place. And only after hearing both sides and listening to pleading without end can he come to a verdict. That is, if there is no alternative. For usually father will first investigate whether the parties cannot "settle out of court." And if father forgets this way out there is apt to be a mother's voice or the voice of an older sister whispering into the children's ears: "Come, why not just settle this between the two of you!"

Thus we see in actual fact how our whole system of civil proceedings comes to development within the circle of brothers and sisters.

The relationship of father and child represents supreme authority, hence justice is upheld by demanding and imposing *punishment*. But the sibling relationship represents the principle of equality, hence personal rights are upheld by demanding restoration or compensation.

And if at last we are asked, "What good is that? All it does is encourage lawsuits and promote a litigious society!" then allow us to counter with the consideration that our present society has not too many but too few civil proceedings. The simple reason for that is that justice is too uncertain, too cumbersome and too costly, with the result that the office of justice of the peace has disappeared from our legal system, and with that the summary justice of wisdom and equity available in small-claims courts.

If you think a decrease in lawsuits would be a blessing for the country, consider this: First, the custom to demand justice vis-à-vis each other is barely known among the uncivilized, does not arise until moral life develops, and is most in vogue in the best of states. Second, to have a thousand justice issues remain unsettled and then just cold-shoulder and ignore each other and for the rest of your life harbor resentment toward each other—is that not ten times worse than together have recourse to a judge and in ten minutes have the matter settled, so that you can both put it behind you and get on with your lives?

But quite apart from that, citizens' zeal for insisting on their rights entails yet another element and enriches the state with a still more precious jewel by stimulating our thirst for *freedom*.

For siblings to be something more than just "father's children" and to discover among themselves the difference between "mine and thine"—this is what arouses enthusiasm from the depth of their soul. Not an enthusiasm for licentious liberty, but for rightful and lawful freedom, for a liberty that sprouts from justice. And not until you have learned to sing, not just of the two poles of equality and fraternity, but of the threefold cord "liberty, equality, and fraternity," will your doxology be complete as you sing the praises of God's ingenious creation that shines forth in the bond between brother and sister.

VII LIBERTY, EQUALITY, FRATERNITY!

"Liberty, equality, fraternity" is not a newly invented slogan but a slogan that has been falsified and misused.

It is not a new invention, because it is taken directly from the heart of family life and is a perfect reflection of the relationship between brothers and sisters. The defining feature of that relationship, after all, is *equality* before the law. From that equality, precisely because it is maintained by justice, is born the sense, the possession, the enjoyment of *liberty*. And what keeps these "equal" children together, despite their zeal for liberty, and what unites them in the end, is the bond of *fraternity*.

The mistake of the men of the Paris Commune and the heroes of the barricades is immediately apparent. They stripped equality of its two guardians and removed both the modifier "equality *before the law*" and the addition "legal equality *among one's peers*." The former they made over into *equality in person and property*, and the latter into *equality with one's superiors*.

There must be *equality before the law*, although it is not possible in every state and under all circumstances. Declaring a state of siege and martial law is a clear illustration. No, equality by means of civil proceedings is a highly desirable situation which can only be established by degrees, as the nations develop morally. Yet it remains every nation's ideal and it received a powerful boost in 1789. Legal equality should be implemented in our country to a much richer and fuller degree than thus far. Where the godless Revolution went wrong was in falsifying the ideal of *equality before the law* by making it over into *equality of property* and so unleashing passions of egoism and greed in total disregard of all standards of justice and right.

When once equality was falsified, it stands to reason that the concept of liberty was also corrupted. For what is liberty? It is to get out from under the *tyranny of violence and arbitrariness* in order to place oneself voluntarily under the *rule of law*. But the mob of the *sansculottes* and the men of the September massacres, by putting aside the law through their false concept of equality, once again erected the tyranny of the fist, the knife, and the dagger—all in the name of liberty.[13]

In the meantime, while fraternity—brotherhood—by virtue of its origin, is intended to draw the ties of blood so close that friction and conflict are overcome, the wise men of our age managed to make of it that blood ties would no longer count for anything and that the meaning of brotherhood was to unite with the international rabble in order to spill, on the scaffold or in the dungeon, rivers of the noblest blood from among one's own people.

We too therefore firmly embrace the banner displaying the beautiful slogan *Liberty, Equality, Fraternity!*—so long as we are allowed to derive it, not from the madness of the revolutionary fanatics, but from the glorious bond woven by the Supreme Wisdom between siblings in a family.

Only then are both liberty and fraternity clarified in an inspiring, noble manner.

Whenever a somewhat weaker, slower child is alone with its brothers and sisters, it is often treated less than kindly: it gets pushed around and yelled at, and it senses it can do nothing about it. But let father or mother once enter, and observe how that ill-treated child cheers up. Father and mother are in the room: that means the return of the protection of the law, with the result that the other children once again acknowledge their shared equality and that the suppressed child is once again *free*.

It is especially in contrast with the school that a child knows how to appreciate this sacred privilege of the home.

At school, as we all know, the stronger boys sometimes bully the weaker ones, a form of tyranny which is scarcely designed to instruct in Christian and civic virtues. On the contrary, it can be incredibly demoralizing, because in school nothing can be done about that taunting and pestering. The pupils do not know "rights." "To tell teacher" is a sure means of getting a merciless drubbing after school hours. Moreover, children tease and taunt each other in school when no one is looking. But once these tormented

---

13. Kuyper refers here to radical partisans of the French Revolution and the series of killings that occurred in Paris from September 2–6, 1792.

little souls come home again, then notice how they revive in that glorious freedom. Not that there is never any teasing or bullying at home, but at home at least you can sue for right. And right makes free.

Now, if this genuine freedom is imprinted on the minds of the upcoming generation, a love of liberty will automatically become a characteristic trait of the citizenry. And if someone asks: "Are there not popular liberties that have to be wrested from the state?" then the answer is: as long as the citizenry refuses to supply the government with accomplices for oppressing the citizens, no government will be in a position to rob us of our popular liberties. It will just not be able to. And the real secret for a nation to flourish in freedom does not lie in undermining authority, overturning thrones, or bringing down its government, but much rather and far more in developing commonly shared liberty so strongly that no ruler or minister can any longer find accomplices to serve as instruments of oppression.

Brotherhood in turn contains a most fruitful element for the life of the state, namely the power of the *corporation*.

There should not be a sudden leap from household to state. Between state and household there must a mediating link. That indispensable mediating link is the corporation. The absence of corporations in a society is a sign that the domestic characteristics in the life of its citizens are not doing their work and that the state as a result oversteps its bounds, doing what is not its task and so cramping people's initiative.

By corporations we mean societies, federations, associations, partnerships, companies, circles, clubs, guilds, and orders that unite a group of citizens on the basis of equality for the purpose of achieving in state or society, in a lawful way, a goal that is important to them. Now whenever that goal contains the slightest trace of a higher, holier, spiritual or even merely idealist notion, is it not customary among all nations to call such a corporation a "brotherhood"? Even the freemasons—who in our opinion are pursuing a goal that is more of a threat to the state—even they speak of a "sacred brotherhood." So do the communists and the men of the International.

This is a clear indication that people are aware, even in the language they use, how the tendency to unite in corporations, to enjoy group settings, to love clubs and small circles, is but an echo of the sense that was imprinted on us in younger years when we grew up in our families.

As we all know, in the circle of the household the high ideals of the brotherly bond is seldom fully satisfied. The struggle of unequal natures and characters to maintain equality of rights ensures, alas, that the company of brothers and sisters cannot but fall far short of the ideals of the sacred fraternal bond. And so it comes about that the young man, whose heart has been imprinted with the desire for such a bond but who found too little sympathy for the bond in the home, tends automatically to look for that ideal brotherhood on more open terrain and in wider circles, among like-minded men who want what he wants, hence obviating any struggle to maintain equality.

And although we readily concede that such love of company, too, can go to extremes, that does not detract from the blessing of the corporative attitude. Everyone knows that no countries have greater freedom than Britain and America and that precisely in those two countries the corporative attitude (which is quite different from cliquishness) has developed most powerfully and splendidly.

Accordingly, we are not in favor of children's auxiliary societies.[14] On the contrary, at that young age it is in the household circle, and only there, that the "society of little brothers and sisters" ought to be the association that aspiring citizens belong to. Without wanting to criticize what others are doing, and without overlooking the excellent intentions with which children's auxiliary societies have been organized, we are still inclined to ask the sponsors of these clubs with all due respect: With young children, ought not the family be the only circle in their lives, their world, their all, in order that at a later age they can develop the corporative attitude all the more energetically?

VIII ORGANIC TIES

Finally, we still need to discuss the relationship between "master and servant" and "mistress and maid." Although there are many families that have no live-in domestics, everyone senses that a fully developed household also has service personnel, a personnel which almost exclusively, at least in our country, confines itself to maids who in three quarters of our families go by the name of kitchen maid, housemaid, linen maid, nursemaid, and also cleaning lady, seamstress, or midwife.

Of these female helpers, only the first four are "in service," while the others are only temporaries for performing specialized services. But however we differentiate between permanent and temporary services, they remain

---

14. That is, a kind of club for children in support of foreign missions.

services, and it is against nature, it is unchristian, and it is disastrous for society if domestic servants talk among each other about having a "job" rather than being "in service."

Operative in the term *job* is the baleful and socially disruptive influence of the principles of the French Revolution. It is also the result of hearing sermons that spiritualize too much and equip too little. Not properly warned, even Christian maids take this godless word on their lips.

It is absolutely not true that being "in service" is a humiliating or shameful expression. On the contrary, *service* is an honorable word. It runs through all the posts in state and society, from high to low. A private, a captain, a colonel, even a general and a field marshal, are "in the service." An admiral of the fleet counts his "years of service" just as well as the humblest sailor. The term *minister* literally means "servant of the Crown." All civil officials are in the "service" of the state. Gentlemen in waiting "serve" in the king's palaces. Pastors are "servants of the divine Word" and along with all ecclesiastical dignitaries are "in the service" of the church. You are being very polite when you ask, "Can I be of *service*?" or "May I offer you my *services*?" and it is even more common to end a polite letter with "Your humble *servant*."

In light of this fact, the pretension of our kitchen maids that the word *service* is degrading is simply ridiculous. But that would be the least of our problems if it did not also pose a most pernicious evil for family, society, and state. For what is the case? In the great expanse of our society the question constantly arises whether all those social components belong together and fit together, hence if anything can be made out of them or that it is all rough-hewn stone that no one can use for constructing anything.

Many years ago our government sent a completely dismantled steamship to Japan. When the collection of parts and pieces and plates arrived in Japan, it looked like a hopeless jumble, and no one knew how a ship and a steam engine could be made out of it. But what did they soon discover? When the shipwright started to sort through the items and checked his list with numbers, it turned out that everything could be joined, fitted together, and made to function. And precisely because one piece *served* to support another piece and screwed it together, what emerged from the chaotic confusion was a unified whole.

That is how things are, literally, in the case of society. The question is: Does God turn out masses of people without any organic cohesion, or does he provide every country and every city with a set of people who as parts of one great mechanism, *assuming it has been properly assembled*, shall form one ingenious organic whole inasmuch as they complement each other, turn out to belong together, fit into each other, and so can *serve* to support and uphold one another?"

Thus, *service* or *job* makes all the difference.

Whoever speaks of a "job" is an unbeliever who fancies she is able of her own free will to create a "job" with this or that lady as she pleases, and can do with that position as she likes. Our class of domestic servants embracing the lie of the *social contract!* Or, if you will, the lie of the free will! Sheer Pelagianism. According to the image of the sandpile—a society of loose grains, a society built of sand.

Service, on the other hand means "to serve in that for which Higher Wisdom created me, gifted me, destined me." It means not to want to be an individual by oneself, relying on one's own resources, but a member of the whole, a cog in the great mechanism, part of an organically cohesive society.

To "take a job" is therefore haughty pride; to want to be "in service" is godly piety. In the former case it is the maid herself who decides her lot; in the latter it is God the Lord who also has our maids at his command and points them to the place they shall occupy.

That is how God's Word wants it.

That is what the church has always taught.

Not until the false principle of the liberal press began to infiltrate the social class of domestic servants did the glorious, sacred term *service* become despised in people's eyes and did they coin the Pelagian and atomistic word *job*.

It so happens that a human being is created in such a way that he cannot possibly be just anything he wants to be. He has an aptitude for a few things, for which someone else in turn is less suited, while that person in turn is suited for something that the first person cannot do. This automatically gives rise to the law that the one must serve the other with what he is able to do, and must let himself be served with what the other can do better than he.

The doctor offers you "medical services," but he in turn lets himself be served by his valet. In this way everything fits into each other and one person serves as an instrument for another person's strength. This joining and fitting gives birth to the wonderful, glorious, organic society.

If things run well and in accordance with God's will, a mistress or master will not say: "I pay my servants, they have a job with me, and that's it." Instead they will realize, first, that they themselves owe that manservant or maidservant a bounden service of their own; and, second, that they are to receive the work performed by these servants as arranged for them by God and prepared and provided for them.

Thus, with this lofty conception all harshness, all tyranny, all humiliation will vanish. God puts a bridle on both maid and mistress and at the same time his commandment sanctifies their relationship.

Thanks to these principles, the Christian church—notably the Reformed churches—created room in the family circle for domestic servants, a situation which on the one hand fosters loyalty and attachment and on the other has led to respect for our servants as creatures of God, as fellow Christians and, still more especially, as helpers assigned to us by God.

However, the liberal press as well as unbelieving ladies, frivolous maids and a lax church have cooperated in ripping that precious relationship out of its natural context. Alas, mistresses and maids now have to discover through daily experience the "blessings" brought on by departing from the Christian order for life and taking up with the revolutionary principles in the hope of making life more agreeable.

But what is much worse, now that "service" in the estimation of our maids has become a "job," turning them from "members of the household" into "hired staff" with whom our women no longer feel any particular bond, now one of the most priceless supports is breaking down that once upheld the organic community of state and society.

Next to the bond of blood, after all, the moral awareness of "serving one another in accordance with divinely appointed talents and callings" is a force that binds the state together. Service in households brings together people who belong to different social classes and who would otherwise be strangers to one another. It unites them in a relationship intended, ordained, and sanctified by God. And it is precisely this relationship of "master and servant" and "mistress and maid" in the sphere of the household that impresses on the mind—of those at the top just as well as of those at the bottom—a sense of duty and a willingness to weave together all those very different and divergent sectors in state and society to which we all belong in our capacity as citizens.

IX THE EVOLUTION OF THE HOUSEHOLD IN HISTORY

With our previous installment about masters and servants this series of articles is complete. It showed how the household is an ingenious instrument in the hand of God to imprint on people all those habits, attitudes, and qualities that cannot possibly be absent if there is to arise among humankind, in those masses of people, an orderly society and a well-regulated state.

We showed that civic spirit, class contentment, and love of country are automatically fostered by the simple yet grand fact that we are not created *de novo*, like Adam, but are born as members of an existing whole into a family. We brought out how interacting with one's father and being subject to him automatically gives rise to respect for authority and a sense of justice, while the mother in the home is the promoter of our constitutional rights and freedoms as she defends what is fragile and fair and vulnerable. We showed how husband and wife in their marital union breed mutual trust, reciprocal accommodation, and a sense of solidarity—three hidden forces that hold the state together. We drew attention to the way the world of brothers and sisters prepares citizens for the glorious ideal of "liberty, equality, fraternity," and we finished by pointing out how the real meaning of "being of service and being served" lies in the all-controlling idea of the state as a moral organism.

If our readers, before we come to our conclusion, would like further evidence that these things are not just spun by us but are so in fact, then let them compare nation with nation and times with times.

History and ethnography show at a minimum that the family household has hardly functioned in that integral manner at all times and in all places. There have been peoples and there have been times when "belonging to a family" was undone a thousand million times by the horrendous practice of human trafficking. Humans would not live their lives where they belonged but where they ended up as a result of plunder and sale.

There are also peoples and there have also been times when marriage between husband and wife broke up in polygamy or when being in service was destroyed in humiliating slavery. In families thus maimed almost beyond recognition, most of the child-rearing and education went on in the absence of father and mother, and slaves strictly separated sisters and brothers from each other.

What remained of a family household after being mutilated, degenerated, and perverted in those ways barely deserved the name of household. And then it stands to reason that given such a maimed and dulled instrument the Lord God can only in a very inadequate way imprint on the hearts those habits and attitudes that are required for a healthy state. Thus everyone will understand that where polygamy, slavery, and human trafficking, each by itself or in combination, have crippled the family household, there society cannot flourish and a constitutional state cannot arise adorned with rights and freedoms.

We for our part have learned from the facts of history and ethnography that the life and status of a state moves in tandem with the life and status of the household. When the household is thriving, a strong and true state develops as well. But when domestic bonds are loosed, the state deteriorates into a tyranny by rulers and abject submission by subjects. Force replaces right!

Just to be clear, we are not talking about the frightful conditions among the Negro peoples in Africa that fills everyone who has studied them with nothing but horror and loathing. These conditions are profoundly immoral, humanly evil, godless to an inconceivable degree. Consequently, little reminds the observer there of anything like a household. And as a result of that, we find no trace there of political life in orderly states and only scandalous savagery of bloodthirsty brutes. Think of Timbuktu![15]

We are not even referring, except in passing, to the despotism of the heathen Asians. We all heard recently about Burma.[16] Nor do we need to rehearse how the Chinese play havoc with children's health and how conquered peoples are dealt with by Chinese warlords. Wives, fathers, loyal servants are unknown in Asia, so how could households ever arise? And without households, how could there arise anything that remotely resembled free and decent governments? If you wish to verify our inadequate sketch, just make a comparison sometime between China and the vastly superior Japan and notice how much higher political life has developed in Edo compared to Peking.[17]

But what we do wish to call attention to is the difference *in Europe and America* between those countries where the household is flourishing

15. Here Kuyper refers to internecine wars involving Timbuktu throughout the nineteenth century. In these comments as elsewhere, Kuyper's comments display a bias that plays into his romanticized understanding of diversity in a fallen world. For more on Kuyper's racial and civilizational judgments from his Eurocentric perspective, see *CG* 1.12.10n4; 1.41.1n3.
16. Kuyper may be referring to the massacre of upwards of 100 members of the royal family as potential candidates for the throne of Burma, conducted by King Thibaw (1859–1916), the last king of the Konbaung dynasty of Burma, purportedly under the guidance of Queen Supayalat (1859–1925). Britain would annex the country in 1885, after the Third Anglo-Burmese War.
17. That is, Tokyo and Beijing.

and those other countries where it is, if not mutilated, at least falling into decline.

Turkey still officially honors polygamy, thus pulling down the household—and look at what becomes of political life in such a state. Marriage fosters trust but polygamy distrust. This explains why in Turkey and in all Islamic countries the whole atmosphere is poisoned by suspicion and why espionage lurks everywhere. It also explains how an Islamic people such as the Achinese[18] can be such fanatical fighters. It makes understandable how an Islamic power such as Turkey can for a long time dominate entire nations through sheer force without ever witnessing the beginnings of a sound and healthy political culture: there just are no households to furnish the necessary ingredients for it. The General Assembly of Istanbul was a most fatal parody of Disraeli's superficial policy.[19] And the same Disraeli is today discovering how impossible it is to erect something like a regular, orderly administration in a country such as Afghanistan where polygamy dominates.[20]

But you find the same contrast also between Christians. An Italian, a Spanish, or a Greek household is the picture of happiness if you compare it to cohabitation among Turks; and indeed the political life of those nations is flourishing if you place it next to the mismanagement and the roguery of the Turkish pashas. But if you are familiar with the English family or the Scottish home and then travel across Austria-Hungary, Spain, or Italy, your heart will sink because neither the sacredness of marriage nor the tenderness of child-rearing nor the loyal devotion of domestic servants is found in those countries. And if you then transpose this to the field of politics, who would get it into his head to compare the Hungarian Diet with the British House of Commons? And how do Sicilian security forces measure

---

18. The Achinese are an ethnic group inhabiting the northern tip of the island of Sumatra who harbored pirates in the Strait of Malacca and fiercely resisted conquest by Dutch imperial forces.

19. The General Assembly or Ottoman Parliament was a bicameral body constituted on December 23, 1876, and dissolved on February 14, 1878. It was the first democratically representative political institution in the Ottoman Empire.

20. Benjamin Disraeli (1804–81) was a leading Victorian conservative politician and prime minister of the United Kingdom. The Second Anglo-Afghan War (1878–80) was prosecuted during his second term of service as prime minister.

up against our police protection? Or, worse, the scandalous history of the Nicoteras and Tiszas against Britain's political integrity?[21]

And if you delve a bit deeper and compare, for example, France with Germany, or the Lutheran with the Reformed lands in Germany—can it then be seriously denied that concubinage is far more common in France than along the Rhine; that in France all "service" has been turned into mere "jobs"; that domestic life in France offers only a very deficient form of upbringing? And then discover in the toiling and plodding of the Waddingtons, the Grévys, and the Gambettas,[22] and in the frightful scenes of 1870,[23] how badly poor France fares in the area of serious political life.

And, not to dwell on the subject for too long, if you then finally ask: "Which countries have developed the greatest aptitude for a healthy, robust, constitutionally shaped political life?"—could you then withhold the prize, even when viewing Germany, from the more Reformed nations such as Scotland, England, Switzerland, Holland, and so on? And if the next question to be answered was: "Where do people live more *inside* and where *outside* the home?"—are you not obliged, if you want to be truthful, to extend the palm of honor to those same countries and to testify about, say, Scotland above Germany, that it is "the more domestic, the more civic-minded"?

X THE DECLINE OF THE HOUSEHOLD UNDER THE INFLUENCE OF THE REVOLUTION

Remarkable, no? For centuries the condition of the household among the noblest nations of our generation had made steady *progress*. But in our century it has suffered marked *decline*.

Till then, the household was seen to unfold, improve, become more refined. But for the last seventy, eighty years that process has not only halted but the household has slid back, sunk lower, lost noticeably in luster.

It would be a mistake, of course, to depict this decline worse than it is, and an even greater mistake to imagine that everything was gold in

---

21. Nicotera and Tisza are towns in southern Italy and Hungary, respectively, that were marked by political unrest.
22. William Henry Waddington (1826–94), Jules Grévy (1807–91), and Léon Gambetta (1838–82) were leading statesmen in the Third French Republic during the unruly 1870s.
23. Here Kuyper alludes to the bloody rule of the Communards in Paris and the equally bloody reconquest of Paris by the French government.

the old days and tinsel nowadays. For one thing, never forget that it took sixty *centuries* for the household to reach the height it gradually attained and that a regression of sixty *years* scarcely needs to be perceptible to still be very real. Bear in mind as well that this is not a question of former bad exceptions and current favorable exceptions, but solely of conditions in general—of what is usually the case, or if you will, of ideas regarding the family household that are common in public opinion.

Now then, when it comes to that, we stand by our charge that the decline in value and meaning of the family household during the last sixty years is gravely disturbing.

Disturbing, in that the significance of domestic life has diminished in proportion as public meeting places such as theaters, clubs, taverns, and pubs have gained in importance.

Disturbing, in that prostitution in all its unholy forms has done frightful damage to the holy bond of marriage.

Disturbing, in that boarding schools have proliferated; the little ones have moved from the living room to the nursery, and children's time with parents has been reduced to only a few hours a day, in part due to excessive amounts of homework assignments.

Disturbing, in that submission, regard, and respect for father and mother have declined drastically and the expression *le père le caissier de par la nature*[24] has more and more become the disdainful slogan of our young people.

Disturbing, in that the servant class has become a band of nomads, a flock of migrant birds which annually—or every half-year, or sometimes even every three months—fly from cage to cage.

Disturbing, last but not least, in that the tendency to make divorce easier, to have one's offspring more and more reared and educated outside the home, to help children become more independent, and to encourage domestic servants in their mania for change—all this is not just having an effect in reality but is greeted with a good-natured smile, sometimes even fervently advocated.

People may then complain loudly that the old habits are eroding, that the solidity of yesterday is no longer found, that loyalty is on the way out, that you can no longer rely on people, that few care about questions of justice,

---

24. That is, "Father will take care of it" or "the old man will cover the tab."

and that respect for one's superiors is all but gone. Yet not a word is said about the fact that these debit entries in the ledger of our society's morality go hand in hand with the deterioration of the household. That the waters of morality are flowing in a trickle instead of streaming in abundance is a fact that no one will deny; but it seems to occur to no one that therefore the fountain must be plugged.

And yet, once you agree that our descriptions are correct and realize that the civic virtues of loyalty, honesty, respect, and so on are especially imprinted on the citizenry by the family household, then surely a child can see that those precious qualities *had to* become rare the moment the household stopped growing those excellent fruits. If less is sowed and planted in the family, must the harvest not also diminish?

Thus it is perfectly transparent how the restlessness of Europe's states, the change in society's certainties, and the decline of moral standards is directly related to the decline in appreciation for the bonds that God has so skillfully woven into the family household between husband and wife, parents and offspring, brothers and sisters, servants and masters, for uniting them into one organic unit, one close-fitting and firmly anchored whole.

The cause of all the woes that Europe and America labor under is *the revolution*. Not this or that riot or mutiny. Nor any particular uprising or revolt. Nor yet the deposition of a prince or a ruler. No, the revolution means the inversion of the thoughts of man and the relationships of life whereby God has been lowered and man has risen to the top.

The revolution was there from the fall into sin, but up until 1789 it stayed in hiding, even for a part in the heathen world, from a certain shame-facedness at being wicked and sinful. Hence it only became "the revolution for *public* life" in 1789, when men began to preach in word and deed that these evil, wicked, and shameful things are actually the good, glorious, and sacred things. First it was: "It's a sin, but let it go." Then it became: "It's not that bad." Next: "It's not really a sin." And finally: "It is actually praise-worthy!" What once was sin became a virtue. What used to be forbidden is now in fashion.

The poison can be administered unrefined and in large doses, as Multatuli[25] has done, or in small, diluted form, as is done in the liberal press. But whatever difference this makes in the swiftness of the process, in substance it is the same. People laud today what used to be denounced, and what used to appear worthy of praise and honor is today the object of scorn and ridicule.

Given that reversal, things could only break down and shatter. People were told the new philosophy was just a question of doubt versus belief and that the revolution stood for popular rights versus royal prerogatives and for political equality versus aristocratic privilege. In retrospect it turned out to be something quite different.

A false principle is like a steam drill. It passes through any material and simply pulverizes whatever comes in its way.

That is what occurred here as well. The revolutionary principle was supposed to be limited to the state, and it quickly crept into society. It was supposed to be confined to the heads, and imperceptibly it slid into the hearts. It was supposed to apply only to church and palace, and before men realized it was busy undermining the foundations of their own house and home.

And so it happened that the unstoppable driving force of the revolutionary principle at last succeeded with the sharpness of a dagger to pierce and slash the certainties of the family household—first, by pushing the cornerstones from their place; then by employing a wrecking crew with levers and crowbars to take it down, under the pretext that a complete "reconstruction" of the family would have to be undertaken anyway.

Once that was accomplished, the family of course stopped inculcating in the citizens-to-be the moral habits of loyalty and respect which they so badly needed. And when these younger, unstable citizens gradually replaced the older generation and took up leading positions, it stands to reason that the state and the society they shaped could only experience the same lack of solidity which they so woefully lacked themselves.

And indeed, even without extraordinary clairvoyance one could foresee that things had to take this course. For this at least was a known fact: the household had never come into its own either in the heathen world

---

25. This is a pseudonym of Eduard Douwes Dekker (1820–87), a free thinker, champion of the labor movement and women's emancipation. He is best known as the author of the classic novel *Max Havelaar* (Amsterdam: J. de Ruyter, 1860), which critiques oppressive policies in the Dutch East Indies.

or in Islam, and the progress made by the household traveled via Ur of the Chaldees to the mount of Calvary, finally to arrive, as the confession of Christ became more purified, in the Reformed countries, where the Christian faith at last attained its purest manifestation.

The household in its noblest manifestation thus proved to be a fruit of the cross of Christ in countries where that cross was confessed in the purest way.

When men set to work in 1789 to expel Christ from the state, and then from society, next from the church, and finally from the household, it was inevitable that after the expulsion of Christ the blossom that had opened up under the warmth of his vital glow could only wither and fall off.

XI HUSBAND AND WIFE

What progress can one possibly make in reconstructing state and society if in the meantime one enthusiastically participates in causing the walls and shields of the household to split by means of the wedge of the revolution?

And yet that is, alas, very much the case!

Even in Christian families you can hear ideas proclaimed and notions taken for granted which in reality are core beliefs of the revolution and which go directly against the ordinances of God.

In saying this, we are not now, in the present context, referring to bad literature creeping into our homes, to the small space that is left for the Word of God, to worldliness in finery and luxury, to a growing love of pleasure, to overindulge in choice foods and drinks, and more of the same. For although each of these trends evidently serves to make us conform to the world and is therefore reprehensible, nevertheless in this series of articles that kind of cancer in our home life is not under discussion. We are here not dealing with sins *done by* a household, but solely with the blight *done to* the household through dislocating its joints and weakening its tissues, hence into the very functioning of its constituent parts and into the character of the natural relations which it calls into being.

And with a view to that we think it is high time that our Christian families come to their senses and make every relationship in the home count again for what it ought to be—not according to Multatuli's wild fantasies, but in keeping with the quiet gravity of God's Word.

That is first and foremost a matter for husband and wife.

Households where the woman is number one and the man plays a subordinate role have become all too common. Such arrangements are sinful. Households like that have been turned inside out by the revolution and are in conflict with God's ordinance.

To be sure, it is a well-known fact that there are exceptional cases in which the woman is the superior one, both mentally and morally; but we also know that such cases are increasing at an alarming rate. It is the result, for one part, of the dissolute lifestyle in which the future heads of households wasted the best years of their youth, even as the young women lived quietly, grew in knowledge and understanding, and practiced prayer. For another part it is the result of the phenomenon that is observed in all declining societies: namely, that nature itself allows its boundaries to become impure as females become mannish and men turn effeminate.

Consequently it is often factually the case that the woman is a stout and robust figure with a keen intellect and a strong personality, while her husband is a weakling in body, soul, and spirit, no longer the manifestation of that majesty and strength which God originally laid on the man as head of the household.

Given these circumstances, once you accept the revolution's false notion that the man is "master in his house" not because God has so appointed him but because he is factually stronger and better—then it speaks for itself that whenever his superiority is lacking his headship will not be acknowledged either. Thanks to that false premise the woman will take over, and since she has superiority she will also assert it.

On the other hand, if you believe with the church of Christ that the revolution's rule is false, that its basic premise is deeply sinful and wicked, and that the man, weak or strong, is master in his house solely *by the grace of God,* that is, exclusively by the fact that God *appointed* him master of his house, then it needs no further analysis that the rule of women is shameful and harmful.

A man who lets his wife be boss in the house is not just cowardly and unmanly; that would be the least of his shortcomings. But he is directly going against an ordinance of his Lord and resisting the will of his God.

He simply may not do this. And the woman, even if she could, as they say, wind her husband around her little finger, may never aspire to it. In fact, even if her husband pushes this on her, the wife must not give in to it—for the simple reason that it is not the husband's authority that is at stake, but the *majesty of God*.

Mark well, our strong protest against effeminacy contains not a word or syllable, not a tittle or iota, for excusing the behavior of those ill-mannered tyrants in the home who in their foolish pride fancy that their authority rests on their personal excellence and is therefore a hobbyhorse that they can ride with childish vanity in celebration of their undisputed power. That is, at the very least, just as sinful, just as revolutionary. And God will judge such rough Goliaths in the home until the stone from the sling sinks deep into their foreheads. Their behavior has nothing to do with God's ordinances for headship; it is rather a caricature and a mockery of it.

A husband, in and of himself, has no edge over his wife. They are both equal. They are both creatures of God. Whatever each has was a pure gift. The fact that the one may have more power, gifts, talents, and so on than the other never entitles either of them to lord it over the other. To possess more talents only obligates one to greater exertion and greater thankfulness.

So whether you look at a man as a creature or as a sinner, by nature he has not the slightest power or authority over his wife. Only the most high God has anything to say about either. Husband and wife are both at his free disposal, since he created them and gave them all they have. Thus if it had pleased God to say to the man: "Your will shall be subject to the woman!" then the woman would have to wield the scepter as queen of the household, even if the man were ten times stronger and wiser. But now that it has pleased God to say to the woman exactly the opposite: *"Your will shall be subject to the man!"* now it has been decided once and for all, in the most explicit terms, that God the Lord has laid a portion of his divine power over the woman *on the husband* and that it is therefore the husband to whom the rule of the household is due. Due to him, not as something inherent in him, but as laid on him from the outside. Not as a gift, therefore, but as a form of stewardship for which he is accountable. Thus also as a power which in cases of illness or travel abroad he can delegate to the one next to him. And also as a power that does not go down with him into the grave but, being quite separate from his person, will then automatically devolve on his wife.

Now, if this is the clear and unmistakable contrast between what the revolution desires and what God has ordained, then you will understand what it means to exhort one another: "Be antirevolutionary also in your house and home!"

The revolution says, "You are the boss because you are the stronger one." God said, "You are the head because I have appointed you to that position."

The revolution says, "Master in my house on my own authority." God said, "The government which shall be upon your shoulders is *my* government that I have placed upon you!"

And finally, the revolution is of the view that "within the bounds of the law I can do in my household whatever I want!" whereas God declared, "You are accountable to me also for the way you rule your household!"

Our conclusion is straightforward.

Even if the woman is so lucky as to have a husband who is in every respect her superior as well as her loving spouse, then she is bound to submit to the will and authority of such a man, not because of his excellence, nor because he is so loving, but solely because of God's will; his superiority and his love only serve to make it easier for her to obey God's will.

And if instead the woman finds herself in the situation that in one or more respects she outweighs her husband, or also if she has reason to complain of his lack of tenderness toward her, then that still may never be an excuse for her to assault the authority that God has placed on her husband by challenging or usurping it. All she needs to remember is that God has not subjected her to that man for the sake of that man, but in order that she, often suffering wrongfully, might find favor with God in obeying his divine ordinance despite the many things that made her obedience so difficult.

XII PARENTS AND CHILDREN

Things are no different between parents and children. Why does a child have to honor his parents, that is, treat them with respect and loyalty? Is it because his parents give him such loving care, because they were always there for him when he was a child and prayed for him with such heartfelt tenderness? Or is there a different, deeper reason for honoring them? Is there a higher duty that compels him to honor his parents?

It is quite common today to hear parents as well as children give the first answer. When children misbehave or rebel and go too far the usual reaction is to reprimand them and to add: "And we have always been so good to you! Father and I used to be up with you all night. We sacrificed our own wants so we could buy you the things you wanted. How can you be so ungrateful now?"

And, inversely, you can hear children reason along these lines whenever parents scold or discipline them: "I could have done so and I would have been nicer to you, but you weren't very nice to me. Remember what I asked you to do? You didn't do it. So how can you expect me to be nice to you?"

And that's how it goes between parents and children, even in the best Christian families. Everything is put on reciprocal love—like a tug of war, very unloving toward one another.

And that is exactly what we must resist with all our might. For it means that we are importing the height of revolution into our homes. For what is assumed in that case is the thoroughly false idea that it depends on father's conduct whether or not his son should honor him. In other words, the assumption is that father has to earn the right to demand his child's obedience by taking good care of him, and that if father turns out to have been negligent in this the son is absolved from honoring him.

This is an untenable position, which implies in addition that the degree of honor with which a child honors his parents is measured against the degree to which his parents have taken care of him. This in turn implies— and here you encounter the revolution in seminal form—that the child is the judge of the father, that he decides whether his parents have done their duty, and, depending on how this judgment turns out, that he rewards them with kindness and love or punishes them with cool indifference or even rebellion.

This must lead to a complete reversal of the order in the household. It puts the child above the father. And the atmosphere in the home is not set by the parents but by the children.

And given the fact that by far most parents are very careless about child-rearing and rightly give cause for complaint, it further leads to a situation where the number of households keeps on increasing in which the children have stopped honoring father and mother on the ground that father and mother have fallen awfully short in their duty as parents.

In a most questionable way, moreover, it leads to situations in which children place mother above father, or father above mother, and in case of unequal parenting to reward them with unequal measures of honor.

This flagrantly revolutionary viewpoint, finally, leads to nothing less than the cancellation of every right of parents to admonish, reprimand, discipline, and punish their offspring. After all, every deficiency in giving due honor to the parents is simply deserved as punishment for their poor conduct, and their dissatisfied children mete this out to them without even so much as an opportunity to lodge an appeal.

Looked at more closely, the system of reciprocal love makes no sense. Yet there is no disguising the fact that it is widespread. Most novels construct domestic life on exactly this false foundation. In most conversations reciprocal love is assumed to be the basis on which we must take our stand. Our writers, pedagogues, and thought leaders (certainly insofar as they are outside Christ, and sometimes despite their better confession) know no better or firmer bedrock for parents and children to live together than this ebb and flow of being nice and not nice toward one another.

Sometimes they will add that "children owe their existence to their parents, that mother carried them under her heart, gave birth to them amid much pain, and nursed them on her breast." But our children are not that dull not to realize two things full well: (1) that this can at most provide a reason for a certain measure of gratitude toward mother who carried and nursed them, but never toward father, and that therefore these circumstances can never count as a basis for honoring their parents; and (2) that all this could never have been deeds of love toward them personally, for the simple reason that "unknown makes unloved" and that therefore there could not have been, before they saw the light of day, any love for them except from natural instinct.

Whatever one may devise to mislead people with the beautiful word *love* and seemingly raise the household to a higher moral level, factually it is again evident that the principles of the revolution necessarily lead to *lowering* the standard of life. And the outcome proves that ever since these inflated and fallacious notions caught on and the views gained acceptance which Multatuli only carried through to their full consequences—that since that time, we say, the honor that children pay their parents has deteriorated rather than improved, and the luster of home and family life has paled.

Hence our appeal: "Be antirevolutionary also in your household!" In the present context this means: let go of this false basis of the revolution and go back to the foundation God has laid in his commandments and ordinances by giving parents *authority* over their offspring.

What we said in the previous installment applies here as well: father and son, mother and daughter, both in their quality as creatures and in their condition as sinners, have just as much and just as little to say over each other. The only One who has authority over children and can command them is God the Lord, since he is their Creator—always with the understanding, that is, that the same authority to which the children are subject holds just as much for father and mother. Thus if father and mother are to have binding authority, there is only one way, one possibility, to acquire it, and that is that God the Lord *appoints* those parents as bearers of a portion of the authority which God alone can exercise over children, and that those children in turn are *commanded* by God to honor this divinely appointed authority not for the sake of the parents, but for the Lord's sake.

It is on this ground that Scripture instills in us—and it is pursuant to Scripture that the Christian church proclaims—that a child must honor its father and mother for the sole reason that God has commanded it, regardless of whether father and mother live up to their mandate or not.

If with this command the child is taught to look at father and mother in and of themselves, then of course it can often find it difficult to honor them; for who can honor a miserable personality or a cruel despot? But if the child instead is taught that it is not called to honor the human qualities of father and mother but only the divine authority of which they are the bearers, then all internal conflict, all moral confusion, all unreasonableness disappears. For then the child's moral sense remains unshaken and unharmed. Then father's and mother's misbehavior can never abolish the commandment. Then a bedrock is found for a child's obedience that will remain immovable, whoever father and mother are and however they behave. And then the child who submits and suffers under the arbitrary rule of poor parents is not bound to any other suffering than to "endure grief, suffering wrongfully" [see 1 Pet 2:19], by which it will find favor with God.

Our rediscovery of the truly Christian and only genuine basis for the relation between parents and children in the home does not at all mean that we should not pay homage to the wonderful beauty of love that parents and children can show each other. On the contrary, it seems to us that history testifies of a better past, when precisely on the basis of divine authority a beautiful, tender, holy life of love developed between parents and their children. It is much *talked about* today, but at that time it was a *fact*.

XIII BROTHERS AND SISTERS

"By virtue of God's ordinance" or "according to the wish and whim of man"—this turned out to be the sharp contrast between the Christian and the revolutionary worldview, both as to the bond between husband and wife and the union of parents and offspring. As the next two installments will show, the same contrast plays itself out in the relation of brothers and sisters and in that of masters and servants.

That brothers and sisters do not always get along is common, and we saw earlier why this has to be so.[26] We minced no words and now repeat them with some emphasis, not in order to cynically amuse ourselves à la Multatuli with the miseries of the human race, but to cut off, once for all, the disappointments that tend to discourage almost all parents as they rear their children. If we are filled with the false illusion that as the children grow up they will live together like a small band of angels, we will be sorely disappointed and will be overcome by a feeling of despair when we hit upon so much that is almost demonic in the world of children. And if we have had the misfortune of getting our children used to the same illusion and preparing them for finding their siblings none but sweet and loving creatures, then the outcome cannot but painfully disappoint them. It will make them interpret as deliberate teasing and biting what is merely the inevitable expression of a different temperament in a child who is born a sinner.

Thus it is certainly not insignificant whether one nurses correct or false notions about the world of children and cultivates such notions in one's children. For if I take the opposite path and believe on the basis of God's Word that my children *must* all be different and, since they are conceived and born in sin, *cannot but* develop this difference in personality in a sometimes painful, sinful manner, then of course there is no reason for me to be disappointed; then my home will not see inflated pseudo-love, and there is even a chance that my children will exceed my expectations. This will encourage me to persevere in bringing them up with care and in praying for them to the only One who is able to command a holier peace in that chaotic world of tantrums, stubborn wills, and youthful passions.

The revolutionary theory of our "angels of children" who are to grow up into goody-goodies will bitterly disappoint: it paralyzes child-rearing, produces grumpiness and discontent, and makes the children always think the worst of each other. The antirevolutionary principles, by contrast, exhort caution; they make us more serious and drive us to prayer. Those principles are in agreement with reality; they help us to stay calm, and instead of preparing us for repeated disappointments will often fill our hearts with joy and gratitude.

Provided, that is—and this is key—provided the children are impressed from an early age with the sense *that they belong together* and that this is

---

26. See above, section V.

so not because they sought each other's company, nor because father and mother picked them out of a group of a hundred children, but solely *because it pleased God the Lord* to have them born as brothers and sisters and so unite them in birth by the same blood.

Remove that sense, and the fraternal tie will snap. For then the centrifugal force of their difference in personality loses its natural counterweight, and nothing will stop the children from scattering in all directions. And they will then become really unhappy and at times drive the parents to desperation.

And then it is easy to resort to a plan that many are already carrying out: namely, that if the children just don't get along, to send one of them to a boarding school or ... worse, to an institution.

We cannot warn enough against tearing the bond between siblings in this manner, and we cannot emphasize enough to have faith in God also for that bond. For if you believe in God's ordinance and in his providential dispensation, including the fact that brothers and sisters should live together, then you know and are firmly convinced that the Lord surrounds us with just such siblings as are necessary to complement, or else to temper, our particular nature. "Those two make such a pair!" a mother will say about two of her little ones who are always together. But in a much higher and holier sense, Christians confess that a brother and a sister in a family are a pair, not so much because they are leaves from the same tree, but inasmuch as the Lord God brought them together in this way—with precisely those personalities—so that they would find themselves surrounded by each other in order to shape and develop each other. Indeed, even if they are "at daggers drawn" the confession that they belong together must be insisted on. For a sibling who annoys you does you a good turn of great value by honing your skill at self-defense and stimulating your energy level.

What must be paramount and beyond dispute for both parents and children is that *the Lord has brought us together* and therefore we belong together and should normally stay together, fighting and playing, quarreling and caring, in one and the same house, under the same roof, if possible even in the same room.

In particular, therefore, the practice that parents so often resort to of "keeping the children out of each other's hair" is as reprehensible as sending a headstrong child to a boarding school.

"What therefore God has joined together, let not man separate" [Mark 10:9] is the great commandment that may not be transgressed even in the children's world.

In the name of better principles we must protest even against the constant expansion of the nursery. It was a custom among the pagan Greeks and Romans to confine the toddlers to the care of a nursemaid, and it is still the custom in the women's quarters of the Muslims. But that is not fit for Christian families. There, consignment to the nursery should not be stretched out as long as possible, but on the contrary should as much as possible be shortened—for one part so that mother will not be supplanted by the mother-for-hire, but for another so that those lively little tykes can perform their natural function as connecting links that keep the older brothers and sisters together. Those little ones do so much without our noticing it! The arrival of yet another little brother or sister, provided they are not packed away to the top floor, has often been an occasion for the family to rekindle tenderness and love for one another.

Now, if you follow this course and imprint on your children as they grow up a deep sense of "we belong together," you will live to see the wonderful blessing this sense yields amid the many complicated relations among siblings.

If divorce were made very easy, as proposed by the Naguets[27] and the Van Houtens[28] of this world, you would be surprised to see how many recently married couples would separate within the first year and how many who stayed together would sour each other's life with the threat of divorce. By contrast, the certain knowledge that "we belong together and have to stay together" would be a powerful force to get over the initial irritations, create space for calmly looking at the good in each other, and gradually, by complementing and polishing each other, turn two different people into a close-knit couple who did at times ask themselves in despair, "What have we begun?"

Nothing makes people calmer than the knowledge that "there is nothing to be done about it." Nothing draws people closer together than the firm

---

27. Alfred Naguet (1834–1916) was a French physician, member of the Assembly, and sponsor of a bill regulating legal divorce "for cause."
28. Samuel van Houten (1837–1930) was a lawyer, atheist, liberal member of the Dutch Parliament, and sponsor of legislative motions promoting contraception and gender equality.

conviction that "we belong together." And nothing has proved so powerful as coaxing a harmonious chord from seven different notes as precisely the profound sense that "what speaks in the warmth of our shared blood is the ordinance and will of God."

So if your children figure that there is always an escape, as in: "Well, if you just can't get along, father will put him out of the house"; or: "If he continues to behave in that way, father will give him a separate place in the house"; or even: "The children have their own room, they don't concern me"; then, we guarantee you, your children will always be restless; in any serious dispute they will make it their object to cause a separation; and nothing will remain of that shared blood that should draw them together.

But if instead, from childhood up, you put in their mind, like a "law of the Medes and Persians,"[29] the knowledge that they cannot and may not be separated, because the Lord has destined them to grow up together; if from the start you make them realize that in your home there is no room for partitions between brothers and sisters and no secluded nooks to withdraw into; and if they know from their youth that the nursery is not a second living room but is only the vestibule for the one and only living room—then, we are not afraid to assure you, the force that draws together will neutralize the force that drives apart, and with the help of God the blood ties shared by all your children will prove to be a force that binds.

XIV MASTERS AND SERVANTS

Again, in a Christian household that is governed by the Word, relations between master and servant and mistress and maid should not reflect the style of the world or the principles of the revolution.

Let no one say that this point is less important than maintaining good relations between husband and wife or parents and children. On the contrary, partly for our family but especially for state and society, the relation that exists between us and our domestic staff is of the utmost importance.

Partly for our family. For who, we ask, will measure the misery that has been poured out over a whole range of families by unmanageable domestics or, inversely, by servants who were ruined as a result of mistreatment? Or who shall calculate the true value of the blessing and peace that we and our children enjoy by having been fortunate in the choice of staff?

---

29. A reference to the irrevocability of a decree, as in the custom of the Medo-Persians.

Yet of much greater importance is the restoration of good relations, that is, of relations willed by God, between ourselves and our domestics *in the interest of state and society*.

For us and our servants to live together under the same roof is to create the closest, most intimate contact that can exist between the different ranks and classes of society. It brings the daughters of the lower classes into immediate contact with some of the noblest and most prominent families in the land. And since the social question, that is, the question how best to regulate the relation between rich and poor, is exercising the best minds in Europe, it would surely be all too thoughtless not to direct attention first of all to the arrangement found in every town and in every village that takes thousands upon thousands from the homes of the less well-off and conveys them into the houses and inner rooms of our well-to-do fellow countrymen.

We are aware that the social question lies dormant at the moment and has ended for the time being in once again revealing the impotence of the working classes. The initial failure of labor strikes and the inefficacy of workingmen's cooperatives have been followed again by a decline in wage levels after they had just begun to rise. But to conclude from this that the social question is over would be a big mistake. We would rather say that the only thing that has failed thus far is the attempt to wrest better conditions along the *normal* route, so that the danger of violent explosions caused by pent-up resentment has increased rather than vanished.

It makes a big difference therefore whether the thousands upon thousands of domestics who are the representatives of the working classes in our homes acquire there an influence for good or an influence for evil, an influence which they will eventually take back to their working-class circles.

This consideration is all the more compelling since the former domestic will soon be a wife and mother in a working-class family and will usually have a proportionally very strong influence there as a result of the increasing refinement she has undergone during her service as well as the increasing physical strength that more nutritious food has imparted to her over a number of years.

Now, if you make the gross error of wanting to arrange the relationship between you and your servants by means of a *contract* (and is that not what the modern, revolutionary, liberal worldview would like to see?), then it is a foregone conclusion that there can never be any peace and that there will always be tension between you and your staff. You will both be pulling at opposite ends of the same stick, where the only thing that counts is who will get the better end of it. *You* will necessarily be out to get the most service possible out of your staff for the lowest possible wages; and *they* will be shrewd enough to perform as little as possible at the highest wage possible. This will turn into a tug of war, and since our young ladies as a rule know little about keeping house and most of them would rather get involved in as few domestic chores as possible so that the demand for maids continues to rise, the outcome can be no other than that the advantage will be on the side of the maid, who will then be able to make the mistress dance to her tune.

That in turn entails that a maid who runs up against a "mistress with a will" will quit the day after, because she is certain that she will be welcomed with open arms, at higher pay, by a mistress who is short a maid. And this in turn will lead to a situation where our maids become migrant birds, flitting from one nest to the next, and what is worse, never entering a service in order to learn, to be trained, to get to be at home with things. Instead, they will be less knowledgeable, less able, and so less an "all-round girl," as they used to say. Thus they will repeatedly give legitimate cause for reprimand; and then, unable to put with "all that nagging and complaining," they will become impertinent and rebellious.

And once it has come to that, things will turn, literally, into a conspiracy—in two ways. A conspiracy will form upstairs in the salons of the ladies at their teas, who will vent their frustration with "those maids of today." And another conspiracy will take shape downstairs, where the maids will have fun in maligning their mistresses—an exercise in lower-class rhetoric in which the poor "mistresses" will never be referred to in any other way than with the derogatory pseudonym "*them.*"

What can be done to remove this evil?

Crack the whip, some people will say. But with what right? What right do you have to browbeat your maid? Because you are richer? Or from a higher class? Or that you can turf her out tomorrow with six weeks' wages? There's no mention of it in her contract. The contract is nullified only if she refuses to work. Nothing more was stipulated by you.

So give in, says another. Indulge your maids! For the sake of peace, let them do their thing. That's just how they are. And the ladies who turn a blind eye enjoy the least trouble, keep their maids the longest, and have nothing but smiling faces.

Neither reaction is acceptable. A tug of war arouses resentment and embitters. Giving in is shirking your duty and showing lack of moral fiber. And with both reactions you will corrupt yourself as well as your staff.

No, here too there is only one correct response: be antirevolutionary in your household! That is to say, learn to bow, and teach your maids to bow, before the Word of your and their God.

If you do that, you will immediately discover how to arrange your rights and duties. It is not you who has authority over your servants, but God the Lord does; and so he also has the power to delegate a portion of that authority to you. Which leads directly to two conclusions with respect to that right.

In the first place, you simply *must* insist on your authority over your maids, regardless of whether or not you find it convenient or would prefer to just let things be. You must insist on it, regardless of whether your maids are willing to listen or grumble about it. Insist you must, even if it means that tomorrow they quit and walk out on you.

But then also, in the second place, you may never exercise that authority in any other way than before the face of God. It is not your authority but his. You are not asking your maids to bow before your pride but before his majesty.

That will not always be easy. Many maids are no longer familiar with the Word of God. And a great many "Christian" girls, who are familiar with it, are fond of that Word when it comes to piety and salvation of the soul, but have never conceived of the possibility that the same Word of God concerns her conduct as a servant as well, and among other things forbids being "argumentative" (Titus 2:9).

On the other hand, there are plenty of "Christian" ladies who put themselves out in aid of "Christian work" among the girls in Sundaland,[30] yet to whom it has never occurred that they also have to treat the girls in their own house, baptized members of Christ's church, with Christian love.

Yet that is what must be done. There is no other solution.

The "girls" must learn again to bow before God's Word, and so know that they are not working for pay but that they are serving the Lord—because God placed them "in service"; because he gave them that kind of work to do; because they are to serve him in that work. They need to learn again to say "yes, Lord" when God exhorts them in his Word to "suffer wrongfully" as a means to obtain a greater measure of grace. When they meet in their small groups they need to spend some time pondering Ephesians 6:5; Colossians 3:22; 1 Timothy 6:1–2; 1 Peter 2:18; and similar passages.

---

30. Sundaland is an area in Southeast Asia including the Malay Peninsula as well as the islands of Borneo, Java, and Sumatra.

But the ladies, too, must learn again to bow before God's Word. They must learn to face their maids and acknowledge that they too are sinners and that a mistress's authority over her maids is only an authority conferred on her by God. They have to be willing to accept again that their maids, too, are "neighbors" whom they are to love as themselves. They have to realize again that God's Word makes them co-responsible for the social and spiritual well-being of their maids. And they must again learn to be an example, despite any inner resistance, of the power of the mind of Christ, in whom there is neither "bond nor free" [see Gal 3:28] but only "the redeemed by one and the same blood."

Where things are done in this way, there everyone will realize their station. The mistresses will exude the kindly attitude and the maids the loyal devotion that used to constitute the strength of the household.

We do not pretend that this would end all bickering. There will always be squabbles. But then there will be the Word of God as the ever-present Judge who can restore the peace. And even in case of a heated row the Word of God will rein in madam's passion and the reminder of a higher Judge will guard the lips of a hot-tempered maid.

At the same time people will realize that to exclude the maids from the family altar,[31] or to have them stay somewhere in the background during that time, will only be to the detriment of the family itself. Similarly, people will realize that allowing their staff time off for attending church services enhances their moral authority. And people will come to understand that to abuse a servant as a beast of burden without a soul brings down the Lord's curse upon the home.

And what speaks even stronger: where everyone knows and keeps their place, there a more serious approach to life will curb the fascination of our maids with fashion and luxuries; there a high degree of intimacy can arise without degenerating into familiarity; there our working-class families will gain a salutary impression of the homes of the well-to-do; and there above all the high and holy God, whose Word alone once again proved able to save, will be praised for his benevolent dispensation by masters and servants alike.

---

31. That is, the practice of closing the meal with a reading from Scripture and prayer.

XV GOD'S WORD, THE ONLY REMEDY

The proof of anything is found in history. Among its sure findings history teaches us one thing that is surest of all: the state falls into decline if decay creeps into society; society gets unhinged whenever the household deteriorates; and the household breaks down whenever it strays from God's Word.

It is useless for you mourners to decry the lethargy of our current political life. You can wail all you want about the moral deterioration of society. And all your homilies against the growing habit of "going out," of being away from home in pursuit of entertainment, are useless. Those are all words without substance, mere sounds that just evaporate into thin air so long as you shrink from naming the final link in the chain of our misery and dare not add *that the household itself is ailing.*

You may sound like an austere ascetic or a sentimental family man when you inveigh against music halls and theaters and admonish "decent folk" to return to hearth and home for finding warmth and hugs for the frozen human heart. But what else are you doing except mocking our winter chill if those "decent folk" leave the music halls for the vaunted hearth to find on the grate, alas, nothing but cinders and for inspiration nothing but ashes.

It is incumbent on every serious moralist to recognize that it is immoral to palm off the pleasure seekers with words such as the "homeliness" and "coziness" of hearth and home. It is wrong to do so. It is the extreme of superficiality.

No, before we bolt the door behind these pleasure seekers we should first carefully inspect that home to find out whether the house is still fit to live in—whether the atmosphere is indeed cozy and the fireplace still has fire in it. And if we then find, inevitably and sadly, that cracks and leaks have begun to make most houses drafty and damp—that many family circles are boring rather than engaging, that the home fires seldom radiate the kind of warmth that can thaw your spirit, relax your muscles, and make you feel comfortable—if this is what we find, was it then such a waste of time for us to have analyzed the household in order to discover what constitutes its makeup and what has caused its decline?

Our conclusion was this: the family household collapses like a house of cards the moment you stop viewing it in direct relationship to the living God.

If you see in the family household a most artistic creation of God's unfathomable wisdom; if you see in every person who belongs to the household a being whom God has made; if you agree with us that all these people have no other authority than what God has granted them and that they may not shirk the duties God has laid on them: then is the structure, the function and the goal of the family household not completely transparent to you?

And inversely, if you separate the family household from God Almighty, if you view it as a human construct, a contract between its members to enable them to regulate their reciprocal rights and duties as they see fit— then, we came to see clearly, then there is no more bond; then literally everything is up for grabs, right down to the most sacred and tender ties; then it is totally understandable that the rising generation regards the parental home as a kind of Alpine hut that you crawl inside of in order to sleep but that you leave again as soon as possible in order to go on "enjoying life."

For this reason we could reach no other conclusion than to recommend with the greatest earnestness: *put your household back on the solid ground of the Word of God.*

Religious sentiments do not avail. Pious prattle is not worth the trouble of hearing. If it is true that the household depends on God and that he alone has the right to regulate the rights and duties of the members of the family, then one had better know what God has determined and ordained with respect to it.

Therefore I cannot do with anything less than his Word. And that Word as a sure, solid, and trustworthy word. Not a word like shifting sand, but a word so sure and trustworthy that I can fully rely on it.

And when I put that Word back on the family altar, it obviously does not just mean that I am to read from it with my loved ones in order to edify and improve *my soul*, but no less to edify and improve *our home*.

Godliness is absolutely not just a promise for the life that is to come, but definitely also for the life here and now. That is why Scripture speaks not merely about matters that concern the soul, but at least just as often about relationships in everyday life. In fact, it does so to such an extent that the apostles in their epistles repeatedly return to hold forth at length about relations between husband and wife, parents and children, masters and servants.

It is a big mistake, therefore, to limit the power of God's Word in the family to the reading of "spiritual" passages. That will often go over the children's heads anyway.

No, to make God's Word a power in your home you should shed light on domestic relations by reading from the household arrangements and national institutions of Israel, the practical admonitions and penitential sermons of the prophets, the incisive language of Jesus, and the concrete instructions of the apostles. Next, you should read about the examples, judgments, and reprimands in the Word in order to reveal to our conscience all kinds of domestic sins. Third, during all domestic disputes you should be able to fall back on the Word. Finally, you should make sure that the way your household is run is in harmony with the instructions in the Word.

To do this therefore requires reading not just from the four Gospels but also from the five books of Moses, not just from the dogmatic openings but also from the practical closings of the Epistles, from texts that edify the soul but also from passages that touch on righteousness in the shop and at the office, in the kitchen, and in the bedroom. God should be present everywhere, in the home as well, by way of his Word.

We confidently recommend this use of Scripture because Christian parents will discover that nothing provides a stronger guarantee against forsaking the faith of the fathers than to combat inflated piety and to honor God's Word in every room in the house.

Religious circles that want to be overly spiritual and expose their children too early to a rigorous scheme of what constitutes "true conversion" have learned to their great sorrow, especially in the last couple of decades, how their children later abandoned the faith and openly denied what their parents once believed.

Recall for a moment the names of those who a mere twenty years ago were considered the future hope of our Christian Netherlands, and you will have to admit that almost all of them have become estranged from the faith of the fathers.

Consider that nowhere more than in Reformed countries it used to be the custom to shun that tendency to be overly spiritual and first of all to relate everyday life, including that of the household, to the Word of God. In living by the Word the family circle in those blessed lands regained some of that patriarchal stamp of old. Is it not noteworthy that the children from those circles mostly remained loyal to the confession of the fathers?

The advice to have the Word of God first of all serve to edify and strengthen your *family household* is not at all intended to push the edification *of the soul* to the background, but much rather to have that spiritual nurture be all the more successful. To be strong and have influence, in whatever field, you have to be of a piece. That is exactly the hidden reason why the soul is so poorly being anchored in the Word if that Word is not also the foundation of the home.

Should those of our fellow countrymen who have lost the habit of bowing before God's Word be of the opinion that our advice is unsound, well then, let them give something else in its place.

Slogans are hollow sounds and offer no material with which to build. To say that we must make the home more welcoming, that we should instill greater earnestness in our children and have love dominate the atmosphere under our roof—that of course means very little.

The difference with us is not that we do not want this, or that we want something else. Surely, everyone wants this. More love! More earnestness! More warmth!

The question is: How to acquire those ingredients? How to bring more love into the home? How to instill greater earnestness? How to make the atmosphere more welcoming?

Our answer has been: artificial means and repeated sermons will not help. To acquire those ingredients you have to restore the normal functioning of the different parts of the household. And for that, you have to be willing to learn from God's Word what that functioning should be.

By bowing to the Word you introduce a spiritual force into your household that will begin to do its work and accomplish for you what you desire.

If you say to someone who is unwell, "Friend, your circulation needs to improve, your breathing needs correction, your digestion needs to adjust!" it will not help your patient. He knows that himself. The question is how to achieve this. If you want to help your ailing friend, you have to call in a person who knows about the composition of the human body and the proper functioning of its parts, who knows how to diagnose the cause and apply the means to remove it.

That is exactly how we have dealt with the household. We have analyzed its component parts and their function, and indicated its ailments and the power to restore it.

We certainly did not do so in the foolish illusion that a series of essays would suddenly reverse household trends. We are profoundly aware, more than anyone else, that a rebirth of family life can only come from the Lord. But the Lord also uses effective instruments. Those instruments include the press. And that press lowers and desecrates itself if it does not make it a point of honor to serve Jesus' kingship.

It has often perturbed us to meet fellow citizens who would pass through fire for "antirevolutionary principles in politics" yet allowed their domestic life to be ruined by the theories of the revolution. Given the gravity of the times, we felt impelled to move for once from the public square to the privacy of the home in order to call out to our Christian people: be antirevolutionary, but first of all in your own home!

XVI THE SCHOOL

In these articles about the significance of the family household for the state we have also spent a few words on the subject of education. Seeing as this could be done only in passing, it was done very briefly. We have learned that this has caused some misunderstanding as to our intention. By way of an appendix to the series that is now finished, we shall broach the subject of schooling one more time, though only insofar as it is a formative power for a healthy development of our political life.

Our Education Act demands that our primary schools be conducive to instructing the nation's children in all "civic and Christian virtues." By *Christian* virtues are understood those virtues that aim at our usefulness for higher life; by *civic* virtues, on the other hand, are understood those virtues that aim at our usefulness for society.

Civic virtues therefore are all those tendencies, habits, and attitudes that must be present in mature citizens if state and society are to run in a decent and orderly fashion. Such virtues would include fidelity, respect, obedience, honesty, contentment, love of liberty, a sense of justice, and so forth. Now, in order to ascertain whether indeed the primary school is the God-ordained means to instill these habits and imprint these attitudes in the children, one does not need to investigate whether the school *is able* to contribute toward these goals, nor whether it sometimes does so owing to favorable circumstances, and even less whether it often does so in the place of those who are properly called to this task. What needs to be examined, rather, is whether the primary school *as such* succeeds in instilling these civic virtues in the children by means of what belongs to its very essence. (Please note that we are not talking about the Christian school in particular, but simply about the school as school.)

That said, we make the same distinction for the school as we did for the household. A family household exerts influence, first of all, through the relations it engenders between husband and wife, parents and children, sisters and brothers, masters and servants. But in the second place the family does so through the characters of the persons that belong to it. In the third place it does so through what is read and said in the household. And not in the least, finally, it does so through the ups and downs that God brings on such a household. Of all these fruits, however, only the first is inherent to the household while the other three are uncertain. For this reason we were able to make mention only of the *first* fruit when discussing the blessing that the household brings to the state. Everything else we therefore left aside.

Similarly, in the case of the school we need to distinguish between fruit and fruit. Thus we can examine in turn (1) What effect does the school have through the relationships it calls into being? (2) What effect does it have through the personalities of teachers and fellow pupils? (3) As well, what effect does it have through what is shown, taught, and said in the school? (4) What effect does it have in those special eventualities that occur within the school or in conjunction with the school?

Meanwhile, of these four fruits only the first and the third can be discussed here. School eventualities are completely unpredictable; and the effect of the teacher's character or that of the pupils can be both positive and negative. Thus we need to examine only the essential relations created by the school, as well as the activities that the school's curriculum offers the children.

Now, if we look more closely at the first, namely, the typical relationships created by the school, then it is obvious that these can be of two kinds only: of children and teacher, and of children among themselves. The fact that there are just these two relationships tells us that as a formative power the school can hardly compare to the family; and if one examines what influence these two relationships will have on the child one can indeed enumerate: obedience, respect, a sense of justice, and so on, but anyone can see right away that what we have here is a weak aftereffect of what the child learns in the child-father relationship (respect) and in the brother-sister relationship (equality). Besides, a person learns just as well in the workshop and the office to respect his superiors and to relate to his peers on an equal footing. So whether the school, too, promotes that feature is irrelevant. The question is simply this: What is the chief instrument that God has provided for instilling these attitudes? And then we answer without hesitation: primarily the family household, the school being a distant second. This comes out best in the case of instilling respect. Would our schoolboys, however well managed, ever really stop being typical schoolboys if the school itself did not sometimes goad them into playing a trick on the teacher?

The contact between child and teacher as well as between child and other children is not sufficiently varied or complex or frequent to have much influence on a child's heart or conscience. At home the contacts are teeming and tumbling in a thousand different forms. But at school it is almost always: Sit down! Stop talking! Don't speak out of turn! Of course in a school it has to be that way. But how can such quenching of a child's life ever have much influence in the *formation* of that life?

Nevertheless, one important element instilled by the school that benefits the state is the element of *order*. To be sure, a good family, too, inculcates order, but order with a thousand exceptions. In the family the members are together in such small numbers that they accommodate each other's idiosyncrasies; here they put the individual above order. But that is exactly what cannot be carried over to the school. At school, order goes before the individual; each one has to adjust to the rhythm of the whole. Now this is the significant feature that the school instills via its two relationships: (1) The teacher is the one who keeps order in the classroom. (2) The other children are the ones who, in school or on the playground, will quickly cure a child of demanding any special treatment. And since the state has a big stake in having its citizens accustomed "to adjust to the rhythm of the whole," we may conclude that every school that instills the sense of order is useful, and that a teacher who cannot keep order is, for that reason alone, a failure.

This kind of orderliness also implies a certain administration of justice. But the school plays only a secondary role in this, after the family. Moreover, this form of justice comes in handy mostly before and after school hours— and when it comes to that, red-blooded boys regard all informers as traitors.

Yet I would not underestimate the importance of the school. For there is still another important element in the school that is of benefit to the state. It lies in the area indicated by the very nature of the school—the area of thinking, knowing, and shaping the mind.

The school exists for teaching and learning. But note that this entails not only instruction but also character formation. To go to school means to grow used to the idea that we ourselves do not know but that someone else does know and has to teach us. This nurtures an excellent moral quality of great value. It kills the self-conceit that one may have of oneself. It makes the child more humble and receptive to taking in what society has acquired before it was born. Thus it strips the child of any false sense of self-sufficiency.

Granted, a wrong atmosphere in the school can cause a child to behave like a know-it-all at home. Nevertheless, the same boy who at home shows off his recently implanted feathers, at school sits quietly in his desk and listens to what he knows he does not know.

But precisely because the school as school is such an inadequate instrument for accustoming the child to moral habits in a *formal* sense, almost everything regarding the school depends on the content of what is taught and on the mind of the teacher—in other words, on the *substance*.

The children are the ones who do not know and whose impressionable minds look up to the teacher. This fact implies that the teacher, both by what he says and by the textbooks and models he assigns, has it almost completely within his power to shape and knead at his discretion the ideas and elementary notions absorbed by the children. No less does he have the power to take the intellectual capacity of the children in connection with their conscience and inner life and either to shut it up within the sphere of the finite and the mundane, or to open it up to what is timeless, grand, ideal, and heroic.

This is the decisive reason why our Christian people must not be satisfied with a primary school that offers no guarantees that those fundamental notions will be sound and that the mind will be directed toward God.

To say, "Reading, writing, and arithmetic have nothing to do with the soul of my child" is the height of superficiality. For even these very simple things cannot be learned without their containing certain ideas and concepts; and depending on whether these ideas are taken from a supply of poison or from the treasury of wisdom, they will either corrupt or enrich your child.

And although we very much fear that there are many Christian schools that teach the children—unintentionally and thoughtlessly—concepts and ideas that stem from the wrong source, nevertheless these are offset by a fund of positive elements; and the mere fact that God's Word is honored and prayer in Jesus' name is held sacred provides a force of incalculable effect which easily bears comparison with the best that the non-Christian school has to offer.

Add to that the influence of the person of the teacher.

No, we do not join those who believe that "the person of the teacher is everything." Such a spiritualistic view was all the rage in the atmosphere of some twenty years ago.[32] But the more practical sense of recent times has reduced this to its proper dimensions. No, the question whether the government school produces citizens who are revolutionary-minded or who instead opt for the ordinances of law and order—that question is first of all decided by the set of ideas instilled in our children. If those ideas in their most general sense are of the same tenor as notions from the liberal catechism (and this is still very much the case in Christian circles), then the child whose mind has been shaped by these ideas will later harbor revolutionary notions about the authority of the state. If you want the coming generation, once grown up, to stick to the eternal principles, then it is essential that our Christian schools adopt as their common possession the ideas and concepts that do not conform to the liberal catechism but to, say, the Heidelberg Catechism.

That said, we cannot emphasize enough that it is certainly the person of the teacher who brings warmth, glow, ardor into our schools—inspiration that turns dull gray into fresh green, melts down what cannot be recast, and makes a child's heart sense the vibrancy of those ideas and concepts.

To be sure, we nurse no illusions on this score. The fact is that to find, just for our country, some twelve thousand of such born teachers is simply to want to reach for the sky. True gold will always be scarce. But at least we are aware that for the training of teachers, facts and drills matter far less than sound insight and a pure heart.

Of course we are not going to argue with those who want to use the school as a tool for evangelism. You can't reason with those people. The significance of the school for the political life of the nation does not even enter their minds. All we can do when facing this evangelical bias is to remind people of the historical fact that our forefathers who included the school when they raised the slogan "The law is a schoolmaster to bring us to Christ!" were quite as successful as the overly spiritual groups of today in shaping the character of their children and preparing them for accepting Christ as their Savior.

---

32. Kuyper is alluding to the reaction of some people at the implementation of the Primary Education Act of 1857, which meant that government schools had to be religiously neutral. No matter, they consoled themselves; it all depends on the teacher how religion will be treated in the classroom.

YOU SHALL NOT COVET

TEXT INTRODUCTION

The Heidelberg Catechism is a manual for basic instruction in Christian doctrine. Published in 1563, the catechism consists of 129 questions and answers and quickly proved useful for faith formation of children and adults alike. As it is divided into fifty-two parts, each "Lord's Day" enables the entirety of the teachings of the catechism to be covered in weekly sermons throughout the year.

At the Synod of Dort, in its 146th session of April 30, 1619, delegates of the participating churches from abroad exhorted the Dutch church "to persevere in the Reformed faith, to pass it on to posterity, and to preserve it until the return of Christ." In reply, the delegates from the Dutch church made a solemn vow, pledging to preach and preserve the Reformed faith, pure and undiluted.

When Kuyper started his commentary on the Heidelberg Catechism in the fall of 1886 in the Sunday paper *De Heraut*, he recalled this vow and subsequently titled his series *E voto Dordraceno*: "from the vow made at Dordt." The title is usually shortened, at Kuyper's own directive—"for ease of citing," he said—to *E Voto*.

The treatment of the Ten Commandments in the Heidelberg Catechism typically follows the pattern of expositing both those things that are forbidden by each commandment and those things that are required. The tenth commandment, "You shall not covet," similarly has both positive duties and negative prohibitions. Lord's Day 44 covers this petition in questions and answers 113 through 115, and Kuyper's exposition of this commandment is broken up into two parts, wherein he treats Q&A 113 first and then concludes with Q&A 114 and 115. Abridgments in these chapters have been identified with ellipses. The chapters on Lord's Day 44a first appeared as three installments in *De Heraut* of May 7, 14, and 28, 1893.

SOURCE: Abraham Kuyper, *E voto Dordraceno*, 4 vols. (Amsterdam: Wormser, 1892–5), 4:254–79. Translated by Ed M. van der Maas. Edited and annotated by Randy Blacketer and Harry Van Dyke.

YOU SHALL NOT COVET

Question 113. *What does the tenth commandment require?*
Answer: *That not even the least inclination or thought against any command-ment of God ever enter our heart, but that with our whole heart we continually hate all sin and take pleasure in all righteousness.*

> *Yet if it had not been for the law, I would not have known sin. I would not*   §1
> *have known what it is to covet if the law had not said, "You shall not covet."*
> Romans 7:7

The tenth and final commandment stands alone and governs *the whole law* as if in retrospect. It is, if you will, the rudder that directs the course of the entire ship of the law. That our Heidelberg Catechism also understands it in this way is apparent from the fact that it spends not a single word on the broader wording of this commandment but rather summarizes its sense and intention: *That not even the least inclination or thought against any commandment of God ever enter our heart, but that with our whole heart we continually hate all sin and take pleasure in all righteousness.*

...

It is much more important that one observe how the rule governing all the other commandments continues in this tenth commandment as well. The rule always seems to be that, out of a whole category of sins, only one is mentioned by name in the commandment of Sinai, not because it is only this sin that is forbidden but rather to condemn in this one sin *the whole category*. From such an entire group of sins *one* is mentioned individually (for example, adultery, stealing, murder, and so on) because it is the most conspicuous, but time and again the intent turns out to be that by mentioning this one sin *the whole group* to which it belongs is subject to God's condemnation. In the case of each commandment, in order to identify to which group, which encompassing category of sin, it represented, we went back to that root of that one sin. And everything that sprouted from that same root of iniquity, in addition to that one sin, proved to be related to that sin and to be judged along with it.

If we now apply the same approach here, then it follows, first, that what is forbidden here is not only coveting something that belongs to our neighbor, but that the prohibition against coveting what is your neighbor's is merely one sin out of an entire class. Second, in order to identify this class, we must ask ourselves, from what root does the urge to covet our neighbor's things arise? And third, since this root lies within the sinful inclination of our inner being, all unholy and sinful inclinations of our hidden self lie condemned along with this one sin. It is not enough, then, to say that all *desiring*, in the bad sense of the term, is forbidden here. This desiring, in turn, also has a root that lies in the inner dynamic of our depraved heart. And so this commandment actually serves to condemn at one stroke all sins, as a group, as a category, as a class, insofar as they arise in our heart from the sinful impulse of our nature. The catechism therefore states correctly that not only all *lust* or *desire*, but also every *thought* against any commandment of God already makes us guilty in our heart. Add to this the second rule, that each commandment of Sinai *commands* as well as *prohibits*, then it follows that this tenth commandment prescribes the positive demand that the inner movements of our heart must always and invariably be movements of righteousness. Or as the catechism expresses it, "that with our whole heart we continually hate all sin and take pleasure in all righteousness."

The tenth commandment undoubtedly sounds somewhat strange if we consider that this commandment, even as the other nine, was a law in Israel that had to be enforced by the government. Yet a governmental requirement can only concern an *external* act, simply because the government cannot judge what takes place in the heart. Sometimes the government can also punish the intent, what it then refers to as "premeditation," but only when this intent has become apparent from writings or words or actions. It will never occur to an earthly judge to sentence someone to prison or death merely because he says that he was intent on stealing without either giving in to that thought or beginning to carry it out. In all of the other nine commandments we can imagine how the magistrate in Israel upheld them, but in the case of this tenth commandment it is utterly inconceivable (at least as long as we stay with the *earthly* magistrate). Even the early church, which took discipline very seriously, never dared to punish any sin against this commandment except where the sin came to expression in word or deed. The same rule was also followed even in the strictest periods of the Reformation. And still today no consistory will consider barring someone from the Lord's Supper because of a sin against this commandment, for the simple reason that it is unable, and it is beyond its authority, to prove this sin.

The fact that this tenth commandment was nevertheless incorporated in the laws of Israel can be explained only from the fact that there existed in Israel, and in Israel alone, a *theocracy*. This does not merely mean that the government in Israel ruled by the grace of God, for this is true in every country. There is not a single government anywhere on earth that can govern otherwise than by the grace of God; this remains true whether the government is that of a king, a federal council, or a president. The holy apostle says that "there is no authority except from God" [Rom 13:1]. Thus, the essence of theocracy does not consist in this at all, and it is utterly absurd if our opponents call the doctrine of *government by the grace of God* a theocratic notion. That doctrine has nothing to do with theocracy and, when properly considered, does not include but excludes theocracy. In fact, every government by the grace of God presupposes that God does *not* rule a nation directly but through a government.

Conversely, theocracy consisted precisely in the fact that the Lord our God governed Israel *personally and directly*, *without* the mediation of others. Thus, God could say to Samuel, "They have not rejected you, but they have rejected me from being king over them" [1 Sam 8:7]. The tenth commandment was related to this theocracy. Only because a theocracy existed in Israel could such a commandment be made part of the laws of Israel. What would have been inconceivable in other nations was natural in Israel, which was governed theocratically by God himself. A commandment that focused exclusively on the hidden realm of the heart could be given to Israel only because God himself was king in Israel, and Israel's King thus was also *the One who knows the heart*. For as soon as desires, evil lusts, or unholy thoughts find outward expression, they fall under commandments one through nine, but no longer under commandment ten. They fall under the tenth commandment only as long as such desire remains privately within us and we alone know that they rose in us and was more or less fostered by us. The tenth commandment is therefore the spiritual key to all the commandments. It punishes our sins, not viewed from the outside but from the inside—not as they become manifest in human sight but as they surge in our heart in the sight of the holy God. Hence the holy apostle exclaimed that he would not have known what it is to covet, had the law not said, "You shall not covet."

This commandment therefore is most closely linked to our *conscience*. It is not as if our conscience were an absolute judge between good and evil. Paul's example already proves otherwise. He himself testified that it was not his conscience but the law that had revealed to him the sinful character of coveting. At times we see that the conscience can stray very far indeed, and therefore it can never be our conscience as such but only God's Word that is the guide for our conduct and our behavior. Our conscience, however, does provide this certainty, in that it tests our existence, our inner intentions, and every expression of our life against that which we at any given moment view as God's requirement. If we err in this latter respect, then of course our conscience also errs, but to the degree that our insight into God's will is pure, then the conscience within us also makes good and sound judgments. But even apart from this, the conscience in us is always making judgements about whether or not we have come into conflict with what we know to be good, not just externally but most certainly also internally.

Thus, the conscience judges rather thoroughly, and even primarily, our *inner* deliberations, and for that reason it is directly related to this tenth commandment. Do not think, therefore, that your conscience is something separate in you, a kind of lawgiver within you, an additional guide who stays with you for a time. A judge does not make the law but applies it, and your conscience within you is and always remains a *judge*. God gave you a consciousness. In this consciousness two things are reflected. First, *God's will*, and second, the image of *your own person*. The conscience then is nothing other than the verdict of your self-awareness as to whether these two are in conflict. Your conscience is therefore a necessary expression of your consciousness in which you as judge render a decision about whether you go free or are struck down by the law. Thus you might indeed call this your internal monitor, because God in fact *compels* you to render this judgment of your conscience. You are not free in this matter. You *must* pass this judgment. And, however much you may mislead others and yourself in daily life, when it comes to your conscience, all self-deception ceases. You see then: this is how it is. To be sure, your knowledge of the law may indeed fail you, and you may have little self-knowledge, and your moral awareness may weaken, which is why the apostle points out that "God is greater than our heart," and that we do not go free even if our conscience does not condemn us [1 John 3:20–22]. But nevertheless, this always remains the case, and in this is the function of your conscience: insofar as you know the will of God, and you know yourself, you must test yourself against that will of God and accordingly either acquit or condemn yourself.

It also follows from this that your consciousness carries out this acquitting or condemning act only to the extent that a certain awareness of the conflict between God's will and your personal existence has penetrated your consciousness. In the kingdom of glory, in which any notion of conflict with the will of God will spontaneously disappear, there will no longer be any conscious expression of your conscience. In a land where there *could* be no sin against justice, no judges would ever be appointed. It also follows that, for Adam in paradise before his fall into sin, there could not be a single act of conscience in his consciousness. Regarding the case of our Savior, it also follows that any act of conscience would be absurd. For how could he, who was himself God, ever personally come into conflict with God? In the case of the Savior, one could speak of a conscience with regard to sin only insofar as he, being our Mediator, bore our sin. This is why he said at his baptism, "Thus it is fitting for us to fulfill all righteousness" [Matt 3:15], and that is why he was in great agony as our Mediator in the garden of Gethsemane. All this certainly sounds strange as long one holds to the un-Reformed position that the conscience is a kind of separate capacity, a notion which our forefathers (with the exception of Perkins)[1] have always opposed. But it appears entirely natural as soon as you confess with our forefathers that the conscience is an *act* of the moral self-consciousness,

---

1. English clergyman William Perkins (1558–1602) was critical of ritualism and sympathetic to Puritanism. While famous for his defense of the doctrine of double predestination, he wrote several significant books on casuistry and the nature of the human conscience as well as the primacy of the human will.

for which the capacity and necessity are given in our consciousness, but a capacity that can only express itself, and a necessity which is only born, when the will of God and our person are no longer one but come to stand over against one another as two. This first came about through sin and can continue only as long as sin is in us. And therefore we say that there was no conscience as such in Adam before the fall, nor was there one in Jesus in his personal existence, nor will it exist among the blessed in the state of glory. But it will exist forever in the place of destruction, where "their worm does not die" [Mark 9:44 NKJV].

...

§2

For from within, out of the heart of man, come evil thoughts,
sexual immorality, theft, murder, adultery, coveting, wickedness,
deceit, sensuality, envy, slander, pride, foolishness.
Mark 7:21-22

Is desiring or coveting in itself something evil? Certainly not. Rather, the person is intended to be empty in oneself and to be filled with what comes to one from the outside. When the psalmist sings, "One thing have I *asked* of the LORD, that will I seek after: that I may dwell in the house of the LORD all the days of my life, to gaze upon the beauty of the LORD and to inquire in his temple" (Ps 27:4),[2] then this holy desire is indeed praiseworthy. When in Psalm 20:5 it is said to the king, "May the LORD fulfill all your *petitions*!" it certainly does not refer to desires that would be sin for him. The exclamation in Psalm 38:9, "O LORD, all my *longing* is before you," or in Isaiah 26:8, "Your name and remembrance are the *desire* of our soul" then it is not an expression of evil lust but of a devout mind. Jesus declares blessed not those who are satisfied but rather those who "hunger and thirst," who thus desire food and drink. Even as the deer sets out with a desire for flowing streams, so David's soul thirsts for the living God [Psa 42:1]. The Lord himself awakens this desire and arouses it when the call goes out, "Come, everyone who thirsts, come to the waters; and he who has no money, come, buy and eat! Come, buy wine and milk without money and without price" [Isa 55:1].

A heart that does *not* desire is dead, dull, withered, without realizing the danger that lies in its stupor. A heart that does not desire does not *pray*.

---

2. We have italicized the words in the quotations that follow from the ESV which in the SV that Kuyper quotes are all rendered with the word *begeerte* (desire, covet).

All prayer is the desiring of something from God. "If any of you lacks wisdom, let him *ask* God, who gives generously to all without reproach" [Jas 1:5]. We should therefore "by prayer and supplication with thanksgiving" let our "*requests* be made known to God" [Phil 4:6]. Everything flows from him: "every good gift comes down from above, from the Father of lights" [see Jas 1:17], and they come to us from "the wells of salvation" [Isa 12:3]. This is why our God wants us to pray to him so that he may not only enrich us with his favor but also fulfill the *desires* which the Holy Spirit himself has cultivated in us. It is therefore far from true that all desires are sinful. Rather, deeply desiring, again and again, is the motivation for real prayer, and a heart without desire lies idle and dull before God. One should not even limit this conclusion to the desire "to behold God's face and be satisfied with his likeness" [see Psa 17:15]. There is also a desire for a measure of good things and happiness in life which is not excessive, a desire that is appropriate, awakened in us by God himself, and therefore quite legitimate. It never counted lawful, for as sinful desire to say, "Give me neither poverty nor riches; feed me with the food that is needful for me" [Prov 30:8]. Even though the Lord's Prayer is primarily spiritual, it nevertheless includes desire: "Give us today our daily bread." And not only does such desiring belong to our nature as human beings here on earth, but also in heaven things will go from glory to glory, and thus every satisfied desire will generate new desires. Without a prior desire there is no enjoyment. Where appetite is absent, bread is not enjoyed in its glory. And where thirst for God wears off, his majesty can no longer be enjoyed.

No one, then, should view desire as something that has been invented by sin or that first came into the world through sin. On the contrary, desire has been created in us. We have been built to desire. For it to be otherwise, we would have to be self-sufficient. But since God created us dependent, in need of all things—dependent on nature for our earthly existence and dependent on fellowship with God and our neighbor for our heart—therefore you cannot think of your nature as separable from needing, desiring, craving that which we do *not* have within ourselves but which must come to us *from outside*. A vacuum has been created in us that seeks to be filled with what belongs to us but which we do not have of ourselves. This is not only true in general but also something that occurs with respect to the individual commandments. For, to mention only the seventh commandment, God himself created Adam in such a way that he needed Eve as helper opposite him; his desire for Eve was therefore not a sinful contrivance of Adam but a trait God created in him.

Thus, what we consistently observed is also confirmed here, that sin has no essence of its own, does not create its own organ, does not generate any power of its own, but always distorts and turns into evil that which God created for good. A human being must desire. That is our nature and essence, and the more briskly the blood flows through our veins, the more forcefully will the desire in us awaken in all areas of life. The evil, then, is not found in this. Rather, the evil is threefold: (1) sin corrupts this desire, diverts it from what must be its focus, and lures it toward that which it may not desire; (2) this desire disrupts the harmony within you; and (3) sin causes you to seek the fulfillment of the desire in a self-willed manner instead of waiting for it from the Lord our God and by means of his ordinances. Thus, sin also consists in the *perversion* of that which is good in itself, turning against God what ought to be directed toward him and be bound to him. And when we consider it carefully, we find that every sinful desire comes from a natural trait which God created in us, but which we direct to another purpose. This disrupts harmony and in this way transgresses its boundaries. Or else it seeks its fulfillment in an illegitimate way that is not *ordained* but *condemned* by God.

This is why our catechism correctly handles the subject when it applies this tenth commandment to all the commandments. For if desire is the stirring of life in us, then a desire must form the basis for every life expression, and when one proceeds through the nine commandments in succession one finds that each of them enters into an area of human life that finds its stimulus in one desire or another: a desire for God, a desire to worship him, a desire for his name, a desire to live in fellowship with him. A desire for domestic order, a desire for a place among others. A desire for marital happiness, a desire for a measure of earthly goods, or a desire for a good reputation in society. A desire always lurks in the background, and every *sinful* desire proceeds from a desire that is fundamentally good, that is created in us and therefore legitimate. In fact, everything we listed does actually belong to our nature's normal life expressions. Adam in paradise was familiar with all these desires without sin being in him. And now, sinning arises in each of these trajectories only because we direct this desire, which is good in itself, toward a wrongly chosen purpose, or let it work in a one-sided and thus disruptive manner, or try to fulfill that desire in a way forbidden by God.

This threefold form of sinful desire requires only a brief word of explanation. There must be, for example, a desire for God within you. You were created for this. But if (1) your soul's desire, however, tuns away from God toward an idol, then the desire in you is corrupted, and sin is within you. Or, (2) this desire for God is created in you in connection with your calling in life, so that your desire for God may also provide you with the inspiration for your life's calling. However, if you disrupt this harmony and your desire for God becomes so one-sided and fanatical that you forsake your life's calling for the sake of your religion, then the harmony has been disrupted and your piety has become sinful. Or finally, (3) there is a desire for God in you, but you try to fulfill that desire not in the way he has ordained, but by self-determined means, then this otherwise holy desire is diverted from its proper course of life and bears a sinful character.

In this way you can personally trace these three forms in which sinful desire manifests itself in each of the other eight other commandments. To take one commandment from the second table, just think of the desire created in you for the love of someone who is not of the same sex. In and of itself, this desire too is holy. God created it within a person. But if this natural trait focuses on some other woman instead of on your own wife, then your desire is adulterated and corrupted. Or, second, if this trait in your nature is so predominantly focused on your own wife that you neglect your children, your occupation, or your earthly duties, then the harmony is broken, and your desire has turned sinful. Or, finally, if you try and satisfy that natural desire outside the marital state, or to force a marriage that is not in accord with God's ordinances, then there is sin in you. Thus, sin always involves a desire that is falsely directed, or a disharmony, or an unlawfulness of the satisfaction involved. These then are the three factors that can color the desire as sinful, give it a sinful stamp, and transform it into sin. But the desire as such always is and always remains a force that is not rooted in sin but in the structure of your nature.

Now then, when you track down the inklings of such a sinful desire in yourself, you cannot say that it begins to work only when you have consciously imagined it, when you have weighed and pondered the imagined fulfillment, and when you then exert your will to seek that fulfillment. On the contrary, sin has already reached the *second* stage by that point, and it acquires an entirely different character. Once the deliberation of the consciousness has come to an end, we have reached a conclusion for ourselves, and the forces of our will have been hitched up to that conclusion, then we have, in fact, already decided to commit adultery, theft, murder, and so forth in our heart, and for the imputation of guilt it matters not whether circumstances outside our will prevent the execution of our will. But then the sin falls under the sixth, seventh, or eighth commandment and not so much under the tenth. The tenth commandment thus only deals with what lies behind an action and, as Jesus says, what comes from the heart, from which flow the springs of life, and also the springs of our sins. You live, but that stream of life within you has a center, a deep-seated source from which it springs. That deep-seated source cannot be precisely identified. God's Word only tells us that it lies *behind the heart*, and, to indicate something that lies even deeper in our being than our heart, it speaks of our *kidneys*.

Yet it is a matter of course that the initial rustling of life in us lies neither in our *heart* nor in our *kidneys* but is found in our soul. It goes out from the soul, and after having received its impulse in the soul, it chooses nerves and blood as its vehicle, creeps into the kidneys, penetrates the heart, goes through the touchstone of our consciousness, and asks for the operative power of our will. Even though we cannot clearly visualize these spiritual things because they have no visible form, nevertheless, there is a positive side: it enables one to distinguish the various stages by establishing certain guideposts. You then will have a line that is drawn from the center of your soul to the circumference of your life. The first stage on that line is the progression of your life from the center of your soul to your kidneys; the second, from your kidneys to your heart; the third, from your heart to your consciousness; the fourth, from your consciousness to your will; and the fifth, from your will to your word or action.

The catechism has taught us that everything that has already become a conscious and fostered *thought*, or is already an *expression of the will*, or has already formed *words* or *deed*, belongs to the other nine commandments. Indeed, the particular driving force that causes the desires that arise in us to penetrate our consciousness already belongs to the rest of the nine commandments. But what lies behind it, in our heart, in our kidneys, and in the center of our soul as impulse, as inclination, as stimulus to falsify its objective, or its proportion, or its choice of means—that is the specific realm of your innermost life over which the tenth commandment reigns supreme. It therefore tells you *not* that you should destroy the longing, the delight, the love, the nostalgia, in short the desire within you, but on the contrary, that you should let this desire work strongly in you, but in this sense: that it would become in you taking "pleasure in all righteousness" (Q. 113), a longing for what God has ordained for you: namely, a love for God's commandments and a desire for the living God. What must not happen is that you spoil, falsify, and abuse this desire, which God created in you as an indispensable element for your ensouled life. That is your sin. And it is not enough to separate this desire from its sinful contaminations; rather, the requirement is that you do *not* leave your desires unused but focus them on "whatever is lovely, whatever is commendable" [Phil 4:8].

...

The saying of Jesus, "everyone who looks at a woman with lustful intent has already committed adultery with her in his heart" [Matt 5:28], should not lead us astray. This word should not be understood to mean that the lustful intent here refers to the first rustlings of the desire in our soul, in our kidneys, or in our heart. On the contrary, the desire that Jesus means is desire at a later stage. The person to whom Jesus refers has already allowed the desire to pass through to his consciousness. He already looks at that specific woman. He has already devoured her with his eyes. An action, a deed, has already taken place in his heart. That is why Jesus says that in his heart he has already committed adultery, even though the terrible completion of the act through secondary causes has not occurred. Jesus therefore pronounces him guilty of breaking the *seventh* commandment.

But no one may claim on this account that the less determinate and less conscious coveting, a desire, which does not yet have this carnal intention, so that you do not yet look at her, would *not* be sin. On the contrary, the unholy desire that lies behind the consciousness and the choice of the will is just as sinful; but it makes one guilty of violating the *tenth* commandment. Every desire, every craving, every longing that arises in us and from us and that is not in conformity with the righteousness and the commandments of God, is and remains unholy, is always unclean, and serves to indicate that it welled up from impure and tainted springs present in the source.

...

Even God's best children notice that sin no longer reigns in them, that another life has awakened in them, that their love and sympathy have shifted, and that holier desires have come to life in them. And yet, no, even they do not experience this in themselves. As the catechism attests, "even the holiest men, while in this life, have only a small beginning of such obedience" (Q. 114).

But it is precisely for this reason that the tenth commandment is so necessary. Many calm souls who live quiet lives know almost no feelings of guilt because they almost never commit any flagrant transgressions of the first nine commandments. But now comes the *tenth* commandment, and yes, here they suddenly must yield and they learn through this tenth commandment to acknowledge that they are guilty of breaking *all* God's commandments. They are powerlessly guilty, because no matter how much they can change, they cannot effect a complete mortification of sin. That will only happen *in death*. Thus, it is precisely though this commandment that their dormant sense of guilt is awakened in them, powerfully so. Once again they feel as if they are facing a "consuming fire." And then the impulse of faith comes again to take refuge in the offer of reconciliation and to flee to him who has said: "Blessed are the pure in heart, for they shall see God" [Matt 5:8].

And when they themselves then feel and acknowledge that "this sinful drive does not come from my will, not from my consciousness, not from my past, but is rooted in my nature, in my selfhood, in the very center of my being," then this sense of guilt descends down into the guilt of our entire race, and the awareness breaks through that the wrath of God already rested on us because we are children of Adam and partakers of his depraved nature, and therefore we belong to the guilty human race.

Nothing but grace can then bring deliverance, and the Holy Spirit alone can comfort us. It is the Holy Spirit who helps us to diminish the upsurge from that evil fountain and to strengthen in us the upwelling from the fountain of salvation. And if the struggle continues until the end, then that very struggle increasingly bears fruit, so that it will be for us as it was for the apostle: "Wretched man that I am! Who will deliver me from this body of death? My desire is to depart and be with Christ" [Rom 7:24; Phil 1:23]. With him, free from sin!

§3   *For all that is in the world—the desires of the flesh and the desires of the eyes and pride in possessions—is not from the Father but is from the world.*
1 John 2:16

It now remains to explain the sin of *coveting in the narrow sense*, which is *specifically* forbidden in the tenth commandment.

This sin is not the general upsurge of an unholy desire or an illicit thought, but specifically the reaching out of our heart, sick with desire, for that which belongs to our neighbor, be it his wife, his house or field, his draught or pack animals, or whatever belongs to your neighbor or is at his disposal and therefore cannot be ours.

This sin touches on the question of equality.

Speaking in the abstract, we might imagine that all people on earth resembled one another exactly, like the tin soldiers in a toy chest. It would also be conceivable that every human being, or every family, had an identical house, an identical piece of land, an exactly equal amount of perfectly identical household goods—a bit like life in a military barracks, but even more monotonous and uniform.

But the fact is that this is *not* the case. Even as no two leaves on a tree are identical, it is equally impossible to find two persons who are exactly alike. All things diverge. There is a wealth of diversity and variation among all things. It is not a poor but a rich God who has called this world into being, and from his overflowing riches he has given everything its *own* form, in endless variety, so that you will not be tired or worn out by the monotony, but so that everyone would seek the highest harmony amid the richest hues of color.

Also related to this is the fact that God's providential administration has not dispensed the lot and happiness *of human beings* according to a specific ration, each in the same measure and in the same way, but that here everything also varies, diverges, and is differentiated. Here we cannot discuss in depth the doctrine about *why* God the Lord ordained it so. Suffice to say, then, that to the extent that people have occasionally been attempted to ensure an equable distribution of fortune and happiness for all within a given circle for a period of time, it always seemed that untenable situations arose, and that these attempts hindered the development of our human nature. It almost seems as if the interminable friction, agitation, and social turbulence which are the natural consequences of the existing inequality are indispensable for a healthy development of our human nature and the life of humanity.

Nevertheless, the fact itself simply cannot be changed. There exist men but also women; adults but also children; strong young people but also weak old men; healthy but also sick people; strong but also weak people; swift but also slow persons; sharp thinkers but also slow-witted people and dreamers; persons with talent but also those without; persons who burn with will-power, but also others who have no willpower whatsoever. There are those for whom everything goes smoothly and those for whom everything goes wrong; people who grow old but also those who die young. There are those who are happily married and those who are unhappily married, as well as those who do not marry at all. Some die childless, others have scarcely enough room at their table for all their offspring. The one lives in a fertile land, the other on a barren heath. In one place the cold nips like in Iceland, in another the sweltering heat is as oppressive as in the tropics. You are a Netherlander, another is born a Turk. In the Netherlands, the one is from Zealand, the other from Frisia. In short, all of life varies and is unequal. There are simply no perfectly identical circumstances. And all these factors together bring about that the share of happiness in life is so much smaller or larger for the one than for the other.

Happiness in life is always relative. Imagine for a moment that no one had ever known happiness greater than what the Eskimos now enjoy: everyone would be content in that condition and they would not be oppressed by any sense of unhappiness, simply because people would not know any better or know anything different, or only that so-and-so had heard something different. That's just how things are, period. But no sooner does another standard of living appear, one somewhat richer and just a bit happier, than it threatens to rob you of your satisfaction and even to take away the share of happiness that you have. It is *the comparison* that gives rise to the evil. Why does he have a greater share and I a lesser one? Am I not just as good as he? Can I not be in his place and he in mine? Why should I settle for my more modest state? Such are the thoughts that arise in your heart. Covetousness begins to do its work. Seeing what our neighbor has, we conceive the idea of an even *higher* state of happiness than we ourselves have, and then one starts to think: if only I had a wife like that, such a house and field, such cattle, and so forth. But when it becomes clear that this cannot and will not happen, the sinful craving intensifies again before long we think: if I only had not a wife like that, but *his* wife, *his* house, *his* field, and all *his* possessions.

And now with such sinful desire you feel how a flood of unrighteousness suddenly inundates your heart. Your contentment with your situation is gone, and the share of happiness that you once had from that moment on loses all flavor and aroma. What you have no longer appeals to you. You would rather be rid of it. And your heart reaches for what you *do not* have, what you *cannot* have and *may* not have. Bitterness begins to fill your heart, resulting in one continual grumbling and complaining. Resentment becomes your dominant mood. And so you always look. You keep looking *at your neighbor*, at the one who received the *greater* share. And you envy him because of that. He is therefore a thorn in your flesh. He irks you because with his greater happiness he casts a shadow on your more meager existence. What he has could just as well become *yours*. And then begins the plotting and brooding and pondering all kinds of stealthy ways and means and secret passages through which we can get hold of what belongs to our neighbor.

This can take on a very specific form. Take, for example, two persons in the country whose farms are adjacent to one another but are unequal in size, unequal in fertility, and unequal in location. And now the less prosperous farmer gazes and stares every morning and every evening at his neighbor, who has better cattle, whose horses look better, whose hayfields are fuller and stand higher, whose wheat has heavier ears. And so envy and resentment go to work and enmities develop that poison life in so many a village.

But the same desire of the senses can also take on a *more general* form. Envy and resentment of many unite, and systematically set a whole class of less fortunate people against a class of more fortunate people. Or in the end it can become a sin that infests *all of society* and gradually divides our generation into two camps: on the one hand those who stand *below* the mean, on the other those who stand *above* it. Thus it is a situation toward which we are moving at present, now that the so-called haves has become a thorn in the side of the have-nots, and the latter ponder and brood on means to remove this annoyance by equalizing the lot of all. This is squarely against God's ordinance and in itself an absolute impossibility! For everyone senses that no matter how much may be understandable in the present socialist agitations, this agitation has in any case become profoundly sinful in its expression, running directly counter to the tenth commandment.

Nevertheless, beware! We must not suggest that this dissatisfaction exists only among the lower classes. The sinful desire, being dissatisfied with one's own state and position and grasping for what was allotted to others, is rather *the* sin of our whole society, a sin which is systematically nurtured. Surely, what else is the system of competition, in which people increasingly seek the pivot that moves the whole of our society, than a constant comparison of what another is or has, with what you are or have, in order to stimulate the desire that you may become what the other is. And when you then have come neck and neck with B, and have overtaken B and left him behind you discover that behind B there is C, and in turn behind C is there is D, and so forth, interminably, until your death—there is always a competitor who surpassed you and whom in turn you want to surpass. The rule you always apply is that to desire what belongs to your neighbor is not a sin but rather the healthy driving force of human life.

The men of science have even gone so far as to view our entire life from the perspective of a battle between the stronger and the weaker, a "struggle for life,"[3] which ends inexorably in the weak succumbing and the strong triumphing. Always wanting to climb higher up. Never being able to rest. Not a moral "ever upward," but an unhealthy desire for a larger share. And then, once you have climbed one rung higher, you take pleasure in the one who stands lower, because the comparison with the one standing lower serves as your yardstick for happiness. Whoever is *above* you weighs you down and makes you unhappy, but whoever is *below* you accentuates your happiness. And thus it agitates endlessly, and gone is the calm and pure happiness that made you content and quieted your heart.

If you ask what sin is primarily at work here, what stands out is that whoever allows this to happen finds fault with God, who, after all, has determined everyone's lot in life. We are *creatures*; we did not make ourselves, and thus the right of that God, who created us, to do with us what he wills and to deal with us according to his good pleasure, must remain unimpeded. He is the one who made people's lot in life not equal but *unequal*.

And now it rests in the nature of things, and it cannot be otherwise, than that where there is inequality of happiness, the one must have a lesser and the other a greater share, the one must stand on a higher and the other a lower rung of life's ladder. Who would stand higher, and who lower, again rested with the Lord, and was his alone to determine. To be sure, a person, through industry or indolence, tidiness or sloppiness, can also increase or diminish one's happiness, but one's position in life is by and large already determined by one's birth, and even the best person can only effect small changes. The one is laid in a royal cradle as a prince, while the other sees the light of day in a slum, wrapped in rags and noticed by no one. And since your birth in one position, and that of another in a higher or lower position, is entirely independent of your will or agency, it can only be traced back to God, and the matter was his and his alone to determine.

---

3. This is an allusion to Charles Darwin, *On the Origin of Species by means of Natural Selection, or The Preservation of Favoured Races in the Struggle for Life* (London: John Murray, 1859), 62.

In fact, therefore, all this discontent with one's state amounts to challenging God's right as your creator to determine your lot. It is an attempt to set God aside and to take the sovereignty that belongs to him alone into your own hands. And in doing so you despotically replace his providence with your will and wish. You do to this unavoidably if you simply omit nine-tenths of your existence. God's providential order extends over our *whole* existence and is designed for that. He governs you not only with regard to the short years of your existence that you spend here, but also with regard to the ages and many more ages that are to come. Connected with this is the fact that many are sometimes hard-pressed in this brief training school, precisely with a view toward a richer existence that will be their portion in the future. But if we omit those ages, and limit our entire existence to those few years we spend here, then of course it is strange and inexplicable, and we cannot accept that we must go through such a difficult training school. It is the attitude of the boy who views school as his entire world and finds it hard and unbearable that he has to sit at a desk for all those hours awhile his older brother and sister can go free.

Both things, then, are connected. Death has come to be seen as the horizon of life, and with it we have severed our actual, our essential existence of ages upon ages. And so we lack any rationale to explain our lot on earth. And because people did not have peace with that inexplicable lot, they pushed aside God's providence and ended up with the language of pride, namely, that we hold our life in our own hands. At best, the, notions of fortune and fate were added to one's lot. But wherever one invoked the help of Lady Luck, the God of one's life was banished. That is why all social agitations, like the current socialist one, *must* always be accompanied by the denial of God. Current socialism is not indifferent to religion; it is decisively hostile to it. It wants to replace God's rule *over* people with another rule, a rule *by* people.

Two things have so far been completely passed by: (1) that all happiness depends on the degree of need, and (2) that even the smallest share of happiness makes you rich, provided you devote yourself to it.

The first point does not require a lengthy discussion. The man who has accustomed himself to the use of strong drink feels unhappy when he cannot get any stimulating liquor, while conversely an as-yet-unspoiled child would be nauseated if you wanted to force strong drink on him. Need is a very elastic thing in a person. There are circles where people sit at the table with happy faces when some potatoes, vegetables, and a piece of bacon come out of the pot. But there are also circles where people would pass on such a meal and would feel unhappy if they had to eat it. On Java the population sleeps on mats on the ground, but for us a bed is indispensable. A black African wears almost no clothes, but a white European living in the same climate would not be able to go outdoors without clothes. In short, needs literally differ from one person to another. Need can be stimulated, overstimulated, and gradually be stretched to the point of becoming insane; but need can also remain proportional to what one has.

If our feeling of happiness stems from satisfying our wishes, then it goes without saying that two people, one of whom has twenty needs and the other only five needs, are both perfectly happy, even though the one enjoys four times as much as the other. The fisherman who has four or five men on his boat is just as happy as the captain who has signed on thirty crewmembers, as long as each has the number of men he needs. The bird that eats only worms is as rich with his worms as the hunting dog with his piece of meat. The horse asks for oats, but the cow is satisfied with her hay. Thus, all need is an elastic concept, and yet your happiness in life depends on the measure of that need. If you have many needs that remain unfulfilled, you feel unhappy. But if your needs are few, yet they are all met, you are rich.

Now, this stimulation of our needs is something partly good, and partly evil. It is most certainly God's will that our sense of need will gradually expand, in order to stimulate us to make an effort and show initiative. In that sense, the increase in our needs is actually a necessity required for all human progress. Without ambition you remain what you are. This is not harmful so long as the expansion of your needs does not go beyond a certain limit and always remains confined to such an extent that it is possible to satisfy these needs after a few years of effort. But if, on the other hand, you stimulate someone's needs so disproportionally that these needs rise far above their status and position, and he *cannot* possibly satisfy them no matter how hard he may struggle, then you have made him *unhappy*, robbed him of his peace, and put him in a position of dependence. There is no need to point out that he who has fewer needs moves much more freely, whereas the man with a thousand needs faces difficulties at every moment and is dependent on the help of others at every point. The infant is in need of everything, and is therefore absolutely dependent, and those who instill many needs into an adult that he cannot satisfy have made that man a child again.

This is precisely where the greatest error lies in contemporary development efforts, namely that we have tried foreign aid. We try to make people advance *too quickly*, thereby expanding their needs out of all proportion. The systems that are currently in vogue are literally designed to increasingly stimulate needs, even the needs of youngsters. And cruelly, without mercy, people do not hesitate to awaken all such needs in poor communities, in which those needs can never be satisfied. For even if one wanted equalize everyone's lot, it would still be completely impossible to satisfy such inflated needs even halfway. Human life is too poor for this. The world *cannot* give us this. On this score, even respect for privacy has suffered. In our Calvinistic era it was the custom in our country for a person who had received a larger share of happiness to enjoy this *in the privacy of his home*, but now everything is on display. The showcases in our shops and stores are arranged in such a way as to stimulate every desire. The public cafés, hotels, and beer halls are a taunt to the one who eats his bread by the sweat of his brow. It all has become a flaunting and showing off—at the expense, of course, of those who are less fortunate. And thus the cement of *contentment* has disappeared from the whole of our social life. Passions are incited, and the result will be, if God does not prevent it, that the flames shoot out into a conflagration, simply because people have so foolishly opposed God's commandment.

That is why we suggested that people in former days were wise when they accepted what they had instead of always hankering after what they lacked. Granted, this is a mystery, but a mystery whose truth is so convincingly demonstrated. Immerse yourself in your domestic life, devote yourself to it, do not run away from it at every turn, and, before you know it as a woman or a girl, you will realize that there are unnoticed treasures of happiness in that quiet domestic life that you had not suspected from a distance. But now if you follow the opposite method, so that you consider the household a secondary matter and always yearn for what is outside, then that household becomes a burden to you, it does not unlock its treasures for you, and the joy in life is gone.

It is the same with your work and your life's occupation. Live in it and for it, devote yourself to it, and that work, that occupation, will blossom because you put your heart into it. It will bear rich fruit and make you happy. A blacksmith who lives to shoe a horse well enjoys it every time a horse enters his shoeing shed, and each horse that leaves well shod gives him a sense of satisfaction. Conversely, if you view your work merely as a means to earn money, so you can later go looking for pleasure with that money, then of course the work has become a burden to you. Then you wonder if you might do *without* that burden and appropriate someone else's money. The only thing that matters to you is that money. Thus, it is precisely the perspective that one does *not* work for money that Jesus provides for God's children. He points us to the birds of the sky that do what their instincts prescribe for them to do and that are nevertheless fed by God. And so it is also his will that God's child should live like a little child in his father's house, doing what father tells him to do, and knowing that father will take care to feed him. This is how our devout people lived at one time. They worked in their divine vocation. They devoted themselves to it with heart and soul. This made them skilled and experienced. And God blessed them. And then they received their bread every morning and every evening *from the hand of God.*

To be content is itself happiness in life. Limitless desire makes you poor and miserable. Even more so, contentment can accept that your neighbor has a greater share, but your covetousness provokes you against your neighbor to whom God gave more. Contentment is thus a support for your moral life, whereas your limitless desiring is a root from which all kinds of immoral and unlawful weeds can sprout. Greed, the apostle says, is the root of all evil, and "greed," as you know, does not mean "miserliness" here, but its original sense of lusting, wanting, desiring.

It is as if the apostle were wants to say: the transgression of the tenth commandment contains the root from which springs the sins against all the other nine commandments.

OUR RELATIONSHIP TO THE LAW

TEXT INTRODUCTION

The Heidelberg Catechism is a manual for basic instruction in Christian doctrine. Published in 1563, the catechism consists of 129 questions and answers and quickly proved useful for faith formation of children and adults alike. As it is divided into fifty-two parts, each "Lord's Day" enables the entirety of the teachings of the catechism to be covered in weekly sermons throughout the year.

At the Synod of Dort, in its 146th session of April 30, 1619, delegates of the participating churches from abroad exhorted the Dutch church "to persevere in the Reformed faith, to pass it on to posterity, and to preserve it until the return of Christ." In reply, the delegates from the Dutch church made a solemn vow, pledging to preach and preserve the Reformed faith, pure and undiluted.

When Kuyper started his commentary on the Heidelberg Catechism in the fall of 1886 in the Sunday paper *De Heraut*, he recalled this vow and subsequently titled his series *E voto Dordraceno*: "from the vow made at Dordt." The title is usually shortened, at Kuyper's own directive—"for ease of citing," he said—to *E Voto*.

The treatment of the Ten Commandments in the Heidelberg Catechism typically follows the pattern of expositing both those things that are forbidden by each commandment and those things that are required. The tenth commandment, "You shall not covet," similarly has both positive duties and negative prohibitions. Lord's Day 44 covers this petition in questions and answers 113 through 115, and Kuyper's exposition of this commandment is broken up into two parts, wherein he treats Q&A 113 first and then concludes with Q&A 114 and 115. Abridgments in these chapters have been identified with ellipses. The chapters on Lord's Day 44b first appeared as five installments in *De Heraut* of June 4, 11, 18, 25, and July 2, 1893.

SOURCE: Abraham Kuyper, *E voto Dordraceno*, 4 vols. (Amsterdam: Wormser, 1892–5), 4:280–88, 297–320. Translated by Ed M. van der Maas. Edited and annotated by Randy Blacketer and Harry Van Dyke.

OUR RELATIONSHIP TO THE LAW

Question 114. *Can those who are converted to God keep these Commandments perfectly?*
Answer: *No, but even the holiest men, while in this life, have only a small beginning of such obedience, yet so that with earnest purpose they begin to live not only according to some, but according to all the Commandments of God.*

Question 115. *Why then does God so strictly enjoin the Ten Commandments upon us, since in this life no one can keep them?*
Answer: *First, that as long as we live we may learn more and more to know our sinful nature, and so the more earnestly seek forgiveness of sins and righteousness in Christ; second, that without ceasing we diligently ask God for the grace of the Holy Spirit, that we be renewed more and more after the image of God, until we attain the goal of perfection after this life.*

> *If we say we have no sin, we deceive ourselves, and the truth is not in us.* §1
> 1 John 1:8

We now come to the issue of *perfectionism*, which our catechism places immediately after the tenth commandment. It is very practical to make such a connection. For it is precisely the tenth commandment that relentlessly strikes at the heart of all perfectionist fanaticism. But because the catechism links a second question to this one about the *use of the law*, we have no choice but to follow this path. For this reason, we are combining question 114, about perfectionism, and question 115, about the use of the law, under the single heading of our *relationship* to the law.

First, then, is *perfectionism*.

Our forefathers in the sixteenth century had to struggle hard against this heresy in Anabaptist regions, because they were primarily the ones who strongly pushed this "system of perfect holiness." Since that time, this overwrought fanaticism has been dormant. For although the Labadists[1] came close to the boundary, and although it cannot be denied that people have dreamed this dream of "perfect holiness already here on earth" for centuries, this heresy did not resurface, at least not in a fixed form, prior to our century. This most recent movement found momentary momentum in this country among a small circle, but it left the scene just as quickly, and this nineteenth-century perfectionism found its true home among the Quakers, the Plymouth Brethren,[2] and the Baptists in England, America, and on the Cape of Good Hope. Since these groups are spiritually related to the Anabaptist movement of the sixteenth century, it is sufficiently apparent that the root of this error lies precisely in the fundamental error of Anabaptism.

Of course, this is not meant to say that the small group that immersed itself in this dream in response to Murray's[3] call even in this country for a short time—and once made a minister exclaim from the pulpit, "I have not sinned for a full year!"—would thus be fundamentally Anabaptist. On the contrary, the movement was, at least in our region, purely Labadist, and it was born from a thirst for a holier standard of behavior. That is why,

---

1. Jean de Labadie (1610-74) was successively a Jesuit, a Reformed clergyman and professor, and, finally, the founder of his own sect of spiritualist pietism.
2. The Plymouth Brethren were a pietist, prophecy-focused sect associated with the dispensational teachings of John Nelson Darby (1800-82).
3. Andrew Murray (1828-1917) was a popular South African pastor and writer who advocated a view of sanctification identified with the "Higher Life" or Keswick movement. See R. A. Lapsley, "The Doctrinal Issues Presented by the Case of Dr. M. H. Houston," *The Presbyterian Quarterly* 48 (April 1899): 253-67.

when painful disappointment soon disillusioned people and the danger of spiritual pride made itself felt, the movement disappeared just as quickly. Even with Pearsall Smith,[4] and at his sanctification meetings, which were attended in large number especially by Baptists and Quakers, the activity still did not at all exhibit perfectionism as a primary characteristic. The author has personally put Question 114 of our catechism before Pearsall Smith, and after having read it he declared that he was prepared to subscribe to its answer.

The driving force of this movement, then, consisted more in the conviction that people could very well live on a higher spiritual plane than most Christians currently do; that most Christians had in fact stood on such a higher plane; and that there had been at least some circles in which this higher spiritual ideal had been realized. This led people to reach for writings that came from such circles. Specifically, many of the writings of Madame de la Motte Guyon[5] found a reception. In this way, people imperceptibly came to use expressions and manners of speaking that were reminiscent of a particular system, but most people used these without perceiving their meaning and import. The main thought and guiding motif was and remained the attempt to raise the standard of the Christian life, and the only theory that was pursued in this context was the notion that the first conversion brought an individual only to the lower plane and that, therefore, after the first conversion a second something had to follow, which was called the sealing or deliverance. This then was seen as a second action of the Holy Spirit that raised one from this lower level to that higher level at which a more sinless life became possible.

This alone shows how strongly this new movement differed from the original Anabaptist movement. For this first period spent on the lower level is, from the Anabaptist perspective, inconceivable once rebirth has taken place. But it was precisely because this sanctification movement was so lacking in fundamental principles that it very quickly lost its strength!

---

4. Robert Pearsall Smith (1827–98) was a lay promoter of the Holiness and Higher Life movements, which included the teachings of a second level of sanctification and perfectionism, despite what Kuyper claims here. In the summer of 1875, Kuyper himself fell under the spell of Pearsall Smith and this movement after attending Pearsall Smith's conference in Brighton, only to be disillusioned at the end of the year when Pearsall Smith was found to be sexually abusing women.

5. Jeanne-Marie Bouvier de la Motte-Guyon (1648–1717) was a Catholic mystic whose teachings were condemned as a form of quietism.

It sought to renew conditions like those that had existed here and there in the first and the sixteenth centuries amid the heroism of persecution. But they wanted to do this in times and circles where any stimulus for such holy heroism was lacking. In the absence of *heroism*, people had to resort to *quietism*, which, far from steeling the moral strength of will, rather weakens and breaks it. And thus it was inevitable that the anxious disappointment that followed and the spiritual pride that peered through the cracks would soon tear down what had been built so artificially, without leaving behind anything other than the ever-praiseworthy phenomenon that Christian brethren now and then gather together to sharpen one another's love and to sanctify their tenor of life once again through exhortation and quiet self-criticism.

But with this the movement lost its distinctive character. It began to be tantamount to what had set the tone of life in the cloister: the longing, the thirst, the attempt to make the reality of Christian existence stand out more strongly than is usually the case in the common life of Christians. Thus, we have seen something similar to the *collegia pietatis* of the Pietists in Germany and to the conventicles and societies in this country, a somewhat closer bond of a few pious brothers and sisters to help one another to progress in the knowledge of God's ways and to exhort them to a holier life, with a stricter conscience in the sight of God.

But if we now look at the question of perfectionism from the perspective of its principles, then it appears to be very different from the original Anabaptist essence. The Anabaptist mindset, as you will recall from what we have said about the incarnation of the Word, rebirth, and shunning, was absolutely dualistic, that is, it set a person's earthly life in direct opposition to one's life of grace.[6] The life of grace is for the true Anabaptist not a *re-creation* but rather an entirely new creation. And there is no connection between the life of grace and the natural life. They are two circles that overlap one another but otherwise have nothing in common. The sphere of the one life is hermetically sealed off from the other life. The Christ does not receive his flesh and blood from the flesh and blood of the Virgin Mary, but God creates new flesh and new blood in Mary's womb. And thus it is the same in rebirth. It is not the old, sinful essence of our depraved nature

---

6. In addition to earlier treatments of Anabaptism in his commentary on the Heidelberg Catechism, Kuyper distinguished Anabaptism from other magisterial reformation traditions in "State and Church," in *On the Church*, 432–35. See also *CG* 2.10, pp. 85–93.

that is transformed and changed into a new nature; rather, a new a new and different life is created within a person's heart. It is not a noble shoot that is grafted onto a wild trunk; rather, the old trunk is cut down and a new sapling is planted in its place. Thus the effect is that the reborn individual no longer has anything to do with war, government, the swearing of oaths, and so forth, all things that belong to the depraved nature. He still lives in a world that lives out of nature, but he avoids this world through the doctrine of *shunning* in order to withdraw back into one's own circle. And thus the Anabaptist also has *his* ideal and he will one day receive his world, but *his* world will only come with the return of the Lord. That which Jan van Leiden sought to realize in Münster[7] was merely an abnormal outgrowth of the otherwise ideal expectation.

It was different with the nudists.[8] This system flowed directly from the essence Anabaptism. Human beings before the fall were not ashamed. The sense of shame came only with sin, and thus clothing is something that belongs to the depraved nature but not to the holy nature. And because, according to the Anabaptist system, rebirth does not function potentially but immediately and actually, it suddenly cuts off the sinful nature and replaces it with a holy nature and it is therefore entirely consistent with this that people threw off their clothing and even in mixed gatherings displayed themselves again like Adam and Eve saw one another in paradise. It is true that presenting oneself thus in the street did not follow from the system, but appearing without clothing in their gathering together did. And we know how still in this century the so-called Latter-Day Saints in South Africa, as well as a few related groups in Brazil, have returned to similar practices.[9] In heaven, in the state of glory, when the elect will appear in their

7. Jan (or John) of Leiden (1509-36) was a revolutionary Anabaptist who led the infamous Münster Rebellion (1534-35), in which he instituted a theocratic system on the German city in anticipation of Christ's return and the inauguration of a millennial kingdom. In preparation for this apocalyptic event, he made the city's inhabitants go naked. In 1535, imperial troops recaptured the city, and Jan of Leiden along with two other Anabaptist leaders were executed and their bodies displayed in cages hung from St Lambert's Church. The cages remain to this day.
8. In the early years of the Reformation a group of radicals ran naked through the streets of Amsterdam proclaiming God's judgment.
9. At least some forms of ritual nudity have historically been an element of Mormon practice and were relatively more prevalent in the nineteenth century than today. See John-Charles Duffy, "Concealing the Body, Concealing the Sacred: The Decline of Ritual Nudity in Mormon Temples," *Journal of Ritual Studies* 21, no. 2 (2007): 1-21.

glorified body, there can be no more be clothing in our sense of the term than there can be external shame. Well then, the Anabaptist believes that he already possesses that heavenly life and, consequently, these excesses came about, which of course eventually resulted in sin and opened the door to antinomianism, but which were initially intended in a good and holy way.

...

And really everything here depends on the correct confession of the omnipotence of God, that is, on the correct insight (which follows from the confession of his omnipotence) that only God can create something and can give something being, so that whatever he does not create *cannot* have its own being or substance. Applied to *sin*, then, this shows that any notion that sin is something that has substance in itself is to be repudiated. Thus, where sin begins to churn in our nature, it is not as if something came into existence apart from God as a new element or component to our nature, but only the *mode of existence* of our nature is changed. This is expressed most clearly when we say that what was first positive was turned into its negative by sin. The strength that is present there remains the same, but it changes direction. This does mean that the sinner lose many gifts and that the one's heart generally sounds false instead of pure notes, and that one can therefore no longer produce harmonies, but the strength that produces tone and sound is not gone. The tongue you received in order to praise God is not cut out but remains in you and continues to give you a voice. But now this voice blasphemes the glory of God.

Sin, therefore, does not have a power of its own through which it could bring about anything in you from itself, but all the strength with which sin operates is power that God wrought in you. Sin is in itself entirely power-less and exclusively speculates with divine capital. But from this it follows that sin cannot break free from the human essence; the human being must remain a *human being*, and that when God's grace comes to the sinner, all aspects of a human being are still present in the person and that, so to speak, all the limbs are still found in him from which the pure body must be constructed again. A sinner is, if you will, a leaking, wrecked ship, insofar as all the curved timbers have worked loose from the keel and all the seams have come apart, but provided you keep in mind that not a single beam or timber has been lost and that therefore not a single new beam or spar needs to be brought in to restore this wrecked ship.

Applied to the *work of grace*, this shows that the work of grace does not mean that he who lost his legs will get new legs, but rather that the crippled person whose legs were lame receives strength in the leg muscles again and now leaps like a deer. The sinner is a blind person—not as if his eyes have been cut out, but such that the light has gone out and now grace does not cause a new eye to be set in an empty socket, but that the same eye that did not see now sees. Grace is healing. The sick person whose vitality has been depleted by a raging fever is gripped in such a way that this same vitality now turns in a different direction so that the fever abates and one's healthy life takes hold again. The dead person stands up, not because another person takes his place, or because he enters someone else's being by way of soul migration, but because God revives the hollow and inoperative vital forces. What became negative through sin is now made positive again. In paradise there were no thistles and thorns; then, through the curse, all kinds of trees that were at first beautiful were transformed so that they brought forth thistles and thorns. And now, through grace, the thistle is not cut out and the thorn burned to be replaced by a myrtle and a pine, but the thorn *becomes* a pine, the thistle becomes a myrtle. And only does it become a sign to the Lord: a sign of his omnipotence, that nothing could destroy his creature and that ultimately his power breaks through again and shines above all.

On this basis, the Christian church confessed that rebirth is not the creation of a second, new being in or beside our being, but the transformation or re-creation of our own and only being in such a way that it returns to its original plan and its original inclination. The intellect remains the same, but the will that was initially bent is now straightened again. The inner life dynamic which diverted itself away from God is now directed back toward God. The blind person sees again with his own eyes, the deaf person hears again with his own ears, the cripple leaps again with the same feet and legs that earlier could a not carry him. And this is comparatively speaking a *new* condition, so that we have become like *new persons*, that we speak as with *new* tongues, and that we, as Paul says in Ephesians 2:15, experience ourselves created as *new persons*. But new here does not in the least mean created *over again*, so that a second creature would slip into the first one. Nature rejuvenates and renews itself every spring, but it is always the same material elements and the same forces that, under the glow of the same sun, manifest themselves in *new forms*. We must therefore completely set aside the whole Anabaptist notion that always dreams of a new essence. The essence remains one. It is *our own* nature that is transformed. Our self before rebirth and our self after remains the same.

But with this arises a second question, namely, *which way is God's way?* Does he create everything suddenly and all at once in its final state as it must be according to his counsel? Or does he follow the organic way, which gradually lets the stalk and the ear grow from the grain of wheat, and the oak tree from the acorn? And then the answer *cannot* be in doubt. In the original creation, of course, everything was created in a state of provisional perfection. At his creation Adam was immediately an adult man. Eve was not a child at first. God did not sow in paradise and then wait for fifty years until the cedars were full-grown, but he created all of paradise in a state of provisional perfection. We speak of *provisional* perfection because paradise was not yet in the state of *glory* that is to come, and because Adam and Eve were holy but not yet partakers of eternal life. Their holiness still had to develop and it was still a possession that could be lost. But considering the state of paradise as God intended it, then yes, the result of creation was complete and perfect in itself.

However, and this is the essential point for us, afterward God the Lord exclusively chose the path of organic growth. Abel is born as an infant. The animals produce young. The oak tree lets its acorns fall into the soil. Everything now springs up from unnoticeably small germs or spores, and these germs contain the potentials or capacities from which it will all come forth. And it does come, *not* suddenly, *not* all at once, but rather very slowly and through steady growth. This is true of the visible creation, but also of the invisible creation in the human being. The child does not speak at first but only cries. It only learns to speak gradually. A newborn child does not yet think but only gradually comes to know, grasp, and enrich his consciousness. And his moral life is also formed in this way, both in the sinful and the non-sinful way. Here there is growth, increase, development. At first it seems to be nothing, as long as everything is still hidden in its potency, or germ; but soon it will emerge and then it manifests its actuality—in activity—which at first lay hidden in potency.

And this is also the way of the Lord in the miraculous work of regeneration. Here also God works with the mystery of the germ. This is shown most clearly when an elect child passes away in its first year of life. In that case, neither father nor mother have observed anything of that work of regeneration. And yet, the Lord has wrought it. The germ, the potentiality, was there. But now this blessed child disappears, and nothing of its regenerated life will appear on earth. Our churches, which baptize young children since they are *members of Christ* already before baptism, see nothing of any regeneration, nothing of faith in the child to be baptized, and yet they baptize and administer the sacrament whose only goal is *to strengthen a faith that is there.* Thus the rebirth is not a planting in us of the tree of life but an outpouring in us of a *seed of God,* a "seed of life," an imperishable *seed,* but always a *seed*—even as the kernel is for the ear of grain and the mustard seed for the mustard tree in whose branches the birds of the heavens will later nestle, but you do not see, notice, or detect anything of that in this smallest of herb seeds.

Applied to the grand work of transformation and recreation, this means that this re-creation, then, has its fixed *starting point* in the new birth, and that in this *seed of God* everything is present that will later find expression in faith and sanctification—but that all this will develop and grow from that seed only slowly and gradually. It does not happen in such a way that it is suddenly finished and complete, but only such that it carries within it the guarantee of being one day complete and finished. It possesses this guarantee in Christ, whose members we are and in whom, as our Head, everything is now already present that later will find expression with us and in us. But the transformation, the renewal, the re-creation is a work of long years. The effect of this is that our nature, taken at any given point in our life, has always been recreated in a certain respect, but *not* yet recreated in another respect and thus the sinful being can still find expression. ...[10]

Yet if it had not been for the law, I would not have known sin. I would not have known what it is to covet if the law had not said, "You shall not covet."   §3
Romans 7:7

In the Heidelberg Catechism the *commandment* stands in between *faith* (with the *sacraments*) and *prayer.* First it takes up the Twelve Articles of Faith with the sacraments. At the end of the catechism comes the Lord's Prayer. And between these two lies the treatment of the law. We are used to this order, and we can stay with it.

---

10. Here ends §1. In §2, which is here omitted, Kuyper comments on the catechism's statement that "even the holiest men, while in this life, have only a small beginning" of obedience to the commandments. He explains how the perfectionism of the holiness movement as well as the popular beliefs in some of the classical conventicles harbor a dangerous self-delusion.

It is nevertheless useful to remember here the fact that neither Luther nor Calvin modeled this sequence. In Luther's Catechism, by contrast, the *commandment* comes first, followed by *faith*, after faith follows *prayer*, and the *sacraments* come only after prayer.[11] And when you look at Calvin's Geneva Catechism, there you do indeed find faith first, then the commandment, and then prayer, but in Calvin's Catechism the sacraments come only after the *Lord's Prayer*.[12] The Westminster Catechism, which was drafted only much later, after all other catechisms, does not completely follow our Heidelberg Catechism; it has the sequence (1) *faith*, (2) *commandment*, (3) *sacraments*, and (4) *prayer*.

These divergent methods of ordering originate in different uses of the *law*. If I take the *law* as a means to maintain discipline until the coming of Christ, then it must of course precede faith, as in Luther. But if, by contrast, the law is seen as rule and guide for the life of gratitude, then it must just as naturally follow after faith, since there can only be spiritual gratitude in believers. Olevianus and Ursinus[13] sensed this clearly and realized that they actually needed to present the law twice: first *before faith* in order to reveal the conscience in the sinner, and then *again after faith*, to point to the rule of gratitude. And if you pay close attention, they do in fact *give the law twice*.

After all, question 4 already reads, "*What does the Law of God require of us?*" This question should of course have been followed by a complete exposition of the law and a complete interpretation of the Ten Commandments. But in order to prevent needless duplication, the only answer given to question 4 is Christ's *epitome* of the law, and the actual treatment of the Ten Commandments comes only here, after the treatment of the Twelve Articles. To us this solution does not seem the best choice. Question 4 speaks of the *knowledge of sin*, before one comes to Christ. In question 92 the same law is presented again, but now after the Christ has been confessed. The fact that question 4 gives the *highest* summary of the law, as actually only a believer understands it, does not square as well with the fact that the substantive condemnation of specific sins—which the unbeliever can also grasp—is not taken up until after the treatment of *faith*. We should not

---

11. The basic order is the same for both Luther's Small Catechism and Large Catechism.
12. This is the general order for Calvin's Catechism (Latin 1545; French 1541).
13. Caspar Olevianus (1536–87) and Zacharius Ursinus (1534–83) are traditionally considered the main coauthors of the Heidelberg Catechism, although scholars have debated the extent of Olevianus's role.

make too much of this. It is only a question of sequence and arrangement to which our Heidelberg Catechism does not attach any doctrinal significance.

When we now come to the use of the law for the elect in the doctrinal sense, then the core substance is and remains that the use of the law is threefold: (1) to hold before a person as in a mirror one's sin, misery, and worthiness of damnation; (2) to drive one out toward what God has offered us in his dear Son; and (3) to be a rule and guide for us in the life of gratitude. The *law* unmasks the sinner; drives one to Christ; and regulates the life of God's children.

Meanwhile, serious dispute has arisen regarding this threefold purpose of the preaching of the law. It is a dispute that can be easily explained when one raises the further question whether this threefold use applies simultaneously or sequentially in time. If one says sequentially in time, then it means that the law first shows you your sin, and with that this first use of the law is finished. Then the law drives you to Christ, and this *second* use continues until you accept the Christ, at which point this use ceases. And then, finally, comes the *third* use, namely, to walk in this law as beloved children and followers of God. If, on the other hand, you say with the catechism that this threefold use is *simultaneous*, then it indicates that even in the converted individual the law perpetually does these three things: it continues to reveal sin, to drive one toward Christ, and to regulate the walk of God's child.

A reaction against this latter perspective arose from two sides. The first was from the side of the Anabaptists, who view conversion in an absolute sense and thus consider a converted person to be one who already has a complete knowledge of sin, who has left that sin behind, who *has* come to Christ, and who therefore only needs a rule for one's walk. Then from the other side there were the antinomians, who asserted and still assert that *the second use precludes the third*. For, so they say, if in Christ we have received redemption and liberation from the law, because he not only *paid* our penalty but also completely *fulfilled* the law for us, then for us there can be no longer be any question of fulfilling the law. If you nevertheless continue to speak of this, then you negate what you previously confessed and deny that Christ has fulfilled the law for you. They then add a second objection, namely, that there is no benefit in preaching the law of God so strictly if you know beforehand that you will not progress beyond a *small beginning* of this perfect obedience on earth.

Yet not *all* antinomians have set aside the preaching of the law. On the contrary, there are also antinomians who are fond of a strict preaching of the law, and even urge it—but *only in appearance*. What they mean is that the content of the Ten Commandments must be extensively and strictly expounded, but *not* as law. On the contrary, they seek in the preaching of the law a preaching of *the promise of God*. When God says to his child, *You shall not steal*, they do not understand this as a commandment but rather as if God wanted to say, "I, your God, will cause you not to steal; my promise is your guarantee. I, your God, will make cause you not to commit adultery; I promise you this and you can rely on it." The repeated *You shall not* then does not mean *You must not* steal, but rather: the result will show that you do not do it because I am preventing you from doing it.

This view sounds so tempting because it contains the perfectly correct truth that it is the Lord who keeps us from stumbling, which is the reason why his children give thanks to him for his preserving grace and lean on his holy promise, "*I will ... cause you* to walk in my statutes" (Ezek 36:27). This is also what Ephesians 2:10 reveals to us: "We are ... created in Christ Jesus for good works, *which God prepared beforehand, that we should walk in them*." Taken in this way, we fully agree with this confession, which we have always put in the foreground, and we are certain that every child of God will say *yes* and *amen* to it. And as long as this and nothing else is meant by it, then yes, then we can say in a moment of blessed comfort with Luther that the *you shall* of the law that comes to us as a commandment resounds in our soul as a *you shall* of holy promise.

However, this view must be opposed, and strenuously opposed, if it is intended in the antinomian way and turns the law itself into a promise, and requires it be preached in God's church as a promise. For then we find ourselves on unholy paths and the Word of God is violated. In the first place, such a notion is an absurdity. If the law were a promise to the child of God that God will ensure that one will not fall into any of these sins, then one *would* never fall into them. By contrast, the sad reality shows that one falls again and again, daily, into small and sometimes into more serious sins, but in any case, with the disappointing result that on this side of the grave there can be at most a small beginning of perfect obedience. In view of this outcome, we would have to say that God does *not* keep his promise, that he breaks this promise to each of his children day after day. And sometimes this breaking of his promises would go so far as to allow his children to fall into sins that are considered shameful even among unbelievers. God then would have said in his law, "Do not ensure that you do not steal. I your God will ensure that you will not steal." And meanwhile, God would more than once fall short in keeping his promises and would allow his children to commit all kinds of minor injustices. This, further, is *impossible*, and those small dishonesties must be explained away. They may not be confessed as real sins, for God ensures that you do not steal. And so you do not steal, even though you have in a less-than-honest way poured money into your purse that belongs to someone else.

But in the second place, and this is our main objection, those who turn the *commandment* into a *promise* start from the notion that a human being is a machine of that God, apart from the person's will, wound up and let run. And this dehumanizes the human being. God created the human person as a being with a moral nature, that is, as a being with a moral sense of self and with the ability to make voluntary choices. Human responsibility and accountably before God flows from this moral sense of self and this ability to make voluntary choices. He does not grow like a tree, and does not walk like an animal, but lives as *human being*. Thus, if God wants to work on a human being, then this work of God must be directed toward a person's *consciousness* and *will*, it must introduce into that consciousness holy thoughts and holy knowledge, and it must change the direction of the person's will.

And it is precisely the preaching of the law that serves precisely this purpose as the means and instrument. The preaching of the law works on our inner consciousness, through this instilling of the knowledge of God's ordinances in us. And the preaching of the law likewise works on our *will* through the earnestness of God's will that encounters us. And thus it is also entirely true that your God preserves you from sin, as long as you do not forget to add that the Lord also does this by having his law preached to you pointedly, not as a comforting *promise* but precisely as a *holy* and *high* commandment. Those who are deceived, then, must also beware. For by severing the nerve of the commandment in the law, and replacing it with the sweet cord of comfort, they proclaim a false peace, cover things over with whitewash, and thwart one of the most powerful efforts by which the Lord God intended, as a rule, to let his children walk on the harness[14] of his love. Anyone who for a time was misled by this sweet language, a language without seriousness, and who finally came out from under it again, has always had to confess that this kind of preaching had *weakened* their

---

14. That is, a harness used to teach a child to walk, commonly used in earlier eras.

moral earnestness. God's child is not a stone or block, no machine that is wound up only to let it run down until God winds it up again. God's child is a *collaborator* with God, that is, the Holy Spirit dwells in a person, and the Holy Spirit works in a person in such a way that the preaching of the law can have its effect on the person and that, thanks to the preaching of the law, made fruitful by the Holy Spirit, one's life is kept in check.

This is precisely the reason why it is such a culpable dereliction of duty when the ministry of the Word falls short in this preaching of the law. The fact that life was in many respects so honorable and sound during the golden age of our churches can in no small part be attributed to the fact that in that period much effort was invested in the preaching of the law, and that the congregation regularly attended this preaching of the law. At that time the preaching of the law was like a fence along the water's edge and like a handrail along a bridge to prevent the members of the church from falling into the water. The preaching of the law was not a human invention. God instituted it, and therefore all honor and glory for the fruit it bore accrued to God. But its actual result was that a helping hand was extended to the congregation and that those who stumbled were straightened up again before they fell and struck the ground.

Today, by contrast, many view the preaching of the law as secondary. What is generally lacking is the more detailed discussion of the various sins in order to unsettle the conscience and to reveal the sinner to himself. A more general preaching of the law seems to be already more than enough. And this preaching then remains so general that most believers think, not entirely erroneously, that they already know this and thus find it not worth it to pay attention such preaching. And in this way, a mighty support is taken away from the life of the congregation. The question, after all, is not whether you know these things (when they are merely are collected entry in your memory) but rather whether they also come before you as a claim demanding payment of a debt, and to place you again and again as sinner before the holy law of your God. This is the only way the conscience is kept awake, the bandage is pulled from the injured body part and the plaster from the injury, and the shock and dismay at your unholy life goes through your soul. Without that preaching of the law in all its meticulousness, point-edness, and strictness, many an ordinary child of God easily imagines that, in comparison with others who live more laxly, one already ranks among the saints, while in reality even one's position among the ordinary saints is under constant threat. And therefore, one cannot insist enough, especially in these turbulent times, that the ministry of the Word strive for moral earnestness, and that it continuously clarify with clear and evident insight into what God wills that our life should be.

But we have an even more serious conflict with the true antinomians who would prefer to exclude the entire preaching of the law from the congregation as not appropriate under the gospel. They tell you that your position on the law itself is wrong. This perspective was good in the covenant of works but cannot be tolerated in the covenant of grace. That the law, far from making us holy, rather incites sin and thus makes us more unholy, because there is a lust for the forbidden in human nature. So they are hostile to the law, which they call a dead letter, whereas they want to walk in freedom of spirit. Furthermore, they say that the law obligates us either to punishment or to obedience; that is, the law has been accounted to us simply as punishment, and that in Christ we have borne and satisfied this punishment, so that rightfully no obedience can be demanded from us anymore. And finally, they even go so far that they come to see sin as the great means that evokes grace. Although sin is in itself something objectionable, it has its unique significance as a means to elicit grace and to make grace increase, entirely in keeping with what people asked already in Paul's day: "Are we to continue in sin that grace may abound?" [Rom 6:1].

This evil antinomianism is sometimes coupled with the dualistic Anabaptist error that opposes flesh against spirit. In that case, a child of God is spiritual, and although one still walks in the flesh, that flesh is not the person. That flesh is someone else who dwells in the person, a kind of old Adam, who clings to the person. That flesh, the old Adam, may sin as much as he likes. It doesn't matter, for that carnal indweller will someday go to hell. And as for the person, a child of God, there is no knowledge of or suffering from this sin, since it transpires apart from the person. It neither touches nor bothers the person. Indeed, the more deeply this old Adam burrows in, the better it is, because it is precisely through this that the contrast between the child of God and that evil doppelganger in the person manifests itself more sharply. And do not let anyone say that such evil talk is unheard of, for it is not unheard of. Even now there are sizeable circles of God's saints in which arguments such as this are passed around and accepted with certain satisfaction.

This entire false doctrine has arisen from the failure to sufficiently discern the *twofold* understanding of the law. We can speak of the law as a rule that indicates what someone must do to earn something and earn a certain reward. But we can also speak of the law as a rule that indicates what must happen in order for life to run well. To take a very simple example: When a little child must take cod-liver oil, it often refuses. But when its mother says, "If you swallow this you get a cookie, otherwise you get a spanking," then the child swallows it, not for the sake of swallowing, much less to become stronger through the cod-liver oil, but out of fear of punishment and for the sake of the compensation, the reward, the sweet that is dangled in front of the child. But when that same child then gets that cookie, it swallows again, this time not for the compensation, the reward but only because swallowing is the self-evident means of enjoying it.

This distinction also applies here. The law is given to the man in paradise with the offer of reward and the threat of punishment. At that time, he despised the reward, deliberately rejected eternal life, and brought the punishment upon himself. We would be forced to sink under this forever if God in his unfathomable mercy had not brought about the mystery of redemption, so that now Christ, for us and in our place, has borne the punishment, paid the penalty, and fulfilled the law. This is therefore a "done deal" in the full sense of the term for all God's elect, and whoever may come to faith confesses this salvation. He knows that Christ stood in his place and that he stands righteous before his God. The fact that we must nevertheless still preach the law in this sense does not at all mean that something must still be added to the unique sacrifice of Christ, as we shall see later. That sacrifice was offered once and perfectly. Nothing can be taken away from it or added to it. The law is still preached in this sense to God's children to make them realize ever more clearly what kind of death and damnation they have escaped and to increasingly disclose to them the riches of grace contained in Christ's sacrifice.

But, quite separately from this, the law also has its *second* meaning that we indicated. The child swallowed spontaneously the second time, because swallowing is life's law for obtaining nourishment. Thus it is ordained by God and is an established fact for every human being. And the same applies here as well. Human beings have received their own human life from God, and that life has not been left to random chance but is bound to fixed laws. This applies to your body, it applies to your thinking, and it applies to your moral and your spiritual life. Everything follows laws; nothing has been left to random chance. There is a law that says that you must breathe carbon dioxide out and oxygen in; whoever does not do this suffocates. There is a law that two times two is four, and if you do not take this into account, your calculations will not add up. There is a law that the spirit of the child of God must pray, and when one does not pray, one's spiritual life withers. And so there is also a law for your moral life, for what you do and what you avoid, and whoever works against this law rather than in harmony with it harms oneself and runs aground.

Of course, after one's rebirth and conversion a child of God remains a *human being*, and thus God's ordinances also remain applicable to *their lives*. Without air a child of God suffocates just like the unconverted. A child of God who does not respect the laws of thought is just as mistaken in one's reasoning as the unconverted. And so a child of God who does not regulate what he does and does not do in accordance with God's law will also run aground just like the unconverted. And this is why a child of God, just like an unconverted person, needs the law of God continuously and earnestly preached in its fullness, that one may see the tracks in which the wheel of one's life must turn if it is to run well and to bring one happiness in life — inner, moral happiness in life. We shall see later how this relates to gratitude. Here we only point to how these two go together: (1) that the law as a means of choosing between reward and punishment is completely over and done, and (2) that the law as rule for our moral life remains indispensable for the child of God until one's death.

And that same time, this actually answers the second objection, that it is not appropriate to maintain such a strict preaching of the law, given the fact that you know beforehand that the child of God cannot keep it perfectly. After all, it is the hallmark of every rule that you must set the bar high to obtain the highest possible compliance with the rule. When new recruits begin to shoot at targets, most of the bullets strike quite a distance outside the target, and only a few will even strike within the circumference of the target, while there is no thought even a single one of them will quickly hit the center or the bullseye of the target. And yet every recruit is told that he not only must aim at the *target* but at the *center* of the target. And this is what he does, even though he does not hit it. And he *must* do this, for if he did not, his shot would deviate much farther still. And so it is precisely this steady aiming at a point that he nonetheless does not hit that is the means to keep him from a still greater deviation, to help him to gradually learn to aim better, and ultimately also to hit the target.

That glory may dwell in our land.
Psalm 85:9

Having fended off antinomianism in our previous chapter, which wants to abolish every use of the law, we now return to the question wherein the right use of the law consists. In this, we should not let ourselves be confused by what the catechism *does not say.* The catechism only speaks of a threefold purpose the preaching of the law intends, namely, revealing our sins, compelling us toward Christ, and showing us the path through life that is pleasing to God.

It is natural that attention is focused on this, and on this alone, and that it does not also speak of the law as a means to restrain sin in the unbeliever. After all, the catechism speaks in the church and to believers. When, therefore, it asks, "Why then does God so strictly enjoin the Ten Commandments upon us, since in this life no one can keep them?" it refers here exclusively to the preaching that takes places in the holy domain of regeneration and of the new life: *the preaching of the law to the children of God.* The strict and steady preaching of the law must help them (1) to increasingly confess their sinful nature, (2) to take ever more intimate refuge in the Mediator, and (3) to be increasingly conformed to the image of God.

But even though this is said well and correctly with regard to God's children, it does not say *all* there is to say. There is also a force that proceeds from the preaching of the law among unbelievers, a force that works upon every human being, whether elect or not. And in fact it is a force that has the effect of reining in debauchery, maintaining a measure of civil justice, and through this keeping human life from complete savagery. Taken in this sense, the preaching of the law has nothing to do with eternal salvation; it does not draw persons toward God's love; and it is the opposite of man's restoration. But it is a rein, a bridle, a bit that is put on him. This is exactly the sense in which Psalm 32:9 exhorts the unwilling and the senseless to reason when it says, "Be not like a horse or a mule, without understanding, which must be curbed with bit and bridle, or it will not stay near you."

It is perfectly true that God the Lord lets this preaching of the law proceed more from the government than from the church. For as a rule these senseless ones do not enter the house of God, and they hear no other preaching of the law than from their father who must threaten and punish them at home; from public opinion, which still disapproves of many kinds of shamelessness and dishonesty; and from criminal law, which imposes punishment on all kinds of wrongdoings. The vast majority by far of the world's population of the earth never receive any other kind of preaching of the law. Do not forget, of course, that all churches across the whole world together comprise at most less than one-third of the earth's inhabitants. More than two-thirds thus stand entirely outside it. And when you look in your own neighborhood and see how many of those who have been baptized truly receive preaching of the law from God's Word and through his church, then half is certainly too high an estimate. The proportion of humanity that receives the law from God's church still very small, and for most people by far the law comes to them not from the church but exclusively from the government and public opinion.

The law that comes to them in this way is of course not the law of the Ten Commandments as presented to us in Exodus 20. But this does not in any way change the essence of the matter. The law of the Ten Commandments is not a new law. The psalmist proclaimed, "Long have I known from your testimonies that you have founded them forever" (Ps 119:152). The foundation of God's law is situated before our creation in his divine wisdom and will. It is woven into our creaturely existence in and through the creation. The awareness and knowledge of the law was created in us when that law was inscribed on Adam's heart. And when the devastation of sin came between Adam and the law to destroy this divine handwriting, the Lord our God, in what is called his general or common grace, held in check this wearing off of his handwriting so that there is still always a remnant of knowledge of the law even in the unregenerated and unconverted. The holy apostle says in his epistle to the Romans that even the Gentiles, although they do not have the law of Sinai, are a law unto themselves and "show that the work of the law is written on their hearts" (Rom 2:15). And indeed, God's people have first been promised that God would write his law in their heart as a fruit of the Holy Spirit, but this is intended in the pure and perfect sense. But in the case of the Gentiles *something* of God's law is still legible on the tablet of their heart, but it is like smudged writing of which you can, at most, still decipher a few lines here and there.

Now, the law of Sinai is *no other* law than that which was originally imprinted on the human heart. It is the same, with only this difference: (1) it now came to human beings *externally*; (2) it was applied to a *specific nation*, Israel; and (3) it did not speak positively, as it did back then, but in a *prohibitive* manner: "You shall *not* kill, you shall *not* steal," and so forth. But for the rest God's will and his law are and remain one. It is always his ordinances that he has established from eternity. If government and public opinion preach this law, then it will be in a very impure fashion. It can also happen that either the government or public opinion—that is, what

Paul calls "their conflicting thoughts accusing or even excusing them"—preaches and imposes something as law that goes against God's ordinances. But God's ordination has nevertheless brought it about that among virtually all nations some traits of his law have still remained visible. This is partly an aftereffect of the tradition from paradise, partly the result of lawgivers such as Solon,[15] whom God has given to the nations; partly also the result of the influence that the calling of Moses and the reputation of Solomon caused to go out from Israel among the nations. In addition, in no small part due to the actions of Emperor Constantine[16] and his successors, all manner of more accurate insight into the law has been transferred from the preaching of the Christian church into what we call Roman jurisprudence. But in whatever way and in whatever form this *common grace* has operated, the purpose and result was that the law of God, in a stronger or weaker manner, still today bridles the people through government and public opinion, reins in the eruption of sin, and thus brings about a certain civil justice which does not accomplish anything for salvation but makes a humane life in human society possible and thus provides a place for the church to find a foothold.

With this in view, the preaching of the law of Sinai by and in the church of Christ is of tremendous significance, in three respects: (1) This preaching spreads a clearer and purer understanding of God's law among the Christian nations, and thereby ennobles public opinion, exerts influence the government's legislation, and thus has the effect that the Christian nations better apply the bridle of God's law in the civil realm as well. (2) These Christian nations, in turn, exert an extraordinary influence on the non-Christian nations; they do this through the higher position of power they occupy; they do this through their colonizing activities, which automatically lead to the abolition of many abominations in those nations; they also do this by preventing, insofar as lies in their power, at least some abominations such as piracy, human trafficking, and so on, among nations that are not subject to them. (3) This preaching of the law also has the effect among members of the church who are still in an unconverted state that the sinful nature is held in check, the domestic life becomes purer, and thus also in this way *civil justice*, called *virtue* among people, is promoted.

---

15. Solon (ca. 630–ca. 560 BC) was an Athenian legislator and legal reformer.
16. Constantine the Great (272–337) granted civil rights and religious liberty to Christians throughout the Roman Empire.

The latter brings us naturally back to our topic proper. If it is true that the preaching of the law still has a deterrent effect on the unconverted in God's church, then here it also is doing the work of general or common grace. This means that, apart from all spiritual effects, it puts a restraint and a rein on the unconverted which keeps them from all kinds of excess and iniquity. If, for example, a young man who is entirely unconverted is as a young man held back from dishonesty, addiction to drink, or fornication because of the customs of the church, the tone of life of the Christian family, through strict mutual supervision, and through the respect for the law, then all this does not affect his eternal life, and no more than a bridle or a bit have been put on the stubborn mule. But when he comes to conversion this has the wonderful effect that he can look back on a less sullied past, that his imagination is not so badly polluted, that his body suffered less, and that his habits breathe more purity of heart.

This is of course not a requirement for conversion. God can pluck someone like a brand from the fire of sin. Conversion springs from nothing other than the root of rebirth and is not even prepared by common grace. But it would harm the honor of God's church if all of the elect who later come to conversion had lived for many years as the dregs of humanity. It is certainly our duty to go to these as well in case God's elect may be hidden among them. If this turns out to be the case, then many of these last will be the first, as happened to a man like Augustine.[17] But it is wonderful that this is not the *rule*, that this first wallowing in the mud only to be admitted later to the tabernacle of the Lord remains the exception. And this is what the church of God has brought about through its strict and steady preaching of the law.

But that is not all there is to this point. For the child of God is not yet completely divested of one's old nature, not even through conversion. Sometimes one does indeed ride on the heights of God's mountains and all external restraints have become unnecessary for the person. But over against this stand days in which the spiritual impulse dozes or even sleeps. There are days when the ear of the spirit is deaf and one's unconverted old nature wickedly works its way up in the person again. And although this revival of the old nature no longer takes on the fearful proportions of the past, still the child of God recognizes every day, indeed, almost every hour, all kinds of unholy thoughts and evil spirits that well up from the evil

---

17. Augustine of Hippo (354–430) is the most influential figure from the patristic era for the Western church. His remarkable conversion is recounted in his *Confessions*.

fountain inside one and that want to come out. Then life is at its highest when the child of God resists with prayer, for the sake of God, from faith, and in the nobility of the Spirit. Then there is a genuine victory. But if the spirit within him is sluggish and the flesh incites one too much, so that there is no question of a spiritual victory, then it is still better that one desists from sin rather than recklessly indulging in it. Certainly, perfect love excludes fear. But what child of God can say that they always stand in this *perfect* love and operates with this perfect love hour after hour? There are times of depression and irritability, moments of passion and vehemence, hours of agitation and extreme tension, when this love has sometimes been pitifully silenced and the child of God would fall into all kinds of terrible situations without the terror of the law.

In that case, the child of God does not abstain from evil out of love for God, not for the sake of Christ, not out of gratitude, not from the impulse of the Spirit. No, it is rather quite basic and pedestrian. It is because the law would come after him, his reputation would be harmed, and the "You shall not" puts a bit in his mouth. This, then, has nothing to do with a "good work" because it did not involve faith, had nothing to do with God's will, and was definitely not in agreement with the law in all respects.[18] But even so, it is an external blessing that the law kept him standing in his wildness, restrained his old nature, and kept him from dishonoring God's name. And therefore the child of God afterward thanks his Father who is in heaven for keeping him on track through the rein of his law even when he was foolish and wanted to do foolish things.

In this way you see how even the external operation of the law, with respect to civil justice, was well supported and buttressed by the preaching of the law—and still is. Therefore, it is unforgivable and very reckless when the church omits this preaching of the law or treats it superficially. It is inevitable, then, that in circles influenced by the antinomian spirit the standard of the moral life is pulled down gradually and imperceptibly.

But of course, no matter how much benefit the preaching of the law produces for *civil* justice among the converted and the unconverted, the proper goal of this preaching of the law remains higher. For that proper goal is *spiritual* in nature and lies in the ever-clearer disclosure of our sinful

---

18. These are the three characteristics of good works according to the Heidelberg Catechism, Lord's Day 33, Q&A 91.

state, in the ever-greater urging us toward the atoning sacrifice of Christ, and in renewing us in the image of God.

But before expounding on these three points in our final chapter, we must first remove a misunderstanding and confront a very serious objection. Holy Scripture, it is said, and especially the epistles of the holy apostle Paul, continually campaign against the law. It is said that the law is obsolete, that it is practically extinct and abolished, and that the saints of God are thus continually called from the law to the gospel. Therefore, they say, it makes no sense to continue to maintain the preaching of the law in the church of Christ in the face of Paul's condemnation of it. You sense the weight of this objection. Paul does indeed say that "by works of the law no human being will be justified," and that "the righteousness of God has been manifested apart from the law" [Rom 3:20–21]. He attests that "the law brings wrath" [Rom 4:15]; that "apart from the law, sin lies dead" [Rom 7:8]; that "our sinful passions" are "aroused by the law" [Rom 7:5]; that "the power of sin is the law" [1 Cor 15:56]; that "the law is not laid down for the just" [1 Tim 1:9]; that the saints of God "are not under law but under grace" [Rom 6:14]; that "where there is no law there is no transgression" [Rom 4:15]; that "sin is not counted where there is no law" [Rom 5:13]; that "through the law I died to the law" [Gal 2:19]; that we "also have died to the law" [Rom 7:4]; that "we are released from the law" [Rom 7:6].

To the question "Why then the law?" (Gal 3:19) he responds, "It was added because of transgressions, until the offspring should come." Well then, the seed has come. And therefore, there is now a new covenant, which "makes the first one obsolete. And what is becoming obsolete and growing old is ready to vanish away" (Heb 8:13).

In order not to be confused by these decisive and definite statements by the apostle Paul we must point to four things. First, Paul *cannot* have intended to represent the law as something wrong, as the cause of sin, and irrelevant for us, for in contrast to the above statements he also makes other, equally decisive statements in which he praises and commends the law: "So the law is holy, and the commandment is holy and righteous and good" [Rom 7:12]. "We know that the law is spiritual" [Rom 7:14]. "I agree with the law, that it is good" [Rom 7:16]. "For I delight in the law of God, in my inner being" [Rom 7:22]. In 1 Timothy 1:8 he repeats again, "Now we know that the law is good, if one uses it lawfully." And in Romans 3:31 he asks, "Do we then overthrow the law by this faith?" and answers concisely, succinctly, and decidedly, "By no means! On the contrary, we uphold the law."

In the second place, we must keep in mind that when Paul speaks of the law, he does not only refer to the moral law as such, but the whole law as given to Israel, including the ceremonial ministry of shadows and the typological institutions of Israel as a nation among the nations. A *shadow must disappear* when the reality itself comes, and thus the ceremonial law was not to be kept after Christ had fulfilled the sole offering of reconciliation. Furthermore, a law given to Israel as a nation and which to that extent bore a typological character *should* not remain in force as soon as the antitype had appeared in the Christ. The only thing that remained was the eternal will of God that he had determined for all humanity in his creation ordinances, and which was the foundation for all of Israel's laws. Paul, striving *against* the law, thus strove against those who wanted to maintain the ceremonial law and the national institutions of Israel even *after* the coming of Christ. And Paul, striving *in favor* of the law, strove for the moral law and for the principles that were the foundation for Israel's national institutions.

In the third place, we must point out that there is an enormous difference between the *law* and the legalist position. This notion in the covenant of works means working for reward, for merit, as a means to be able to claim salvation. Of this Paul says that it is unprofitable, that it has led to nothing but disappointment, that it did not help people advance but rather set them back. This is something that still applies in full force to anyone who would again seek to restrict the freedom of God's children and diminish God's grace through all kinds of regulations such as, "Do not handle. Do not taste. Do not touch." But the law as the expression of God's ordinances has *nothing* to do with this. The law as rule of life is and remains in force for eternity. It is a lamp for our feet and a light on our path. Our entire delight is in the law [see Psa 119:77].

Finally, we must not forget that it is something quite different whether I stand in my own strength or am guided in the law by the Spirit of the Lord. The law should be written on our heart. Had it remained in our heart it would never have come to stand before us as an external law. Now God writes his law once again in the hearts of his children, but he also does this with the help of the external law, and this is why he has his law preached so strictly. Everything Paul says *against* the law he says to those who try to fulfill the law as it exists, actually, as an external law, in their own strength. But everything he says *in favor of* the law he says about God's eternal ordinances, as they are in themselves, as they ought to be written on the tablets of our heart, as it is imprinted on the tablets of our heart through the preaching of the law, and as it is, thanks to the Holy Spirit, fulfilled in us and through us.

> *There is no fear in love, but perfect love casts out fear. For fear has to do* §5
> *with punishment, and whoever fears has not been perfected in love.*
> 1 John 4:18

When *love* comes, *fear* automatically gives way, and the legalist position, which involved fear of punishment, is automatically vanquished. As long as Adam in paradise continued to be steadfast in love for his God he also knew no terror or fear. It was not the threatened punishment that repulsed him, but the offered reward that drew him. In the sinner, by contrast, it is *fear* that is at work. This fear came with the first awakening in the troubled soul of the spiritual function; we call this the conscience. Then a reproach slices through the soul. You *should not* have acted in this way. You acted against your God. You violated the peace with God Almighty. And then the heart shudders and trembles. Later on, when the sinner has gotten used to this life outside God, it will not be felt quite as strongly. But this terror and fear must have been strong when Adam suddenly fell from *love* into *fear*, and he was shocked at himself as he now stood over against his God. The first pang of his conscience as Adam experienced it in his innermost being after his fall must therefore have been the most frightening manifestation of conscience that ever was. The sudden conflagration in human awareness. The draining away of the stream of God's love, leaving us solely with terror. This is not unlike the sudden failure of the lights at a huge public meeting, when the terror of darkness strikes the heart of all.

This fear of the law, then, cannot be overcome unless love returns. This cannot come from our side. A sinner runs into one's doom out of worry, even as a horse that has broken loose runs into the fire. But love can indeed come from the side of God. And it did so. It came in Christ. Only there lies that unfathomable mystery of justification. Suddenly, the terror of the law and of eternal death had stricken Adam in the heart, and just as suddenly that fear is taken away again through justification. Christ says, "Father, I have found forgiveness for him," and the saved one rejoices and exults, "I am redeemed," and the *Abba, dear Father*, resounds through all the rooms and halls of his soul.

This had to happen suddenly. This fear could not depart gradually in order to let love re-enter little by little. As long as we view someone as a brute even to the smallest degree, then even the first beginning of love cannot awaken. Love only comes when fear can be cast out. And when this love comes from the side of God, with all the resourcefulness of divine love, and suddenly transforms the conscience that spoke evil and condemned persons into a conscience that says good things and absolves persons of condemnation, then this deep divine love sparks such a warm glow of gratitude and affection in us that the love of a person for one's God surpasses itself. Each person can then measure one's own spiritual condition according to this love, like a spiritual thermometer. This love, if it ignites and burns well, emits warmth, radiates a holy glow, and that glow reveals what is in a person.

Having put this in the foreground, we now can answer the question that the catechism poses, namely, whether after the elimination of that terror of the law in our conversion, and the emergence in us of the glow of love, the law can still exert a formative influence on us, or that we must then say, "Now that I have been converted the law does not help me anymore. I am free of the terror, and love is what stimulates me automatically to do what is good. I breathe, I live, I work, I speak because I believe, and so out of gratitude." It is obvious that justification is most certainly a settled matter that can never be repeated; that the justified individual is set free in life and in death; and that all that comes after can never cause one to lose eternal life, simply because no one can ever bring any accusations against such a person. But it does not follow in the least from this that one who has come to conversion has already completely grasped the work of justification in its very depth, nor that in that first moment one has already fully appropriated the sacred treasure that lies in the saving work of Jesus.

Certainly, the love of God expels fear, but the apostle adds: *perfect* love. You must not understand this to mean that love must first reach its *highest* perfection before it begins to expel fear. Then there would be no comfort in it. Or who does not feel that one always remains at a distance from that highest point, or at least enjoys it only for a moment. Indeed, in the moment of conversion, a child of God has tasted that perfect love. To believe for the first time in that perfect love that expels all fear, believing it in its deep and full sense—that *is* your conversion. But God's child also knows that that love does not always burn with equal brightness. That love will later become numb again. Sometimes little more is left of it than embers covered with ashes in which at most a small spark still glows. That spark will not go out, for precisely at the moment that it would go out, the lid of the extinguishing pot is suddenly lifted, the fresh wind of God's holy breath blows in your heart, and the coal revives. But in any case, the loving condition of the soul toward its God is neither constant nor suddenly perfected. There is rising and falling, and there is also an ascent in this love.

If this love recedes, fades, or grows fainter, then fear automatically returns, the conscience wakes up again and becomes angry, stings and reproaches us again, and often this goes so far that the child of God, even after one's conversion, begins to doubt one's standing again. This is nothing but a return of fear and a receding of love. Commonly, this is a consequence of the child of God thinking too much that one's Father in heaven was there *for the child's sake*, and not thinking enough that the child exists for *the sake of the Father*. His calling is not just to proclaim *Soli Deo Gloria* in the world, but also putting *Soli Deo Gloria* into practice in one's own heart. Without this it is not the true, pure love, sanctified by God himself. It remains love in which the primary stress falls on one's own happiness, and it does not become the self-denying love which loses itself in the worship of him who appears radiantly from Zion. And then God has such a child undergo spiritual treatment once again, and withdraws his love somewhat, lets his grace go into hiding, and so gradually changes his child's heart so that it becomes capable of true love. It is no longer "I am holy" but *"Hallowed be your name"*; no longer "I am saved" but *"Your kingdom come"*; no longer "I keep your law" but *"Your will be done."* For any who pray the Lord's Prayer in truth, and can pray it in its real sequence, they indeed love their God and have denied themselves for their God.

Thus, the relationship of the soul of the child of God to one's Father in heaven gets a *history*. At first it does not have one. For justification is like a bolt of lightning that strikes the heart at the same time that faith sinks in. All this is central. It is complete at once. You are either justified or you are not. But after this begins the life of the child of God with one's Father in heaven. After this comes the effort of one's heart to penetrate into that mystery of justification and to understand its application to oneself. And in this history, this long path, three things are necessary for the children of God: (1) that they gradually learn to better understand how deep the ruin was from which God snatched them away, (2) how wonderful the means of salvation was that God devised, and (3) how one must behave as a child of God in the house of one's heavenly Father in order to join with such holy company. It is for these three things that God uses *his* law.

First, this law repeatedly shows you more clearly and vividly the deadly peril from which you have been saved.

Do not take this mechanistically and say that this happens to all in the same way. And most of all, do not demand that it happen in others as it happened in and to you. Sadly, there are children of God who, already before their conversion, had become acquainted with all of that deep and terrible nature of sin through their own horrible sins or through the sins of their companions. But this is not true of most. Most of God's children are kept from this before their conversion through the blessing of the covenant of grace. They were raised Christian and already from an early age they were accustomed to the service of the Lord. When people like this come to conversion, for them it does not have the intense character as it does with others. It happens more quietly. But this also means that their knowledge of sin is much smaller in scope. This does not mean that it is more superficial, for their conscience functions more delicately, more tenderly, whereas the conscience of the others, those who were sinners in days past, has lost much of its sensitivity. But the conviction of sin is less defined in those who made the quiet transition. They feel horrific terror before God's majesty, but they do not know how to account for it. They certainly had heard in the past, and they understood in the hour of their conversion, that they are sinners before their God, and they have felt the chill breath of eternal death waft over their soul. But this knowledge of sin, and of their own worthiness of damnation, and of the deadly peril in which they stood, is by no means complete. They would not be able to endure this all at once. They simply cannot imagine that, and parroting others does not help in spiritual matters.

Therefore one must never say that no one shares in Christ unless one has entirely realized the full length and breadth, the depth and height of one's own worthiness of damnation. One might imagine that this is true, but in reality it never happens this way. The terror of eternal death will initially strike more deeply in one person than in another. But there is not a single individual who does not come to a deeper insight over time. Thus, there is progress, although not in justification, for that remains finished once and for all and perfect in its eternal center, but there is progress in knowledge and insight into what that justification has been for us. There is an ever-maturing insight into human nature, into the nature of sinners, and into the nature of our own *selves*. We certainly have felt our guilt in all its gravity at the moment of our conversion, but then it fell from our shoulders and no one could estimate the weight of that guilt. But *after* this, the light of knowledge rises above. The law now returns, no longer as the angry drover it once was, no longer as the all-demanding tyrant who wants to bring us to salvation but can never do it, but as the light that is kindled above the depth of the abyss to tell us and show us *how deep* that abyss actually was. At first, we could not fathom it, our eye was not yet trained for this, we had no benchmark in our perception. But now that we grow older and our awareness becomes clearer, now that our understanding grows, specifically our spiritual understanding of the law, now we measure with that law in hand ever more accurately and clearly the depth of that abyss in which we would have sunk, and the depth of ruin in which we were confined with our soul and our soul's entire existence. And so this law enriches us. It makes us all the happier. For thanks to this law we know ourselves to be freed by our God from ever more damnation and guilt.

Coupled with this is a second enrichment. All that the children of God possess is in their Savior. Our life is hidden *with Christ* in God. We are blessed with all spiritual blessings in heaven *in Christ*. Nothing is ever added to this and nothing is ever taken away from it. Just as your justification is what it is suddenly and all at once, and can increasingly unfold in your awareness but can never become less or more, so it is also with your treasure in Christ. What you have in him you have all at once and completely. It is finished. Nothing *can* be added to it. You cannot have half a Christ. Whoever has him, has him completely. He who does *not* have him completely does *not* have him. But whether you have immediately grasped the glory given to you in Christ in its fullness it is something quite different. And then the answer is, of course, not by a long shot.

The one who converts to one's Savior is like the poverty-stricken man who suddenly inherits a million dollars. What did he inherit? A million dollars. And this million is put before him on the table in the form of one thousand bills of one thousand dollars each. He stares and gazes at that paper. He feels that he is suddenly wealthy, immeasurably rich. But that is all he comprehends. He does not yet see gold or silver. It is all still paper. All this must gradually be exchanged. He must first gradually become more aware, realize its scope, and thus must, with the help of others, gradually begin to realize what a million dollars actually is. And even then, he is still far from comprehending all that he has received. For then comes the second question, namely, what must he do with this money?

And it is only when that question has also been answered and he begins to enjoy what he received, that his understanding of his treasure becomes more and more complete. And this is exactly how it is with the treasure the children of God received in their Savior. Then you feel and realize that in your Jesus you have become infinitely rich and you are overjoyed, assured of all salvation. But this does not yet mean that you understand it. At first it is all still paper money to you. A stack of large-denomination bills which you put away but you still cannot take it all in. Only gradually must one bill after the other be exchanged for silver and gold. And only then you gradually come to a clearer awareness of and deeper insight into all that was encompassed in the holy, glorious name of Jesus. This is the first step. And then comes the second step, namely, coming to enjoy your treasure, to appropriate and apply to yourself what is included in that treasure, until at last you really know in your own soul's enjoyment and experience, what the divine treasure is that was hidden in the work of the Mediator.

And this is the second grace which God effects in his child through *the law*. He does this partly through the ceremonial law. For the ceremonial law demonstrated to Israel through visual pedagogy what would come in the Messiah, and thus also demonstrates to us what has come in Christ. The apostles therefore point continually back to the ceremonial sacrifices, and it provides no small enrichment of the knowledge of his Christ to God's child if one sees what is given in Christ on Golgotha in the shadows of the old covenant. But God also pursues this instruction of his child through the moral law. For the more the spiritual knowledge of the law opens up for one, the more one learns to understand the sickness of one's own soul, the worm in one's own heart. And since the goal of all the work of Christ is the healing of our wounds, and since there is thus a direct relationship between Christ's redemptive work and the nature of our wounds, then, necessarily, the sinner's spiritual self-knowledge also opens one's eyes to the beautiful proportion found in the work of redemption. One then begins to understand how perfectly that redemption was geared to our sinful condition; how in every respect that sacrifice of Christ provides all that is indispensable for our salvation; and how everything—even for the future—has been given in Christ to make our salvation perfect, including in the reality of its results. The one who rejects this divine instruction can say that Christ is their Savior, but that does not know *how*, and settles for a inaccessible mystery. But for those who receive divine instruction in this from the law, they gradually obtain clarity and transparency, insight and discernment, and thus their soul becomes ever richer in the admiration and worship that make them rejoice and praise.

This is to be explained especially from the fact that the one who sees more in Christ also applies more from Christ to oneself, practices it, experiences its blessings, enjoys it, and in so doing learns to appreciate it. Many live outside this. They go around like they are in a well-stocked pharmacy that contains medicines for every illness and ointments for every wound, but, year in and year out, they never take anything except from two or three very familiar shelves. Quinine against fever, chamomile to open up the skin, rhubarb to expel evil substances. But they have no understanding of any of the finer ingredients and so they do not touch them. This is what many people do with their Savior. Yes, they know that with him there is *atonement* for their guilt, *help* against temptation, a *promise* of glory, and they accept these three doctrines, and apply them and use them, but they keep their distance from all the hidden treasure that is in Christ. They know that there is much more in him, but they have no understanding of this, they have no power over this. They dare not approach it. And thus, while they do have Christ, they use him sketchily and in part. But if through their spiritual understanding of the law their diagnosis of sin has become richer, and through this the correct understanding of the salvation in Christ, then they automatically also come to the finer balm of Gilead and their enjoyment becomes so much greater.

And now finally the third point, namely, that the Holy Spirit uses *the law*, comprehended spiritually, to gradually *renew God's child into the image of God*. You do not do this yourself; it is the Holy Spirit in you who does it. But neither does the Holy Spirit treat you like a block of marble from which the sculptor conjures a statue, but as a born-again child of God who must be stimulated to self-insight and self-motivation. He works in you the willing and the doing, but in such a way that you then also will and work. And to bring you to this point he leads you into knowledge, the spiritual knowledge of God's law. Then that law, in the fullness of its characteristics, draws an image, an image of the person of God in that person's perfection which thus ultimately coincides with the image of the Son of God when that insight becomes perfectly clear. The law in its full effect applied to human beings is similar to the Christ. In highest fullness, the law and the Christ are one. Thus, the law interprets the Christ to you, and Christ shows you the unity of the law in its fullness. The Holy Spirit captivates you with this exalted, holy image. He tries to appeal to you with the law. He draws you through it, and just as the light draws the stem laden with buds toward it, straightens it, and makes the buds on that stem open up, so also is the working of this Sun of righteousness. What was still turned away in you he draws to himself. What was sagging he lifts up. The buds that were still closed and had neither color nor fragrance he causes to come out, to take on color from him, and he gives them a delightful fragrance.

This does not happen suddenly. Rather, it goes very slowly. There is so much that resists and opposes. There are so many vines and creepers that have twisted around the stem and must be removed. There are so many detrimental insects that want to spoil the buds. There is so much frigid wind. On earth, therefore, we cannot progress beyond a beginning of the conformity the image of the Son. But that means that progress, growth, and flourishing are indeed present. Every child of God could commit all kinds of sin in the past which today they can no longer do, and conversely they do many things which were entirely impossible for them in the past. Thus they do not shed their character, they do not become neutral model humans, nor do they mutilate their human nature. But the development of their character is different than it was in the past. A balance now enters their soul's existence. A measure of holy, divine peace sometimes rustles deep inside them. A power radiates from them, albeit it a very small power, but nevertheless a power of love, a power that is sanctifying, a power that breaks down sin and attempts to work on building the walls of God's holy Zion.

But here a struggle takes place, a struggle between the Holy Spirit and our *ego* at the bottom of our heart. For you can resist the Holy Spirit in this instruction and in this transformation into God's image, and you can grieve him, work against him. Or, on the contrary, you can be willing and teachable, and, like the horse in battle, comply with the rider's directions. And it is precisely this that depends so much on your entry into God's law. If you live by this law, pay attention to it, enter into it with spiritual knowledge, then your sensibility and inclination toward the perspective of the Spirit is changed and that willing and working that the Spirit works in you then comes automatically. And because practice brings about *habit*, that *holy habit* gradually emerges in you that makes living out of love for your God a matter of course.

And if this brings to a close the exposition of the law of God and of its lawful use ordained of God, then we must not proceed to the last section, *on prayer*, without a word of earnest exhortation to the ministers of the Word and to God's people among us to send out this power of the law more spiritedly and more richly and fruitfully than they have until now. No, the law does not lie beyond the experience of the heart. Rather, it is precisely in the path of the law that the healthy, true spiritual experience of grace finds this fresh and vibrant way that distinguishes it from all false mysticism.

A truth that remains objective is like a medicine on the bedside table which we refuse to take. The medicine *must* be absorbed by us, it *must* be given to us by the ministers, and God's people *must* appropriate it. And this does not happen through all kinds of personal stories, but it happens when, as our catechism requires, the *law of God* in all its glory, in all its meticulousness, and in all its spiritual understanding is used in order that God's children, each in their own situation, may gain increasingly more insight into their sin and perdition, may see more and more the riches in Christ and appropriate them from the Mediator, and thus, as a fruit of this, their whole soul's existence is increasingly renewed into the image of God.

BIBLIOGRAPHY

van Apeldoorn, L. J. *Geschiedenis van het nederlandsche huwelijksrecht voor de invoering van de fransche wetsgeving*. Amsterdam: Uitgeversmaatschappij, 1925.

Bacote, Vincent E. *The Spirit in Public Theology: Appropriating the Legacy of Abraham Kuyper*. Grand Rapids: Baker Academic, 2005.

Ballor, Jordan J., ed. *Makers of Modern Christian Social Thought: Leo XIII and Abraham Kuyper on the Social Question*. Grand Rapids: Acton Institute, 2016.

Barnett, Samuel A. "The Poor of the World: India, Japan, and the United States." *Fortnightly Review* 54, no. 320, 1 August 1893, 207–22.

Barnett, Samuel and Henrietta. *Practicable Socialism: Essays on Social Reform*. London: Longmans, Green, 1894.

Bartholomew, Craig G. *Contours of the Kuyperian Tradition*. Downers Grove, IL: IVP Academic, 2017.

Bavinck, Herman. *The Christian Family*. Translated by Nelson D. Kloosterman. Grand Rapids: Christian's Library Press, 2012.

Benedict, Philip. *Christ's Church Purely Reformed: A Social History of Calvinism*. New Haven: Yale University Press, 2003.

Bishop, Steve and John H. Kok, eds. *Abraham Kuyper: A Collection of Readings on the Life, Work, and Legacy of Abraham Kuyper*. Sioux Center, IA: Dordt College Press, 2013.

Bohatec, Josef. *England und die Geschichte der Menschen- und Bürgerrecht*. 3rd ed. Edited by Otto Weber. Graz: Böhlau, 1956.

Bolt, John. "The Holland-American Line of Liberty." *Journal of Markets & Morality* 1, no. 1 (Spring 1998): 35–59.

———. *A Free Church, A Holy Nation: Abraham Kuyper's American Public Theology*. Grand Rapids: Eerdmans, 2001.

Bonte, H. W. F., ed. *Kramer's Algemeene Kunstwoordentolk*. 4th ed. Gouda: Van Goor, 1886.

Bratt, James D. *Dutch Calvinism in North America: A History of a Conservative Subculture*. Grand Rapids: Eerdmans, 1984.

———. *Abraham Kuyper: Modern Calvinist, Christian Democrat*. Grand Rapids: Eerdmans, 2013.

Wood, John Halsey. *Going Dutch in the Modern Age: Abraham Kuyper's Struggle for a Free Church in the Nineteenth-Century Netherlands*. Oxford: Oxford University Press, 2013.

———. "Abraham Kuyper." In *Christianity and Family Law: An Introduction*. Edited by John Witte Jr. and Gary S. Hauk, 291–306. Cambridge: Cambridge University Press, 2017.

Butterfield, Herbert. *Christianity and History*. New York: Charles Scribner's Sons, 1949.

Calvin, John. *Commentarii in Quatuor Euangelistas*. Vol. 6, *Opera omnia*. Amsterdam: Joannem Jacobi Schipper, 1667.

———. *Commentary on a Harmony of the Evangelists Matthew, Mark, and Luke*. Vol. 1. Translated by William Pringle. Edinburgh: Calvin Translation Society, 1845.

"A Century of Christian Social Teaching: The Legacy of Leo XIII and Abraham Kuyper," *Journal of Markets & Morality* 5 (2002): 1–304.

Conradie, Ernst N., ed. *Creation and Salvation: Dialogue on Abraham Kuyper's Legacy for Contemporary Ecotheology*. Leiden: Brill, 2011.

da Costa, Isaäc. *Bezwaren tegen de geest der eeuw*. Leiden: L. Herdingh, 1823.

———. "Een Gebed voor den 'Heraut.'" In *Da Costa's Kompleete Dichtwerken*, 3:395. Haarlem: Kruseman, 1863.

Darwin, Charles. *On the Origin of Species by means of Natural Selection, or The Preservation of Favoured Races in the Struggle for Life*. London: John Murray, 1859.

Duffy, John-Charles. "Concealing the Body, Concealing the Sacred: The Decline of Ritual Nudity in Mormon Temples." *Journal of Ritual Studies* 21, no. 2 (2007): 1–21.

Van Dyke, Harry. "Abraham Kuyper and the Continuing Social Question." *Journal of Markets & Morality* 14, no. 2 (Fall 2011): 641–46.

Gedenkboek. Opgedragen door het feestcomité aan Prof. Dr. A. Kuyper. Bij zijn vijf en twintigjarig jublileum als hoofdredacteur van "De Standaard" (Amsterdam: Herdes, 1897), 59–77.

de Génestet, Petrus Augustus. "XCII. Verdraagzaamheid." In *Dichtwerken*. Edited by C. P. Tiele. Amsterdam: Kraay, 1869.

Godet, F. L. *A Commentary on the Gospel of St. Luke*. Vol. 1. Translated by E. W. Shalders. Edinburgh: T&T Clark, 1875.

von Haller, Karl Ludwig. *Restauration der Staats-Wissenschaft*. 6 vols. Winterthur: Steinerische Buchhandlung, 1816–34.

Harinck, George and Hans Krabbendam. *Sharing the Reformed Tradition: The Dutch-North American Exchange, 1846–1996*. Amsterdam: VU Uitgeverij, 1996.

Harinck, George and Hans Krabbendam, eds. *Breaches and Bridges: Reformed Subcultures in the Netherlands, Germany, and the United States*. Amsterdam: VU Uitgeverij, 2000.

Harmon, Andrew M. "Common Grace and Pagan Virtue: Is Kuyperian Tolerance Possible?" *The Kuyper Center Review* 2 (2011): 302–14.

Hegel, G. W. F. *The Philosophy of Right*. Translated by Alan White. Indianapolis: Focus, 2002.

Heslam, Peter S. *Creating a Christian Worldview: Abraham Kuyper's Lectures on Calvinism*. Grand Rapids: Eerdmans, 1998.

Himes, Brant M. *For a Better Wordliness: Abraham Kuyper, Dieterich Bonhoeffer, and Discipleship for the Common Good*. Eugene, OR: Wipf & Stock, 2018.

Hittinger, Russell. "Pope Leo XIII." In *Modern Christian Teachings on Law, Politics, and Human Nature*. Edited by John Witte Jr. and Frank S. Alexander, 39–73. New York: Columbia University Press, 2005.

Horwitz, Paul. *First Amendment Institutions*. Cambridge: Harvard University Press, 2013.

Hulsman, Gerrit. *Moderne wetenschap of bijbelsche traditie?* Utrecht: Kemink & Zoon, 1897.

Jellinek, George. *Die Erklärung der Menschen- und Bürgerrechte: Ein Beitrag zur modernen Verfassungsgeschichte*. Leipzig: Duncker & Humblot, 1895.

Jonker, A. J. Th. *Kalvinistische ingenomenheid met Rome aan Kalvijn zelve getoetst*. Rotterdam: Bredée, 1889.

Kievits, H. A. *Oefeningen in het zuiver schrijven der Nederduitsche taal*. Tiel: Wermeskerken, 1840.

Kocken, W. H. C. *De Vraag: Wat is the Moerdijk geschied?* Utrecht: J. Bijleveld, 1873.

van der Kooi, Cornelius and Jan de Bruijn, eds. *Kuyper Reconsidered: Aspects of His Life and Works*. Amsterdam: VU Uitgeverei, 1999.

Kuyper, Abraham. *Wat moeten wij doen, het stemrecht aan onszelven houden of den kerkraad machtigen?* Culemborg: Blom, 1867.

———. *Eenvormigheid, de vloek van het moderne leven*. Amsterdam: H. de Hoogh, 1869.

———. *De "Nuts"-Beweging*. Amsterdam: H. Höveker, 1869.

———. *Conservatisme en orthodoxie*. Amsterdam: H. de Hoogh, 1870.

———. *Het modernisme een fata morgana op christelijk gebied*. Amsterdam: H. de Hoogh, 1871.

———. *Liberalisten en Joden*. Amsterdam: Wormser, 1878.

———. *De Leidsche professoren en de executeurs der Dordtsche nalatenschap*. Amsterdam: Kruyt, 1879.

———. *Antirevolutionair óók in uw huisgezin*. Amsterdam: Kruyt, 1880.

———. *Bede om een dubbel "corrigendum"*. Amsterdam: Kruyt, 1880.

———. *Souvereiniteit in eigen kring; rede ter inwijding van de Vrije Universiteit, den 20sten October 1880 gehouden, in het koor der Nieuwe Kerk te Amsterdam*. Amsterdam: Kruyt, 1880.

———. *"Strikt genomen": het recht tot universiteitsstichting*. Amsterdam: Kruyt, 1880.

———. Introduction to *Geschiedenis der Martelaren*. Doesburg: Van Schenk Brill, 1883.

———. *Het Conflict Gekomen*. Amsterdam: Kruyt, 1886.

———. *Niet de vrijheidsboom maar het kruis. Toespraak ter opening van de tiende Deputatenvergadering in het eeuwfeest der Fransche Revolutie*. Amsterdam: Wormser, [1889].

———. *E voto Dordraceno*, 4 vols. Amsterdam: Wormser, 1892-5.

———. *De Christus en de Sociale nooden en Democratische Klippen*. Amsterdam: Wormser, 1895.

———. *Varia Americana*. Amsterdam: Höveker and Wormser, 1897.

———. *Encyclopaedie der heilige Godgeleerdheid*. 3 vols. Kampen: Kok, 1909.

———. *Dictaten Dogmatiek*. Vol. 5. 2nd ed. Kampen: Kok, 1913.

———. "De pers als vredesapostel." *Grotius: Internationaal Jaarboek* (June 1913): 54-65.

———. "The Ordinances of God." In *Political Order and the Plural Structure of Society*. Edited by James W. Skillen and Rockne M. McCarthy, 242-57. Atlanta: Scholars Press, 1991.

———. "Calvinism: Source and Stronghold of Our Constitutional Liberties." In *Abraham Kuyper: A Centennial Reader*. Edited by James D. Bratt, 279-322. Grand Rapids: Eerdmans, 1998.

———. *Conservatism and Orthodoxy: False and True Preservation* (1870). In *Abraham Kuyper: A Centennial Reader*. Edited by James D. Bratt, 65-85. Grand Rapids: Eerdmans, 1998.

———. *Modernism: A Fata Morgana in the Christian Domain* (1871). In *Abraham Kuyper: A Centennial Reader*. Edited by James D. Bratt, 87-124. Grand Rapids: Eerdmans, 1998.

———. *Uniformity: The Curse of Modem Life* (1869). In *Abraham Kuyper: A Centennial Reader*. Edited by James D. Bratt, 19-44. Grand Rapids: Eerdmans, 1998.

———. *Our Worship*. Translated and edited by Harry Boonstra et al. Grand Rapids: Eerdmans, 2011.

———. *On the Church*. Edited by John Halsey Wood Jr. and Andrew M. McGinnis. Bellingham, WA: Lexham Press, 2016.

———. *On Education*. Edited by Wendy Naylor and Harry Van Dyke, 17-28. Bellingham, WA: Lexham Press, 2019.

———. *On Business & Economics*. Edited by Peter S. Heslam. Bellingham, WA: Lexham Press, 2021.

Lapsley, R. A. "The Doctrinal Issues Presented by the Case of Dr. M. H. Houston." *The Presbyterian Quarterly* 48 (April 1899): 253-67.

Leroy-Beaulieu, Anatole. "Le Règne de l'argent." *Revue des deux mondes* 122, 15 March 1894, 241-60.

Lossius, Kaspar Friedrich. *Gumal and Lina; Or, An Instructive and Entertaining History Designed Chiefly for Use in the Religious Education of Young People*. Translated by S. B. Moens. 2 vols. London: Smallfield, 1817.

Lugo, Luis E., ed. *Religion, Pluralism, and Public Life: Abraham Kuyper's Legacy for the Twenty-First Century*. Grand Rapids: Eerdmans, 2000.

Macaulay, Thomas Babington. *Critical and Historical Essays Contributed to the Edinburgh Review*. Vol. 3 Leipzig: Bernh. Tauchnitz Jun., 1850.

de Maistre, Joseph. *Considérations sur la France*. London, 1797.

Maurice, Frederick Denison. *Social Morality: Twenty-One Lectures Delivered in the University of Cambridge*. London: Macmillan, 1869.

McConnell, Michael W. "Establishment and Toleration in Edmund Burke's Constitution of Freedom." *Supreme Court Review* (1995): 393-462.

McGoldrick, James E. *God's Renaissance Man: The Life and Work of Abraham Kuyper*. Auburn, MA: Evangelical Press, 2000.

McKee, Elsie Anne. *Diakonia in the Classic Reformed Tradition and Today*. Grand Rapids: Eerdmans, 1989.

———. *The Pastoral Ministry and Worship in Calvin's Geneva*. Geneva: Librairie Droz, 2016.

Milton, John. *Areopagitica; A speech of Mr. John Milton For the Liberty of Unlicenc'd Printing*. London, 1644.

Mommsen, Theodor. *Römische Geschichte*. 3 vols. Leipzig: Reimer & Hirzel, 1854-56.

———. *Römisches Staatsrecht*. 3 vols. Leipzig: S. Hirzel, 1871-76.

Mouw, Richard J. *He Shines in All That's Fair: Culture and Common Grace*. Grand Rapids: Eerdmans, 2002.

———. *Abraham Kuyper: A Short and Personal Introduction*. Grand Rapids: Eerdmans, 2011.

———. *The Challenges of Cultural Discipleship: Essays in the Line of Abraham Kuyper*. Grand Rapids: Eerdmans, 2011.

———. "Volume Introduction: A Comprehensive Theology of 'Commonness.'" In Abraham Kuyper, *Common Grace*. 3 vols. Edited by Jordan J. Ballor and Stephen J. Grabill/J. Daryl Charles. Translated by Nelson D. Kloosterman and Ed M. van der Maas, 1:xviii-xxx. Bellingham, WA: Lexham Press, 2015-2020.

Olson, Jeannine E. *Calvin and Social Welfare: Deacons and the Bourse Française*. London: Associated University Presses, 1989.

Plato. *The Republic of Plato*. Translated by John Llewelyn Davies and David James Vaughan. Cambridge: Macmillan, 1852.

Le Play, Frédéric. *De la réforme sociale en France*. 2 vols. Paris: Henri Plon, 1864.

———. *L'Organisation de la famille*. Paris: Téqui, 1871.

de Pressensé, Edmond. *L'Église et la Révolution française: Histoire des relations de l'Eglise et de l'état de 1789 à 1802*. Paris: Ch. Meyrueis, 1864.

de Pressensé, Edmond. *Religion and the Reign of Terror*. Translated by John P. Lacroix. New York: Carlton & Lanahan, 1869.

van Prinsterer, G. Groen. *Nederlandsche Gedachten*. 1st series. 4 vols. The Hague: Vervloet, 1829–32.

———. *Archives ou Correspondance inédite de la Maison d'Orange-Nassau*. 1st series. 9 vols. Leiden: Luchtmans, 1835–47.

———. *Adviezen in de Tweede Kamer der Staten-Generaal*. Leiden: Luchtmans, 1840.

———. *Handboek der Geschiedenis van het Vaderland*. 5 vols. Leiden: Luchtmans, 1841–46.

———. *Ongeloof en Revolutie*. Leiden: Luchtmans, 1847.

———. *Grondwetherziening en Eensgezindheid*. Amsterdam: Johannes Müller, 1849.

———. *Adviezen in de Tweede Kamer der Staten-Generaal*. Utrecht: Kemink en Zoon, 1856.

———. *Archives ou Correspondance inédite de la Maison d'Orange-Nassau*. 2nd series. 5 vols. Utrecht: Kemink et fils, 1857–61.

———. *Nederlandsche Gedachten*. 2nd series. 6 vols. Amsterdam: Höveker, 1867–76.

———. *Ongeloof en Revolutie*, 2nd ed. Amsterdam: H. Höveker, 1868.

———. *Nederlandsche Gedachten*. Amsterdam, 1874.

———. *Groen van Prinsterer. Schriftelijke Nalatenschap*. Edited by L. J. van Essen. Vol. 7. The Hague: Nijhoff, 1980.

———. *Briefwisseling*. The Hague: Nijhoff and Instituut voor Nederlands Geschiedenis, 1992.

———. *Unbelief and Revolution*. Edited and translated by Harry Van Dyke. Bellingham, WA: Lexham Press, 2018.

Rousseau, Jean-Jacques. *Letter to Beaumont, Letters Written from the Mountain, and Related Writings*, ed. Christopher Kelly and Eve Grace. Translated by Christopher Kelly and Judith R. Bush. Hanover, NH: Dartmouth College, 2001.

Rutgers, Abraham. "Halleluja, eeuwig dank en ere." In *Evangelische Gezangen*. Amsterdam: Johannes Allart, 1806.

Stahl, Julius. *Die Philosophie des Rechts*. 3rd ed. Vol. 2 Heidelberg: Mohr, 1856.

Stephen, James Fitzjames. *Liberty, Equality, Fraternity*. London: Smith, Elder, 1873.

Thorbecke, J. R. *Aanteekeningen op de Grondwet*. 2nd ed. Vol. 2. Amsterdam: Johannes Müller, 1843.

Tuininga, Matthew J. *Calvin's Political Theology and the Public Engagement of the Church: Christ's Two Kingdoms*. Cambridge: Cambridge University Press, 2017.

Uhlhorn, Gerhard. *Der Kampf des Christenthums mit dem Heidenthum: Bilder aus der Vergangenheid als Spiegelbilder für die Gegenwart*. Stuttgart: Meyer & Zeller, 1874.

VanDrunen, David. *Natural Law and the Two Kingdoms: A Study in the Development of Reformed Social Thought*. Grand Rapids: Eerdmans, 2010.

VanTil, Kent A. "Abraham Kuyper and Michael Walzer: The Justice of the Spheres." *Calvin Theological Journal* 40 (2005): 267–89.

Vree, Jasper and Johan Zwaan, eds. *Abraham Kuyper's* Commentatio *(1860): The Young Kuyper about Calvin, a Lasco, and the Church*, 2 vols. Leiden: Brill, 2005.

de Vries, John Hendrik. "Biographical Note." In Abraham Kuyper, *Lectures on Calvinism*. Grand Rapids: Eerdmans, 1981.

van der Vyver, Johan D. *Leuven Lectures on Religious Institutions, Religious Communities and Rights*. Leuven: Peeters, 2004.

Wells, David F., ed. *Reformed Theology in America: A History of its Modern Development*. Grand Rapids: Eerdmans, 1997.

Witte, John Jr. *The Reformation of Rights: Law, Religion, and Human Rights in Early Modern Calvinism*. Cambridge: Cambridge University Press, 2007.

————. "Prophets, Priests, and Kings of Liberty: John Milton and the Reformation of Rights and Liberties in England." *Emory Law Journal* 57 (2008): 1527–1604.

————. *From Sacrament to Contract: Marriage, Religion, and Law in the Western Tradition*. 2nd ed. Louisville, KY: Westminster John Knox, 2012.

————. *A New Reformation of Rights: Calvinism and the Rise of Modern Human Rights* (forthcoming).

Witte, John Jr. and Robert M. Kingdon. *Sex, Marriage and Family in John Calvin's Geneva*. 2 vols. Grand Rapids: Eerdmans, 2005, 2020.

Wolterstorff, Nicholas P. "Abraham Kuyper (1837–1920)." *Modern Christian Teachings on Law, Politics, and Human Nature*. Edited by John Witte Jr. and Frank S. Alexander, 288–327. New York: Columbia University Press, 2005.

ABOUT ABRAHAM KUYPER (1837–1920)

Abraham Kuyper's life began in the small Dutch village of Maassluis on October 29, 1837. During his first pastorate, he developed a deep devotion to Jesus Christ and a strong commitment to Reformed theology that profoundly influenced his later careers. He labored tirelessly, publishing two newspapers, leading a reform movement out of the state church, founding the Free University of Amsterdam, and serving as prime minister of the Netherlands. He died on November 8, 1920, after relentlessly endeavoring to integrate his faith and life. Kuyper's emphasis on worldview formation has had a transforming influence upon evangelicalism, both through the diaspora of the Dutch Reformed churches, and those they have inspired.

In the mid-nineteenth-century Dutch political arena, the increasing sympathy for the "No God, no master!" dictum of the French Revolution greatly concerned Kuyper. To desire freedom from an oppressive government or heretical religion was one thing, but to eradicate religion from politics as spheres of mutual influence was, for Kuyper, unthinkable. Because man is sinful, he reasoned, a state that derives its power from men cannot avoid the vices of fallen human impulses. True limited government flourishes best when people recognize their sinful condition and acknowledge God's divine authority. In Kuyper's words, "The sovereignty of the state as the power that protects the individual and that defines the mutual relationships among the visible spheres, rises high above them by its right to command and compel. But within these spheres ... another authority rules, an authority that descends directly from God apart from the state. This authority the state does not confer but acknowledges."

ABOUT THE CONTRIBUTORS

Matthew J. Tuininga (Ph.D., Emory University) is associate professor of moral theology at Calvin Theological Seminary. His research focuses on religion, society, and politics in American history, and he is the author of *Calvin's Political Theology and the Public Engagement of the Church: Christ's Two Kingdoms* (Cambridge).

John Witte Jr. (J.D., Harvard University; Dr. Theol. h.c., Heidelberg) is Robert W. Woodruff Professor of Law, McDonald Distinguished Professor of Religion, and director of the Center for the Study of Law and Religion at Emory University. A leading specialist in legal history, human rights, religious freedom, marriage and family law, and law and religion, he has published 300 articles, 17 journal symposia, and 40 books.

SUBJECT INDEX

A

Adam, 297, 337, 338, 340, 344, 375, 381
  Eve and, 339–40, 361, 364
  old, the, 371
adultery, xxxvii, 282, 340–41, 343
advertisers, 215, 255
Africa, Africans, 69, 298, 350
Alexander the Great, 90
almsgiving, 16, 33, 40
Ambrose of Milan, 95
America. *See* United States.
Amsterdam, 113, 144–45, 146
Anabaptists, 358–61, 363, 367
  dualism, 360, 371
  nudists, 361–62
anarchy, anarchism, 44, 76
antinomianism, 362, 367–68, 371, 374, 378
antirevolutionaries, 83–84, 90, 97–98,
  153
  Christianity, protection of, 190–91
  civility, 73–74
  class egotism, 76–77
  household, 268–70, 271
  Jesus Christ and, 102–3
  Milton, John, 166–68, 170–71, 181
  Roman Catholic Church and, 80,
    109–10
  universal suffrage, 63–64

Anti-Revolutionary Party (ARP), 53–54,
  85–86, 99, 102, 106, 232, 245
  historical and national character,
    100–102
  principles, Christian, 99–100, 103–4,
    125–27
  public opinion, 104–5
  Réveil, 96–97, 125–26
  speech, freedom of, 211–22
  unity, 223–24, 225–26
anti-Semitism, 8, 71
aristocrats, aristocratic, 24, 106, 303
  period of democracy, 50–51, 52, 68–69,
    70, 75
Asian despotism, 90, 91–92, 298
association, assembly, freedom of,
  184–85, 186–88
Association for Higher Education on a
  Reformed Foundation, 113, 115n2
atheism, 62–64, 168–69
Augustine of Hippo, 377
authority, 317–18
  fathers, 274–75, 276–78, 284
  government, 155–56, 335
  parents, 118, 309–10
  Roman Catholic Church, 160–61,
    162–63, 164, 168–69, 189
Austria, 88, 89, 200

SCRIPTURE INDEX

Old Testament

Extra Biblical Texts